ENGAGING PRIVACY AND INFORMATION TECHNOLOGY IN A DIGITAL AGE

James Waldo, Herbert S. Lin, and Lynette I. Millett, *Editors*

Committee on Privacy in the Information Age

Computer Science and Telecommunications Board

Division on Engineering and Physical Sciences

NATIONAL RESEARCH COUNCIL
OF THE NATIONAL ACADEMIES

THE NATIONAL ACADEMIES PRESS
Washington, D.C.
www.nap.edu

THE NATIONAL ACADEMIES PRESS   500 Fifth Street, N.W.   Washington, DC 20001

NOTICE: The project that is the subject of this report was approved by the Governing Board of the National Research Council, whose members are drawn from the councils of the National Academy of Sciences, the National Academy of Engineering, and the Institute of Medicine. The members of the committee responsible for the report were chosen for their special competences and with regard for appropriate balance.

Support for this project was provided by the W.K. Kellogg Foundation, Sponsor Award No. P0081389; the Alfred P. Sloan Foundation, Sponsor Award No. 2001-3-21; the AT&T Foundation; and the Carnegie Corporation of New York, Sponsor Award No. B 7415. Any opinions, findings, conclusions, or recommendations expressed in this publication are those of the author(s) and do not necessarily reflect the views of the organizations or agencies that provided support for the project.

Library of Congress Cataloging-in-Publication Data

Engaging privacy and information technology in a digital age / James Waldo, Herbert S. Lin, and Lynette I. Millett, editors.
　　p. cm.
　　Includes bibliographical references and index.
　　ISBN 978-0-309-10392-3 (hardcover) — ISBN 978-0-309-66732-6 (pdf)   1. Data protection. 2. Privacy, Right of—United States. I. Waldo, James. II. Lin, Herbert. III. Millett, Lynette I.
　　QA76.9.A25E5425 2007
　　005.8--dc22
　　　　　　　　　　　　　　　　　2007014433

Copies of this report are available from the National Academies Press, 500 Fifth Street, N.W., Lockbox 285, Washington, DC 20055; (800) 624-6242 or (202) 334-3313 (in the Washington metropolitan area); Internet, http://www.nap.edu.

Printed in the United States of America

THE NATIONAL ACADEMIES
Advisers to the Nation on Science, Engineering, and Medicine

The **National Academy of Sciences** is a private, nonprofit, self-perpetuating society of distinguished scholars engaged in scientific and engineering research, dedicated to the furtherance of science and technology and to their use for the general welfare. Upon the authority of the charter granted to it by the Congress in 1863, the Academy has a mandate that requires it to advise the federal government on scientific and technical matters. Dr. Ralph J. Cicerone is president of the National Academy of Sciences.

The **National Academy of Engineering** was established in 1964, under the charter of the National Academy of Sciences, as a parallel organization of outstanding engineers. It is autonomous in its administration and in the selection of its members, sharing with the National Academy of Sciences the responsibility for advising the federal government. The National Academy of Engineering also sponsors engineering programs aimed at meeting national needs, encourages education and research, and recognizes the superior achievements of engineers. Dr. Wm. A. Wulf is president of the National Academy of Engineering.

The **Institute of Medicine** was established in 1970 by the National Academy of Sciences to secure the services of eminent members of appropriate professions in the examination of policy matters pertaining to the health of the public. The Institute acts under the responsibility given to the National Academy of Sciences by its congressional charter to be an adviser to the federal government and, upon its own initiative, to identify issues of medical care, research, and education. Dr. Harvey V. Fineberg is president of the Institute of Medicine.

The **National Research Council** was organized by the National Academy of Sciences in 1916 to associate the broad community of science and technology with the Academy's purposes of furthering knowledge and advising the federal government. Functioning in accordance with general policies determined by the Academy, the Council has become the principal operating agency of both the National Academy of Sciences and the National Academy of Engineering in providing services to the government, the public, and the scientific and engineering communities. The Council is administered jointly by both Academies and the Institute of Medicine. Dr. Ralph J. Cicerone and Dr. Wm. A. Wulf are chair and vice chair, respectively, of the National Research Council.

www.national-academies.org

vi

Preface

Privacy is a growing concern in the United States and around the world. The spread of the Internet and the seemingly unbounded options for collecting, saving, sharing, and comparing information trigger consumer worries; online practices of businesses and government agencies present new ways to compromise privacy; and e-commerce and technologies that permit individuals to find personal information about each other only begin to hint at the possibilities.

The literature on privacy is extensive, and yet much of the work that has been done on privacy, and notably privacy in a context of pervasive information technology, has come from groups with a single point of view (e.g., civil liberties advocates, trade associations) and/or a mission that is associated with a point of view (e.g., regulatory agencies) or a slice of the problem (e.g., privacy in a single context such as health care).

Many of the groups that have looked at privacy have tended to be singular in their expertise. Advocacy groups are typically staffed by lawyers, and scholarship activities within universities are conducted largely from the perspective of individual departments such as sociology, political science, or law. Business/management experts address demand for personal information (typically for marketing or e-commerce). Although a few economists have also examined privacy questions (mostly from the standpoint of marketable rights in privacy), the economics-oriented privacy literature is significantly less extensive than the literature on intellectual property or equitable access. In an area such as privacy, approaches from any single discipline are unlikely to "solve" the problem, making it important to assess privacy in a manner that accounts for the implications of technology, law, economics, business, social science, and ethics.

Against this backdrop, the National Research Council believed that the time was ripe for a deep, comprehensive, and multidisciplinary examination of privacy in the information age: How are the threats to privacy evolving, how can privacy be protected, and how can society balance the interests of individuals, businesses, and government in ways that promote privacy reasonably and effectively?

A variety of conversations in late 2000 with privacy advocates in nonprofit organizations, and with private foundation officials about what their organizations have not been supporting, and ongoing conversations with computer scientists and other analysts who focus on information technology trends indicated a dearth of analytical work on the subject of online privacy that incorporated expertise about key technologies together with other kinds of expertise. Without adequate technical expertise, information technology tends to be treated as a black box that has impacts on society; with such expertise, there can be a more realistic exploration of interactions among technical and nontechnical factors and of design and implementation alternatives, some of which can avoid or diminish adverse impacts.

For these reasons, the National Research Council established the Committee on Privacy in the Information Age. The committee's analytical charge had several elements (see Chapter 1). The committee was to survey and analyze the causes for concern—risks to personal information associated with new technologies (primarily information technologies, but from time to time biotechnologies as appropriate) and their interaction with nontechnology-based risks, the incidence of actual problems relative to the potential for problems, and trends in technology and practice that will influence impacts on privacy. Further, the charge called for these analyses to take into account changes in technology; business, government, and other organizational demand for and supply of personal information; and the increasing capabilities for individuals to collect and use, as well as disseminate, personal information. Although certain areas (e.g., health and national security) were singled out for special attention, the goal was to paint a big picture that at least sketched the contours of the full set of interactions and tradeoffs.

The charge is clearly a very broad one. Thus, the committee chose to focus its primary efforts on fundamental concepts of privacy, the laws surrounding privacy, the tradeoffs in a number of societally important areas, and the impact of technology on conceptions of privacy.

To what end does the committee offer such a consideration of privacy in the 21st century? This report does not present a definitive solution to any of the privacy challenges confronting society today. It does not provide a thorough and settled definition of privacy. And it does not evaluate specific policies or technologies as "good" or "bad."

Rather, its primary purpose is to provide ways to think about privacy, its relationship to other values, and related tradeoffs. It emphasizes the need to understand context when evaluating the privacy impact of a given situation or technology. It provides an in-depth look at ongoing information technology trends as related to privacy concerns. By doing so, the committee hopes that the report will contribute to a better understanding of the many issues that play a part in privacy and contribute to the analysis of issues involving privacy.

In creating policies that address the demands of a rapidly changing society, we must be attuned to the interdependencies of complex systems. In particular, this must involve trying to avoid the unwitting creation of undesirable unintended consequences. We may decide to tolerate erosion on one side of a continuum—privacy versus security, for example. Under appropriate conditions the searching of travelers' bags and the use of behavioral profiles for additional examination are understandable. But with this comes a shift in the continuum of given types of privacy.

Perhaps most importantly, the report seeks to raise awareness of the web of connectedness among the actions we take, the policies we pass, the expectations we change. In creating policies that address the demands of a rapidly changing society, we must be attuned to the interdependencies of complex systems—and whatever policy choices a society favors, the choices should be made consciously, with an understanding of their possible consequences.

We may decide to tolerate erosion on one side of an issue—privacy versus security, for example. We may decide it makes sense to allow security personnel to open our bags, to carry a "trusted traveler" card, to "profile" people for additional examination. But with such actions come a change in the nature and the scope of privacy that people can expect. New policies may create a more desirable balance, but they should not create unanticipated surprises.

To pursue its work, the National Research Council constituted a committee of 16 people with a broad range of expertise, including senior individuals with backgrounds in information technology, business, government, and other institutional uses of personal information; consumer protection; liability; economics; and privacy law and policy. From 2002 to 2003, the committee held five meetings, most of which were intended to enable the committee to explore a wide range of different points of view. For example, briefings and/or other inputs were obtained from government officials at all levels, authorities on international law and practice relating to policy, social scientists and philosophers concerned with personal data collection, experts on privacy-enhancing technologies, business representatives concerned with the gathering and uses of personal data, consumer advocates, and researchers who use personal data. Several papers were commissioned and received.

As the committee undertook its analysis, it was struck by the extraordinary complexity associated with the subject of privacy. Most committee members understood that the notion of privacy is fraught with multiple meanings, interpretations, and value judgments. But nearly every thread of analysis leads to other questions and issues that also cry out for additional analysis—one might even regard the subject as fractal, where each level of analysis requires another equally complex level of analysis to explore the issues that the previous level raises. Realistically, the analysis must be cut off at some point, if nothing else because of resource constraints. But the committee hopes that this report suffices to paint a representative and reasonably comprehensive picture of informational privacy, even if some interesting threads had to be arbitrarily limited.

This study has been unusually challenging, both because of the nature of the subject matter and because the events that occurred during the time the report was being researched and written often seemed to be overtaking the work itself. The temptation to change the work of the committee in reaction to some news story or revelation of a pressing privacy concern was constant and powerful; our hope is that the work presented here will last longer than the concerns generated by any of those particular events.

The very importance of the subject matter increases the difficulty of approaching the issues in a calm and dispassionate manner. Many members of the committee came to the process with well-developed convictions, and it was interesting to see these convictions soften, alter, and become more nuanced as the complexities of the subject became apparent. It is our hope that readers of this report will find that the subject of privacy in our information-rich age is more subtle and complex than they had thought, and that solutions to the problems, while not impossible, are far from obvious.

The committee was highly diverse. This diversity reflects the complexity of the subject, which required representation not just from the information sciences but also from policy makers, the law, business, and the social sciences and humanities. Such diversity also means that the members of the committee came to the problem with different presuppositions, vocabularies, and ways of thinking about the problems surrounding privacy in our increasingly interconnected world. It is a testament to these members that they took the time and effort to learn from each other and from the many people who took the time to brief the committee. It is easy in such situations for the committee to decompose into smaller tribes of like-thinking members who do not listen to those outside their tribe; what in fact happened was that each group learned from the others. The collegial atmosphere that resulted strengthened the overall report by ensuring that many different viewpoints were represented and included.

Much of this collegial atmosphere was the result of the work of the staff of the National Research Council who guided this report. Lynette Millett started the study and has been invaluable through the entire process. Herb Lin injected the energy needed to move from first to final draft, asking all of the questions that needed to be asked and helping us to craft recommendations and findings that are the real reason for the report. The committee could not have reached this point without them.

Special thanks are due to others on the CSTB staff as well. Marjory Blumenthal, CSTB's former director, was pivotal in framing the project and making it happen. Janice Sabuda provided stalwart administrative and logistical support throughout the project. David Padgham and Kristen Batch provided valuable research support and assistance.

Outside the NRC, many people contributed to this study and report. The committee took inputs from many individuals in plenary sessions, including both scheduled briefers and individuals who attended and participated in discussions. The committee also conducted several site visits and informational interviews and commissioned several papers. The committee is indebted to all of those who shared their ideas, time, and facilities. The committee thanks the following individuals for their inputs and assistance at various stages during the project: Anita Allen-Castellitto, Kevin Ashton, Bruce Berkowitz, Jerry Bogart, Bill Braithwaite, Anne Brown, David Brown, Bruce Budowle, Lee Bygrave, Michael Caloyannides, Cheryl Charles, David Chaum, Ted Cooper, Amy D. Corning, Lorrie Cranor, Jim Dempsey, George Duncan, Jeff Dunn, Ed Felten, Michael Fitzmaurice, Michael Froomkin, Moya Gray, Rick Gubbels, Van Harp, Dawn Herkenham, Julie Kaneshiro, Orin Kerr, Scott Larson, Edward Laumann, Ronald Lee, David Lyon, Kate Martin, Patrice McDermott, Robert McNamara, Judith Miller, Carolyn Mitchell, Jim Neal, Pablo Palazzi, Kim Patterson, Merle Pederson, Priscilla Regan, Joel Reidenberg, Jeff Rosen, Mark Rothstein, Vincent Serpico, Donna Shalala, Martha Shepard, Eleanor Singer, David Sobel, Joe Steffan, Barry Steinhardt, Carla Stoffle, Gary Strong, Richard Varn, Kathleen Wallace, Mary Gay Whitmer and the NASCIO Privacy Team, and Matthew Wynia.

Finally, we must acknowledge the contribution of Lloyd Cutler, who served as co-chair of the committee from the time of its inception to the time of his death in May 2005. Lloyd was an active and energetic member of the committee, who insisted that we think about the principles involved and not just the particular cases being discussed. The intellectual rigor, curiosity, and decency shown and demanded by Lloyd set the tone and the standard for the committee as a whole. We were fortunate to have him as part of our group, and we miss him very much.

William Webster, *Chair*
Jim Waldo, *Vice Chair*
Committee on Privacy in the Information Age

Acknowledgment of Reviewers

This report has been reviewed in draft form by individuals chosen for their diverse perspectives and technical expertise, in accordance with procedures approved by the National Research Council's Report Review Committee. The purpose of this independent review is to provide candid and critical comments that will assist the institution in making its published report as sound as possible and to ensure that the report meets institutional standards for objectivity, evidence, and responsiveness to the study charge. The review comments and draft manuscript remain confidential to protect the integrity of the deliberative process. We wish to thank the following individuals for their review of this report:

Hal Abelson, Massachusetts Institute of Technology,
Ellen Clayton, Vanderbilt University Medical Center,
Peter Cullen, Microsoft Corporation,
George Duncan, Carnegie Mellon University,
Beryl Howell, Stroz Friedberg, LLC,
Alan Karr, National Institute of Statistical Sciences,
Michael Katz, University of California, Berkeley,
Diane Lambert, Google, Inc.,
Susan Landau, Sun Microsystems Laboratories,
Tom Mitchell, Carnegie Mellon University,
Britton Murray, Freddie Mac,
Charles Palmer, IBM, Thomas J. Watson Research Center,
Emily Sheketoff, American Library Association,

Robert Sparks, Independent Consultant, El Dorado Hills, California,
Peter Swire, Ohio State University, and
Alan Westin, Independent Consultant, Teaneck, New Jersey.

Although the reviewers listed above have provided many constructive comments and suggestions, they were not asked to endorse the conclusions or recommendations, nor did they see the final draft of the report before its release. The review of this report was overseen by Stephen Fienberg, Carnegie Mellon University. Appointed by the National Research Council, he was responsible for making certain that an independent examination of this report was carried out in accordance with institutional procedures and that all review comments were carefully considered. Responsibility for the final content of this report rests entirely with the authoring committee and the institution.

Contents

xv

PART II
THE BACKDROP FOR PRIVACY

PART III
PRIVACY IN CONTEXT

PART IV
FINDINGS AND RECOMMENDATIONS

APPENDIXES

Executive Summary

Privacy has many connotations—control over information, access to one's person and property, and the right to be left alone have all been included under this rubric. In political discourse, the term "privacy" has been used to refer to physical privacy in the home or office, the ability to make personal reproductive decisions without interference from government, freedom from surveillance, or the ability to keep electronic communications and personal information confidential. For many, privacy is regarded as a fundamental value and right, tied to ideals of autonomy, personal worth, and independence. Privacy is often seen as a necessary condition for keeping personal and public lives separate, for individuals being treated fairly by governments and in the marketplace, and for guaranteeing spaces where individuals can think and discuss their views without interference or censure.

Philosophical approaches to the study of privacy have centered on the elucidation of the basic concept and the normative questions around whether privacy is a right, a good in itself, or an instrumental good. Economic approaches to the question have centered around the value, in economic terms, of privacy, both in its role in the information needed for efficient markets and in the value of information as a piece of property. Sociological approaches to the study of privacy have emphasized the ways in which the collection and use of personal information have reflected and reinforced the relationships of power and influence between individuals, groups, and institutions within society.

Key to any discussion of privacy is a clear specification of what is at stake (what is being kept private) and the parties against which privacy is being invoked (who should not be privy to the information being kept private). For example, one notion of privacy involves confidentiality or secrecy of some specific information, such as preventing disclosure of an individual's library records to the government or to one's employer or parents. A second notion of privacy involves anonymity, as reflected in, for example, the unattributed publication of an article or an unattributable chat room discussion that is critical of the government or of an employer, or an unidentified financial contribution to an organization or a political campaign.

These two simple examples illustrate a number of essential points regarding privacy. First, the party against which privacy is being invoked may have some reason for wanting access to the information being denied. A government conducting a terrorist investigation may want to know what a potential suspect is reading; an employer may be concerned that an article contains trade secrets or company-proprietary information and want to identify the source of that information. Privacy rights are invoked to prevent the disclosure of such information. Second, some kind of balancing of competing interests may be necessary. Third, balancing is a task that is essentially political—and thus the political and societal power of various interest groups is critical to understanding how tradeoffs and compromises on privacy develop.

DRIVERS OF CHANGE IN NOTIONS OF PRIVACY

This report focuses on three major drivers of the vast changes affecting notions, perceptions, and expectations of privacy: *technological change, societal shifts,* and *discontinuities in circumstance.*

• *Technological change* refers to major differences in the technological environment of today as compared to that existing many decades ago (and which has a major influence on today's social and legal regime governing privacy). The hardware underlying information technology has become vastly more powerful; advances in processor speed, memory sizes, disk storage capacity, and networking bandwidth allow data to be collected, stored, and analyzed in ways that were barely imaginable a decade ago. Other technology drivers are just emerging, including sensor networks that capture data and connect that data to the real world. Increasingly ubiquitous networking means that more and more information is online. Data stores are increasingly available in electronic form for analysis. New algorithms have been developed that allow extraction of information from a sea of collected data. The net result is that new kinds of data are being collected and stored in vast quantities and over long periods of time, and obscurity or difficulty of access are increasingly less practical as ways of protecting privacy. Finally, because information technologies are continually dropping in cost, technologies for collecting and analyzing personal information from multiple, disparate sources are increasingly available to individuals, corporations, and governments.

- *Societal shifts* refer to evolutionary changes in the institutions of society—the organizations and the activities and practices that make use of the technological systems described above—and to the transformation of social institutions, practices, and behavior through their routine use. To an unprecedented degree, making personal information available to institutions and organizations has become essential for individual participation in everyday life. These information demands have increasingly appeared in licensing; administration and conferring of government or private sector benefits to particular classes of people (e.g., veterans, the unemployed, those with low income, homeowners); providing of services; employment; and retailing.

- *Discontinuities in circumstance* refer to events and emergent concerns that utterly transform the national debate about privacy in a very short time (and thus do not allow for gradual adjustment to a new set of circumstances). The most salient example in recent years concerns the events of September 11, 2001, which transformed the national environment and catapulted counterterrorism and national security to the very top of the public policy agenda. But the SARS outbreak in 2003 hinted at the potential for global pandemic on a very short time scale with some other disease, and measures to prevent pandemic outbreaks are receiving greater attention today. In the past, the Watergate scandals of 1972-1973, the Church Committee Hearings of 1976 (also known as the Hearings of the United States Senate Select Committee to Study Governmental Operations with Respect to Intelligence Activities), and the attack on Pearl Harbor in 1941 could also be seen as watershed events with dramatic changes in the environment for privacy.

These multiple drivers suggest how our attitudes toward privacy are context dependent. It is difficult to hold a precise view of what privacy is, absent consideration of what kind of information is sought, who seeks it, and how it is to be collected, protected, and used. There are, for example, some things one might not mind the government knowing that one would object to an employer knowing (and vice versa). And there are other things that one would not object to either of them knowing, but would not want passed on to aunts and uncles, just as there are things that one would like to keep within the family. Determining what should (1) be left to the realm of ethics and common courtesy, (2) be incentivized or discouraged, or (3) be formalized in regulation or law is yet another balancing question that comes up when contemplating privacy.

Taken together, these drivers point to an environment for privacy that is quite different from what existed in the era that led to the formation of many of today's expectations and assumptions about the nature of privacy and the role that privacy plays in individual lives and in society. As the environment changes, it is easy to see how understandings and a status quo developed prior to those changes can be upended. Thus, there is no immutable standard for what degree of privacy can be expected—suggesting that battles once fought and settled in one era may need to be refought and settled anew in another.

UNDERSTANDING PRIVACY TRADEOFFS

Privacy is a complex issue because multiple interests are at stake. Indeed, if the information had no value to anyone (either at the moment of collection or in the future), the protection of privacy would be a non-issue; the information would not be gathered in the first place.

But this is not the case. In many ways, both large and small, benefits do accrue from the collection of some kinds of information. These benefits lead to pressures against privacy measures that might impede the collection of such information. In some cases, these pressures are the result of *specific uses* for the information collected—that is, privacy concerns sometimes emanate from specific uses of information rather than the fact of collection itself. From a privacy protection standpoint, this in turn highlights a major problem for individuals—knowing those ultimate uses can be difficult or impossible.

Some of the most complex tradeoffs—and the ones most controversial or difficult to manage—involve a tradeoff of the interests of many individuals against the interests of a collective society. An individual's interest in keeping his or her medical records private—an interest shared by many individuals—may pose a tradeoff when community needs for epidemiological information are concerned or when emergency care for the individual is necessary without explicit consent. Video surveillance may deter crime but also poses a privacy risk if male camera operators use the cameras to focus on private parts of women's bodies. While law enforcement authorities believe that it is helpful to know the identities of individuals interested in reading about terrorism or bomb making, librarians and many state legislatures are concerned about ensuring a free, unfettered, and unmonitored flow of information to all library patrons that could be jeopardized if individuals' reading habits are potentially the subject of government investigation or even monitoring. Surveillance by government authorities can inhibit legal and legitimate social and political gatherings.

However, the fact that tradeoffs are sometimes necessary should not be taken to mean that tradeoffs are always necessary. In some cases, careful design and planning will minimize the tradeoffs that are needed to attend to societal needs without compromising personal information. An example might be a design decision for a system to discard data immediately after it has been used for the purpose at hand—in many instances, privacy concerns are strongly mitigated by the non-retention of data.

This perspective makes clear that the social context in which privacy is experienced has shifted in recent years. Identifying balances that people are comfortable with in legal affairs, security provisions, behavioral norms, and relationships will require an ongoing dialogue involving numerous stakeholders and constituencies. Expectations of privacy formed in the preindustrial age were not sufficient after the industrial revolution, and it should not be surprising that notions of privacy developed during the industrial age should show signs of stress in the new information age. It is at just such times of changing capabilities and expectations that we need to examine the core of our notions of privacy to ensure that what is most important survives the transitions.

TOOLS FOR PROTECTING PRIVACY

There are many pressures to diminish privacy, regardless of how the term is defined, but there are also a number of tools available to help protect privacy. These tools fall into three generic categories:

• *Personal unilateral actions (self-help).* When information collectors rely on individuals themselves to provide personal information, these individuals can take action to withhold that information. They can refuse to provide it at all, or they can provide false, misleading, or incomplete information. A common example is an affinity card, which entitles the holder to a discount on store products. Affinity cards are typically provided to an individual upon receipt of a completed application, which usually involves a questionnaire about income, demographics, and spending habits. There is often no verification of the information provided or sanction applied for inaccurate information, and so many individuals simply provide inaccurate information. Withholding information also works to protect privacy, although it may also deny one certain benefits, such as a license or a job. Neither of these approaches is well advised, of course, when there are excessively negative and severe consequences to withholding or providing false information.

• *Technology.* Technical measures can protect privacy as well, although a relevant question is who decides to implement any given technical measure. From an individual standpoint, encryption and anonymizers are today the primary privacy-protecting technologies. That is, encryption of personal information can be used to ensure that such information can only be accessed with the express permission of the subject of that information, and that communications cannot be seen by others than those taking part in the communication. Anonymizers (e.g., anti-spyware tools, anonymous browsers) allow an individual to explore cyberspace (e.g., using e-mail, viewing Web sites) with a high degree of anonymity. In addition, anti-spam and anti-phishing technologies help individuals to be left alone and reduce the leakage of personal information. Technical safeguards to protect privacy are also available to the collectors of personal information, who may wish to protect such information to make individuals more willing or more comfortable about sharing information with them. For example, technologies are being developed that can screen out individuating characteristics in large-scale public data-gathering systems such as video cameras, and some statistical methods and data-mining algorithms have been developed that facilitate the anonymization of information without changing the important statistical properties of the information taken in the aggregate.

• *Policy.* Policy measures, by which are meant actions that information collectors can or must take, are arguably the most important privacy protection tool. That is, privacy is much more an issue of who is permitted to see an individual's personal information than of technologically restricting access to that information. People may be concerned about personal health and medical information being improperly disclosed, but this problem may arise at least as much as a result of policy decisions to make such information broadly accessible to relevant parties as from the activities of hackers breaking into medical databases. Policy measures fall into five generic categories:

—*Limits on the information collected and stored (data minimization).* For example, often the most "obvious" efforts to enhance public safety or security are highly privacy-invasive (e.g., collect all possible data about individuals and mine it extensively). However, it may be possible, with some thoughtfulness early on, to collect a much more limited set of information that will still satisfy a given purpose. Collected information, once used, can also be deleted to prevent further use. Of course, such limits will be strongly resisted by information collectors who do not know in advance of collection the specific purposes for which they need information, and who see information as an opportunity to develop a resource that might be useful for an extended time. Note also that limits need not be formulated in all-or-nothing terms. Limits may be imposed in the form of differential levels of access for different individuals, varying time windows for access (both when data are made available and for how long), or access for certain purposes but not for others.

—*Limits on outsider access.* By definition, an outsider is a party external to the organization that collects the information in question. Outsiders can be denied access through both technical and procedural means. Technical means include measures such as encryption and access control mechanisms that prevent unauthorized access; procedural means include regulation-based restrictions on who receives information.

—*Prevention of internal abuse.* Even organizations with the best of intentions may have insiders (e.g., employees) who do not use the information collected in accordance with organizationally approved purposes. For example, a law enforcement agent may use a national criminal database to investigate an individual for personal reasons, in violation of departmental policy. In such instances, frequent audits to uncover improper access and penalties for improper access are essential elements of preventing such use.

—*Notification.* It is generally believed that violations of privacy are in some sense worse when they occur without the knowledge of the individual in question; thus, notification when unauthorized access occurs can be regarded as a privacy protection measure.

—*Correction.* The opportunity to review information collected and to ensure that it is at least correct protects the individual against decisions being made on the basis of incorrect information.

A BASIC ANALYTICAL FRAMEWORK
FOR UNDERSTANDING PRIVACY

The notion of privacy is a basic starting point for this framework, and as suggested in the introduction, three essential questions arise:

- What is the information that is being kept private (and with whom is that information associated)?
- From whom is the information being withheld?
- What purposes would be served by withholding or not withholding the information, and whose interests do those purposes serve?

A Worked Example of Privacy Tradeoffs

To illustrate how basic privacy tradeoffs arise, this report considers privacy and the U.S. library community. The issue of privacy in libraries is considered not because it is more important than privacy in other domains (e.g., in health care or law enforcement), but because it provides an opportunity to introduce in a concrete manner some of the basic tradeoffs.

The library community has a long historical commitment to protecting the privacy of its patrons, formalized more than five decades ago and integrated into a core set of shared beliefs. This community was also an early adopter of information technology as a way of furthering its mission of offering full access to all information to libraries' patrons. Since many libraries are publicly funded in one way or another, this community is also directly subject to shifts in the political landscape. This combination makes this community one of the most active, articulate, and thoughtful of the various factions taking part in the debates about privacy.

The framework of questions posed above provides a starting point for the discussion of library privacy.

• What is the information that is being kept private (and with whom is that information associated)? The information that is being kept private is the borrowing history of reading materials of library patrons who are identifiable by name or the names of all individuals who have had access to specific reading materials. (Such information is protected under the laws of many states.) "Borrowing history" can include computer access to information as well.

• From whom is the information being withheld? According to the librarians' code of ethics, borrowing records should be kept private from all parties except as necessary to provide fiscal accountability for materials borrowed (you fail to return a book, you pay for it).

• What purposes would be served by withholding or not withholding the information, and whose interests do those purposes serve? The rationale underlying the withholding of borrowing information is the belief that citizens are served best when they can obtain information and access to society's scientific, cultural, and historical legacy without interference or observation from other parties, and disclosure of that information might subject patrons to pressure and outside influence. Moreover, because there is no general social consensus about information that is or is not desirable for people to have (the primary exceptions being materials judged to constitute child pornography), librarians believe that leaving the choice of subjects to the individual's own choosing maximizes the benefit to society as a whole. As for disclosure of information on borrowing, the interests served depend on who has access and for what reasons access is being sought. For example, parents may wish to know if a teenage daughter is reading about sex, or law enforcement authorities may wish to know if a person of interest is reading about guns or radical politics.

From this example, several themes emerge.

First, the direct interests of the individual differ from those of the parties seeking the information.

Second, a long history of privacy concerns in the library community provides the basic context against which today's current concerns about privacy are judged and assessed.

Third, technological advances in the library domain—coupled with change in the social and political milieu in which libraries operate—reopen once-settled arguments and compromises that have historically been made between privacy and other values. Law enforcement authorities have sought information about reading habits of patrons in the past, but debates over library privacy have been reopened as records of Internet access in libraries become important to criminal or intelligence investigations.

In order to compare how these issues play out in other domains, the next section illustrates three other important scenarios.

Elaboration of the Issues

Although other parties have many reasons for using personal information of individuals, four stand out as being of particular significance. One reason is economic—by using personal information about individuals, various profit-making enterprises can enhance their revenue streams, sometimes quite substantially. A second is medical—detailed information about patients enables higher-quality and less expensive health care than would otherwise be possible. A third is public safety and national security—collection of information about criminals, criminal activities, and terrorists enables law enforcement and national security authorities to protect the public more effectively. A fourth is research—statistical trends derived from collections of personal information are often of importance to public policy makers. Privacy tradeoffs related to each of these reasons are explored below.

Economic Drivers

A good example of how economic drivers affect privacy can be found in the area of the definition, protection, and enforcement of intellectual property rights in the networked digital environment. Deep privacy issues arise in this domain because digital rights management technologies (DRMTs)—originally intended to help limit illegal distribution of copyrighted digital materials—also enable very-fine-grained control over what legitimate users may do with materials in their possession (e.g., how many times a document can be read, or whether it can be forwarded). Of particular concern from a privacy perspective, DRMTs could also be used to monitor what intellectual property and information an individual uses and how. Information can be collected about how many times you read a document, how long you spend listening to a piece of music, how often you visit a particular place on the Internet, or what kinds of changes you make to information and when—among many other things. Such fine-grained information collection and monitoring of what many perceive to be critical components of their intellectual and emotional selves (the books we read, the music we listen to, the movies that we watch) might have a dramatic impact on people's perceptions of their individual privacy.

In the case of DRMTs, the economic benefit today arises not from the collection of this information about user behavior per se, but from the primary applications of DRMTs to charge fees for various services for access to protected materials (printing, storage, multiple simultaneous access, and so on). That is, publishers have found that DRMTs are enablers for a different and more profitable business model, although in the future certain parties might also find significant economic interest in what could be gleaned from such information such as from targeted marketing based on user interests). Privacy concerns arise because of the potential for these DRMTs to collect detailed information on user behavior regarding the digital content they consume and thus all of the consequences that could result if DRMTs were in fact used in this way.

Medical Drivers

Health and medical privacy has traditionally been considered a core privacy right. The experience of policy makers in implementing the privacy regulations of the Health Insurance Portability and Accountability Act (HIPAA) serves as a case study in some of the subtleties of privacy, showing the difficulty of determining the line between what should be private and what can be disclosed (and with whom and for what purposes such sharing can take place); the difficulties of placing the appropriate procedures and technologies in place to ensure the required levels of privacy; and the various costs of such privacy regulations. The health and medical communities are also on the leading edge of several possible future privacy issues, having to do with the appropriate use of information that can be gathered from sources such as DNA analysis. These issues call into question even the notion of whose privacy is involved, since the information contained in a person's DNA concerns not only that person but also the set of people who share that person's genetic lineage. The same may be true to a lesser extent for health habits and infectious diseases, the presence of which often correlates with family membership.

Privacy issues arise in the health and medical domain primarily as the result of a concern about the consequences should personal health and medical information be disclosed or disclosable. One source of concern is social—there is stigma associated with certain medical conditions, and disclosure of those conditions potentially subjects individuals with them to discrimination and to being socially ostracized. A second is economic—disclosure of information about an individual's health to insurance companies can be used to deny him or her health insurance (or increase the price of such insurance), and disclosure of such information to an employer may affect his or her employment prospects with that employer. And underlying these social and economic concerns is the fact that candor between a patient and his or her health care provider is essential for good care.

An interesting middle ground is the disclosure of personal health information for research purposes (e.g., to determine effective courses of medical treatment). For such purposes, individual names need not be associated with the information being collected, although unique identifiers may be needed to track individuals longitudinally. In this context, some people may regard collection of information as benign from a privacy standpoint, while others may regard it as intrusive.

More generally, this example illustrates that concerns about privacy—in many domains—often relate to the stated reasons for which the information is gathered, the intention of the gatherers, and the subsequent uses to which the information is put. Something can be seen either as an invasion of privacy or as an attempt to give better service, depending on the motives, results, explanations offered, safeguards provided, and trust relationships that hold between the individuals and the companies that are gathering and using the information.

Law Enforcement and National Security Drivers

Law enforcement and national security authorities need information about criminals, criminal activities, and terrorists if these authorities are to carry out their missions. And if collection of information could be precisely limited to these targets there would be little controversy.

But criminals and terrorists do not wear brightly colored shirts announcing that they are actual or potential criminals and terrorists. As a rule, criminals and terrorists wish to blend in with the law-abiding population so that they do not come under suspicion and thus have a freer hand to plan and operate. Thus, any information collection directed at criminals and terrorists potentially gathers information about law-abiding citizens, and striking the appropriate balance between acknowledging the law enforcement/national security need for collecting information and protecting the privacy of law-abiding citizens has been an especially copious source of public policy controversy since September 11, 2001. Of course, this is not a new tension; indeed, it has existed far longer than this country. What makes this subject of particular importance for this study is the confluence of the technology that makes it possible for privacy to be eroded far more extensively than ever before with the historical context that makes the claims for security more persuasive.

There are many reasons that law-abiding individuals might be concerned about the collection of their personal information, but three are worthy of particular mention. First, these individuals may be concerned that such information might be abused. By giving government officials the ability to collect personal information, citizens must take on faith that such abilities will be exercised only for proper reasons, such as the investigation of a crime, and not for improper ones, such as the settling of personal vendettas. Second, government knowledge about certain activities often has a chilling effect on such activities, even if such activities are entirely legal—an example might be planning a public protest about government action. Third, many individuals do not want government authorities to collect personal information simply on the theory that such collection raises their profile and makes it more likely that they might be erroneously singled out in some manner to their detriment even if they have done nothing illegal.

FINDINGS AND RECOMMENDATIONS

Argumentation for the findings and recommendations is provided in Chapter 10 of the report. Recommendations are presented in boldface below.

The committee found that the meaning of privacy is highly contextual, and it can vary depending on the specific circumstances at hand, such as the situation and relationships at issue, the intentions of the parties involved, and the historical context, technology, and political environment. Despite this contextual meaning, privacy is an important value to be maintained and protected, because the loss of privacy often results in significant tangible and intangible harm to individuals and to groups. Privacy is most important to people when they believe the entity receiving their personal information is not trustworthy and that they may be harmed by sharing that information.

At the same time, privacy is not an absolute good in itself. Tradeoffs against other desirable societal values or goods are sometimes inevitable.

Privacy-invasive solutions to public policy problems may be warranted under some circumstances. However, when they are implemented as measures of first rather than last resort, they generate resistance that might otherwise be avoided if other alternatives were tried first.

Businesses, researchers, and government agencies find value in the exploitation of personal information, and they have further developed many mechanisms—both voluntary and intrusive—for obtaining personal information. Moreover, because these entities often develop new ways of using personal information in pursuit of their organizational goals and missions, there emerge many pressures for the repurposing of data that have already been collected. Changing social trends and sentinel events such as the 9/11 attacks put additional strong pressures on privacy.

The changing information technology environment has also helped to compromise privacy, although some developments in information technology and other technologies do have considerable potential to enhance it. In addition, technology-based privacy enhancement rests on firmer ground to the extent that technologists attend to privacy considerations throughout the life cycle of personal information that is collected rather than just at the beginning of the collection process.

The committee is concerned about the nature of public debates about privacy and its relationship to other societal interests. For example, the committee found that there is often a lack of clarity about the privacy interests involved and too often a tendency to downplay and to be dismissive of the privacy issues at stake. When privacy is at issue, the committee found that bland assurances that privacy will not be harmed offered by policy makers can do more to raise skepticism than honest presentation and assessment of tradeoffs.

To facilitate a more thoughtful public debate, the committee articulated a number of principles. The first was that the debate should avoid demonization. Most threats to privacy do not come from fundamentally bad people with bad intentions. Demonization tends to make compromise and thoughtful deliberation difficult. Second, the debate should account for context and nuance; taking nuance and context into account will often be necessary if common ground is to be found. Third, the debate should respect the complexity inherent in the problem. Privacy is a complicated issue, and it is a moving target, as the numerous social and technical factors with which it is intertwined change over time. Thus, initiatives that have policy implications and solutions to identified privacy problems are more likely to be successful if they can begin with modest and simple steps that provide feedback to guide and shape further actions. Fourth, decision makers must be aware of long-term costs and risks. In particular, it is costly to retrofit privacy features into a system (such as the addition of query audit trails to deter inappropriate use by employees), and such fixes are often necessary when inadvertent violations of privacy occur that might have been prevented if those features had been available in the first place. (There are also the costs associated with unfavorable publicity and possible economic liability.) Thus, it often makes sense to ensure that adequate technology-based enforcement of privacy policies is a part of a system's initial design.

In order to enhance privacy, individual, organizational, and public policy actors have roles to play.

Individuals can take a number of steps to enhance the privacy of their personal information and to become better informed about the extent to which their privacy has been compromised, although the effectiveness of these measures is bound to be limited. The committee thus recommends that **if policy choices require that individuals shoulder the burden of protecting their own privacy, law and regulation should support the individual in doing so.**

Firms and other organizations can design and implement self-regulatory regimes for protecting the privacy of the personal information they collect. Self-regulation is limited as a method for ensuring privacy, although it nevertheless offers protections that would not otherwise be available to the public. The committee offers a number of concrete recommendations to enhance the effectiveness of privacy policies. Specifically, **organizations with self-regulatory privacy policies should take both technical and administrative measures to ensure their enforcement, routinely test whether their stated privacy policies are being fully implemented, produce privacy impact assessments when they are appropriate, strengthen their privacy policy by establishing a mechanism for recourse if an individual or a group believes that they have been treated in a manner inconsistent with an organization's stated policy, and establish an institutional advocate for privacy.**

The committee found that governmental bodies have important roles to play in protecting the privacy of individuals and or groups and in ensuring that decisions concerning privacy are made in an informed fashion. However, the U.S. legal and regulatory framework surrounding privacy is a patchwork that lacks consistent principles or unifying themes. Accordingly, the committee concluded that a less decentralized and more integrated approach to privacy policy in the United States could bring a greater degree of coherence to the subject of privacy. Two recommendations follow from this conclusion. First, the committee recommends that **the U.S. government should undertake a broad systematic review of national privacy laws and regulations.** Second, the committee recommends that **government policy makers should respect the spirit of privacy-related law.**

The principles of fair information practice for the protection of personal information were first enunciated in a 1973 report of the U.S. Department of Health, Education, and Welfare. In reviewing the privacy landscape, the committee found that these principles are as relevant and important today as they were in 1973. Thus, the committee recommends that **principles of fair information practice should be extended as far as reasonably feasible to apply to private sector organizations that collect and use personal information.** Given the growing importance of repurposing collected personal information, the committee also recommends that **to support greater transparency into the decision-making process regarding repurposing, guidelines should be established for informing individuals that repurposing of their personal information might occur, and also what the nature of such repurposing would be, and what factors would be taken into account in making any such decision.** In addition, the committee recommends that **the principle of choice and consent should be implemented so that individual choices and consent are genuinely informed and so that its implementation accounts fairly for demonstrated human tendencies to accept without change choices made by default.**

Furthermore, although a number of laws do protect the privacy of personal information in government hands, the use of private sector data aggregators is a gray area, and the committee recommends that **the U.S. Congress should pay special attention to and provide special oversight regarding the government use of private sector organizations to obtain personal information about individuals.**

As for the government use of personal information, the committee found that because the benefits of privacy often are less tangible and immediate than the perceived benefits of other interests such as public security and economic efficiency, privacy is at an inherent disadvantage when decision makers weigh privacy against these other interests. The committee concluded that, to reduce this inherent disadvantage, governments at federal, state, and local levels should establish mechanisms for the institutional advocacy of privacy within government. Accordingly, the committee recommends that **governments at various levels should establish formal mechanisms for the institutional advocacy of privacy within government,** and furthermore that **a national privacy commissioner or standing privacy commission should be established to provide ongoing and periodic assessments of privacy developments.**

Finally, the committee found that the availability of individual recourse for recognized violations of privacy is an essential element of public policy regarding privacy. Accordingly, it recommends that **governments at all levels should take action to establish the availability of appropriate individual recourse for recognized violations of privacy.**

Part I

Thinking About Privacy

Chapter 1 ("Thinking About Privacy") introduces many of the concepts needed for an informed discussion about privacy. The chapter underscores that privacy is an elusive concept, even though many people have strong intuitions about what it is. Indeed, privacy is seen to be a concept that acquires specific meaning only in the context of specific circumstances and settings. Notions of privacy are influenced by many factors, including technological change, societal and organizational change, and changes in immediate circumstances. Relevant technical issues include concepts of false positives and false negatives, the nature of personal information, the distinction between privacy and anonymity, fair information practices, and reasonable expectations of privacy.

1

Thinking About Privacy

Just as recent centuries saw transitions from the agricultural to the industrial to the information age and associated societal and technological changes, the early 21st century will continue to pose dynamic challenges in many aspects of society. Most importantly from the standpoint of this report, advances in information technology are proceeding apace. In this rapidly changing technological context, individuals, institutions, and governments will be forced to reexamine core values, beliefs, laws, and social structures if their understandings of autonomy, privacy, justice, community, and democracy are to continue to have meaning. A central concept throughout U.S. history has been the notion of privacy and the creation of appropriate borders between the individual and the state. In the latter 19th century, as industrial urban society saw the rise of large bureaucratic organizations, notions of privacy were extended to the borders between private organizations and the individual. This report focuses on privacy and its intersections with information technology and associated social and technology trends.

1.1 INTRODUCTION

One of the most discussed and worried-about aspects of today's information age is the subject of privacy. Based on a number of other efforts directed toward analyzing trends and impacts of information technology (including the evolution of the Internet, a variety of information security issues, and public-private tensions regarding uses of information and information technology), the National Research Council saw a need for a comprehensive assessment of privacy challenges and opportunities and thus established the Committee on Privacy in the Information Age. The committee's charge had four basic elements:

• To survey and analyze potential areas of concern—privacy risks to personal information associated with new technologies and their interaction with non-technology-based risks, the incidence of actual problems relative to the potential, trends in technology and practice that will influence impacts on privacy, and so on;
• To evaluate the technical and sociological context for those areas as well as new collection devices and methodologies—why personal information is at risk given its storage, communication, combination with other information, and various uses; trends in the voluntary and involuntary (and knowing and unknowing) sharing of that information;
• To assess what is and is not new about threats to the privacy of personal information today, taking into account the history of the use of information technology over several decades and developments in government and private sector practices; and
• To examine the tradeoffs (e.g., between more personalized marketing and more monitoring of personal buying patterns) involved in the collection and use of personal information, including the incidence of benefits and costs,[1] and to examine alternative approaches to collection and use of personal information.

Further, in an attempt to paint a big picture that would at least sketch the contours of the full set of interactions and tradeoffs, the charge called for these analyses to take into account changes in technology; business, government, and other organizational demand for and supply of personal information; and the increasing capabilities for individuals to collect and use, as well as disseminate, personal information. Within this big picture, and motivated by changes in the national security environment since the September 11, 2001, attacks on the World Trade Center and the Pentagon, the committee addressed issues related to law enforcement and national security somewhat more comprehensively than it did other areas in which privacy matters arise.

To what end does the committee offer this consideration of privacy in the 21st century? Most broadly, to raise awareness of the spider web of connectedness among the actions we take, the policies we pass, the

---

[1]Throughout this report, the term "benefits and costs" should be construed broadly, and in particular should not be limited simply to economic benefits and costs.

expectations we change, the "flip side" of impacts policies have on privacy. There should not be unintended consequences to privacy created by policies we write or change to address the continuing shifts in our society. We may decide to tolerate erosion on one side of a continuum—privacy and security sometimes pose a conflict, for example. We may decide it makes sense to allow security personnel to open our bags, to carry a "trusted traveler" card, to accept "profiling" of people for additional examination. But we should not be surprised by the erosion of our own and other people's privacy by this shift in the continuum. Policies may create a new and desirable equilibrium, but they should not create unforeseen consequences.

The goals here are not to evaluate "good" and "bad," whether in changes in the continuums privacy moves on, policies, technologies, and laws. Rather, the committee hopes that this report will contribute to a recalibration of the many issues that play a part in privacy and will contribute to the analysis of issues involving privacy. The degree of privacy traded for security or public health, for example, should be a result of thoughtful decisions following public discussion in which all parties can participate. Only then will the policies that emerge from the pressures at work during the early years of the 21st century be understood in their impacts on privacy.

To be clear, the committee does not claim that this report presents comprehensive solutions to the many privacy challenges confronting society today. Nor does it provide a thorough and settled definition of privacy. Debate will continue on this complicated and value-laden topic for the foreseeable future. This report does provide ways to think about privacy, its relationship to other values, and related tradeoffs. It emphasizes the need to understand context when evaluating the privacy impact of a given situation, piece of legislation, or technology. And it provides an in-depth look at ongoing information technology trends as related to privacy concerns.

1.2 WHAT IS PRIVACY?

The committee began by trying to understand what privacy is, and it quickly found that privacy is an ill-defined but apparently well-understood concept. It is ill-defined in the sense that people use the term to mean many different things. Any review of the literature on privacy will reveal that privacy is a complicated concept that is difficult to define at a theoretical level under any single, logically consistent "umbrella" theory, even if there are tenuous threads connecting the diverse meanings. Specifying the concept in a way that meets with universal consensus is a difficult if not impossible task, as the committee found in doing its work.

At the same time, the term "privacy" is apparently well understood in the sense that most people using the term believe that others share their particular definition. Nonetheless, privacy resists a clear, concise definition because it is experienced in a variety of social contexts. For example, a question may be an offensive privacy violation in one context and a welcome intimacy in another.

The committee believes that in everyday usage, the term "privacy" generally includes reference to the types of information available about an individual, whether they are primary or derived from analysis. These types of information include behavioral, financial, medical, biometric, consumer, and biographical. Privacy interests also attach to the gathering, control, protection, and use of information about individuals. Informational dimensions of privacy thus constitute a definitional center of gravity for the term that is used in this report, even while recognizing that the term may in any given instance entail other dimensions as well—other dimensions that are recognized explicitly in the discussion.[2]

The multidimensional nature of privacy is explicated further in Chapter 2, and a theme that becomes apparent is the situational and contextual nature of privacy—that is, it depends on a number of specific factors that often do not cleanly and clearly overlap, rather than being identified by a sweeping universal calculus or definition.

Moreover, privacy in any given situation may be in tension with other values or desires of the individual, subgroups, and society at large. Privacy, like most other values in modern democratic societies, is not an absolute but rather must be interpreted and weighed alongside other socially important values and goals. How this balancing (which need not mean equivalent weighing) is to be achieved is often the center of the controversy around privacy, because different people and groups balance in different ways these values that are in tension.

A further complication is that participants in the balancing debate often confuse the needs of privacy with other values that might be tied to privacy but that are, in fact, distinct from it. For example, concerns over whether an individual's HIV status should be private may in fact reflect, in part, a concern about his or her ability to obtain health insurance.

In short, as with most interesting and contentious social topics, where privacy is concerned there are both costs and benefits, and these vary by the group, context, and time period in question, as well as by the means used to measure them. Sometimes, tradeoffs are inevitable (Box 1.1 pro-

---

[2]The term "private" can have both descriptive and normative meanings. To describe information as "private information" might mean "information that is not accessible to others," or it could mean "information that should not be accessible to others." Generally the context will specify the meaning, but these two different meanings are noteworthy.

BOX 1.1
Some Illustrative Tradeoffs in Privacy

• Government or privately controlled cameras monitoring the movement of ordinary citizens in public places for the stated purpose of increasing public safety.
• Government collection of data on peoples' political activities for the stated purpose of increasing public safety or homeland security.
• Collection by a retailer of personal information about purchases for the stated purpose of future marketing of products to specific individuals.
• Collection by a bank of personal financial information about an individual for the stated purpose of evaluating his or her creditworthiness for a loan.
• Aggregation by insurers of medical data obtained through third parties for the stated purpose of deciding on rates or availability of health insurance for an individual.
• Provision of information to law enforcement agencies about library patrons (including who they are and what they read or saw in the library) for the stated purpose of increasing public safety or homeland security, and a prohibition of discussing or acknowledging that this has been done.
• Availability of public government records (including criminal records, family court proceedings, real estate transactions, and so on, and formerly only available in paper format) on the World Wide Web for the stated purpose of increasing the openness of government.
• Geographic tracking of cell-phone locations at all times for the stated purpose of enabling emergency location.

Note also that privacy concerns are often grounded in information that may be used for purposes other than a stated purpose. Indeed, in each of the examples given above, another possible—and less benign—purpose might easily be envisioned and thus might change entirely one's framing of a privacy issue.

---

vides some illustrative examples). Advocates for various positions who argue vigorously for a given policy thus run the risk of casting their arguments in unduly broad terms. Though rhetorical excesses are often a staple of advocacy, in truth the factors driving the information age rarely create simple problems with simple solutions.

Perhaps the best known of the general tradeoffs in the privacy debate is that which contrasts privacy with considerations of law enforcement and national security. At this writing, there is considerable debate over the Bush administration's use of warrantless wiretapping in its counterterrorism efforts against al-Qaeda. Furthermore, the USA PATRIOT Act, passed in the immediate wake of the September 11, 2001, attacks on the World Trade Center and the Pentagon and extended and amended in early 2006, changed a number of privacy-related laws in order to facilitate certain law enforcement and national security goals. (Chapter 9 contains an extensive discussion of these issues.)

But the law enforcement/national security versus privacy debate is hardly the only example of such tradeoffs that are being made. Box 1.1 provides some illustrations. Privacy concerns interact with the delivery of health care and the information needed to contribute to public health as well as the information needed to discover and understand risk factors that any individual may have. Privacy concerns interact with the ability to do long- and short-term sociological studies. Techniques that are believed to increase productivity and profitability may come at a cost to the privacy interests of many consumers and workers. Privacy concerns also are reflected in the debates about new forms of intellectual property.

Privacy concerns also interact with sociological and policy research. In order to conduct these kinds of research, substantial amounts of personal information are often necessary. However, in general, these data never have to be associated with specific individuals. This situation contrasts sharply with the societal needs described above: law enforcement authorities are interested in apprehending a specific individual guilty of criminal wrongdoing, national security authorities are interested in identifying a particular terrorist, or a business wants to identify a specific customer who will buy a product. For these reasons, protected data collections such as those found in social science data archives and census public-use files serve the interests of groups and communities with less controversy; when controversy does exist, it usually relates to whether the data contained in these files and archives are sufficiently anonymized, or to specific nonstatistical uses of these data.

Tradeoffs are also not limited to the value of information to an organization versus the value of privacy to an individual—they also arise in the same situation of an individual alone. For example, an individual might regard his or her personal information as a commodity that can be traded freely in exchange for some other good or service of value—and thus he or she might well be willing to provide personal information on shopping habits at a chain drugstore or supermarket in exchange for a 2 percent discount on all purchases. Furthermore, even if the tradeoffs do appear to pit value to an organization against value to an individual, some would argue that there is benefit to the individual as well (albeit not specific benefit to him or her) if the organization can be construed as "all or most of society." This point is discussed in greater detail in Section 6.4.

Not only are these tradeoffs complex, difficult, and sometimes seemingly intractable, but they are also often not made explicit in the discussions that take place around the policies that, when they are enacted, quietly embody the value tradeoffs. Clarifications on these points would not necessarily relieve the underlying tensions, but they would likely help illuminate the contours of the debate. A major purpose of this report is to contribute to that illumination.

1.3 AN ILLUSTRATIVE CASE

In early 2005, a firm known as ChoicePoint announced that "a crime committed against ChoicePoint . . . MAY have resulted in [consumer] name[s], address[es], and Social Security number[s] being viewed by businesses that are not allowed access to such information."[3] Specifically, ChoicePoint reported that "several individuals, posing as legitimate business customers, recently committed fraud by claiming to have a lawful purpose for accessing information about individuals, when in fact, they did not." ChoicePoint explained its business as verifying for its business customers information supplied by individuals as part of a business transaction, often as part of an application for insurance, a job, or a home loan.

ChoicePoint notified approximately 143,000 individuals that their personal information might have been compromised. In early 2006, the U.S. Federal Trade Commission (FTC) announced that ChoicePoint would pay $15 million in fines and other penalties for lax security standards in verifying the credentials of its business customers. Furthermore, the FTC noted that "this breach occurred because ChoicePoint failed to implement reasonable and appropriate procedures for approving new customers and for monitoring existing ones."[4] It also said that more than 800 cases of identity theft arose from this breach in security.

For purposes of this study, the truth or falsity of the FTC's allegations about ChoicePoint's security practices per se is not relevant. But what is relevant is that the personal information of more than 143,000 individuals was released to parties that did not have a lawful purpose in receiving that information, and that a number of cases of identity theft arose from this release.

Several questions immediately come to mind:

1. How is ChoicePoint able to aggregate such voluminous information? The data that ChoicePoint collects on individuals includes criminal histories, Social Security numbers, and employment histories.

---

[3]"Choicepoint's Letter to Consumers Whose Information Was Compromised," *CSO Magazine*, available at http://www.csoonline.com/read/050105/choicepoint_letter.html.

[4]Federal Trade Commission, "ChoicePoint Settles Data Security Breach Charges; to Pay $10 Million in Civil Penalties, $5 Million for Consumer Redress," available at http://www.ftc.gov/opa/2006/01/choicepoint.htm.

2. Why do ChoicePoint and other similar firms collect such voluminous data on individuals?

3. What was the harm suffered by the individuals whose identities were not stolen? Eight hundred individual cases of identity theft were attributed to the breach, a number corresponding to about ½ of 1 percent of the 143,000 individuals involved.

4. To what extent were individuals notified by ChoicePoint surprised by the existence of such aggregations of personal data?

Question 1 points to the availability of great quantities of personal information on a large scale to organizations that have no direct involvement in the creation of the data. ChoicePoint is not the primary collector of such information; it is an aggregator of it. It also points to the fact that information collected for one purpose (e.g., a job application with a certain employer) can be "repurposed" and used for an entirely different purpose (e.g., verification of job history in connection with a background investigation).

Question 2 points to a demand on the part of private businesses and government agencies for personal information about its employees and customers. Indeed, such information is so important to these businesses and government agencies that they are willing to pay to check and verify the accuracy of information provided by employees and customers. (Note also that by insisting that employees and customers provide personal information, these businesses and agencies often add to the personal information that is available to data aggregators.)

Question 3 focuses attention on the value of privacy and the nature of the harm that can accrue to individuals when their privacy is breached even if they have not been the victims of identity theft. In this case, the answer is that these individuals suffer the same harm that Damocles experienced when he was partying and feasting under the sword. No physical harm came to Damocles, yet the cost to his sense of well-being was high indeed. A person whose privacy has been breached is likely to be concerned about the negative consequences that *might* flow from the breach, and those kinds of psychological concerns constitute a type of actual though intangible harm entirely apart from the other kinds of tangible harm that the law typically recognizes. A second kind of intangible harm experienced by Damocles might have been his reluctance to engage in dancing and making loud noises that might have caused the thread holding the sword to break—a so-called chilling effect on his activities and behaviors. In short—harm need not be tangible to be real or actual.[5]

---

[5]Nor is "harm" a concept that is relevant only to individuals. As Section 2.3 addresses in greater detail, certain kinds of harm may relate to groups or to society as a whole. Group or

Question 4 alerts us to issues involving the commodification of personal information and its being treated as a kind of marketable property to be used as those who come to possess it choose. Question 4 also calls attention to several collateral issues surrounding privacy. In this case, the issue is the role of notification in privacy, and whether notification that personal information is being collected about an individual in any sense ameliorates any breach of privacy that might be associated with that collection. Given legal requirements to notify individuals after privacy violations have been documented, are such violations thus less likely?

Questions and issues such as these recur frequently in this report, although in no sense do these examples exhaust the kinds of questions and issues that arise. Privacy provides a useful filter through which to think about individual and societal benefits and costs.

1.4 THE DYNAMICS OF PRIVACY

Privacy is part of a social context that is subject to a range of factors. While a relationship between privacy and society has always existed, the factors (or pressures) affecting privacy in the information age are varied and deeply interconnected. These factors, individually and collectively, are changing and expanding in scale with unprecedented speed in terms of our ability to understand and contend with their implications to our world, in general, and our privacy, in particular. Some of these factors include the volume, magnitude, complexity, and persistence of information; the expanding number of ways to collect information; the number of people affected by information; and the geographic spread and reach of information technology.

1.4.1 The Information Age

What is meant by the term "information age," and what are the factors so profoundly affecting the dynamics of privacy? With respect to the information age, a great deal has been written about the fact that almost no part of our lives is untouched by computing and information technology. These technologies underlie new ways of collecting and handling information that in turn have ramifications throughout society, as they mediate much private and public communication, interaction, and transactions. They are central components of contemporary infrastructures involving (but certainly not restricted to) commerce, banking and finance, utilities, communications, national defense, education, and entertainment.

---

societal harms may be related to individually suffered harm, but are conceptually separate notions.

BOX 1.2
Large-scale Factors Affecting Privacy

Technological Change	*Societal Trends*	*Discontinuities in Circumstance*
• Ubiquity	• Globalization	• Catastrophic attacks
• Connectivity	• Mobility	in 2001 on the World
• Data collection	• Virtuality	Trade Center/Pentagon
• Storage	• Urbanization	• Watergate scandal in
• Computational power	• Constant accessibility	1972-1973
• Commoditization of	• Litigiousness	• Church Committee
hardware	• Demographics/Aging	Hearings of 1976
• Software usability	• New ways of living	(also known as the
• Encryption	and communicating	Hearings of the
• Privacy-relevant	• Increases in social	United States Senate
biotechnology	networking	Select Committee to
• Extensions of human	• Increased societal	Study Governmental
senses	interdependence	Operations with Respect
• Portability of data	• Increase in electronic	to Intelligence Activities)
and communications	communication	• Attack on Pearl Harbor
devices	literacy	in 1941
• Persistence of	• Increase in	• Invention in 1995 of the
information	expectations for	World Wide Web[1]
• Affordability of data	information availability	• National and
and communications	• Linked monetary	international health
• Advances in sensor	systems	threats (SARS and
technology	• Linked production	avian flu)
	systems	

[1]The World Wide Web is a product of technology trends, but it was also the primary driving force underlying the explosion of easy-to-use Internet applications that ultimately made enormous amounts of information—personal and otherwise—publicly accessible.

This brief characterization of the information age highlights the three major factors, indeed drivers, of the vast changes affecting current notions, perceptions, and expectations of privacy: *technological change, societal shifts,* and *discontinuities in circumstances* (Box 1.2).

Technological change (Column 1 in Box 1.2) refers to major differences in the technological environment of today as compared to that existing many decades ago (differences that have a major influence on today's social and legal regime governing privacy). Column 2 in Box 1.2 identifies a number of trends that set a large-scale social and cultural context for discussions of privacy. Societal shifts refer to evolutionary trends in society writ large. Discontinuities in circumstances (Column 3 in Box 1.2) are events and emergent concerns that transformed the national debate about privacy in a very short time (and thus did not allow for gradual adjustment to a new set of circumstances).

Society is thus experiencing the effects of changes in these factors. For example:

- Changes in technology have enhanced access to information and images previously available to the public but then much more difficult to access. New technologies that extend the senses have made new kinds of data available as a result of covert "soft surveillance." The fact that such surveillance permits the collection of personal information without the consent or knowledge of the subject offers temptations for misuse.
- Changes in business models, which are increasingly based on the notion of greater customization of services and products, a process that in turn requires large amounts of personal information so that the appropriate customization can be employed.
- Changes in expectations of security following the terrorist attacks of 2001 have reduced people's expectations of the privacy rights of foreign nationals and U.S. citizens in this country, as did the attack on Pearl Harbor in 1941. Similarly, the post-Watergate revelations of government abuse of records containing personal information increased people's expectations of the privacy rights to which they were entitled.

Subsequent chapters characterize these rapid changes in some detail. For the purposes of this introduction to thinking about privacy, it is sufficient to note that each of these changes is having significant impacts on society. However, in combination, these changes are key drivers of the information society and underlie fundamental changes in how we, as individuals and as a society, grapple with privacy, business activities, social interaction, and information. These systemic and profound changes in turn have a most direct influence on the dynamics of privacy—and indeed privacy's salience as a topic of importance to this committee and to citizens generally.

1.4.2 Information Transformed and the Role of Technology

Technological advancements, coupled with changes in other areas, combine to make the privacy challenge particularly vexing. Technological change is, of course, not new. The printing press has been described as a precursor to the World Wide Web; e-mail and cell phone text messaging have revolutionized interpersonal and group correspondence. Affordability and advances in sensor technologies have broadened the volume and scope of information that can be practically acquired. The privacy debate in the United States itself has part of its roots in the technological changes involving the press and technology for photography—Warren and Brandeis, in their landmark 1890 *Harvard Law Review* paper,[6] were responding to, as they put it, "recent inventions and business methods."

The business method at issue was the popular press, and the most striking of the recent inventions—the technology—was the unposed photograph. Suddenly, it was easy to take spontaneous and often uninvited photos of people—which Warren and Brandeis denounced as "invad[ing] the sacred precincts of private and domestic life"—and to show the results to a large, literate, curious, and gossipy audience.[7]

What makes information special is that it is reproducible. In digital form, information can be copied an infinite number of times without losing fidelity. Digitized information is also easy to distribute at low cost. Today, in the information age, the sheer quantity of information; the ability to collect unobtrusively, aggregate, and analyze it; the ability to store it cheaply; the ubiquity of interconnectedness; and the magnitude and speed of all aspects of the way we think about, use, characterize, manipulate, and represent information are fundamentally and continuously changing. Consider concepts of:

- *Information search.* Within half a generation we have moved from dusty card catalogues and file drawers full of rolls of microfiche to warehouses of servers connected to the worldwide Internet that allow, among many other things, much of the Internet to be searched for keywords at the click of a button.
- *Information production.* In just the world of publishing alone, we have moved from mimeographs and hand distribution for the truly dedicated amateur to parents creating, modifying, and publishing entire photo and video albums of their children in ways that are accessible almost instantly around the globe. Blogging enables many of us to publish nearly anything we want on the Internet.
- *Information manipulation.* The ways in which information can be manipulated have expanded—both in terms of capability and also in terms of who has access to the tools that allow such manipulation. Photo-editing software and sound-editing technologies are now bundled with many common personal computers. What might have taken hours to

---

[6]Samuel D. Warren and Louis D. Brandeis, "The Right to Privacy," *Harvard Law Review* IV (December 15, No. 5):195, 1890, available at http://www.lawrence.edu/fac/boardmaw/Privacy_brand_warr2.html.

[7]George Radwanski, Address to the Privacy Lecture Series, Toronto, Ontario, March 26, 2001, available at http://www.privcom.gc.ca/speech/02_05_a_010326_2_e.asp.

correct or modify in the days of the professional darkroom or recording studio can now be trivially accomplished by anyone with a PC.

• *Information storage.* In many cases, records containing information are no longer thrown away. It has become less expensive to keep the data on larger, cheaper storage devices than to cull the information accurately so as to remove data. As a result data that has outlived its original use is retained and becomes subject to future unanticipated uses.

• *Information acquisition.* It is easier today than ever before to acquire many kinds of information about individuals. Sensors such as video surveillance cameras and radio-frequency ID tags are rapidly dropping in cost and are increasingly ubiquitous in the environment. Cell phones are capable of localizing to an accuracy of 100 meters the real-time whereabouts of the individuals carrying them. Electronic fare cards for public transportation often identify entry and exit points, along with the time of day.

• *Information analysis.* Sophisticated algorithms are increasingly capable of finding patterns buried in large quantities of data. Basic statistics of data can be generated on board sensor platforms, or even the sensors themselves, before even being transmitted to a central point of analysis. And the ingenuity of users knows few bounds, as such users find new ways of using information already collected for new purposes.

Trends in information technology have made it easier and cheaper by orders of magnitude to gather, retain, and analyze information. Other trends have also enabled access to *new* kinds of information that historically would have been next to impossible to gather about another individual. For example, certain kinds of data acquisition devices are already widely deployed (e.g., video cameras). The cost of such devices is dropping, which will enable even more ubiquitous deployment. And it will be increasingly easy to collect information from them as they are deployed not as standalone devices but in networks. Such devices have many socially beneficial applications, ranging from health care monitoring to monitoring of weather and geophysical variables to traffic control. But even if the data from these systems are not intended to monitor human interaction and behavior, they can often be repurposed to do exactly that. Moreover, information about human behavior can be inferred from seemingly innocuous data (such as heat sources in buildings or the way a person walks).

Still another effect of new information technologies is the erosion of privacy protection once provided through obscurity or the passage of time; e.g., youthful indiscretions can now become impossible to outlive as an adult. For much of the past, the effects of data collection were not a major issue, perhaps because the relevant data were inaccessible for practical purposes or individual pieces of data were stored in different locations so that patterns contained within the potentially aggregated data were difficult to find. Often either the sheer volume of input would overwhelm the method of analysis or the patterns would be lost in a sea of data. It is not quite the case that data were inaccessible, but they were contained in the form of, for example, public records stored in filing cabinets in county clerks' basements, and were in practice expensive and difficult to access.

Today and increasingly in the future, electronic storage of information is less expensive and potentially more persistent than paper storage.[8] Also, information systems have moved from isolated systems to clustered systems of users and machines to what now is becoming a mesh of interconnected information and analysis systems, which can share information and work collectively, leading to a much greater ease of data aggregation. Once data is aggregated, new and more powerful techniques and technologies for analyzing information (generically known as data mining) will make it much easier to extract and identify personally identifiable patterns that were previously protected by the vast amounts of data "noise" around them. Furthermore, as the interrelationships between systems become more closely identified, the issues of ownership, control, prerogative, and privacy also become more difficult to discern or manage.

Similarly worrisome to many is the emergence of biometric identification, the use of information technologies to measure and record biological or physiological characteristics of the human body for identification purposes. Such characteristics can include DNA sequences, gait, retinal patterns, fingerprints, and so on. The primary significance of biometrics in a privacy context is that certain markers are selected for large-scale use because they are believed to be more or less invariant over an individual's lifetime. (Whether this is in fact the case in any given instance can be a subject of great debate.)

The comments above should not be taken to mean that the advance of technology has only negative effects on privacy. As the discussion in Chapter 3 indicates, some advances in technology can promote or enhance privacy. For example, technology enables the maintenance of audit trails

---

[8]Whether paper or electronic storage is in fact more persistent in the long run (measured in decades) is not known with certainty. Whereas paper is a very simple and enduring medium, today's high-capacity CD-ROMs and DVDs may be largely unusable in 10 years. The problem of electronic media obsolescence as it affects access to stored information can be addressed by periodically rewriting the information onto new media, but such rewriting presents logistical challenges that can be daunting for individuals and organizations alike. (On the difficulties faced by organizations, see National Research Council, *LC21: A Digital Strategy for the Library of Congress*, National Academy Press, Washington, D.C., 2000.)

that can keep track of who accesses what data. The possibility of accessing sensitive data improperly on an anonymous basis often presents a strong temptation for doing so, and the keeping of audit logs can often deter such activity. However, such privacy-protecting technologies must be deployed in order to enhance privacy, and because they generally have no operational or business value other than protecting privacy, it is often the case that such protective technologies are not deployed.

1.4.3 Societal Shifts and Changes in Institutional Practice

Focusing solely on technological advancements provides an incomplete view of how values, understandings, and expectations shift over time. Important consideration must be given to societal institutions—the organizations and the activities and practices that make use of the technological systems described above—and to the transformation of social institutions through their routine use.

Modern society is characterized, in part, by a multitude of demands for personal information not just from families and one's immediate community but also from governments and institutions. Whether these demands are the result of new technologies searching for problems to solve at lower cost, or whatever they serve to stimulate the growth of new technologies, is open to question—as with most such questions, the most likely answer is "some of both."[9] But what is clear today is that making personal information available to institutions and organizations is absolutely essential for individual participation in everyday life.

Consider, for example, the information demands involved in:

- Licensing practices, of which the driver's license is the most ubiquitous example. To obtain a driver's license, an individual must provide personal information (e.g., name, address, and so on) as well as proof of driving ability. But over time, a driver's license comes to contain a driver's history of moving violations and accidents as well. Furthermore, a driver's license is a de facto ID standard for many purposes, ranging from admission to facilities and air travel to check cashing. Though auto-

---

[9]As one example, a string of technological innovations that shaped, and were shaped by, the development of the modern bureaucracy between 1890 and 1939 is described in James Beniger, *The Control Revolution: Technological and Economic Origins of the Information Society*, Harvard University Press, Cambridge, Mass., 1986. The duality of causation is reflected quite well in the example of the use of Herman Hollerith's punch card system to increase the efficiency of the 1890 census. While Hollerith's machines cannot be blamed, there is little doubt that they were an integral part of the transformation of the national government's data gathering, processing, and distribution activities.

mated systems are not in place today to collect driver's license numbers in all of these applications, they could be—and the volume of personal information about spending habits, locations, travel, and so on that might be assembled through such systems is rather large. For other licensing applications, such as licenses needed for various professions, other kinds of information may be needed, such as various histories of education, records of previous practice, and customer complaints and/or disciplinary actions taken. To receive an amateur radio operator's license, a person—regardless of age—must allow his or her name and address to be posted on the Internet.

• Many benefits in society are conferred by law only to particular classes of people (e.g., veterans, the unemployed, those with low income, homeowners). Establishing eligibility and verifying claims require individual information. In response to concerns about fraud, administering government agencies are asking for more information and have increasingly turned to computer matching involving diverse databases. In contrast, such agencies rarely do computer matching to identify potential clients who are not utilizing benefits to which they are entitled.

• Many private sector institutions make distinctions between categories of people. For example, the granting and the terms of credit to individuals both depend heavily on many of the details of their financial history (e.g., records of payment, length of time at particular addresses, employment record, income). Admissions to many institutions of higher education depend on a detailed history and record of an individual's curricular and extracurricular activities.

• Many institutions require personal information as a condition of providing service at all. In some cases, the need for personal information is intrinsic to the service itself—health care services for an individual are perforce information-intensive, and given societal pressures to deliver more effective health care at lower cost, are likely to become more so in the future. In other cases, the need for personal information is externally motivated—for example, as a matter of regulation for the purpose of inhibiting money laundering, banks are legally required to collect and file information from customers that is not intrinsically connected to the provision of financial services.

• Employers are demanding more information about employees as they seek to validate employment credentials, to better match a person to a job, and to avoid liability suits. Would-be employees submit extensive application forms documenting previous work histories and education; once hired, they are often subject to drug tests and location checks to help ensure that they are continuing to observe the conditions of their employment. On the job, intensive work monitoring has increased, particularly as individuals work with computers and or work in areas subject to video surveillance. This may go beyond monitoring of work products per se, to the monitoring of behavior unrelated to work and sometimes behavior off-duty.

• Retailers of goods and services galore are seeking to provide more personalized products and targeted attention to their customers. From customization of goods and services to individual needs targeted at marketing specific products to selected audiences likely to buy them, detailed personal information about the preferences and habits and buying histories of customers is an enabler for personalization.

• Members of the public demand information as well. Through the legislative process, previously private information such as physician malpractice histories, sexual offender status, and political contributions are now public—and more importantly, easily available—for all to see.

• Individuals demand more information from each other in many contexts. For example, it is common that individuals—especially young people—using social networking sites post large amounts of personal information. No one forces these people to do so, and yet the social context of the sites' use provides a strong impetus for doing so.

The examples above illustrate current information demands. They also suggest how our attitudes toward privacy are context dependent. It is difficult to hold a broad view, absent consideration of what kind of information is sought, who seeks it, and how it is to be collected, protected, and used. There are, for example, some things one might not mind the government knowing that one would object to an employer knowing (and vice versa). And there are other things that one would not object to either of them knowing, but would not want passed on to aunts and uncles, just as there are things that one would like to keep within the family. Determining what should be left to the realm of ethics and common courtesy, what should be incentivized or discouraged, and what should be formalized into a code of law is yet another balancing question that comes up when contemplating privacy.

A further complicating factor is the changing nature of expectations about the revelation and concealment of personal information. Social and cultural trends over the last century (perhaps accelerated during the 1960s) have softened traditional beliefs that opposed the easy revelation of certain kinds of personal information. Although many individuals do seek a certain measure of privacy in their lives (e.g., they purchase homes with privacy-protecting features such as enclosed porches or obscuring bushes), there has been a lessening or outright ending of reticence in mass culture as seen in the popularity of reality television shows and talk show confessionals. In addition, an emphasis in some parts of society on sharing and building trust and community through openness in communication and discussion may conflict with privacy notions regarding what is (or should be) kept as "personal information" and what should be revealed.

Finally, in some cases personal information is used to determine a category into which a given individual might fall, and what is of interest to another party is the category rather than the person.[10] The availability of personal information enables the assignment of an individual to one or more categories, such as those who share a characteristic such as age, race, or genetic marker. For example, the popularity of geo-demographic targeting for the marketing of goods and services at the neighborhood level reflects a determination that there is quite a bit of predictive utility in the differences between 100 types of communities definable at the ZIP + 4 level of precision.[11] Political parties use personal information to determine how to target their voter turnout efforts towards those most likely to vote for their candidates.[12]

Undertaken in the context of selling different products based on a zip code's socioeconomic status indicators, such a practice may be benign. Nevertheless, it is important to consider the implications of less benign applications, such as political campaigns run on a similar basis, in which different messages are targeted to different geographical areas, or redlining—the practice of denying service (or increasing the cost of service) to people in selected geographic areas—which may serve as a proxy for race, ethnicity, or income. Such issues reflect the potential for an information-based ability for discrimination of many different kinds—against individuals and against groups—in the name of increasing efficiency. (Note that this notion of discrimination is not necessarily confined to discrimination against categories of people protected by law.)

1.4.4 Discontinuities in Circumstance and Current Events

Current events can be important factors in shaping attitudes toward privacy.

---

[10]Geoffrey C. Bowker and Susan L. Star, *Sorting Things Out: Classification and Its Consequences*, MIT Press, Cambridge, Mass., 1999.

[11]See the discussion of geo-demographic clustering and commercial services offered by Claritas Corporation in Mark Monmonier, *Spying with Maps*, University of Chicago Press, 2002.

[12]See, for example, Chris Cillizza and Jim VandeHei, "In Ohio, a Battle of Databases," *Washington Post*, September 26, 2006, p. A-1.

1.4.4.1 National Security and Law Enforcement

The events of September 11, 2001, have led to a renewed emphasis on homeland security and how best to achieve it in the United States. The primary focus of homeland security is now prevention of deliberate catastrophically harmful incidents rather than prosecution of those responsible for such acts. Prevention and disruption of a terrorist act are much more difficult than is prosecution of those responsible after the act, primarily because investigative activities can be focused much more precisely, working backward from the event.

This new focus has resulted in a number of privacy-relevant changes in the policy environment. One of the most important changes has been to elide the traditional separation of law enforcement and national security intelligence gathering. But this change poses numerous challenges, the most important of which is the final disposition of "law enforcement" information versus "national security" information. Law enforcement officials operate in a prosecutorial role, which means that "law enforcement" information must be usable in open court, along with information about its origins and provenance. "National security intelligence" information is often tied to the sources and methods used to gather it, most of which must remain secret if they are to be productive sources in the future. This means, for example, that it is not generally feasible to allow individuals about whom information has been collected to challenge the accuracy of such information, or even to notify these individuals about the fact of such collection.

A second change has been a greater willingness to focus information-gathering efforts on the continental United States. Although they were foreign citizens, the September 11 hijackers operated from U.S. soil and used U.S. airliners flying from U.S airports to strike U.S. targets. Thus, attention has been focused on identifying other possible terrorist cells operating in the United States by detecting their operational "signatures" through domestically focused information gathering and analysis. While the concerns of law enforcement and national security officials regarding the possibility of U.S.-based terrorist operations cannot be discounted, the mere fact of including information about U.S. persons within the scope of counterterrorist operations inevitably raises privacy concerns as well.

These issues are addressed at greater length in Chapter 9.

1.4.4.2 Disease and Pandemic Outbreak

In recent years, concerns about pandemic disease outbreaks have also advanced to the top of the public policy agenda. By definition, pandemics result from the emergence of a new disease (or a variant of an old one) that is both infectious in humans and highly contagious. Pandemics have occurred throughout human history, but the cost and time required to travel great distances have diminished now to the point where long-distance travel is within the reach of a large part of the world's population. Along with increased cultural exchange and commerce, this rapid and accessible travel, especially by airplane, has increased the chances for rapid spread of communicable diseases across local and national borders. A person may become infected with a disease and fly to a foreign country before even realizing that he or she is sick—an especially relevant point when the symptoms of the disease in question take a long time to appear.

As this report is written, world scientists are monitoring two diseases in particular, SARS and the avian (bird) flu. In both cases, the public health response calls for rapid detection of a medical anomaly and, if possible, identification of the location and direction of spread of the disease so that, for example, quarantine and inoculation zones can be established to stem the spread of disease.

The options available from a public health standpoint to prevent pandemic outbreaks originating from outside national borders are limited. The volume of air traffic is so large that it cannot be shut down or even seriously attenuated without enormous economic consequences. Thus, the only other option is to monitor closely for the outbreak of disease in other nations and to seek to prevent those who are disease carriers from crossing one's own national borders.

Although individuals seeking to enter the United States have fewer and more limited privacy protections than they would if they were already present in-country, monitoring and obtaining information on the health of individuals have implications for privacy. Monitoring for the outbreak of disease can entail the acquisition of a great deal of personal information so that public health officials can track a disease as it spreads. But even more (potentially) invasive is the idea of obtaining information from travelers (who may be either foreign nationals or one's own citizens returning from abroad) in order to differentiate them into disease carriers and nondisease carriers. Thus, in the pursuit of public health, nations have sometimes required individuals seeking to enter to undergo tests for HIV, fill out detailed medical questionnaires, take medical examinations at the border, and undergo (sometimes covert) thermal scans that detect the presence of fever.

1.5 IMPORTANT CONCEPTS AND IDEAS RELATED TO PRIVACY

Debates over privacy often make use of specialized concepts whose intuitive meaning is not necessarily clear on the face of it. Moreover, these debates are often conducted without much cognizance of the topic's long history in the public policy sphere. This section addresses key concepts, and Section 1.6 addresses important historical lessons.

1.5.1 Personal Information, Sensitive Information, and Personally Identifiable Information

Personal information can be regarded as the set of all data that is associated with a specific individual, e.g., date of birth, gender, address, name of first pet, favorite chocolate, high school of graduation, geographical location at 3:14 p.m. on March 30, 2005, and on and on and on. The specific value of any given element in that set (e.g., a date of birth January 2, 1957) can almost always be associated with more than one individual (many people were born on January 2, 1957).

Personal information thus has meaning only through the ways in which it associates or differentiates an individual from others. The value of any given data element (call that data element D_1) divides the set of all human beings in the universe into two subsets—a set S_1 comprising those with whom the value of D_1 can validly be associated, and the complement of that set. Multiple data (D_2, D_3, D_4...) result in sets S_2, S_3, S_4. Combining the values of personal data elements D_1, D_2, D_3, D_4 means taking the intersection of S_1, S_2, S_3, S_4 (call the intersection S_I, and the number of people in S_I the bin size. In general, S_I has more than one person in it (i.e., the bin size is more than one). In the case when the bin size is one, S_I has exactly one person in it, and the data values associated with S_I can be said to uniquely specify a specific individual.

Several points are worth noting here:

- Privacy is perforce a relative concept. In a specific context, I may feel that my "privacy" is adequately protected if I can be identified within a bin size of 1,000; you may feel that your privacy is adequately protected only if you can be identified within a bin size of 10,000.
- Certain combinations of data elements can be particularly—and surprisingly—effective in reducing bin size. For example, 87 percent of the U.S. population can be uniquely specified by knowledge of his or her 5-digit ZIP code of residence, gender, and date of birth.[13] None of these individual pieces of information are individually identifying, but most of

---

[13] Latanya Sweeney, *Uniqueness of Simple Demographics in the U.S. Population*, LIDAP-WP4, Laboratory for International Data Privacy, Carnegie Mellon University, Pittsburgh, Pa., 2000.

the general public would be surprised by their collective power in identifying individuals.[14]

• A person's identity (whether defined by the individual in question or others labeling him or her) is defined by some subset of personal information. By convention and for legal purposes, that subset generally includes the name of the person in question. But people often operate with multiple identities (or may have identities imposed upon them)—one's identity as a parent, as an employee, as a Social Security recipient, as a member of America Online with several screen names, and so on. Reconciling multiple identities is, in essence, the process of taking the union of all of these subsets, although efforts to link multiple identities through a common identifier are often controversial. (Also, knowing a person's name will not necessarily permit access to that person if his or her location (whether in real space or in cyberspace) is unknown.)

• In general, it is the values of data elements and combinations thereof that specify unique individuals, not the data elements themselves. In some cases, "unique identifiers"—if genuinely unique—could be said to specify unique individuals. For example, ruling out the case of identical twins, an individual's complete genomic sequence (the specific sequence of all 3 billion DNA base pairs) could specify a unique individual. Barring errors and fraud, the Social Security number was originally intended to be a unique identifier. But in general, no one data element specifies a unique individual.

• Unique identifiers require special protection from a privacy perspective. Because it is a data element (and not a specific value) that can be used to uniquely specify an individual, a unique identifier for a person can greatly facilitate the linkage of other information about that person and hence the collection of large amounts of information under that one identifier. When such unique identifiers fall into criminal hands, and especially when it is impossible to revoke an identifier and obtain a new one, impersonation, identity theft, and even location tracking become much easier to accomplish.

• The value of any given data element may or may not be permanently associated with a given individual. An individual's date of birth does not change, but an individual's weight does. Matters of historical

---

[14]Date of birth is an especially powerful tool for reducing bin size. Knowing the day of the year splits the population into 366 groups. Knowing the year of birth splits the population into an additional 90 to 100 years, depending on one's estimate of the age of the oldest individuals. Thus, date of birth alone splits a population into some 32,940 to 36,600 bins. A 5-digit ZIP code splits the population into 100,000 bins. These attributes taken together constitute approximately 3.5×10^9 bins, a number that is about 10 times the population of the United States. Thus, Sweeney's empirical result is not entirely surprising.

fact, if recorded correctly and accurately, do not change and thus are permanent, although their meaning is subject to interpretation and those interpretations may change—e.g., what to make of an individual who undergoes a sex change operation. Names and addresses do change with some frequency, although one may be able to make some general socio-demographic inferences with knowledge of such changes over time. An individual's DNA sequence does not change throughout his or her life-time, but the longevity and stability of many other biometric indicators have not been definitively established.

Individuals vary considerably in their privacy demands or expecta-tions for different kinds of data and for the same individual data element in different situations. That is, in one situation, an individual may regard a particular data element as highly private (one that might require a large bin size) and in a different situation regard the same data element as not at all private (i.e., he would be perfectly fine with a bin size of one). Relevant situational factors may include:

- *The specific value of the data element and whether or not it stigmatizes or disadvantages.* For example, an HIV-positive individual may require a bin size of one million to feel that his HIV status is private; an HIV-negative individual may feel entirely comfortable with a bin size of one (i.e., being identified with certainty as being HIV-negative).
- *The stated purpose for which any given data element is requested.* The closer the fit between the goals of the supplier and the requester of infor-mation and between the information requested and the goal, the more likely it is to be provided. In most doctor-patient contexts, the patient is only too glad to offer information. If a newspaper's Web site asks a visitor her income, she may refuse to provide it, whereas she would willingly supply that same information in filling out an online application for a mortgage. Note also that if there is an incentive or reward for supply-ing personal information, many consumers sell that information more cheaply than their statements about the value of their personal informa-tion would lead one to expect.
- *The accessibility of the given data element.* Data that are public and hard to access (e.g., paper records, such as property taxes or divorce pro-ceedings, that are kept in the physical facilities of many jurisdictions) are very different from data that are public and very easy to access (e.g., the same public information posted online). The ease or difficulty of finding a particular type of data element may also contribute to accessibility.
- *The transience of the given data element.* For example, when informa-tion is stored in paper form, it may be discarded eventually because it is expensive to store. There may be different privacy implications if the data

element is available only for an instant (e.g., a conversation being heard in real time), for one hour, one year, one decade, or one century.[15]

The above discussion also illuminates the distinction between three categories of information—personal information, sensitive information, and personally identifiable information.[16]

- Personal information is the set of all information that is associated with a specific person X. Personal information is thus defined in a technical or objective sense.

- Sensitive information is the set of personal information that some party believes should be kept private. If the party is the person associated with that information (call that person X), the set is defined by personal preferences of X, and X's definition of private (which may be highly context dependent and linked to particular cultural standards regarding the revelation or withholding of information). Note that context may reflect a temporal aspect as well. In some circumstances, one might regard a certain item of personal information as less sensitive if it referred to his or her information "state" in the past rather than in the present. (For example, I may regard my physical location now as being a more sensitive item of information than my physical location 3 weeks ago.) The converse may be true as well. The party defining "sensitive information" may also be a party other than person X. This other party may take into account the interests and preferences of person X, but may also be taking other factors into consideration. For example, person X may prefer that her criminal record be kept private, but most criminal records are regarded legally as public information. Who defines what information should count as "sensitive" is often a controversial matter.

- Personally identifiable information (PII) refers to any information that identifies or can be used to identify, contact, or locate the person to whom such information pertains. This includes information that is used in a way that is personally identifiable, including linking it with identi-

---

[15]Privacy is not necessarily a monotonically decreasing function of the holding period. Personal information held for 100 years after the death of the person involved is arguably nonsensitive as far as that person is concerned, although it may be highly sensitive to grandchildren if it contains genetic or severely stigmatizing information. The converse may be true as well.

[16]These and some additional distinctions are discussed in Gary T. Marx, "Varieties of Personal Information as Influences on Attitudes Towards Surveillance," in R. Ericson and K. Haggerty, eds., *The New Politics of Surveillance and Visibility*, University of Toronto Press, 2006; and "Identity and Anonymity: Some Conceptual Distinctions and Issues for Research," in J. Caplan and J.T. Torpey, *Documenting Individual Identity: The Development of the State Since the French Revolution*, Princeton University Press, Princeton, N.J., 2000.

fiable information from other sources, or from which other personally identifiable information can easily be derived, including, but not limited to, name, address, phone number, fax number, e-mail address, financial profiles, Social Security number, and credit card information.[17] Although PII is also said to not include information collected anonymously, the discussion above suggests both that the ability to make an identification may depend on the specific values of the PII in question and on the ability to aggregate data in ways that reduce significantly or even eliminate the anonymity originally promised or implied. Thus, information that previously was not PII may at a later date become PII as new techniques are developed or as other non-PII information becomes available.

1.5.2 False Positives, False Negatives, and Data Quality

In many societies, alleged criminals are tried by jury. In any given trial, the jury finds a defendant either innocent or guilty (apart from jury deadlocks). If a defendant found guilty did not in fact commit the crime for which he or she is being tried, the result is a "false positive." If a defendant found innocent did in fact commit the crime for which he or she is being tried, the result is a "false negative."

False positives and false negatives arise in any kind of classification exercise.[18] For example, a credit-card-issuing bank examines personal information of potential clients and classifies them as good credit risks (likely to pay their bills) and bad credit risks (unlikely to pay their bills). Some individuals identified as good credit risks will, in fact, not pay their bills—these are the false positives. Some individuals identified as bad credit risks would, in fact, pay their bills—these are the false negatives. These errors can arise either from the problems in the data or from the classification mechanism. For example, if the credit card company has information on two John Smith's mixed together, it is easy to see how a classification of John Smith might be erroneous. However, even if the data are entirely accurate, mistaken classifications are still possible, even though they would be less likely than in the case of conflated data.

Or, an intelligence analyst examines financial transactions and phone records of a set of individuals, searching for possible indications of terrorist planning. He classifies them as "unlikely to be involved in terrorist activity" and "likely to be involved in terrorist activity," and sends only

---

[17]This definition is a commonly used one, although the precise wording may vary depending on the user in question.

[18]An extensive treatment of false positives and false negatives (and the tradeoffs thereby implied) can be found in National Research Council, *The Polygraph and Lie Detection*, The National Academies Press, Washington, D.C., 2003.

those in the latter category up the chain of command for further investigation. A false positive is someone in the latter category who, upon further investigation, has no terrorist connection at all. A false negative is someone in the former category who should have received further investigation but did not.

Two important points arise in this discussion.

• For a given database and given analytical approach, false positives and false negatives are in some sense complementary. More precisely, for a given database, one can drive the rate of false positives to zero, or the rate of false negatives to zero, but not simultaneously. For example, it is easy to identify all individuals who are bad credit risks—just deny everyone credit. This approach catches all of the bad credit risks—but also results in a huge number of false negatives. Decreases in the false positive rate are inevitably accompanied by increases in the false negative rate, and vice versa, though not necessarily in the same proportion. However, if the quality of the data is improved, or if the classification technique is improved, it is possible to reduce both the false positive rate and the false negative rate.

• Identifying false negatives in any given instance may be problematic. In the case of credit card issuers, the bank will probably not issue cards to the bad credit risks. Thus, it may never learn that these individuals are in fact creditworthy—and these individuals may forevermore be saddled with another declination of credit on their records without being given the chance to prove their creditworthiness. In the case of the terrorist investigation, it is essentially impossible to know if a person is a false negative until he or she commits the terrorist act.

False positives and false negatives are important in a discussion of privacy because they are the language in which the tradeoffs described in Section 1.2 are often cast. Banks obtain personal information on individuals for the purpose of evaluating their creditworthiness. All of these individuals surrender some financial privacy, but some do not receive the benefit of obtaining credit, and some of those not receiving credit are deserving of credit. A law enforcement official may obtain personal information on individuals searching evidence of criminal activity. All of these individuals surrender some privacy, and those who have not been involved in criminal activity have had their privacy violated despite the lack of such involvement.

Data quality is the property of data that allows them to be used effectively, economically, and rapidly to inform and evaluate decisions.[19]

---

[19]Alan F. Karr, Ashish P. Sanil, and David L. Banks, "Data Quality: A Statistical Perspec-

Typically, data should be correct, current, complete, and relevant. Data quality is intimately related to false positives and false negatives, in that it is intuitively obvious that using data of poor quality is likely to result in larger numbers of false positives and false negatives than would be the case if the data were of high quality.

Data quality is a multidimensional concept. Measurement error and survey uncertainty contribute (negatively) to data quality, as do issues related to measurement bias. But in the context of using large-scale data sets assembled by multiple independent parties using different definitions and processes, many other issues come to the fore as well.

It is helpful to distinguish between issues related to data quality in a single database and data quality associated with a collection of databases. Data quality issues for a single database include (but are not limited to) missing data fields; inconsistent data fields in a given record, such as recording a pregnancy for a 9-year-old boy; data incorrectly entered into the database, such as that which might result from a typographical error; measurement error; sampling error and uncertainty; timeliness (or lack thereof); coverage or comprehensiveness (or lack thereof); improperly duplicated records; data conversion errors, as might occur when a database of vendor X is converted to a comparable database using technology from vendor Y; use of inconsistent definitions over time; and definitions that become irrelevant over time.

Data quality issues for multiple databases include all of those issues for a single database, and also syntactic inconsistencies (one database records phone numbers in the form 202-555-1212 and another in the form 2025551212); semantic inconsistencies (weight measured in pounds vs. weight measured in kilograms); different provenance for different databases; inconsistent data fields for records contained in different databases on a given data subject; and lack of universal identifiers to specify data subjects.

1.5.3 Privacy and Anonymity

Privacy is an umbrella concept within which anonymity is located. A vandal may break a window, but his or her identity may not be directly

---

tive," *Statistical Methodology* 3:137-173, 2006; Thomas C. Redman, "Data: An Unfolding Quality Disaster," *DM Review Magazine*, August 2004, available at http://www.dmreview.com/article_sub.cfm?articleId=1007211; Wayne W. Eckerson, "Data Warehousing Special Report: Data Quality and the Bottom Line," May 1, 2002, available at http://www.adtmag.com/article.aspx?id=6321&page=; Y. Wand and R. Wang, "Anchoring Data Quality Dimensions in Ontological Foundations," *Communications of the ACM* 39(11):86-95, November 1996; and R. Wang, H. Kon, and S. Madnick, "Data Quality Requirements Analysis and Modelling," Ninth International Conference of Data Engineering, Vienna, Austria, 1993.

known. Someone may send an unsigned or pseudonymous e-mail, or make a charitable contribution. Anonymity may involve a protected right, as in the delivery of political messages. Or it may simply be an empirical condition generated by stealth or circumstance. Unsigned graffiti illustrates the former and "faceless" individuals in a crowd the latter.

The distinction between privacy and anonymity is clearly seen in an information technology context. Privacy corresponds to being able to send an encrypted e-mail to another recipient. Anonymity corresponds to being able to send the contents of the e-mail in plain, easily readable form but without any information that enables a reader of the message to identify the person who wrote it. Privacy is important when the contents of a message are at issue, whereas anonymity is important when the identity of the author of a message is at issue. Depending on the context, privacy expectations (and actualities apart from the rules) may extend to content or the identity of the sender or to both.

The relationship between privacy and anonymity can be made more formal. If personal information about an individual is denoted by the set P, the individual has privacy to the extent that he or she can keep the value of any element in the set private. Consider then another set Q, a subset of P, which consists of all elements that could be used—individually or in combination—to identify the individual. The anonymity of the individual thus depends on keeping Q private.

For example, one might define a number of different sets: the set of all people with black hair, the set of all people who work for the National Academies, the set of all people who type above a certain rate, and so on. Knowledge that an individual is in any one of these sets does not identify that individual uniquely—he or she is thus "anonymous" in the usual meaning of the term. But knowledge that an individual is in all of these sets—that is, considering the intersection of all of these sets—might well result in the ability to identify the individual uniquely (and hence in the loss of anonymity).[20]

Note also that anonymity is often tied to the identification of an individual rather than the specification of that individual. A person may be specified by his or her complete genomic sequence, but in the absence of databases that tie that sequence to a specific identity the person is still anonymous. A fingerprint may be found on a gun used in a murder, but the fingerprint does not directly identify the shooter unless the fingerprint

---

[20]More precisely, Q is the set of all subsets of P that could be used to identify the individual. Imagine that elements P_2, P_4, P_{17} of P could be used together to identify the individual, as could elements P_2, P_3, P_{14} taken together, and elements P_3, P_7, P_{14}. Then anonymity would require that these three sets be kept private, that is $\{P_2, P_4, P_{17}\}$, $\{P_2, P_3, P_{14}\}$, and $\{P_3, P_7, P_{14}\}$. In practice, this might well imply keeping private the union of all these sets $\{P_2, P_3, P_4, P_7, P_{14}, P_{17}\}$.

is on file in some law enforcement databank. In short, the specification of a unique individual is not necessarily the same thing as identifying that individual.[21]

An additional consideration is that "identification" usually means unique identification—using any of these sets would result in a bin size of one. In other words, in the usual discussion of anonymity, an anonymous person is someone whose identity cannot be definitively ascertained. However, for some purposes, a bin size of three would be insufficient to protect his or her identity—if a stool pigeon for an organized crime syndicate were kept "anonymous" within a bin size of three, it is easy to imagine that the syndicate would be perfectly willing and able to execute three murders rather than one. Here again is a situational factor that contributes to the relative nature of such concepts.

The anonymity dimension of privacy is central to the problem of protecting data collected for statistical purposes. For example, many agencies of the federal government collect information about the state of the nation—from the national economy to household use of Medicare—in order to evaluate existing programs and to develop new ones. That information is often derived from data collected by statistical agencies or others under a pledge of confidentiality. A most critical data source is microdata, which includes personal information about individuals, households, and businesses, and a central concern of the federal statistical agencies is that the responses provided by information providers will be less candid if their confidentiality cannot be guaranteed.[22] (This issue is addressed at greater length in Section 6.8.)

This issue also arises explicitly, although in a somewhat different form, in contemplating the significance of an organization's privacy—that is, information about an organization with whom a number of individuals may be associated. Information about an organization can reveal information about individuals, although it may not be uniquely associated with an individual. For example, if a survey of employers shows that a company pays a large amount in employee health care benefits to medi-

---

[21]It is worth noting that despite the common "intuitively obvious" usage of the term "identity," identity is fundamentally a social construct and thus has meaning only in context. I may know a person who sends me e-mail only by his or her e-mail address, but the identity "JohnL7534@yahoo.com" may be entirely sufficient for our relationship—and it may not matter if his first name is really John, whether his last name begins with L, or even whether this person is male or female. In this sense, specification might be regarded as a decontextualized identification.

[22]See, for example, National Research Council, *Expanding Access to Research Data: Reconciling Risks and Opportunities*, The National Academies Press, Washington, D.C., 2005; National Research Council, *Private Lives and Public Policies: Confidentiality and Accessibility of Government Statistics*, National Academy Press, Washington, D.C., 1993.

cal care providers that specialize in treating AIDS, then it can be inferred that some employees of that company have AIDS. This fact may have significance for all of the employees—those with AIDS may face a greater likelihood of having their status revealed, and those without AIDS may face higher health care premiums in the future if their past employment history becomes known.

1.5.4 Fair Information Practices

Fair information practices are standards of practice required to ensure that entities that collect and use personal information provide adequate privacy protection for that information. These practices include notice to and awareness of individuals with personal information that such information is being collected, providing individuals with choices about how their personal information may be used, enabling individuals to review the data collected about them in a timely and inexpensive way and to contest that data's accuracy and completeness, taking steps to ensure that the personal information of individuals is accurate and secure, and providing individuals with mechanisms for redress if these principles are violated.

Fair information practices were first articulated in a comprehensive manner in the U.S. Department of Health, Education, and Welfare's 1973 report *Records, Computers and the Rights of Citizens.*[23] This report was the first to introduce the Code of Fair Information Practices (Box 1.3), which has proven influential in subsequent years in shaping the information practices of numerous private and governmental institutions and is still well accepted as the gold standard for privacy protection.[24]

From their origin in 1973, fair information practices "became the dominant U.S. approach to information privacy protection for the next three decades."[25] The five principles not only became the common thread running through various bits of sectoral regulation developed in the United States, but they also were reproduced, with significant extension, in the guidelines developed by the Organisation for Economic Co-operation and

---

[23]U.S. Department of Health, Education, and Welfare, *Records, Computers and the Rights of Citizens*, Report of the Secretary's Advisory Committee on Automated Personal Data Systems, MIT Press, Cambridge, Mass., 1973.

[24]Fair information principles are a staple of the privacy literature. See, for example, the extended discussion of these principles in D. Solove, M. Rotenberg, and P. Schwartz, *Information Privacy Law*, Aspen Publishers, 2006; Alan Westin, "Social and Political Dimensions of Privacy," *Journal of Social Issues* 59(2):431-453, 2003; Helen Nissenbaum, "Privacy as Contextual Integrity," *Washington Law Review* 79:101-139, 2004; and an extended discussion and critique in Roger Clarke, "Beyond the OECD Guidelines: Privacy Protection for the 21st Century," available at http://www.anu.edu.au/people/Roger.Clarke/DV/PP21C.html.

[25]Westin, "Social and Political Dimensions of Privacy," 2003, p. 436.

BOX 1.3
Codes of Fair Information Practice

Fair information practices are standards of practice required to ensure that entities that collect and use personal information provide adequate privacy protection for that information. As enunciated by the U.S. Federal Trade Commission (other formulations of fair information practices exist),[1] the five principles of fair information practice include:

- *Notice and awareness.* Secret record systems should not exist. Individuals whose personal information is collected should be given notice of a collector's information practices before any personal information is collected and should be told that personal information is being collected about them. Without notice, an individual cannot make an informed decision as to whether and to what extent to disclose personal information. Notice should be given about the identity of the party collecting the data, how the data will be used and the potential recipients of the data, the nature of the data collected and the means by which it is collected, whether the individual may decline to provide the requested data and the consequences of a refusal to provide the requested information, and the steps taken by the collector to ensure the confidentiality, integrity, and quality of the data.
- *Choice and consent.* Individuals should be able to choose how personal information collected from them may be used, and in particular how it can be used in ways that go beyond those necessary to complete a transaction at hand. Such secondary uses can be internal to the collector's organization, or can result in the transfer of the information to third parties. Note that genuinely informed consent is a sine qua non for observation of this principle. Individuals who provide personal information under duress or threat of penalty have not provided informed consent—and individuals who provide personal information as a requirement for receiving necessary or desirable services from monopoly providers of services have not, either.
- *Access and participation.* Individuals should be able to review in a timely and inexpensive way the data collected about them, and to similarly contest that data's accuracy and completeness. Thus, means should be available to correct errors, or at the very least, to append notes of explanation or challenges that would accompany subsequent distributions of this information.
- *Integrity and security.* The personal information of individuals must be accurate and secure. To assure data integrity, collectors must take reasonable steps, such as using only reputable sources of data and cross-referencing data against multiple sources, providing consumer access to data, and destroying untimely data or converting it to anonymous form. To provide security, collectors must take both procedural and technical measures to protect against loss and the unauthorized access, destruction, use, or disclosure of the data.
- *Enforcement and redress.* Enforcement mechanisms must exist to ensure that the fair information principles are observed in practice, and individuals must have redress mechanisms available to them if these principles are violated.

---

[1]See http://www.ftc.gov/reports/privacy3/fairinfo.htm.

Development (OECD). These principles are extended in the context of OECD guidelines that govern "the protection of privacy and transborder flows of personal data" and include eight principles that have come to be understood as "minimum standards . . . for the protection of privacy and individual liberties."[26] They also include a statement about the degree to which data controllers should be accountable for their actions. This generally means that there are costs associated with the failure of a data manager to enable the realization of these principles.

1.5.5 Reasonable Expectations of Privacy

A common phrase in discussions of privacy is "reasonable expectation of privacy." The phrase has a long history in case law, first introduced in *Katz v. United States*, 389 U.S. 347 (1967), that reflects the fact that expectations are shaped by tradition, common social practices, technology, law, regulations, the formal and informal policies of organizations that are able to establish their own rules for the spaces that they control, and the physical and social context of any given situation. Expectations of privacy vary depending on many factors, but place and social relationships are among the most important.

Historically, the home has been the locale in which the expectation of privacy has been the most extensive and comprehensive. Yet there are different zones of privacy even within the home, and within the sets of interpersonal relationships that are common to one's home. While customs vary across cultures and individual families, there is a well-distributed sense of the nature of these spatial boundaries within the home. Kitchens and living rooms are common or relatively public spaces within the home, and they are places into which outsiders may be invited on special occasions. Bedrooms and bathrooms tend to be marked off from the more public or accessible spaces within the home because of the more intimate and personal activities that are likely to take place within them.

In U.S. workplaces, individuals have only very limited expectations of privacy. The loss of privacy begins for many with the application, and reaches quite personal levels for those jobs that require drug tests and personality assessments. On the other hand, privacy does not evaporate entirely on the job. Closets may be provided for the storage of personal effects, and depending on the relative permanence of assigned spaces, desk drawers may be treated as personal space. The presence or absence

---

[26]Marc Rotenberg, *The Privacy Law Sourcebook 2001*, Electronic Privacy Information Center, 2001, pp. 270-272.

of doors within workspaces affects the ability of workers to control direct observation by others.

Technology also affects reasonable expectations of privacy. Technology can be used to enhance human senses and cognitive capabilities, and these enhancements can affect the ability to collect information at a distance. The result is that space is not the marker it once was for indicating boundaries between private and public interactions. In the case of information technology, the "objects" about which one is private (digital objects such as electronic files or streams of bits as communications) are quite distinct from objects that were originally the focus of privacy concerns (physical, tangible objects made of atoms). Thus, Kerr argues, for example, that the well-established history of Fourth Amendment law governing permissible searches (and also reasonable expectations of privacy) must be rethought in light of the manifest differences between physical and digital objects.[27]

Critical events such as the terrorist attacks of 2001 have dramatically increased the level of personal and records surveillance that travelers encounter. Heightened concern about threats of violence means that searches of personal effects are becoming more common at sporting events, popular tourist sites, and even schools.

Formal and informal policies that define the boundaries between the public and the private also help to shape our expectations of privacy that develop over time. Privacy policies are not only established by legislatures, administrative agencies, and the courts. Individual firms, trade unions, professional associations, and a host of other institutional actors have also developed policies to govern the collection and use of personal information. Individuals also have policies, or norms, that govern the ways in which they will interact with organizations and with other individuals. Indeed, individuals' reciprocal behavior with respect to asking for, and offering, information is conditioned by custom and manners that are no less significant for not being less formal than the written policies.

Cross-cultural differences with respect to expectations of privacy can be noted. For example, compared to Western cultures, a number of Eastern cultures place a far lower value on certain kinds of privacy in the home, and an Asian child often grows up with very different expectations of privacy than might an American child.

Finally, the concept of "reasonable expectations of privacy" has a normative meaning as well as a descriptive meaning. For example, in

---

[27]Orin Kerr, "Searches and Seizures in a Digital World," *Harvard Law Review* 119:531, 2005. Kerr's normative reformulation of Fourth Amendment law calls for maintaining "the specific goals of specific doctrinal rules in light of changing facts," although he clearly recognizes that other normative reformulations are possible.

a world where electronic surveillance technologies make surveillance easy to conduct on a wide scale, one could argue that no one today has a "reasonable expectation" that his or her phone calls will not be tapped. But both statutory law (e.g., Title III in the U.S. Code) and case law (e.g., *Katz v. United States*, 389 U.S. 347 (1967)) stipulate that under most circumstances, an individual *does* have a reasonable expectation that his or her phone calls will not be tapped.

1.6 LESSONS FROM HISTORY

In the history of the United States, a number of societal shifts have taken place that relate to contemporary visions of privacy (Appendix A). For example, a move from primarily rural to a more urban (or suburban) society resulted in changes to the scale of one's community and increased one's proximity to strangers. In addition, the impact of information technologies is often to compress time and distance in the social sphere, and one result has been an increasingly diminished utility of time and space as markers of the boundaries between private and public space. Associated changes in how trust is developed and sustained have all shaped our understanding and appreciation of the value of privacy and the limits on it in a more impersonal society.

Furthermore, there is an increased appetite on the part of many sectors of society for information collection and analysis and verification. The kinds of interactions individuals have with institutions and with each other have changed as a result. Increased societal needs, increased interdependence, new kinds of risks, ever greater complexity, and an increase in the number of rules one needs to be aware of to move safely and smoothly through society have radically altered the kinds of interactions individuals have with institutions and with each other. Both private organizations and government agencies are increasingly concerned with the ability to document compliance and discover violations. This is a major motivation for collection of information about individuals and about organizations.

As the discussion in Appendix A (on the history of surveillance and privacy in the United States) suggests, a number of lessons can be gleaned from history. The first is that surveillance has been intensifying as society has grown more complex.[28]

The second lesson is that each technological advance in the spheres

---

[28]Living in small towns or tightly knit communities is often associated with lesser degrees of privacy (where "everyone knows everyone else's business"). But lesser privacy in these communities is not generally the result of explicit acts of surveillance or information gathering—rather, it is a by-product of routine day-to-day living.

of sensing, communication, and information processing invites greater surveillance, and often those invitations are accepted. The invention of the telegraph led almost immediately to the invention of wiretapping. The invention of automated fingerprint matching led to the FBI's integrated automated fingerprint identification system. The development of the computer resulted in unprecedented record-keeping power, and the emergence of networking technology has further increased that power. This is not to suggest that technologies make things happen on their own, but they do facilitate the activities and ambitions of those who might use them and who can afford the costs of those new technologies.

The third lesson is that times of crisis or war are often marked by contractions in the scope of civil liberties. Often, when U.S. government leaders have come to believe that the security or the core interests of the nation were being threatened from without, the government has increased its surveillance of groups within its borders. In case after case whether British Loyalists, or Japanese-Americans, or Arab-Americans, the unequal weight of government surveillance on these groups has been justified on the basis of alleged links between the groups in question and threats to the national interest. Moreover, as the putative threat from these groups has faded with history, actions taken against these groups have generally been regarded with a degree of retrospective shame.

The fourth lesson is that although U.S. conceptions of privacy can be traced historically, the meaning of the concept has been highly varied and vague, and there has never been an agreed-upon meaning. One result is that the legal and regulatory framework surrounding privacy has been a patchwork without a unifying theme or driving principles. This state of affairs in the United States contrasts sharply with those of certain other nations (notably the member states of the European Union) that often take a more comprehensive approach to privacy-related issues. This point is discussed further in Chapter 4.

1.7 SCOPE AND MAP OF THIS REPORT

This report examines privacy from several perspectives and offers analysis and ways of thinking through privacy questions at the same time that it provides a snapshot of the current state of affairs.

Part I is this chapter (Chapter 1).

Part II includes Chapters 2 through 5, which are primarily expository. Chapters 2 and 3 seek to lay the groundwork for what privacy is and how it affects and is affected by societal and technological complexities. Chapters 4 and 5 address the legal landscape of privacy in the United States and the political forces shaping that landscape throughout recent history.

Part III (Chapters 6 through 9) considers privacy in context, examining privacy issues in different sectors of society. Chapter 6 looks at institutional practice in privacy broadly in several different sectors. Chapter 7 provides a more in-depth look at health and medical privacy. Chapter 8 explores privacy and the U.S. library community and also mentions the issue of intellectual property and privacy (where technology, policy, and privacy intersect strongly). Chapter 9 looks at law enforcement and national security.

Part II can be skipped without loss of continuity if the reader wishes to consider the various case studies first in Part III. However, Parts I and II supply important background information that provides a context for Part III.

Part IV consists of a single and final chapter (Chapter 10) and provides the bulk of the report's look to the future. It examines mechanisms and options for privacy protection and presents the report's findings and recommendations.

Appendix A presents a short history of surveillance and privacy in the United States. Appendix B provides a look at international considerations.

Part II

The Backdrop for Privacy

Chapter 2 ("Intellectual Approaches and Conceptual Underpinnings") provides a primer on privacy as an intellectual concept from the perspective of three disciplines—philosophy, economics, and sociology. Philosophical approaches to the study of privacy have centered on the elucidation of the basic concept and the normative questions around whether privacy is a right, a good in itself, or an instrumental good. Economic approaches to the question have centered around the value, in economic terms, of privacy, both in its role in the information needed for efficient markets and in the value of information as a piece of property. Sociological approaches to the study of privacy have emphasized the ways in which the collection and use of personal information have reflected and reinforced the relations of power and influence between individuals, groups, and institutions within society. That there is such a multiplicity of legitimate intellectual approaches to the study of privacy suggests that no one discipline captures, or can capture, the richness and texture of its various nuances, and what appear at first to be very slight or subtle differences turn out to have deep implications in practice.

Chapter 3 ("Technological Drivers") examines the vast changes enabled by information technology by exploring the ramifications of increased connectivity and ubiquity, data gathering, ever-growing computational power and storage capacity, and more-sophisticated sensors; what architecture choices mean for social values such as privacy; and what kind of control (or lack of control) technology enables for individuals. Such change has dramatically altered the on-the-ground realities within which the concept of privacy is necessarily embedded. The net result is that new kinds of data are being collected and stored in vast quantities and over long periods of time, and obscurity or difficulty of access are increasingly less practical as ways of protecting privacy. Finally, because information technologies are continually dropping in cost, technologies for collecting and analyzing personal information from multiple, disparate sources are increasingly available to individuals, corporations, and governments.

Chapter 4 ("The Legal Landscape in the United States") provides a detailed overview of the legal landscape in the United States. The foundation of privacy law in the United States is, of course, the U.S. Constitution, and the First, Fourth, and Ninth Amendments of the Constitution have important implications for privacy, and specifically constrain the applicability of federal and state law regarding certain privacy-related issues. In addition, there are a large number of federal laws (and regulations and executive orders) that address privacy in one form or another, so many in fact that what emerges is an ad hoc patchwork of law that lacks strong coherence or unifying themes. State laws regarding privacy and common law and private causes of action (privacy torts) add to this patchwork but do not rationalize it. Finally, in a global economy, the need to conduct commerce across international borders suggests that the United States cannot ignore foreign law regarding privacy—and foreign law regarding privacy is often much more comprehensive than domestic law.

Chapter 5 ("The Politics of Privacy Policy in the United States") addresses the question of how privacy policy is made. Privacy advocates use public opinion as a lever to generate concern and action. In addition, a number of reports over the past several decades have served to catalyze public action. Judicial decisions—important in interpreting existing law—are also the most important, and perhaps the only, forum in which competing goals and values are explicitly weighed and balanced against each other. Finally, corporate policy regarding privacy—even if it is established by default or inattention—has potentially enormous impact on the privacy actually enjoyed by individuals, because such policies often delve into areas of privacy that are minimally addressed by existing law.

2

Intellectual Approaches and Conceptual Underpinnings

The concept of privacy has a long intellectual history. Many have written attempting to characterize privacy philosophically, sociologically, psychologically, and legally. This chapter provides a brief sampling of some major intellectual perspectives on privacy, along with some analysis of how these different perspectives relate to one another. These perspectives illustrate some common themes while demonstrating the difficulty inherent in characterizing privacy, no matter what intellectual frameworks or tools are used.

Note also that this chapter—as well as this report—focuses on privacy as it relates to information. The informational dimensions of privacy are clearly central, but at the same time some have argued that the concept of privacy must be broader than that; for example, the U.S. Supreme Court has held that a right to choose an abortion or to receive information about contraceptives is founded on privacy protections implied in the Constitution. The discussion below is not intended to address these non-informational dimensions of privacy and mentions them only in passing as they may help to illuminate some of the issues surrounding the notion of privacy and the ethical and moral dimensions of the general privacy debate.

2.1 PHILOSOPHICAL THEORIES OF PRIVACY

2.1.1 A Philosophical Perspective

Philosophical works on privacy generally focus on two central tasks.[1] The first is to attempt to answer the question, What is privacy?, by giving a precise definition or analysis of the concepts involved. The second is to explain why we value privacy and why privacy should be respected by others, whether those others are individuals, organizations, or governments.

It is useful to distinguish these two tasks by calling the first a descriptive account of privacy and the second a prescriptive or normative account of privacy. These tasks are conceptually distinct, and maintaining the distinction between them allows a rich set of questions to be asked.

For example, a descriptive analysis does not need to justify the ethical questions surrounding privacy as part of the analysis of the concept. Once a descriptive analysis of privacy has been accomplished, the normative aspects of the concept can then be discussed based on that description, and the discussion may well—and properly—include ethical questions.

Further, normative accounts of privacy may depend on subtle differences in the descriptive analysis that are either stated or presumed, and that can be masked if the two tasks are intertwined. So, for example, a descriptive account of privacy may show that there are cases where privacy conflicts with other values. Such a conflict may lead to the decision that not all violations of privacy are to be avoided. But if descriptive and prescriptive accounts of privacy were merged, such an analysis might be precluded from the outset since our prescriptive account might hold that all reductions of privacy count as moral violations.

Any descriptive account of privacy will have to correspond to the perceptions and intuitions of most people about clear cases of the concept. So, for example, an analysis of the concept that held that privacy is a binary property that an individual either has or has totally lost would not be acceptable, as it violates the commonly held intuition about degrees of privacy and the loss of some privacy. A descriptive account that adequately deals with clear cases can then be used to elucidate less clear cases, and can then be used as a base for prescriptive discussions about privacy. So, for example, starting from a descriptive analysis of privacy that acknowledges that there are levels or degrees to privacy, it is then possible to address the prescriptive question of where a particular loss or

---

[1] Note that the discussion in Section 2.1.1 draws not only on the writings of professional philosophers, but also on other work that undertakes explicit conceptual analysis devoted to exploring what privacy is, what a right to privacy consists in, and why we ought to protect it.

gain of privacy is good or bad, problematic or not, and for whom and for what time period and under what conditions.

Much of the philosophical work on privacy has been stimulated by contentious activities in realms such as law, policy, institutional practices, and specific or novel applications of technology. In such a context, the prescriptive aspects of privacy are the most commonly discussed. What descriptive work has been done is often in the context of clarifying the basic concepts as part of a discussion of a particular normative view.

2.1.2 Privacy as Control Versus Privacy as Restricted Access

The most common descriptive accounts of privacy reflect two basic views: (1) privacy as restrictions on the access of other people to an individual's personal information and (2) privacy as an individual's control over personal information[2] such as information on health status. While related, these two views can also be seen as distinct.

Political science professor emeritus Alan Westin's take on privacy was (and remains) an influential example from the group that defines privacy in terms of control. Indeed, Westin can be credited with developing one of the very first formulations of so-called informational privacy in the late 1960s, and his definition of privacy has proven quite useful to scholars as society has moved more fully into the information age: "Privacy is the claim of individuals, groups, or institutions to determine for themselves when, how, and to what extent information about them is communicated to others."[3]

In *Privacy and Freedom*, Westin took an interdisciplinary approach to analyzing the nature and functions of privacy, its roles in society, and new technologies for surveillance, as well as the push for new privacy standards and protections. As part of the overall theory put forth in the book, Westin defines four distinct functions of (or reasons for wanting) privacy—personal autonomy, emotional release, self-evaluation, and limited/protected communication—as well as four distinct states of privacy—*solitude*, freedom from observation; *intimacy*, closeness among a small group of people; *anonymity*, freedom from being identified in public settings; and *reserve*, the freedom to withdraw from communication. As he describes it, these states are subject to constant change, depending on one's personal needs and choices about what to reveal and what not to reveal at a given time. Indeed, for Westin, the importance of this control over information disclosure, "both to [an] individual's self-development

---

[2]A second use of "control" refers to an external agency with the power to compel a person to disclose personal information. "Control" in this section is not used in this sense.
[3]See Alan Westin, *Privacy and Freedom*, Atheneum, New York, 1967, p. 7.

and to the exercise of responsible citizenship, makes the claim to privacy a fundamental part of civil liberty in democratic society."[4] Westin's model of informational privacy and his ideas regarding privacy more generally have informed most subsequent scholarly discussions of privacy and have often acted as a crucial jumping-off point for the work of other researchers.[5]

In more recent years, much of Westin's work has been somewhat less philosophical in nature, involving surveys to assess the attitudes of U.S. consumers and Internet users toward privacy, often in association with Harris Interactive (previously Louis Harris and Associates)—work that has earned him both praise and criticism. In contrast to traditional university-based research, this work has often been done in cooperation with commercial interests.

In his survey research, Westin has suggested that Americans hold differing views regarding the value of certain aspects of privacy. For example, based on his analysis of surveys over a number of years, he groups consumers into one of three categories:

- *Privacy fundamentalists*—those who reject trading information for special offers, who prefer only opt-in approaches, and who would prefer to see more legislative approaches to privacy protection;
- *Privacy unconcerned*—consumers who are comfortable with trading their information for almost any consumer value; and
- *Privacy pragmatists*—people who take time to weigh the benefits and risks associated with providing their personal information.

Westin goes on to suggest that the "privacy pragmatists" are the largest group, at over 60 percent of U.S. consumers, and are thus a group deserving of focused attention from businesses and policy makers. His survey work has also shown that of the four states of privacy he identified in his earlier research, intimacy is the most important state to Americans, followed by solitude, reserve, and anonymity (in that order).

Westin's empirical research also led him to identify three phases in the state of U.S. consumer attitudes toward privacy: 1961 to 1979, 1980 to 1989, and 1990 to 2002.[6] He notes that privacy has gone from "a modest matter for a minority of consumers in the 1980s to an issue of high

---

[4]Alan F. Westin, "Social and Political Dimensions of Privacy," *Journal of Social Issues* 59(2):431-453, 2003.

[5]For an additional perspective on the impact of Westin's privacy work, see Stephen Margulis, "On the Status and Contributions of Westin's and Altman's Theories of Privacy," *Journal of Social Issues* 59(2):411-429, 2003.

[6]These three phases, as well as the baseline period leading up to them (1945 to 1960), are described in detail in Westin, "Social and Political Dimensions of Privacy," 2003.

intensity expressed by more than [75 percent] of American consumers in 2001,"[7] citing driving factors like increasing distrust of institutions and fears surrounding the potential abuse of technology.

Analyses of privacy in terms of individuals' control over their personal information are far more common than those that are based on access, and hence are rarely backed by systematic argument. Arguments based on the "privacy as control" perspective tend to concentrate on the extent of what must be controlled for privacy to be maintained. At one extreme is the position that says that all that needs to be controlled is information about the individual per se (e.g., health status). More general analysis includes other aspects of an individual's life, such as control over the receipt of information (such as information concerning birth control, argued in *Griswold v. Connecticut*, 381 U.S. 479 (1965)) or the control over one's body (the crux of *Roe v. Wade*, 410 U.S. 11 (1973)).

Theorists supporting the access-based definition of privacy have offered explicit explanations for their analysis, based on the ability of that analysis to explain situations that cannot be explained by a control-based theory. One such class of situations is exemplified by a person choosing to reveal intimate details of his life on national television. On the basis of the "privacy as control" theory, he could not reasonably claim that he had less privacy as the result of doing so because he chose to reveal those details. However, on the basis of the "privacy as restricted access" theory, he would have less privacy, because the information given on the show had become accessible to the entire audience.

American University philosopher Jeffrey Reiman has presented a case in which the control theory would say that privacy had been violated but our intuitions say that no such violation has occurred. He points out that societies often regulate certain public activities, by requiring, for example, that bathrooms are used or that clothing is worn in public. Such requirements diminish the control of individuals over the information that they can allow to others, but the laws are also seen as privacy enhancing. Thus control over information cannot be the exclusive defining characteristic of privacy. However, laws and related expectations regarding disclosure and non-disclosure of personal information do limit the access to information by others, which is just the sort of thing that the access-based models of privacy would predict.

Although the issue of whether privacy is best seen as a question of access or a question of control is the primary disagreement in much of the philosophical literature, it is hardly the only point of dispute. Another

---

[7]Alan Westin, 2001, Testimony before the House Committee on Energy and Commerce's Subcommittee on Commerce, Trade, and Consumer Protection, May 28, available at http://energycommerce.house.gov/107/hearings/05082001Hearing209/Westin309.htm.

basic question has to do with what aspects of a person's life are relevant to the question of privacy. Ruth Gavison, professor of human rights at the Hebrew University in Jerusalem, defines privacy along three axes: the first has to do with access to information about the person (secrecy), the second has to do with knowledge of the person's identity (anonymity), and the third has to do with access to the physical proximity of the person (solitude).[8] University of Pennsylvania professor of law Anita Allen's early work distinguished among informational privacy (limited access to information, confidentiality, secrecy, anonymity, and data protection), physical privacy (limited access to persons, possessions, and personal property), and decisional privacy (limited intrusion into decision making about sex, families, religion, and health care).[9]

2.1.3 Coherence in the Concept of Privacy

The wide variation in the accounts of privacy has led some commentators to question the whole endeavor of giving a descriptive account of privacy. For example, Yale professor of law Robert Post writes, "Privacy is a value so complex, so entangled in competing and contradictory dimensions, so engorged with various and distinct meanings, that I sometimes despair whether it can be usefully addressed at all."[10] Some of the commentators who question the descriptive accounts of privacy have argued for a general skepticism toward the coherence of the concept of privacy, while others have claimed that the concept is best understood not as a single concept but rather as a combination of other, more basic rights.

A radical example of this second approach is the analysis of MIT philosopher Judith Jarvis Thompson, who argues that privacy is neither distinctive nor useful.[11] In fact, says Thompson, privacy is not a coherent concept in itself, but rather a catchall that reduces, in various cases, to more primitive concepts that are more easily understood, such as property, contracts, and bodily rights. Treating privacy as a concept distinct from these others simply confuses the issues surrounding the more basic concepts.

A less radical approach admits that privacy is a distinct concept but argues that it is impossible to clearly analyze because of the excess baggage that the concept has accumulated over time. Indeed, this baggage is seen to make the overall concept of privacy incoherent. This approach

---

[8]Ruth Gavison, "Privacy and the Limits of Law," *Yale Law Journal* 89:421-471, 1980.

[9]Anita Allen, "Constitutional Law and Privacy," in Dennis Patterson, ed., *A Companion to Philosophy of Law and Legal Theory*, Oxford University Press, Blackwell, England, 1996.

[10]Robert C. Post, "Three Concepts of Privacy," *Georgetown Law Journal* 89(6):2087, 2001.

[11]Judith Jarvis Thomson, "The Right to Privacy," *Philosophy & Public Affairs* 4:295-314, 1975.

suggests reducing and simplifying the distinct claims, interests, and values that common usage covers in the term "privacy" to a few basic concepts (or a single, much reduced, concept). Some aspects of the general concept of privacy are reducible to more fundamental concepts, and some aspects do not belong within the rubric of privacy and should be dropped altogether. In this approach, what remains should be a coherent and useful concept of privacy, even if it does not reflect current use of the term.

An even weaker form of reductionism is willing to accept a multidimensional concept of privacy, made up of several non-reducible parts that relate to each other in some fundamental way. For example, Judith DeCew argues that privacy covers information, physical and mental access to oneself, and decision-making autonomy.[12] These concepts are distinct, and therefore the concept of privacy is in some way made up of others that are more basic. However, DeCew argues that there is a coherence to these concepts that makes the notion of privacy important in its own way; the whole is greater than the sum of the parts.

New York University professor of culture and communication Helen Nissenbaum's approach to privacy is based on the idea that social norms governing information flow depend on context.[13] A judgment that a given action or practice violates privacy is a function of the context in which the activity takes place, what type of information is in question, and the social roles of the people involved. Social contexts, such as health care, education, commerce, religion, and so on, are governed by complex social norms, including informational norms that specify the principles of transmission governing the flow of information.

These norms prescribe how certain types of information about specific individuals acting in specific roles ought to flow from party to party. In a health care context, for example, one such norm might specify that patients are obliged to share health-related information with physicians who are treating them; another norm for that context specifies that physicians may not release that information to anyone else. In a context of friendship, friends share information not out of any obligation but through choice, and the flow of information is generally reciprocal. The term "contextual integrity" is applied to those circumstances in which informational norms are respected.

According to Nissenbaum's theory of contextual integrity, these informational norms establish an expectation against which certain actions and practices are evaluated. In particular, they provide a guide to evaluating

---

[12]Judith DeCew, *In Pursuit of Privacy: Law, Ethics, and the Rise of Technology*, Cornell University Press, Ithaca, N.Y., 1997.

[13]See, for example, Helen Nissenbaum, "Privacy as Contextual Integrity," *Washington Law Review* 79(1):119-158, 2004.

new socio-technical practices, which are judged to respect or violate contextual integrity on the bases of several key factors:

- The governing context;
- Whether the new practice changes the types of information at issue;
- Whether the new practice causes a shift in who is involved as senders, receivers, and subjects of this information; and
- Whether new patterns of information flow fit with the relevant principles of transmission.

When new technologies or socio-technical practices are disturbing from a privacy standpoint, the reason is that they are seen as violating standing informational norms. Under certain circumstances, norms may be revisited and revised: critical events, such as the September 11 attacks, may demand a revision of informational norms governing public spaces; the outbreak of an epidemic may demand that norms of information flow in the medical health care context be revisited; emergence of online dating might also result in a shift of the norms governing information flow. Nevertheless, a systematic and comprehensive strategy for evaluating whether change should be resisted or embraced starts with the important first step of revealing how, if at all, standing norms have been breached or are threatened.

The theory of contextual integrity augments dominant approaches to privacy by introducing a middle layer of social analysis missing from theories analyzing privacy as a fundamental human right or value and also from theories placing privacy interests among a whole set of moral and non-moral interests to be weighed and traded in the course of political decision making. By bringing social norms to the foreground through contexts, roles, and transmission principles, this social approach adds a dimension of thought that can help address some of the critical challenges posed by new practices, and can help illuminate many of the intractable puzzles and stand-offs regularly faced in traditional approaches to privacy, for example, cultural and historical differences.

Gary T. Marx, MIT professor emeritus, offers a related approach emphasizing the importance of defining terms and identifying contextual variation.[14] Examining context can guide empirical inquiries and help identify assumptions often buried within normative arguments. Among

---

[14]Gary T. Marx, *Windows into the Soul: Surveillance and Society in an Age of High Technology*, University of Chicago Press, forthcoming, and various articles by Gary Marx on privacy, equality, soft surveillance, borders, the public and the private, ethics, varieties of personal information and anonymity, available at http://garymarx.net.

the most relevant factors in his situational or contextual approach are the following:

* Keeping distinct (yet noting relationships among) the family of concepts encompassing personal information—e.g., privacy and publicity, public and private, personal and impersonal information, surveillance, secrecy, confidentiality, anonymity, pseudo-anonymity, and identifiability and being clear about which concepts (whether as factors to be explained or to be approached as social issues) are being discussed;
* The nature of the means or techniques used (contrast the unaided and aided senses—e.g., directly overhearing a conversation with intercepting electronic communication on the Internet);
* The goals (contrast collecting information to prevent a health epidemic with the spying of the voyeur);
* The location (contrast personal information obtained from the home with that gathered on a public street);
* The type of information-protective border that is crossed (contrast crossing the borders of the physical person as in a body cavity search, with crossing via aggregation the de facto borders resulting from the disaggregation of information in scattered databases);
* The direction of a personal border crossing (compare taking information from a person as with drug testing or a photo with imposing information on a person as with spam or subliminal sounds);
* The type of personal information involved (contrast a general characteristic such as gender or age with information that may be stigmatizing, intimate, and/or offer a unique and locatable identity);
* The form of the data itself (contrast a third party's written account of an event with the same event revealed by a hidden video camera);
* The roles and relationships among those involved (contrast parents gathering personal information on children or an ill family member with an employer or merchant gathering information on employees or customers); and
* The conditions of information collection, involving, e.g., informed consent, adequate security, reciprocity, sharing in the benefits, and so on.

This approach yields a number of hypotheses about the patterning of normative expectations with respect to privacy behavior and helps give structure to the intuitive understandings of privacy mentioned below in this chapter.

The multidimensional nature of personal information and the related contextual and situational variation prevent reaching any simple conclusions about how crossing personal informational borders will, or should, be judged. Thus, the intellectual approach is one of contingency rather than absolutism.

Although the conceptual questions surrounding the notion of privacy are important, it is not necessary to resolve these matters here. It is sufficient to observe that in all of these various perspectives, personal information—information about us—plays a central role, and questions of access to and use of such information are important. The challenges posed for privacy in the information age—by technological advancement, societal shifts, and critical or signal events—fall squarely within the scope of most dominant accounts of privacy and do not require resolution of some of the more difficult conceptual questions concerning the full scope or borders of the concept.

2.1.4 Normative Theories of Privacy

The philosophical works that attempt to characterize the concept of privacy see that activity as necessary for addressing the important normative questions surrounding privacy. These normative questions concern the value of privacy and include such issues as why privacy is important, both to the individual and to society; why we should individually and as a society protect privacy; and how and to what extent and in what ways with what costs and benefits privacy should be protected.

This last issue arises because of the need to consider privacy in relation to other values that may be in conflict with it. For example, maximizing privacy will constrain the information available to others, and in so doing may decrease efficiency, or security, or other things that society or various subgroups value. Deciding how much privacy to allow or require sometimes entails a tradeoff with respect to other values, and understanding the nature of those tradeoffs is necessary before one can think in a systematic fashion about decisions involving tradeoffs.

One position on the value of privacy is that it is a fundamental human right, like the right to liberty or life. In this view, privacy is an intrinsic good in itself, and a life shorn of privacy is less meaningful than one that has some measure of privacy. The fundamentalist position holds that privacy is tied to a cluster of rights, such as autonomy and dignity. These are tied together in such a way that the combination allows a human life to be more essentially human than if they are missing. Carried to its logical extreme, if privacy is an intrinsic (and absolute) good, then there are no cases in which any lack of privacy can be justified.

A more common view holds privacy to be of instrumental rather than intrinsic value; that is, the value of privacy derives from the value of other, more fundamental values that privacy allows. In the instrumentalist view, the value of privacy comes because it sustains, promotes, and protects other things that we value. In this view, privacy can be traded off or limited because doing so will promote other values that we hold dear.

One example of the instrumentalist view holds that the value of privacy derives from the need for privacy to allow autonomy in the individual. Unlike the fundamentalist, who claims that privacy is a basic right on the same level as autonomy, the instrumentalist will claim that autonomy (the ability to control our actions and make free choices) is a fundamental value that is aided by privacy. Without privacy, in this view, the individual could be manipulated or coerced in such a way as to lose autonomy. People with no sense of privacy are less able to define and pursue the goals and ends that are meaningful to them. The actions of such an individual are more likely to be dictated by what others think than by his or her own decisions. But privacy, in this view, is not a fundamental right; if the autonomy of the individual could be guaranteed without a guarantee of privacy, there would be no need (in this view) to ensure privacy.

Another instrumentalist view holds that the value of privacy is derived from the fact that privacy contributes to fairness. It is because of privacy that we can ensure a level playing field in the information that is known by each of the two parties in an interaction. Without privacy, it would be easy for the more powerful (rich, devious) of the parties to hold extra information about the other party, disadvantaging that party in the interactions. Without privacy, the party with the greatest resources can get an unfair information advantage over other parties, ensuring the maintenance of the power or resource disparity.

Privacy has also been identified as an instrument needed for other, less tangible, goods. Arguments have been presented that tie privacy with such things as the ability to define relationships with others and the ability to sustain intimacy. Respect for privacy, in such views, is needed to demonstrate to individuals that they have control of their minds and their bodies. Without privacy there could be no such demonstration of respect, and without such respect the intimacy needed for personal relationships would be impossible.

All of this chapter's previous discussions of the value of privacy concentrate on that value to the individual. There have been other approaches that try to see privacy through the lens of the society or group of which the individual is a part. Some discussions, for example those by communitarians, call attention to possible negative consequences of privacy.

For example, Amitai Etzioni contrasts certain privacy interests of individuals against what he identifies as the common good, or the well-being of the society as a whole.[15] In most cases in which the interests of an individual are assessed against the interests of the collective, Etzioni

---

[15]Amitai Etzioni, *The Limits of Privacy*, Basic Books, New York, 1999.

insists that the collective interests must prevail. Protecting the privacy of individuals makes it harder for the society to enforce laws and ensure good public health, and it makes the overall economy less efficient. In this view, privacy has a negative value to the overall community in many settings, even if it has some value to individuals within that society. Because people tend to see only their own point of view, privacy has historically been seen to be valuable. Etzioni's view holds that if the price society sometimes pays for individual privacy were clearer, privacy would be given less importance by society.

Similar arguments are set forth by Anita Allen-Castellito, who suggests that individuals are "accountable" to a number of "others" including employers, family members, and in some instances, members of a racial or ethnic group.[16] Accountability means that we may reasonably be expected to "answer for" our behavior to others with whom we have a meaningful relationship. In her view, we are not entitled to say "it is none of your business" when some people inquire into our reasons for acting in some way that might place others, or the relationship or the person we care about, at risk.

There are also communitarians who hold that privacy is actually of value to society as a whole. While it is true that the lack of information about the individual required by privacy may have drawbacks in the areas of public health, law enforcement, and the economy, it is argued that privacy is needed to ensure the best results to society in all of these areas. Without privacy, for example, public health authorities would obtain less accurate reporting of disease and be less sure that those who have communicable diseases would seek treatment. While privacy may impede law enforcement, it is also required to insulate citizens from governmental tyranny and to ensure the general health of liberal democracy. Citizens with faith in government and law enforcement are more likely to be cooperative when they perceive that power is limited by decent rules. While aspects of the economy might be more efficient if there were no privacy, such a state of affairs would favor those able to obtain the most information, tending to ensure that unfair distributions of wealth and privilege would be perpetuated.

As is often the case with ethical and philosophical discussions, the value of these debates over privacy is not so much that we can find an answer to our questions, but rather that the issues becomes clearer and more precisely identified.

For example, the descriptive debate concerning the nature of privacy shows the difficulty of saying just what privacy is in a single simplistic

---

[16]Anita L. Allen-Castellito, *Why Privacy Isn't Everything: Feminist Reflections on Personal Accountability*, Rowman and Littlefield, Oxford, 2003.

definition. While we can be reasonably sure that privacy is a matter of individuals' control over information about themselves, it is less clear whether the emphasis should be on control over the gathering of that information, the access to that information after it has been gathered, the use of the information that has been gathered, or on all equally.

In addition, the debate about the normative status of privacy shows that it is sometimes unclear why we should value privacy, and what sort of value privacy has. It does seem clear that privacy must be balanced with other values that we have (at least some of the time), but the mechanisms for establishing such a balance are far from clear. Indeed, as the debates about the value of privacy for the individual or the group show, different circumstances can lead to very different decisions about the value of privacy. The debate has brought forward examples where claims to privacy are used to protect behavior that we find of great value, and examples where claims to privacy are used to protect behavior we abhor. The advantages and disadvantages will also have differential impact on the group or individual in question.

2.2 ECONOMIC PERSPECTIVES ON PRIVACY[17]

2.2.1 The Rationale for an Economic Perspective on Privacy

Normative discussions of privacy emphasize the notion of privacy as something of value, which has led some to attempt to look at privacy through the lens of economic theory. Rather than philosophizing about what societal values are being balanced, an economic perspective on privacy regards privacy as something that people value in varying degrees under varying circumstances (Box 2.1). To the extent that the value of privacy can be imagined in meaningful quantitative terms, an economic approach provides a framework for specifying some of the various costs and tradeoffs privacy is presumed to involve.

Thus, one starting point is the idea brought forth in Section 1.2 that privacy inherently involves tradeoffs, and understanding the nature and scope of tradeoffs is squarely in the domain of economics. A second starting point is a growing awareness that personal information about individuals, their interests, their buying tendencies, and so on has commercial value. Indeed, as Culnan and Bies suggest, consumers' personal

---

[17]This section is based largely on Kai-Lung Hui and I.P.L. Png, 2006, "The Economics of Privacy," in Terry Hendershott, ed., *Handbook of Information Systems and Economics*, Elsevier, forthcoming; and Alessandro Acquisti, *The Economics of Privacy*, available at http://www.heinz.cmu.edu/~acquisti/papers/acquisti_privacy_economics.ppt.

BOX 2.1
Personal Information as an Economic Good

Consider the passing of personal information in some kind of transaction between the subject of the information and the recipient.

- The amount of personal information can be increased by recombinations and analysis of existing data.
- The individual generally does not know how, how often, or for how long the information provided will be used.
- Other parties who may gain access to the information are not known to the individual.
- The value of personal information to the individual is highly uncertain, and is often determined by events or circumstances extant after the transaction.
- Individuals often place different values on the protection and on the sale of the same piece of information.
- The information, as information, is generally non-rivalrous (use of the information by one party generally does not prevent its use by another party). Personal information is also often non-excludable (other parties often cannot be prevented from using the information).

SOURCE: Adapted from Alessandro Acquisti, *The Economics of Privacy*, available at http://www.heinz.cmu.edu/~acquisti/papers/acquisti_privacy_economics.ppt.

---

information is at the center of the tension between many corporate and consumer interests.[18]

Finally, from a policy standpoint, economics is relevant because much of the public policy debate about privacy involves a consideration of the positive or negative market effects (whether real or potential) of government privacy regulation. For example, one long-running debate concerns using "opt-in" or "opt-out" approaches for permitting the sharing of consumer information among organizations. (Opt-in regimes do not collect information unless the individual explicitly takes steps to allow it; opt-out regimes collect information unless the individual explicitly takes steps to disallow it.) Opt-in is largely seen as an undue burden by the business world, whereas many privacy advocates see consumer opt-in (which, in a sense, places consumers in the position of owner of their own information) as the best approach for protecting consumers' privacy.

---

[18]Mary J. Culnan and Robert J. Bies, "Consumer Privacy: Balancing Economic and Justice Considerations," *Journal of Social Issues* 59(2):323-342, 2003.

In considering the economics of privacy, Alessandro Acquisti notes that privacy issues actually originate from two different markets: a market for personal information and a market for privacy. The market for personal information focuses on economically valuable uses for personal information and how such information can be bought, sold, and used in ways that generate value. Consider, for example, companies that may need to make decisions about extending credit to individuals. These companies may engage the services of credit bureaus that provide personal financial information regarding these individuals that is relevant to determining their creditworthiness. Or a company may use personal information about the tastes and buying preferences of its customers so that it can tailor its products more precisely to customer needs or market its products with greater efficiency. In general, personal information can be regarded as an economic good.

The market for privacy can be conceptualized as the market for goods and services that help consumers enhance or protect the privacy of their personal information. For example, they may buy products based on privacy-enhancing technologies, or adopt privacy-enhancing strategies, or patronize companies that promise to keep their customers' personal information protected and private.

The sections below describe four economic perspectives on privacy: a "privacy as fraud" perspective, a perspective based on assigning to individuals the property rights to their personal information, a perspective based on regulation, and a perspective based on behavioral economics.

2.2.2 Privacy as Fraud

First appearing in the late 1970s, one school of thought about the economics of privacy asserts that government facilitates the free flow of personal information for commercial uses in the interests of promoting and maximizing market efficiency.[19] In this view, both consumers and sellers benefit: consumers benefit when sellers have access to useful information about them, and sellers benefit from being able to get the best return on their advertising or marketing approaches and ultimately make more sales. For example, having information about a given consumer's interest in golf might help a travel agency tailor vacation offerings or packages that would interest or benefit that consumer, as well as allow the agency

---

[19]Among the pioneering economic and legal studies with a focus on privacy are Richard Posner, "An Economic Theory of Privacy," *Regulation* (May/June):19-26, 1978; Richard A. Posner, "The Economics of Privacy," *American Economic Review* 71(2):405-409, 1981; and George J. Stigler, "An Introduction to Privacy in Economics and Politics," *Journal of Legal Studies* 9:623-644, 1980.

to save money by not wasting resources in reaching out to people with no interest in such things.

However, as Hui and Png have noted, this approach "may not work efficiently" as it is predicated on, among other things, sellers having perfect information about consumers.[20] Such is rarely the case, as relevant consumer information is often inaccurate, too costly, or simply too difficult to obtain. Moreover, access to information about buyers (especially transaction information) can also allow sellers to engage in so-called price discrimination, whereby consumers willing to pay a higher price for a given good or service will be charged a higher price. For example, Odlyzko describes how one computer manufacturer offered the same system for sale to small businesses, health care companies, and state and local governments at respectively lower prices.[21]

In addition, this approach can also lead to certain external effects that consumers often view as undesirable. Indeed, many consumers perceive unsolicited marketing appeals of a type enabled by the sharing of information (e.g., an unsolicited phone call about a tailored golfing vacation package when one has no interest whatsoever in a golfing vacation) as intrusions into their privacy and hence as becoming costs that they must bear.[22] Generally, research suggests that this approach tends to favor sellers over consumers and often results in undesirable externalities for consumers.

In the context of this approach, privacy involves the "withholding or concealment of information"[23]—the ability of buyers to keep personal information away from sellers. Advocates of this approach assert that because efficient markets depend on the free flow of information, privacy thus renders markets less efficient.[24] For instance, a buyer would choose to hide discrediting or negative information out of self-interest rather than allowing that information to be used in the decision-making process of the seller, particularly if it would raise the cost of the good or service for

---

[20]Kai-Lung Hui and I.P.L. Png, "The Economics of Privacy," in Terry Hendershott, ed., *Handbook of Information Systems and Economics*, Elsevier, forthcoming.

[21]Andrew Odlyzko, "Privacy, Economics, and Price Discrimination on the Internet," 2003, available at http://www.dtc.umn.edu/~odlyzko/doc/privacy.economics.pdf.

[22]As a general matter, it is not evident whether privacy leads to more or fewer intrusions such as telemarketing calls. Increased information allows firms to better target their marketing efforts. On the one hand, marketing efforts become more effective, so that firms engage in more of them. On the other hand, because firms target, a consumer is less likely to get a worthless call.

[23]Posner, "An Economic Theory of Privacy," 1978, p. 19.

[24]Stigler, "An Introduction to Privacy in Economics and Politics," 1980.

the buyer.[25] In this view, privacy would create inefficiencies and impose restraints on businesses, and ultimately, would lower the general welfare. Furthermore, in this view, market forces would create the necessary balance between the opposing interests of buyers and sellers for the most efficient allocation of personal information for maximum benefit.

2.2.3 Privacy and the Assignment of Property Rights to Individuals

After the initial economic analyses in the late 1970s and 1980s, privacy reappeared in the economic literature in the mid-1990s,[26] as the "dot-com" IT sector expanded and markets for personal information grew. In these analyses, assignment of property rights to information was proposed as one way to control or improve the use of personal information:[27] consumers would "own" their personal information and would be free to share it in whatever manner they chose. For example, some might choose to restrict commercial access to their personal information entirely, whereas others might choose to sell some or all of their personal information or make it available in exchange for some other benefit.

From the "privacy as fraud" perspective, the assignment of property rights to information would distort the free market for information, shifting society away from an economically efficient equilibrium and reducing overall societal welfare. For example, granting workers property rights to their personal information might allow them to conceal information from employers. Individual workers might benefit in the short term, but employers—being denied valuable information—would make less efficient employment decisions and in the long run might be able to offer fewer jobs, resulting in fewer opportunities for these workers overall.

Assigning property rights to personal information would result largely in an opt-in market for information sharing, whereby sellers would have access to the information only of those consumers who chose to make it available. This approach would arguably free consumers from some of the negative effects permitted by a more free market approach (e.g.,

---

[25]It is this point that makes the "privacy as fraud" school of thought significantly different from a free market school. In a completely free market, individuals would be free to spend money to conceal information. Rather, the "privacy as fraud" school stipulates that the government acts to *prevent* such concealment.

[26]Economic literature in the mid-1990s emphasizing privacy aspects includes Roger Clarke, "Computer Matching by Government Agencies: The Failure of Cost/Benefit Analysis as a Control Mechanism," *Information Infrastructure & Policy* 4(1):29-65, 1995; Eli Noam, "Privacy and Self-Regulation: Markets for Electronic Privacy," and Hal Varian, "Economic Aspects of Personal Privacy," both in *Privacy and Self-Regulation in the Information Age*, U.S. Department of Commerce, 1997; and Kenneth Laudon, "Markets and Privacy," *Communications of the ACM* 39:9, 1996.

[27]Varian, "Economic Aspects of Personal Privacy," 1997.

costs/intrusions from unsolicited marketing appeals), but it might also mean that consumers would not benefit as much from tailored goods and services from sellers or that sellers would be forced to pass along higher costs associated with less efficient marketing.

Hermalin and Katz have found that privacy can be efficient in certain circumstances but that privacy property rights—personal control over one's personal information—are often worthless.[28] Suppose, for example, that a job candidate has the right to withhold health information from a potential employer. Such silence would likely be inferred by the employer to mean that the candidate's health is poor. The same holds true for a job candidate who declines to answer a question about whether he was in prison: The employer would likely assume that the candidate has served a prison term. If an employer assumes the worst about a potential employee who chooses to exercise his or her privacy rights, then the right to remain silent can be completely valueless, and anyone other than those with the most to hide will "voluntarily" reveal their personal information. To protect privacy in such settings, it may be necessary that public policy make it mandatory for everyone to remain silent about their personal information.

2.2.4 The Economic Impact of Privacy Regulation

Whereas the assignment of property rights can have value in resolving privacy issues in contexts where the collectors and users of personal information and the information owners can enter into contractual arrangements, there are many situations in which such contractual arrangements are difficult to manage. Such situations are generally handled through regulatory and tort law, and economic analyses of such laws make it possible to understand some of their economic impact.

Hui and Png argue that privacy regulation is most appropriate when many information providers (consumers) are highly sensitive to the gathering of their personal information. (In this context, regulation refers to restrictions, and possibly prohibitions, on the sale or use of personal information for commercial purposes.) When this is so, regulation works efficiently and overall welfare is maximized because consumers can avoid the cost of understanding the privacy policy of each individual information gatherer. By contrast, regulation is highly inefficient when most consumers do not care very much about protecting their personal information; under these circumstances, information collectors will avoid the cost of protecting the personal information they gather.

---

[28]Ben Hermalin and Michael Katz, "Privacy, Property Rights & Efficiency: The Economics of Privacy as Secrecy," *Quantitative Marketing and Economics* 4(3, September):209-239, 2006.

One argument in favor of regulation is that it may be a more effective form of commitment than contractual arrangements.[29] Hui and Png argue that under some circumstances, sellers benefit from privacy guarantees provided to consumers. A privacy guarantee assures the consumer that his information will not be further shared with a third party, thus making a privacy-sensitive consumer more likely to make a purchase from a seller. In this setting, the efficiency of regulation emerges from eliminating uncertainty on the consumer's part about whether his personal information will be shared with other parties. An example is the privacy of patient health information. Because candor is required for effective provision of health care services, privacy guarantees for patient health information promote healthier individuals—and healthier individuals enhance overall community health.

Yet there are contexts in which privacy guarantees detract from overall welfare. Hui and Png suggest that although the "do not call" list has helped to reduce the volume of telephone solicitors, it may not be possible to control spam e-mail in the same way. One reason is that the majority of spam e-mail likely comes from illicit spammers in any event, and these individuals are unlikely to obey a law that requires senders of spam to consult with a "do not spam" list. Even worse, spammers might find ways of obtaining the e-mail addresses on the "do not spam" list, thus rendering the law counterproductive.

Hui and Png conclude that the key issue is how to balance the interests of sellers and consumers, and note that a sweeping "okay to use" or "do not use" solution will not work across all contexts. When it is feasible to determine the benefits and costs of information use, one approach is industry-specific regulation.

2.2.5 Privacy and Behavioral Economics

In 2004, some of the first work on a behavioral economic perspective on privacy appeared. Behavioral economics seeks to integrate insights from psychology with neoclassical economic theory and to understand the economic implications of behavior that does not conform to the calculating, unemotional, utility-maximizing characteristics of Homo economicus.

In a privacy context, it has been observed that despite consumer concern about privacy, survey results point to broad discrepancies between

---

[29]Although private contracts can represent a stronger commitment than does public policy (which can be unilaterally changed), a regulatory approach to privacy protection has the dual advantages of greater enforceability and broad applicability and relevance across the entire population.

attitudes of individuals and their actual behavior toward privacy protection.[30] Given the lack of consumer demand, markets for privacy-protecting goods and services (e.g., anonymizers) will continue to remain small, and other self-regulating markets relying on consumer behavior for input may not sufficiently protect consumer privacy.[31]

Moreover, research in social psychology and behavioral economics indicates that the "default condition" of many choices is very "sticky"— that is, most people find it easier to accept a default choice made on their behalf regarding a putative decision than to change that choice, even if the default choice is less advantageous to them than changing that choice.[32]

Recent work by Acquisti is illustrative, offering an explanation for the well-known discrepancy between individuals' attitudes and their behavior when it comes to online privacy.[33] Acquisti argues that contrary to traditional economic analyses that assume that individuals are fully rational, forward-looking, Bayesian updaters who take into account how current behavior will influence their future well-being and preferences, individuals instead demonstrate various forms of psychological inconsistencies (self-control problems, hyperbolic discounting, present-biases). Furthermore, the ability to make fully informed decisions regarding one's privacy is extremely difficult after personal information has been transmitted to a third party and can continue to change hands, without the individual's knowledge, for any length of time.

To provide further insight on individual decision making, Acquisti relies on the concept of immediate gratification,[34] an individual's preference for well-being earlier rather than later and the tendency to engage in desirable activities over undesirable activities, even if the choice may result in negative future consequences. Furthermore, an individual's preferences are also inconsistent over time (i.e., preferences for the future activities will change as the date to undertake the activity approaches)

---

[30]See, for example, studies cited in Section 8 in Hui and Png, "The Economics of Privacy," forthcoming.

[31]Alessandro Acquisti, "Privacy, Economics, and Immediate Gratification: Why Protecting Privacy Is Easy, But Selling It Is Not," in *Proceedings of the 2004 BLACKHAT Conference*, Las Vegas, Nev., July 2004.

[32]See, for example, William Samuelson and Richard Zeckhauser, "Status Quo Bias in Decision Making," *Journal of Risk & Uncertainty* 1:7-59, 1988; B.C. Madrian and D.F. Shea, "The Power of Suggestion: Inertia in 401(k) Participation and Savings Behavior," *Quarterly Journal of Economics* 116(4):1149-1187, 2001.

[33]Alessandro Acquisti, "Privacy in Electronic Commerce and Economics of Immediate Gratification," pp. 21-29 in *Proceedings of the ACM Electronic Commerce Conference* (EC 04), ACM Press, New York, 2004.

[34]Immediate gratification is related to other types of psychological distortion described in economic and psychological literature that include time inconsistency, hyperbolic discounting, and self-control bias.

and are disproportionate (i.e., perception of risks will vary for near-term and longer-term consequences). In relating this to an individual's online behavior, he suggests that individuals want to protect their privacy in principle but put off to some time in the future the effort required, rather than taking immediate action.

Combining these two sets of factors reveals broader consequences for individual privacy protection. Acquisti suggests that individuals tend to dismiss possible future consequences of revealing personal information for an immediate reward, but also lack complete information to grasp the magnitude of the risk—because each instance of revealing personal information can be linked together, resulting in "a whole that is more than the sum of its parts." Acquisti concludes that more attention will have to be paid to behavioral responses to privacy protections, rather than focusing on protecting privacy solely through informational awareness and industry self-regulation.

Acquisti's conclusions have deep privacy implications. For example, one principle of fair information practice (see Box 1.3) is that of choice and consent. But the principle itself is silent on whether the appropriate choice should be opt-in or opt-out. Under the canons of traditional economic analysis and the rational actor model, these regimes are essentially equivalent (under the assumption that there are no transaction costs associated with either choice). But there are impassioned arguments about whether opt-in or opt-out consent better reflects the willingness of data subjects to provide information without limitations on its secondary use—and these arguments are rooted in a realization that in the real world, the default choice makes a huge difference in the regime that will end up governing most people. Those who advocate opt-out regimes know that most people will not take the trouble to opt out, and thus they can be presumed to "want" to allow information to be collected. Those who advocate opt-in regimes know that most people will not take the trouble to opt in, and that their privacy (in this case, their immunity to having information collected) will thus be protected.

Behavioral economics calls into question how to determine the value that consumers place on their personal information. Hui and Png suggest that one important factor is that the information owners are unlikely to fully take into account the benefit of their information to the parties wanting their information.[35] This has both a societal consequence (in that overall welfare is reduced as these parties are unable to exploit that information) and personal consequences (in that they may thus exclude

---

[35]Kai-Lung Hui and I.P.L. Png, "The Economics of Privacy," in Terry Hendershott, ed., *Handbook of Information Systems and Economics*, Elsevier, forthcoming.

themselves from being offered certain goods or services that they might desire). In addition, information owners are likely to attach too high a price to their personal information, which might excessively raise the barrier to potential buyers of the information, and there is often a significant discrepancy between what consumers report being willing to pay to protect their personal information and what they are willing to accept to allow the use of their personal information. Hui and Png go on to suggest that consumers often attach a high price to their personal information when discussing privacy and personal information, but often readily part with their personal information "in exchange for even small rewards or incentives."[36]

Finally, the findings of behavioral economics have implications for the various critiques of how fair information principles have been implemented in the United States.[37] At the heart of these critiques is the oft-expressed concern that the Federal Trade Commission (FTC), the government agency with responsibility for the protection of certain privacy rights, at least for consumers in the United States, has compressed these fair information practices into a limited construct referred to as "notice and choice." Most often, the provision of notice is satisfied by largely unintelligible industrial sector "boilerplate" language that is not subject to review by the FTC, and the default choice is framed in terms of consumers' opting out of some subcomponent as standard business practice, unless specific legislation establishes informed affirmative consent as the default.[38] Behavioral economics thus implies that a default opt-out choice will not result in a regime that would be affirmatively chosen under a default opt-in choice.

---

[36]See Section 6 in Hui and Png, "The Economics of Privacy," forthcoming.

[37]See for example, Marc Rotenberg, "Fair Information Practices and the Architecture of Privacy (What Larry Doesn't Get)," *Stanford Technology Law Review*, Volume 1, 2001 (online journal available at http://stlr.stanford.edu/STLR/Articles/01_STLR_1/index.htm); Robert Gellman, "Does Privacy Law Work?," in P. Agre and M. Rotenberg, eds., *Technology and Privacy: The New Landscape*, MIT Press, Cambridge, Mass., 1997; and R. Clarke, "Beyond the OECD Guidelines," Xamax Consultancy Pty Ltd., 2000.

[38]The special and highly contested case of telecommunications policy, in which customer proprietary network information (CPNI) could be released only with explicit consumer permission, is one such example. The Federal Communications Commission (FCC) issued an order interpreting the "approval" requirements in February 1998 (available at http://www.fcc.gov/Bureaus/Common_Carrier/Orders/1998/fcc98027.txt). Under the FCC's rule, telephone companies must give customers explicit notice of their right to control the use of their CPNI and obtain express written, oral, or electronic approval for its use. The rule was unsuccessfully challenged by a potential competitor, U.S. West, 182 F.3d 1223 (10th Cir. 1999).

2.3 SOCIOLOGICAL APPROACHES

Sociological approaches to the study of privacy have emphasized the ways in which the collection and use of personal information may reflect and reinforce the relationships of power and influence between individuals, groups, and institutions within society. This emphasis on power relationships is an important factor characterizing the behavior of institutional actors in modern societies.[39] There are also important distinctions to be drawn with the work of those scholars who focus on structural or institutional relationships and those who focus on the cognitive, affective, behavioral, and social process responses of individuals.

Surveillance from this perspective is generally understood to refer to the systematic observation of individuals undertaken in an effort to facilitate their management and control. Some scholars concerned with surveillance emphasize the ways in which surveillance technology has changed over time, while others focus on the ways in which old and new surveillance techniques are used in the exercise of control over individuals in their roles as employees, consumers, and citizens. Still others emphasize the ways in which the use of surveillance techniques becomes a commonplace activity within more and more varied organizational and institutional contexts. Still others focus on interpersonal uses among families, friends, and strangers and the role of the mass media.[40]

An important but distinct body of work within this scholarly tradition is one that focuses on a variety of surveillance techniques used by

---

[39]Within sociology there are different perspectives on surveillance. More technologically oriented observers might prefer to talk about the "capture" of transaction-generated information (see, for example, Philip E. Agre, "Surveillance and Capture: Two Models of Privacy," *The Information Society* 10(2):101-127, 1995). On the other hand, David Lyon (in *Surveillance Society: Monitoring Everyday Life*, Open University Press, 2001) argues that "rather late in the day sociology started to recognize surveillance as a central dimension of modernity, an institution in its own right, not reducible to capitalism, the nation-state, or even bureaucracy." Gary T. Marx ("Seeing Hazily, But Not Darkly, Through the Lens: Some Recent Empirical Studies of Surveillance Technologies," *Law and Social Inquiry* 30(2):339-399, 2005) notes limitations on an exclusive focus on power and control as the defining elements. There are also goals involving protection, documentation, planning, strategy, and pleasure (e.g., as entertainment and to satisfy curiosity).

[40]One surprisingly relatively unstudied and unregulated type here that arouses strong social concern is the voyeur secretly gathering data. See, for example, C. Calvert, *Voyeur Nation: Media, Privacy and Peering in Modern Culture*, Westview, Boulder, Colo., 2000; and a "true fiction" case in which the protagonist Tom Voire engages in, or is the victim of, more than 100 kinds of questionable personal information practices, as described in Gary T. Marx, "Forget Big Brother and Big Corporation: What About the Personal Uses of Surveillance Technology as Seen in Cases Such as Tom I. Voire?" *Rutgers Journal of Law & Urban Policy* 3(4):219-286, 2006.

the police and security forces.[41] However, debates continue among scholars of surveillance who contest evidence and claims about the extent to which there is a meaningful possibility of limiting, resisting, or reversing the trend toward more complete social control and domination through surveillance.

Another important distinction within sociology is a focus on the macro level of grand theory examining the structural or institutional relationships versus a focus on the cognitive, affective, and behavioral responses of individuals who are subject to surveillance. This latter approach makes it easier to test theories empirically. Among those taking a macro-level approach, David Lyon also brings a long historical view to his assessment of the role of surveillance in society. He integrates a number of insights from an evolving cultural studies tradition to study that which is referred to as the postmodern condition. He provides examples to illustrate the ways in which "dataveillance," or the analysis of transaction-generated data, reduces the need for access to a physical or material body in order to gather information and intelligence about the past, present, or future behavior of data subjects.[42]

Priscilla M. Regan has proposed framing privacy as a collective concern rather than as an individualistic one.[43] She gives three reasons for arguing that privacy has value not only to individuals but also to society in general. First, she believes that all individuals value some degree of privacy and have some common perceptions about privacy. Second, she notes that privacy is a value that supports democratic political systems. Third, she asserts that technology and market forces make it hard for any one person to have privacy without all persons having a similar minimum level of privacy. She also conceptualizes personal information as a resource that is available to multiple parties, is difficult to prevent others from using, and is subject to degradation as a result of overuse. Thus, she argues, personal information as a resource is subject to some of the same kinds of excessive-use pressures as are resources such as clean air and edible ocean fish. Privacy can be framed as preventing the overuse of personal information, and thus she argues that public policies to support privacy would have much in common with policies that address the issue of common-pool resources such as air and fish.

Scholars working from within a Marxist or neo-Marxist tradition

---

[41]Richard Ericson and Kevin Haggerty, *Policing the Risk Society*, University of Toronto Press, 1997; and Gary T. Marx, *Undercover: Police Surveillance in America*, University of California Press, 1988.

[42]Lyon, *Surveillance Society*, 2001.

[43]P.M. Regan, "Privacy as a Common Good in the Digital World," *Information, Communication and Society* 5(3, September 1):382-405, 2002.

engage the development of surveillance techniques as a response of capitalists to continuing crises of over- and underproduction. As the logic of capital is extended to more and more activities, surveillance facilitates coordination and control.[44] Anthony Giddens, who extends the analyses of surveillance, combines the grand theories begun by Michel Foucault and Max Weber with empirical data in an effort to cross these distinctions.[45] Scholars influenced by Giddens have focused on surveillance as an aspect of rationalization within government[46] and corporate bureaucracies.[47]

In terms of understanding how individuals perceive surveillance processes, Irwin Altman's work reflects a psychological emphasis and contributes not only concepts and measures of desired and realized levels of privacy, but also behavioral insights that are useful in cataloging the resources available to individuals that allow them to exercise more or less control over the boundaries between themselves and others.[48]

Finally, and in addition to his identification and assessment of important trends, critical events, and important distinctions between segments of the population (Section 2.1.2), Westin's analyses have provided insights into the ways in which privacy policies emerge in response to public concerns. But critics have suggested that for a number of reasons, including the influence of corporate sponsors and a concern with assessing the public's response to the issue of the day, Westin's empiricism has stretched its theoretical foundations beyond its useful limits.[49]

The work within sociology on surveillance (and, by extension, its relationship to privacy) considers the effect of surveillance on individuals and society. These effects can occur even in the absence of actual surveillance if the individuals believe that they are being observed—these are intangible effects in the sense that they affect individuals' states of mind, but are no less real. This feeds into the worries about the impact of tech-

---

[44]Frank Webster and Kevin Robins, *Information Technology: A Luddite Analysis*, Ablex, 1986.

[45]See, for example, Anthony Giddens, *The Nation State and Violence: Volume Two of a Contemporary Critique of Historical Materialism*, Polity Press, Cambridge, Mass., 1985. This work integrates an understanding of bureaucracy from Max Weber (see Reinhard Bendix, *Max Weber, an Intellectual Portrait*, Doubleday, 1960) and panoptic surveillance from Michel Foucault (*Discipline and Punish: The Birth of the Prison*, Vintage Books, 1979).

[46]Christopher Dandeker, *Surveillance Power and Modernity*, Polity Press, Cambridge, Mass., 1990.

[47]Oscar H. Gandy, Jr., *The Panoptic Sort: A Political Economy of Personal Information*, Westview, 1993.

[48]Stephen T. Margulis, "On the Status and Contribution of Westin's and Altman's Theories of Privacy," *Journal of Social Issues* 59(2):411-429, 2003.

[49]Oscar H. Gandy, Jr., "The Role of Theory in the Policy Process: A Response to Professor Westin," pp. 99-106 in Charles Firestone and Jorge Reina Schement, eds., *Towards an Information Bill of Rights and Responsibilities*, The Aspen Institute, 1995.

nology advances, since many of those advances enable the observation of an individual without the knowledge of the person being observed. Even if these beliefs are groundless, they can change the behavior of the individual. Sociological studies attempt to understand these effects.

Sociological perspectives on privacy also examine the consequences that flow from the lack of privacy. For example, although one could define privacy as "that which can be lost under excessive surveillance," sociological analyses would highlight the point that under excessive surveillance far more is lost than just privacy. Human dignity, equal opportunity, social justice, and equality for groups with historical disadvantages—among other values—can suffer as a result of excessive and inappropriate surveillance. On the other hand and somewhat ironically, surveillance may also be a factor in documenting wrongs. (For example, a tape from a video surveillance may inadvertently capture an incident of police misconduct.) To approach the topic using only the language of privacy is to miss some of the pressing social, ethical, and political issues raised by contemporary surveillance. Alternatively, one might formulate issues of human dignity, equal opportunity, social justice, and racial parity as being some of the areas in which societal or group harms may result from a loss of (individual) privacy.

It is helpful to consider some of the distinctions between personal identity and externally constructed identification.[50] For example, David Phillips accepts the critical distinction between identity and identification,[51] noting the differences in agency that usually locate within bureaucratic organizations the power to impose identification on someone. Furthermore, Phillips clarifies the distinctions between nominal, indexical, and descriptive forms of identification:

• Nominal identification refers to the names people have been given. Such names often do not provide unique identification in that more than one person can have the same name. Additional data can reduce the number of persons to whom these data apply. Biometric data are assumed to reduce the range of associations rather dramatically.

• Indexical identification associates information about place and time in order to enable a particular person to be "identified" in some way.

• Descriptive identification refers to the ways in which identification can be based on an association of attributes, behaviors, and locations with other markers.

---

[50]Oscar H. Gandy, Jr., "Exploring Identity and Identification in Cyberspace," *Notre Dame Journal of Law, Ethics and Public Policy* 14(2):1085-1111, 2000.

[51]David J. Phillips, "Privacy Policy and PETs: The Influence of Policy Regimes on the Development and Social Implications of Privacy Enhancing Technologies," *New Media & Society* 6(6):691-706, 2004.

Descriptive identification plays an important role in the identification of groups, and such identification can enable and justify discriminatory actions that reduce the space for autonomous action that people might otherwise enjoy. Such issues are often discussed under the heading of group privacy.

Group privacy is not a new concept,[52] although most of the attention that has been paid to the concept in the past has been focused on the freedom of association. Privacy scholars have begun to argue that group privacy should also be understood as a right of self-determination that is increasingly limited by the use of transaction-generated information to define group membership on the basis of behavioral rather than biological attributes. Developments in genetic research may or may not establish linkages between biology and behavior, but the emerging concern with behavioral identification is different.

The reason is that behavioral identification or characterization of groups can be done covertly. Persons who are members of groups defined on the basis of biological markers (age, race, gender) have some opportunity to mobilize and petition for rights on the basis of a common identity. Persons who are members of groups that have been identified and defined on the basis of statistical analyses are less likely to be aware of the identities of others in their group, even if they manage to discover the nature of their own classification. These ascriptive groups often have names that are used only by the organizations that produce them.[53]

Because the existence of such groups is rarely made public, and little effort is made to inform group members of their status, they are less likely to organize politically to press for their rights. To the extent that members of social groups that have traditionally been victims of discrimination are also members of statistically derived groups of "disfavored others," it seems likely that their social position will reflect the impact of cumulative disadvantage.[54]

An important cluster of concerns is inherent in an information-based ability to discriminate against persons as individuals or as members of groups in the name of increasing efficiency and economic competitiveness

---

[52]Edward J. Bloustein, *Individual and Group Privacy*, Transaction Publications, 1978. Also relevant is S. Alpert, "Protecting Medical Privacy: Challenges in the Age of Genetic Information," *Journal of Social Issues* 59(2):301-322, 2003.

[53]The names for communities produced by users of geo-demographic targeting techniques may be interpreted by the general public, but those names are rarely made public because people so identified are often angered when they learn of their identification. Examples might be a group characterized as "shotgun and pickups" or "Volvo-driving Gucci lovers."

[54]The concept of cumulative disadvantage is examined in considerable detail in R.M. Blank, M. Dabady, and C.F. Citro, eds., *Measuring Racial Discrimination*, The National Academies Press, Washington, D.C., 2004.

or meeting other socially desirable goals.[55] The ability to discriminate has the potential to reinforce differences in power and privilege within social systems. Discrimination is an exercise in social sorting, and such sorting relies heavily on personal information. Sorting occurs for all kinds of reasons—some benign and some insidious—but social sorting can mean that individuals in some categories will face more limitations on their opportunities to choose than will individuals in other categories. On the other hand, the protection of privacy means that some personal information will not be available for such sorting.

As a matter of national policy, it is illegal to make certain decisions (e.g., on employment, housing) on the basis of categorical distinctions regarding race, gender, religion, and certain aspects of lifestyle. At the same time, many believe that attention to these very factors is appropriate as a tool to overcome historic and persistent disadvantage. But the conflicts are clear, and the sociological and cultural challenge is thus to determine what kinds of information about persons are and are not appropriate to use and under what conditions. New contested means of classification and identification are likely to continually appear and to be challenged as values conflict. There is no simple answer to such questions, but discussion of and openness with respect to the factors used in social sorting for public policy purposes are of the utmost importance.

2.4 AN INTEGRATING PERSPECTIVE

The discussion above of philosophical, economic, and sociological perspectives on privacy indicates that understanding privacy in the information age requires consideration of a variety of approaches, methods, and ideas. Taken as a whole, the privacy literature is a cacophony, suggesting that trying to define privacy in the abstract is not likely to be a fruitful exercise. Indeed, a number of varied and sometimes incommensurate perspectives on privacy were reflected in the committee. But the committee also found common ground on several points among its members, witnesses, and in the literature.

The first point is that privacy touches a very broad set of social concerns related to the control of, access to, and uses of information—this report emphasizes privacy as access to and control over information about individuals. An interesting question is whether privacy is a concept relevant to information about groups of people, although of course for many

---

[55]See, for example, Frederick Schauer, *Profiles, Probabilities, and Stereotypes*, Harvard University Press, Cambridge, Mass., 2003, and Bernard E. Harcourt, "Rethinking Racial Profiling: A Critique of the Economics, Civil Liberties, and Constitutional Literature, and of Criminal Profiling More Generally," *University of Chicago Law Review* 71(Fall):1275-1381, 2004.

purposes a group can be treated as an individual (e.g., corporations are given the legal right to make contracts and to sue and be sued as legal persons).

Second, to the extent that privacy is a "good thing to have," it sometimes conflicts with other good things to have. Thus, needs for privacy must sometimes be balanced with other considerations—complaints of some privacy advocates or privacy foes about excessive or inappropriate balancing notwithstanding. How this balance is to be achieved is often the center of the controversy around privacy. Complicating the effort to find the appropriate balance is the tendency to confuse the needs of privacy with other values that might be tied to privacy but are, in fact, distinct from it and the differential impact of policies on various social groups and over time. For example, the privacy of personal health information is often related to concerns about discriminatory access to heath care; this point is discussed further in Box 7.1 in Chapter 7.

Third, privacy in context is much more understandable than privacy in the abstract. As the literature illustrates, agreement on a broad analytical definition of privacy in the abstract is difficult if not impossible. But discussions of the privacy implications of specific events and practices are easier to understand and discuss. One approach to grounding a discussion of privacy in context is the use of anchoring vignettes (Box 2.2). The anchoring vignette technique can be useful for understanding the impact of any given technology on privacy by posing a set of grounded, scenario-specific questions that can be answered with and without the presence of that technology. It can also be helpful for understanding public perceptions of privacy in various contexts. In this report, the technique is used in multiple ways to illustrate and to help unpack intuitions about privacy in different contexts.

Knowing a context for privacy discussions does not result in an over-arching theoretical definition of privacy. Nor does it represent an agreement about the level of privacy that is appropriate in any given situation. However, knowing the relevant dimensions of privacy and what "more" or "less" privacy might mean in the specific context of each dimension does clarify the discussion, and the anchoring vignette technique is one useful approach to obtain such knowledge.

The context-sensitive nature of privacy makes it clear that questions about privacy necessarily imply specifying privacy "from whom," "about what," "for what reasons," and "under what conditions." For example, a set of possible privacy violators might include one's employer; family; friends, acquaintances, and neighbors; researchers; businesses; and government. Associated with each of these potential violators is an "about what"—a (different) set of information types that might arise with any given possible privacy violator. For example, in the context of an employer

---

BOX 2.2
The Anchoring Vignette Approach
to Grounding Discussions of Privacy

Developed by committee member Gary King and others, an anchoring vignette is a brief description of a specific situation involving personal information.[1] Organized into related sets in which a range of privacy considerations are manifest, the vignettes help to collect, articulate, and organize intuitions about privacy in a more precise and empirical fashion; clarify assumptions about privacy; empirically document views on privacy; and serve as a good tool for illustrating, expressing, and communicating existing concepts of privacy.

Vignettes have been extensively used for conducting actual surveys and in helping develop actual survey instruments, but in the context of this report they help to define the concepts so that all participants in a privacy discussion have the same frame of reference. Although they are not intended to suggest a particular policy to adopt, anchoring vignettes help to provide a lingua franca for privacy and so they may be of use to citizens in attaining a better understanding of public policy regarding privacy. The vignettes form a continuum along which various policy scenarios can be placed and in that sense can help to frame questions that might be asked about any given policy.

To illustrate, consider the issue of privacy with respect to criminal charges. A set of useful vignettes might be as follows:

1. [Jonathan] was arrested on charges of assault and battery last year. He lives in a county that stores records of criminal charges at the police headquarters, where there is no public access.

---

[1]Gary King, Christopher J.L. Murray, Joshua A. Salomon, and Ajay Tandon, "Enhancing the Validity and Cross-cultural Comparability of Survey Research," *American Political Science Review* 98(1):191-207, 2004, available at http://gking.harvard.edu/files/abs/vign-abs.shtml. See also Gary King and Jonathan Wand, "Comparing Incomparable Survey Responses: New Tools for Anchoring Vignettes," *Political Analysis*, forthcoming, 2007, available at http://gking.harvard.edu/files/abs/c-abs. shtml. Extensive examples and other information can be found at the Anchoring Vignettes Web site, at http://gking.harvard.edu/vign/. The committee thanks Dan Ho and Matthew Knowles, who assisted in the development of material on anchoring vignettes presented to the committee during its open data-gathering sessions.

---

as a possible privacy violator, one might be concerned about surveillance of work or about drug testing. By contrast, in the context of friends, acquaintances, and neighbors as possible privacy violators, one might be concerned about personal secrets, nudity, sex, medical information, and invasiveness.[56]

The kinds of social roles and relationships involved are as central as

---

[56]In thinking through who might be a possible privacy violator, it also helps to consider parties with whom one might be willing to share information. Although in some sense, one is the complement of the other, in practice the complement is more likely to be fuzzy, with zones of more gray and less gray rather than sharp boundaries between black and white.

2. [Monali] was arrested on charges of assault and battery last year. She lives in a county that maintains all records of criminal charges for public inspection at the county courthouse.

3. [David] was arrested on charges of assault and battery last year. He lives in a county that maintains all records of criminal charges at the county courthouse for public inspection and in an electronic database, to which any police officer or county official has access.

4. [Andrea] was arrested on charges of assault and battery last year. She lives in a county that posts all criminal charges on the Internet. The Web page includes pictures and detailed profiles of all arrested.

Our intuitions about privacy in each of these situations reflect our answers to questions such as, How much privacy does the individual have in this situation?, Does David have more privacy than Andrea?, and so on. We can also ask how much privacy the individual *should* be granted in the situation.

One way to think about these vignettes is to imagine being asked a survey question about each vignette or even about yourself: *How much privacy [does "Name"/do you] have? (a) unlimited, (b) a lot, (c) moderate, (d) some, (e) none?* The imagined survey context helps to make the examples concrete and clarifies how they are to be read. Although such vignettes are often used for survey research, defining privacy from the bottom up does not involve administering a survey or necessarily asking these questions of others.

For each set of anchoring vignettes (denoting privacy in one specific context), different people will have different views about what thresholds delineate levels of privacy below which violations should be considered undesirable, unethical, illegal, or immoral. Agreement on normative issues like these will always be difficult to achieve. The anchoring vignette-based approach to privacy thus does not resolve all normative issues, but it helps to clearly define the playing field.

Note also that vignettes can be modified to illustrate different scenarios. For example, the above scenario can be modified by substituting "convicted" for "arrested on charges" and "convictions" for "charges." It is likely that such changes might cause at least some people to reevaluate their answers.

the goals, location, type of technology, and data involved, and the conditions under which personal information is collected and used. Indeed, what constitutes privacy, what information should be private, and what individuals or institutions are posing potential threats to that privacy are all questions subject to considerable debate. A related set of questions involves the circumstances under which privacy can be seen to go too far. Under some conditions the failure to discover or reveal personal information can be harmful socially (e.g., in the case of potential for exposure to deadly contagious diseases or a person with a history of violent and abusive behavior).

3

Technological Drivers

Privacy is an information concept, and fundamental properties of information define what privacy can—and cannot—be. For example, information has the property that it is inherently reproducible: If I share some information with you, we both have all of that information. This stands in sharp contrast to apples: If I share an apple with you, we each get half an apple, not a whole apple. If information were not reproducible in this manner, many privacy concerns would simply disappear.

3.1 THE IMPACT OF TECHNOLOGY ON PRIVACY

Advances in technology have often led to concerns about the impact of those advances on privacy. As noted in Chapter 1, the classic characterization of privacy as the right to be left alone was penned by Louis Brandeis in his article discussing the effects on privacy of the then-new technology of photography. The development of new information technologies, whether they have to do with photography, telephony, or computers, has almost always raised questions about how privacy can be maintained in the face of the new technology. Today's advances in computing technology can be seen as no more than a recurrence of this trend, or can be seen as different in that new technology, being fundamentally concerned with the gathering and manipulation of information, increases the potential for threats to privacy.

Several trends in the technology have led to concerns about privacy. One such trend has to do with hardware that increases the amount of information that can be gathered and stored and the speed with which that information can be analyzed, thus changing the economics of what it is possible to do with information technology. A second trend concerns the increasing connectedness of this hardware over networks, which magnifies the increases in the capabilities of the individual pieces of hardware that the network connects. A third trend has to do with advances in software that allow sophisticated mechanisms for the extraction of information from the data that are stored, either locally or on the network. A fourth trend, enabled by the other three, is the establishment of organizations and companies that offer as a resource information that they have gathered themselves or that has been aggregated from other sources but organized and analyzed by the company.

Improvements in the technologies have been dramatic, but the systems that have been built by combining those technologies have often yielded overall improvements that sometimes appear to be greater than the sum of the constituent parts. These improvements have in some cases changed what it is possible to do with the technologies or what it is economically feasible to do; in other cases they have made what was once difficult into something that is so easy that anyone can perform the action at any time.

The end result is that there are now capabilities for gathering, aggregating, analyzing, and sharing information about and related to individuals (and groups of individuals) that were undreamed of 10 years ago. For example, global positioning system (GPS) locators attached to trucks can provide near-real-time information on their whereabouts and even their speed, giving truck shipping companies the opportunity to monitor the behavior of their drivers. Cell phones equipped to provide E-911 service can be used to map to a high degree of accuracy the location of the individuals carrying them, and a number of wireless service providers are marketing cell phones so equipped to parents who wish to keep track of where their children are.

These trends are manifest in the increasing number of ways people use information technology, both for the conduct of everyday life and in special situations. The personal computer, for example, has evolved from a replacement for a typewriter to an entry point to a network of global scope. As a network device, the personal computer has become a major agent for personal interaction (via e-mail, instant messaging, and the like), for financial transactions (bill paying, stock trading, and so on), for gathering information (e.g., Internet searches), and for entertainment (e.g., music and games). Along with these intended uses, however, the personal computer can also become a data-gathering device sensing all of these activities. The use of the PC on the network can potentially generate data that can be analyzed to find out more about users of PCs than they anticipated or intended, including their buying habits, their reading and listening preferences, who they communicate with, and their interests and hobbies.

Concerns about privacy will grow as the use of computers and networks expands into new areas. If we can't keep data private with the current use of technology, how will we maintain our current understanding of privacy when the common computing and networking infrastructure includes our voting, medical, financial, travel, and entertainment records, our daily activities, and the bulk of our communications? As more aspects of our lives are recorded in systems for health care, finance, or electronic commerce, how are we to ensure that the information gathered is not used inappropriately to detect or deduce what we consider to be private information? How do we ensure the privacy of our thoughts and the freedom of our speech as the electronic world becomes a part of our government, central to our economy, and the mechanism by which we cast our ballots? As we become subject to surveillance in public and commercial spaces, how do we ensure that others do not track our every move? As citizens of a democracy and participants in our communities, how can we guarantee that the privacy of putatively secret ballots is assured when electronic voting systems are used?

The remainder of this chapter explores some relevant technology trends, describing current and projected technological capacity and relating it to privacy concerns. It also discusses computer, network, and system architectures and their potential impacts on privacy.

3.2 HARDWARE ADVANCES

Perhaps the most commonly known technology trend is the exponential growth in computing power—loosely speaking the central processor unit in a computer will double in speed (or halve in price) every 18 months. What this trend has meant is that over the last 10 years, we have gone through about seven generations, which in turn means that the power of the central processing unit has increased by a factor of more than 100. The impact of this change on what is possible or reasonable to compute is hard to overestimate. Tasks that took an hour 10 years ago now take less than a minute. Tasks that now take an hour would have taken days to complete a decade ago. The end result of this increase in computing speed is that many tasks that were once too complex to be automated can now be easily tackled by commonly available machines.

While the increase in computing power that is implied by this exponential growth is well known and often cited, less appreciated are the economic implications of that trend, which entail a decrease in the cost of computation by a factor of more than 100 over the past 10 years. One outcome of this is that the desktop computer used in the home today is far more powerful than the most expensive supercomputer of 10 years ago. At the same time, the cell phones commonly used today are at least as powerful as the personal computers of a decade ago. This change in the economics of computing means that there are many more computers in simple numbers than there were a decade ago, which in turn means that the amount of total computation available at a reasonable price is no longer a limiting factor in any but the most complex of computing problems.

Nor is it merely central processing units (CPUs) that have shown dramatic improvements in performance and dramatic reductions in cost over the past 10 years. Dynamic random access memory (DRAM), which provides the working space for computers, has also followed a course similar to that for CPU chips.[1] Over the past decade memory size has in some cases increased by a factor of 100 or more, which allows not only for faster computation but also for the ability to work on vastly larger data sets than was possible before.

Less well known in the popular mind, but in some ways more dramatic than the trend in faster processors and larger memory chips, has been the expansion of capabilities for storing electronic information. The price of long-term storage has been decreasing rapidly over the last decade, and the ability to access large amounts of such storage has been increasing. Storage capacity has been increasing at a rate that has outpaced the rate of increase in computing power, with some studies showing that it has doubled on average every 12 months.[2] The result of this trend is that data can be stored for long periods of time in an economical fashion. In fact, the economics of data storage has become inverted. Traditionally, data was discarded as soon as possible to minimize the cost of storing that data, or at least moved from primary storage (disks) to secondary storage (tape) where it was more difficult to access. With the advances in the capacities of primary storage devices, it is now often more expensive to decide how to cull data or transfer it to secondary storage (and to spend the resources to do the culling or transferring) than it is to simply store it all on primary storage, adding new capacity when it is needed.

The change in the economics of data storage has altered more than just the need to occasionally cull data. It has also changed the kind of

---

[1]On the other hand, the speed with which the contents of RAM chips can be accessed has not increased commensurately with speed increases in CPU chips, and so RAM access has become relatively "slower." This fact has not yet had many privacy implications, but may in the future.

[2]E. Grochowski and R.D. Halern, "Technological Impact of Magnetic Hard Disk Drives on Storage Systems," *IBM Systems Journal* 42(2):338-346, July 2003.

data that organizations are willing to store. When persistent storage was a scarce resource, considerable effort was expended in ensuring that the data that were gathered were compressed, filtered, or otherwise reduced before being committed to persistent storage. Often the purpose for which the data had been gathered was used to enhance this compression and filtering, resulting in the storing not of the raw data that had been gathered but instead of the computed results based on that data. Since the computed results were task-specific, it was difficult or impossible to reuse the stored information for other purposes, part of the compression and filtering caused a loss of the general information such that it could not be recovered.

With the increase in the capacity of long-term storage, reduction of data as they are gathered is no longer needed. And although compression is still used in many kinds of data storage, that compression is often reversible, allowing the re-creation of the original data set. The ability to re-create the original data set is of great value, as it allows more sophisticated analysis of the data in the future. But it also allows the data to be analyzed for purposes other than those for which it was originally gathered, and allows the data to be aggregated with data gathered in other ways for additional analysis.

Additionally, forms of data that were previously considered too large to be stored for long periods of time can now easily be placed on next-generation storage devices. For example, high-quality video streams, which can take up megabytes of storage for each second of video, were once far too large to be stored for long periods; the most that was done was to store samples of the video streams on tape. Now it is possible to store large segments of real-time video footage on various forms of long-term storage, keeping recent video footage online on hard disks, and then archiving older footage on DVD storage.

Discarding or erasing stored information does not eliminate the possibility of compromising the privacy of the individuals whose information had been stored. A recent study has shown that a large number of disk drives available for sale on the secondary market contain easily obtainable information that was placed on the drive by the former owner. Included in the information found by the study was banking account information, information about prescription drug use, and college application information.[3] Even when the previous owners of the disk drive had gone to some effort to erase the contents of the drive, it was in most cases fairly easy to repair the drive in such a way that the data that the drive had held

---

[3]Simson L. Garfinkel and Abhi Shelat, "Remembrance of Data Past: A Study of Disk Sanitization Practices," *IEEE Security and Privacy* 1(1):83-88, 2003.

were easily available. In fact, one of the conclusions of the study is that it is quite hard to really remove information from a modern disk drive; even when considerable effort has been put into removing the information, sophisticated "digital forensic" techniques can be used to re-create the data. From the privacy point of view, this means that once data have been gathered and committed to persistent storage, it is very difficult to ever be sure that the data have been removed or forgotten—a point very relevant to the archiving of materials in a digital age.

With more data, including more kinds of data, being kept in its raw form, the concern arises that every electronic transaction a person ever enters into can be kept in readily available storage, and that audio and video footage of all of the public activities for that person could also be available. This information, originally gathered for purposes of commerce, public safety, health care, or for some other reason, could then be available for uses other than those originally intended. The fear is that the temptation to use all of this information, either by a governmental agency or by private corporations or even individuals, is so great that it will be nearly impossible to guarantee the privacy of anyone from some sort of prying eye, if not now then in the future.

The final hardware trend relevant to issues of personal privacy involves data-gathering devices. The evolution of these devices has moved them from the generating of analog data to the generation of data in digital form; from devices that were on specialized networks to those that are connected to larger networks; and from expensive, specialized devices that were deployed only in rare circumstances to cheap, ubiquitous devices either too small or too common to be generally noticed. Biometric devices, which sense physiological characteristics of individuals, also count as data-gathering devices. These sensors, from simple temperature and humidity sensors in buildings to the positioning systems in automobiles to video cameras used in public places to aid in security, continue to proliferate, showing the way to a world in which all of our physical environment is being watched and sensed by sets of eyes and other sensors. Box 3.1 provides a sampling of these sensing devices.

The ubiquitous connection of these sensors to the network is really a result of the transitive nature of connectivity. It is not in most cases the sensors themselves that are connected to the larger world. The standard sensor deployment has a group of sensors connected by a local (often specialized) network to a single computer. However, that computer is in turn connected to the larger network, either an intranet or the Internet itself. Because of this latter connection, the data generated by the sensors can be moved around the network like any other data once the computer to which the sensors are directly connected has received it.

The final trend of note in sensing devices is their nearly ubiquitous

---

BOX 3.1
A Sampling of Advanced Data-gathering Technologies

- Pervasive sensors and new types of sensors (e.g., "smart dust")
- Infrared/thermal detectors
- GPS/location information
- Cell-phone-generated information
- Radio-frequency identification tags
- Chips embedded in people
- Medical monitoring (e.g., implanted heart sensors)
- Spycams and other remote cameras
- Surveillance cameras in most public places
- Automated homes with temperature, humidity, and power sensors
- Traffic flow sensors
- Camera/cell-phone combinations
- Toys for children that incorporate surveillance technology (such as a stuffed animal that contains a nanny-cam)
- Biometrics-based recognition systems (e.g., based on face recognition, fingerprints, voice prints, gate analysis, iris recognition, vein patterns, hand geometry)
- Devices for remote reading of monitors and keyboards
- Brain wave sensors
- Smell sensors

However, it should also be noted that data-gathering technologies need not be advanced or electronic to be significant or important. Mail or telephone surveys, marketing studies, and health care information forms, sometimes coupled with optical scanning to convert manually created data into machine-readable form, also generate enormous amounts of personal and often sensitive information.

---

proliferation. Video cameras are now a common feature of many public places; traffic sensors have become common; and temperature and humidity sensors (which can be used as sensors to detect humans) are in many modern office buildings. Cell phone networks gather position information for 911 calling, which could be used to track the locations of their users. Many automobiles contain GPS sensors, as part of either a navigation system or a driver aid system. As these devices become smaller and more pervasive, they become less noticeable, leading to the gathering of data in contexts where such gathering is neither expected nor noticed.

The proliferation of explicit sensors in our public environments has been a cause for alarm. There is also the growing realization that every computer used by a person is also a data-gathering device. Whenever a computer is used to access information or perform a transaction, information about the use or transaction can be (and often is) gathered and stored. This means that data can be gathered about far more people in far more circumstances than was possible 10 years ago. It also means that such information can be gathered about activities that intuitively appear to occur within the confines of the home, a place that has traditionally been a center of privacy-protected activities. As more and more interactions are mediated by computers, more and more data can be gathered about more and more activities.

The trend toward ubiquitous sensing devices has only begun, and it shows every sign of accelerating at an exponential rate similar to that seen in other parts of computing. New kinds of sensors, such as radio-frequency identification (RFID) tags or medical sensors allowing constant monitoring of human health, are being mandated by entities such as Walmart and the Department of Defense. Single-sensor surveillance may be replaced in the future with multiple-sensor surveillance. The economic and health benefits of some ubiquitous sensor deployments are significant. But the impact that those and other deployments will have in practice on individual privacy is hard to determine.

3.3 SOFTWARE ADVANCES

In addition to the dramatic and well-known advances in the hardware of computing have come significant advances in the software that runs on that hardware, especially in the area of data mining and information fusion/data integration techniques and algorithms. Owing partly to the new capabilities enabled by advances in the computing platform and partly to better understanding of the algorithms and techniques needed for analysis, the ability of software to analyze the information gathered and stored on computing machinery has made great strides in the past decade. In addition new techniques in parallel and distributed computing have made it possible to couple large numbers of computers together to jointly solve problems that are beyond the scope of any single machine.

Although data mining is generally construed to encompass data searching, analysis, aggregation, and, for lack of a better term, archae-ology, "data mining" in the strict sense of the term is the extraction of information implicit in data, usually in the form of previously unknown relationships among data elements. When the data sets involved are volu-minous, automated processing is essential, and today computer-assisted data mining often uses machine learning, statistics, and visualization techniques to discover and present knowledge in a form that is easily comprehensible.

Information fusion is the process of merging/combining multiple sources of information in such a way that the resulting information is more accurate or reliable or robust as a basis for decision making than any single source of information would be. Information fusion often involves the use of statistical methods, such as Bayesian techniques and random effects modeling. Some information fusion approaches are implemented as artificial neural networks.

Both data mining and information fusion have important everyday applications. For example, by using data mining to analyze the patterns of an individual's previous credit card transactions, a bank can determine whether a credit card transaction today is likely to be fraudulent. By combining results from different medical tests using information fusion techniques, physicians can infer the presence or absence of underlying disease with higher confidence than if the result of only one test were available.

These techniques are also relevant to the work of government agencies. For example, the protection of public health is greatly facilitated by early warning of outbreaks of disease. Such warning may be available through data mining of the highly distributed records of first-line health care providers and pharmacies selling over-the-counter drugs. Unusually high buying patterns of such drugs (e.g., cold remedies) in a given locale might signal the previously undetected presence and even the approximate geographic location of an emerging epidemic threat (e.g., a flu outbreak). Responding to a public health crisis might be better facilitated with automated access to and screening analyses of patient information at clinics, hospitals, and pharmacies. Research on these systems is today in its infancy, and it remains to be seen whether such systems can provide reliable warning on the time scales needed by public health officials to respond effectively.

Data-mining and information fusion technologies are also relevant to counterterrorism, crisis management, and law enforcement. Counterterrorism involves, among other things, the identification of terrorist operations before execution through analysis of signatures and database traces made during an operation's planning stages. Intelligence agencies also need to pull together large amounts of information to identify the perpetrators of a terrorist attack. Responding to a natural disaster or terrorist attack requires the quick aggregation of large amounts of information in order to mobilize and organize first-responders and assess damage. Law enforcement must often identify perpetrators of crimes on the basis of highly fragmentary information—e.g., a suspect's first name, a partial license number, and vehicle color.

In general, the ability to analyze large data sets can be used to discern statistical trends or to allow broad-based research in the social, economic, and biological sciences, which is a great boon to all of these fields. But the ability can also be used to facilitate target marketing, enable broad-based e-mail advertising campaigns, or (perhaps most troubling from a privacy perspective) discern the habits of targeted individuals.

The threats to privacy are more than just the enhanced ability to track an individual through a set of interactions and activities, although that by itself can be a cause for alarm. It is now possible to group people into smaller and smaller groups based on their preferences, habits, and activities. There is nothing that categorically rules out the possibility that in some cases, the size of the group can be made as small as one, thus identifying an individual based on some set of characteristics having to do with the activities of that individual.

Furthermore, data used for this purpose may have been gathered for other, completely different reasons. For example, cell phone companies must track the locations of cell phones on their network in order to determine the tower responsible for servicing any individual cell phone. But these data can be used to trace the location of cell-phone owners over time.[4] Temperature and humidity sensors used to monitor the environment of a building can generate data that indicate the presence of people in particular rooms. The information accumulated in a single database for one reason can easily be used for other purposes, and the information accumulated in a variety of database can be aggregated to allow the discovery of information about an individual that would be impossible to find out given only the information in any single one of those databases.

The end result of the improvements in both the speed of computational hardware and the efficiency of the software that is run on that hardware is that tasks that were unthinkable only a short time ago are now possible on low-cost, commodity hardware running commercially available software. Some of these new tasks involve the extraction of information about the individual from data gathered from a variety of sources. A concern from the privacy point of view is that—given the extent of the ability to aggregate, correlate, and extract new information from seemingly innocuous information—it is now difficult to know what activities will in fact compromise the privacy of an individual.

3.4 INCREASED CONNECTIVITY AND UBIQUITY

The trends toward increasingly capable hardware and software and increased capacities of individual computers to store and analyze information are additive; the ability to store more information pairs with the increased ability to analyze that information. When combined with these

---

[4]Matt Richtel, "Tracking of Mobile Phones Prompts Court Fights on Privacy," *New York Times*, December 10, 2005, p. A1.

two, a third technology trend, the trend toward increased connectivity in the digital world, has a multiplicative effect.

The growth of network connectivity—obvious over the past decade in the World Wide Web's expansion from a mechanism by which physicists could share information to a global phenomenon, used by millions to do everything from researching term papers to ordering books—can be traced back to the early days of local area networks and the origin of the Internet: Growth in the number of nodes on the Internet has been exponential over a period that began roughly in 1980 and continues to this day.[5] Once stand-alone devices connected with each other through the use of floppy disks or dedicated telephone lines, computers are now networked devices that are (nearly) constantly connected to each other.

A computer that is connected to a network is not limited by its own processor, software, and storage capacity, and instead can potentially make use of the computational power of the other machines connected to that network and the data stored on those other computers. The additional power is characterized by Metcalfe's law, which states that the power of a network of computers increases in proportion to the number of pair-wise connections that the network enables.[6]

A result of connectivity is the ability to access information stored or gathered at a particular place without having physical access to that place. It is no longer necessary to be able to actually touch a machine to use that machine to gather information or to gain access to any information stored on the machine. Controlling access to a physical resource is a familiar concept for which we have well-developed intuitions, institutions, and mechanisms that allow us to judge the propriety of access and to control that access. These intuitions, institutions, and mechanisms are much less well developed in the case of networked access.

The increased connectivity of computing devices has also resulted in a radical decrease in the transaction costs for accessing information. This has had a significant impact on the question of what should be considered a public record, and how those public records should be made available. Much of the information gathered by governments at various levels is considered public record. Traditionally, the costs (both in monetary terms and in terms of costs of time and human aggravation) to access such

---

[5]Raymond Kurzweil, *The Singularity Is Near*, Viking Press, 2005, pp. 78-81.

[6]See B. Metcalfe, "Metcalfe's Law: A Network Becomes More Valuable as It Reaches More Users," *Infoworld*, Oct. 2, 1995. See also the May 6, 1996, column at http://www.infoworld.com/cgi-bin/displayNew.pl?/metcalfe/bm050696.html. The validity of Metcalfe's law is based on the assumption that every connection in a network is equally valuable. However, in practice it is known that in many networks, certain nodes are much more valuable than others, a point suggesting that the value may increase less rapidly in proportion to the number of possible pair-wise connections.

public records have been high. To look at the real estate transactions for a local area, for example, required physically going to the local authority that stored those records, filling out the forms needed for access, and then viewing the records at the courthouse, tax office, or other government office. When these records are made available through the World Wide Web, the transaction costs of accessing those records are effectively zero, making it far easier for the casual observer to view such records.

Connectivity is also relevant to privacy on a scale smaller than that of the entire Internet. Corporate and government intranets allow the connection and sharing of information between the computers of a particular organization. The purpose of such intranets is often for the sharing of information between various computers (as opposed to the sharing of information between the users of computers). Such sharing is a first step toward the aggregation of various data repositories, combining information collected for a variety of reasons to enable that larger (and richer) data set to be analyzed in an attempt to extract new forms of information.

Along with the increasing connectivity provided by networking, the networks themselves are becoming more capable as a mechanism for sharing data. Bandwidth, the measure of how much data can be transferred over the network in a given time, has been increasing dramatically. New network technologies allowing some filtering and analyzing of data as it flows through the network are being introduced. Projects such as SETI@home[7] and technologies like grid computing[8] are trying to find ways of utilizing the connectivity of computers to allow even greater computational levels.

From the privacy point of view, interconnectivity seems to promise a world in which any information can be accessed from anywhere at any time, along with the computational capabilities to analyze the data in any way imaginable. This interconnectivity seems to mean that it is no longer necessary to actually have data on an individual on a local computer; the data can be found somewhere on another computer that is connected to the local computer, and with the seemingly unlimited computing ability of the network of interconnected machines, finding and making use of that information is no longer a problem.

Ubiquitous connectivity has also given impetus to the development of digital rights management technologies (DRMTs), which are a response to the fact that when reduced to digital form, text, images, sounds, and other forms of content can be copied freely and perfectly. DRMTs harness the power of the computer and the network to enforce predefined limits on

---

[7]Available at http://setiathome.ssl.berkeley.edu/.
[8]Available at http://www.gridforum.org/.

the possible distribution and use of a protected work. These predefined limits can be very fine-grained. They can include:

• Limits on the number of times that protected information is viewed or on the extent to which protected information can be altered;
• Selective permissions that allow protected information to be read but not copied, printed, or passed along electronically except to selected parties;
• Selective access to certain portions of protected information and denial of access to others;
• Tracking of the parties that receive protected information and what they did with it (e.g., what they read, when they read it, how many times they read it, how long they spent reading it, to whom they forwarded it); and
• Enforcement of time windows during which certain access privileges are available.

DRMTs are a particularly interesting technological development with a potential impact on privacy. Originally developed with the intent of enhancing privacy, their primary application to date has been to protect intellectual property rights. But some applications of DRMTs can also detract from privacy. For example, DRMTs offer the potential for institutional content owners to collect highly detailed information on user behavior regarding the texts they read and the music they listen to, a point discussed further in Section 6.7. And in some instances, they have the potential to create security vulnerabilities in the systems on which they run, exploitation of which might lead to security breaches and the consequent compromise of personal information stored on those systems.[9]

On the other hand, DRMTs can—in principle—be used by private individuals to exert greater control over the content that they create. An individual could set permissions on his or her digital document so that only certain other individuals could read it, or could make a copy of it, and so on. Although, this capability is not widely available today for individuals to use, some document management systems are beginning to incorporate some such features.

---

[9]An example is the recent Sony DRM episode, during which Sony's BMG Music Entertainment surreptitiously distributed software on audio compact disks that was automatically installed on any computer that played the CD. This software was intended to block the copying of the CD, but it had the unintentional side effect of opening security vulnerabilities that could be exploited by other malicious software such as worms or viruses.

3.5 TECHNOLOGIES COMBINED INTO
A DATA-GATHERING SYSTEM

Each of the technology trends discussed above can be seen individually as having the potential to threaten the privacy of the individual. Combined into an overall system, however, such technologies seem to pose a far greater threat to privacy. The existence of ubiquitous sensors, generating digital data and networked to computers, raises the prospect of data generated for much of what individuals do in the physical world. Increased use of networked computers, which are themselves a form of activity sensor, allows the possibility of a similar tracking of activities in the electronic world. And increased and inexpensive data storage capabilities support retention of data by default.

Once stored, data are potentially available for analysis by any computer connected via a network to that storage. Networked computers can share any information that they have, and can aggregate information held by them separately. Thus it is possible not only to see all of the information gathered about an individual, but also to aggregate the information gathered in various places on the network into a larger view of the activities of that individual. Such correlations create yet more data on an individual that can be stored in the overall system, shared with others on the network, and correlated with the sensor data that are being received.

Finally, the seemingly unlimited computing power promised by networked computers would appear to allow any kind of analysis of the data concerning the individual to be done thoroughly and quickly. Patterns of behavior, correlations between actions taken in the electronic and the physical world, and correlations between data gathered about one individual and that gathered about another are capable, in principle, of being found, reported, and used to create further data about the individual being examined. Even if such analysis is impractical today, the data will continue to be stored, and advances in hardware and software technology may appear that allow the analysis to be done in the future.

At the very least, these technology trends—in computation, sensors, storage technology, and networking—change the rules that have governed surveillance. It is the integration of both hard and soft technologies of surveillance and analysis into networks and systems that underlies the evolution of what might be called traditional surveillance to the "new" surveillance.[10] Compared to traditional surveillance, the new surveillance is less visible and more continuous in time and space, provides fewer

---

[10]The term originates with Gary Marx, "What's New About the 'New' Surveillance?," *Surveillance & Society* 1(1):9-29, 2005; and Gary Marx, "Soft Surveillance: The Growth of Mandatory Volunteerism in Collecting Personal Information," in T. Monahan, *Surveillance and Security: Technological Politics and Power in Everyday Life*, Routledge, 2006.

opportunities for targets to object to or prevent the surveillance, is greater in analytical power, produces data that are more enduring, is disseminated faster and more widely, and is less expensive. (Table 3.1 presents some examples.) Essentially all of these changes represent additional surveillance capabilities for lower cost, and exploitation of these changes would bode ill for the protection of privacy.

3.6 DATA SEARCH COMPANIES

All of the advances in information technology for data aggregation and analysis have led to the emergence of companies that take the raw technology discussed above and combine it into systems that allow them to offer directly to their customers a capability for access to vast amounts of information. Search engine services, such as those provided by Google, Yahoo!, and MSN, harness the capabilities of thousands of computers, joined together in a network, that when combined give huge amounts of storage and vast computational facilities. Such companies have linked these machines with a software infrastructure that allows the finding and indexing of material on the World Wide Web.

The end result is a service that is used by millions every day. Rather than requiring that a person know the location of information on the World Wide Web (via, for example, a uniform resource locator (URL), such as www.cstb.org), a search engines enables the user to find that information by describing it, typically by typing a few keywords that might be associated with that information. Using sophisticated algorithms that are the intellectual property of the company, links to locations where that information can be found are returned. This functionality, undreamed of a decade ago, has revolutionized the way that the World Wide Web is used. Further, these searches can often be conducted for free, as many search companies make money by selling advertising that is displayed along with the search results to the users of the service.

While it is hard to imagine using the Web without search services, their availability has brought up privacy concerns. Using a search engine to assemble information about an individual has become common practice (so common that the term "to Google" has entered the language). When the Web newspaper, cnet.com, published personal information about the president of Google that had been obtained by using the Google service, Google charged Cnet with publishing private information and announced that it would not publicly speak to Cnet for a year in retribution.[11] This

---

[11]Carolyn Said, "Google Says Cnet Went Too Far in Googling," *San Francisco Gate*, August 9, 2005, available at http://sfgate.com/cgi-bin/article.cgi?file=/c/a/2005/08/09/GOOGLE. TMP&type=business.

TABLE 3.1 The Evolution of Surveillance over Time

Dimension	Traditional Surveillance	The New Surveillance
Relation to senses	Unaided senses	Extends senses
Visibility of the actual data collection, who does it, where, and on whose behalf	Visible	Reduced visibility, or invisible
Consent	Lower proportion involuntary	Higher proportion involuntary
Cost	Expensive per unit of data	Inexpensive per unit of data
Location of data collectors and analyzer	On scene	Remote
Ethos	Harder (more coercive)	Softer (less coercive)
Integration	Data collection as separate activity	Data collection folded into routine activity
Data collector	Human, animal	Machine (wholly or partly automated)
Where data reside	With the collector, stays local	With third parties, often migrates
Timing of data collection	Single point or intermittent	Continuous (omnipresent)
Time period of collection	Present	Past, present, future
Availability of data	Frequent time lags	Real-time availability
Availability of data collection technology	Disproportionately available to elites	More democratized, some forms widely available
Object of data collection	Individual	Individual, categories of interest
Comprehensiveness	Single measure	Multiple measures
Context	Contextual	Acontextual
Depth	Less intensive	More intensive
Breadth	Less extensive	More extensive
Ratio of knowledge of observed to observer	Higher (what the surveillant knows the subject probably knows as well)	Lower (surveillant knows things that the subject doesn't)
Identifiability of object of surveillance	Emphasis on known individuals	Emphasis also on anonymous individuals, individual masses
Realism	Direct representation	Direct and simulation
Form	Single medium (likely narrative or numerical)	Multiple media (including video and/or audio)
Who collects data?	Specialists	Specialists, role dispersal, self-monitoring
Analysis of data	More difficult to organize, store, retrieve, analyze	Easier to store, retrieve, analyze
Ease of merging data	Discrete non-combinable	Easy to combine
Communication of data	More difficult to send, receive	Easier to send, receive

SOURCE: G.T. Marx, "What's New About the New Surveillance?," *Surveillance & Society* 1(1):9-29, 2002, available at www.surveillance-and-society.org/articles1/whatsnew.pdf.

is an interesting case, because the information that was obtained was accessible through the Web to anyone, but would have been difficult to find without the services offered by Google. Whereas in this case privacy could perhaps have been maintained because of the difficulty of simply finding the available information, the Google service made it easy to find the information, and made it available for free.

A second privacy concern arises regarding the information that search engine companies collect and store about specific searches performed by users. To service a user's search request, the specific search terms need not be kept for longer than it takes to return the results of that search. But search engine companies keep that information anyway for a variety of purposes, including marketing and enhancement of search services provided to users.

The potential for privacy-invasive uses of such information was brought into full public view in a request in early 2006 by the Department of Justice (DOJ) for search data from four search engines, including search terms queried and Web site addresses, or URLs, stored in each search engine's index but excluding any user identifying information that could link a search string back to an individual. The intended DOJ use of the data was not to investigate a particular crime but to study the prevalence of pornographic material on the Web and to evaluate the effectiveness of software filters to block those materials in a case testing the constitutionality of the Child Online Protection Act (COPA).[12]

The four search engines were those associated with America Online, Microsoft, Yahoo!, and Google. The first three of these companies each agreed to provide at least some of the requested search data. Google resisted the original subpoena demanding this information; subsequently, the information sought was narrowed significantly in volume and character, and Google was ultimately ordered by a U.S. District Court to provide a much more restricted set of data.[13] Although the data requested did not include personally identifiable information of users, this case has raised a number of privacy concerns about possible disclosures in the future of the increasing volumes of user-generated search information.

Google objected to the original request for a variety of reasons. Google asserted a general interest in protecting its users' privacy and

---

[12]Attorney for Alberto R. Gonzales, McElvain Declaration in *Gonzales v. Google, Inc.* (subpoena request), available at http://i.i.com.com/cnwk.1d/pdf/ne/2006/google-doj/notice. of.stark.declaration.pdf.

[13]Antone Gonsalves, "Judge Hands Google Mixed Ruling on Search Privacy," *Internet Week*, March 17, 2006, available at http://Internetweek.cmp.com/showArticle.jhtml?artic leID=183700724. The findings based on the search data were to serve as part of the government's case in defending the constitutionality of the Child Online Protection Act, a law aimed at protecting minors from adult material online.

anonymity.[14] Additionally, Google believed the original request was overly broad, as it included all search queries entered into the search engine during a 2-month period and all URLs in Google's index. In negotiations with the DOJ, the data request was reduced to a sampling of 50,000 URLs and 5,000 search terms by the DOJ.[15]

In considering only the DOJ's modified request, the court decided to further limit the type of data that was released to include only URLs and not search terms. Several of the privacy implications considered in this ruling included the recognition that personally identifying information, although not requested, might be available in the text of searches performed (e.g., such as searching to see if personal information is on the Internet, such as Social Security numbers or credit card information, or to check what information is associated with one's own name, so-called vanity searches). The court also acknowledged the possibility of the information being shared with other government authorities if text strings raised national security issues (e.g., "bomb placement white house").[16]

Although this case was seen as a partial victory for Google and for the privacy of its users, the court as well as others acknowledged that the case could have broader implications. Though outside its ruling, the court could foresee the possibility of future requests to Google, particularly if the narrow collection of data used in the DOJ's study was challenged in the COPA case.[17] However, others have suggested that this case underscores the larger problem of how to protect Internet user privacy, particularly as more user-generated information is being collected and stored for unspecified periods of time, which makes it increasing vulnerable to subpoenaed requests.[18]

Many of the concerns about compromising user privacy were illustrated graphically when in August 2006, AOL published on the Web a list of 20 million Web search inquiries made by 658,000 users over a 3-month

---

[14]Declan McCullagh, "Google to Feds: Back Off," CNET News.com, February 17, 2006, available at http://news.com.com/Google+to+feds+Back+off/2100-1030_3-6041113.html ?tag=nl.

[15]Order Granting in Part and Denying in Part Motion to Compel Compliance with Subpoena Duces Tecum, United States District Court for the Northern District of California, San Jose Division, Court Ruling No. CV 06-8006MISC JW, p. 4, available at http://www.google.com/press/images/ruling_20060317.pdf.

[16]United States District Court for the Northern District of California, San Jose Division, Court Ruling, pp. 18-19.

[17]United States District Court for the Northern District of California, San Jose Division, Court Ruling, p. 15.

[18]Thomas Claburn, "Google's Privacy Win Could Be Pyrrhic Victory," InformationWeek, March 22, 2006, available at http://www.informationweek.com/showArticle.jhtml;jsessionid =LMWTORMPFH2B4QSNDBCSKH0CJUMEKJVN?articleID=183701628.

period.[19] AOL sought to anonymize users by substituting a code number for their login names, but the list of inquiries sorted by code number shows the topics in which a person was interested over many different searches. A few days later, AOL took down the 439-megabyte file after many complaints were received that the file violated user privacy. AOL acknowledged that the publication of the data was a violation of its own internal policies and issued a strongly worded apology. Some users were subsequently identified by name.[20]

A related kind of IT-enabled company—the data aggregation company— is discussed further in Chapter 6.

3.7 BIOLOGICAL AND OTHER SENSING TECHNOLOGIES

The technology trends outlined thus far in this chapter are all well established, and technologies that follow these trends are deployed in actual systems. There is an additional trend, only now in its beginning stages, that promises to extend the sensing capabilities beyond those that are possible with the kinds of sensors available today. These are biological sensing technologies, including such things as biometric identification schemes and DNA analysis.

Biometric technologies use particular biological markers to identify individuals. Fingerprinting for identification is well known and well established, but interest in other forms of biometric identification is high. Technologies using identifying features as varied as retinal patterns, walking gait, and facial characteristics are all under development and show various levels of promise. Many of these biometric technologies differ from the more standard and currently used biometric identification schemes in two ways: first, these technologies promise to allow the near-real-time identification of an individual from a distance and in a way that is non-invasive and, perhaps, incapable of being detected by the subject being identified; second, some of these mechanisms facilitate automated identification that can be done solely by the computer without the aid of a human being. Such identification could be done more cheaply and far more rapidly than human-mediated forms of identification.

Joined into a computing system like those discussed above, such identification mechanisms offer a potential for tracing all of the activities of an individual. Whereas video camera surveillance now requires human watchers, automated face-identification systems could allow the logging

---

[19]Saul Hansell, "AOL Removes Search Data on Group of Web Users," *New York Times,* August 8, 2006.
[20]Michael Barbaro and Tom Zeller, Jr., "A Face Is Exposed for AOL Searcher No. 4417749," *New York Times,* August 9, 2006.

of a person's location, which could then be cross-referenced with other information gathered about that individual, all without the knowledge of the person being tracked. Such capabilities raise the prospect of a society in which everyone can be automatically tracked at all times.

In addition to these forms of biometric identification is the technology associated with the mapping and identification of human DNA. The mapping of the human genome is one of the great scientific achievements of the past decade, and work is ongoing in understanding the phenotypic implications of variations at specific sites within the gnome. A full understanding of these relationships would allow use of a DNA sample to obtain information not only about the individual from whom the DNA was taken, but also about individuals genetically related to that individual. Just what information will be revealed by our DNA is currently unknown, but there is speculation that it might indicate everything from genetic predisposition to certain kinds of disease to behavioral patterns that can be expected in an individual. Much of this information is now considered to be private, but if it becomes easily accessible from our own DNA or from the DNA of our relatives, issues will arise as to how that information should be treated or even who the subject of the information really is.

3.8 PRIVACY-ENHANCING TECHNOLOGIES

Although much of the discussion above concerns advances in technology that potentially threaten privacy, technology is not inherently destructive of privacy. Technology developments can help with limiting access to or control of information about people. These fall into two categories: those that can be used by the individual whose privacy is being enhanced, and those that can be used by an information collector who wishes to protect the privacy of the individuals about whom information is being collected.[21]

3.8.1 Privacy-enhancing Technologies for Use by Individuals

One cluster of technologies allows individuals to make basic data unavailable through the use of cryptography. Data about a person is made private by encrypting that data in such a way that the data cannot be decrypted without the consent and active participation of the person who provides the decryption key; this is known as the confidentiality

---

[21]A useful reference, and one on which much in this section is based, is Lorrie Faith Cranor, *The Role of Privacy Enhancing Technologies*, AT&T Labs Research, available at http://www.cdt.org/privacy/ccp/roleoftechnology1.shtml.

application of cryptography. Despite considerable work on decryption technologies, the cost to decrypt an encrypted data set without access to the decryption keys can currently be made almost arbitrarily high in comparison to the cost of encrypting the data set.

However, such technologies are not universally accepted as an appropriate approach to the problem of protecting privacy. In particular, they allow the hiding of data from everyone, including those who some feel should be able to see the data, such as law enforcement agencies or intelligence-gathering branches of the government. In addition, they make it impossible for the data to be accessed in cases when the owner of the data is unable to participate. It would be impossible, for example, for emergency medical personnel to gain access to protected medical information if the subject of the records (and holder of the decryption key) were unconscious.

Other privacy-enhancing technologies that are usable by individuals facilitate anonymization in certain contexts. For example, some anonymization technologies allow e-mail or Web surfing that is anonymous to Internet eavesdroppers for all practical purposes. These technologies can also exploit national boundaries to increase the difficulty of breaking the anonymity they offer—identifying information stored on a server located in Country A may be difficult or impossible for authorities in Country B to obtain because of differing legal standards or the lack of a political agreement between the two nations. This same technology, however, can also hide the identity of those who use the networks to threaten or libel other members of the network community. Although it can facilitate privacy, anonymity can also help to defeat accountability. Since law enforcement is based on the notion of individual accountability, law enforcement pressures to restrict the use of anonymizing technologies are not unexpected. Anti-spyware technologies stem the flow of personal information related to one's computer and Internet usage practices to other parties, thereby enhancing privacy.

Another category of privacy-enhancing technologies includes those that assist users in avoiding spam e-mail, that prevent spyware programs from being installed, or that alert individuals that they might be the subject of "phishing" attacks.[22] Anti-spam technologies promote the privacy of those who believe that being left alone is an element of privacy. Phish-alerting technologies enhance privacy by warning the individual that he

---

[22]"Phishing" is the act of fooling someone into providing confidential information or into doing something under false pretenses. A common phishing attack is for an attacker to send an e-mail to someone falsely claiming to be a legitimate enterprise in an attempt to trick the user into providing private information (e.g., a login name and password for his bank account) that can be used by the attacker to impersonate the victim.

or she may be about to divulge important personal information to a party that should not be getting it.

None of the technologies above are focused on privacy per se, which relates to the protection of personal information. For example, encryption provides confidentiality of stored information or information sent over a network—any information, not just personal information. Anonymizing technologies protect only a subset of personal information—personal information that can be used to identify an individual.

3.8.2 Privacy-enhancing Technologies for Use by Information Collectors

Privacy-enhancing tools that can be used by information collectors include anonymization techniques that can help to protect privacy in certain applications of data mining.

3.8.2.1 Query Control

Teresa Lunt has undertaken some work in the development of a privacy appliance[23] that is based on a heuristic approach to query control and can be viewed as a firewall that is placed in between databases containing personal information and those querying those databases. Programmed by a party other than the querying party, the appliance is intended to prevent:

- Direct disclosures (e.g., by withholding from query results data such as names, Social Security numbers, credit card numbers, addresses, and phone numbers);
- Inferences of identity based on the combined results of multiple queries. This requires the maintenance of a log of earlier queries and a determination of whether any given query can yield an inference of identity; if so, the appliance is intended to prevent that query result from being returned.
- Access to sensitive statistics. If a statistic will reveal information about an individual or if sensitive information can be inferred from a statistical summary, the appliance should block access to that statistic (if, for example, a statistical query is computed over too few records).

In those instances where identifying information must be obtained (e.g., in order to identify the would-be perpetrator of a terrorist event),

---

[23]Privacy Appliance, Xerox PARC, information available at http://www.parc.com/research /projects/privacyappliance/.

individuals with proper authorization such as a court order could be granted privileges to override the blocking by the appliance.

The query control approach draws from the broader literature on approaches to privacy protection and disclosure limitation. Nonetheless, it also poses some unresolved issues for which further research is needed.

• A lesson from the literature on the statistics of disclosure limitation is that privacy protection in the form of "safe releases" from separate databases does not guarantee privacy protection for information in a merged database.[24] It is not known how strongly this lesson applies to the query control approach, especially given the fact that the literature addresses aggregate data, whereas questions of privacy often involve identification of individuals.

• The query control approach assumes that it is possible to analyze a log of previous queries to determine if any given query can yield an inference of identity. While this result is clearly possible when the previous queries are simple and relatively few, the feasibility of such analysis with a large number of complex queries is at present not known.

• Still to be determined are the scope and the nature of analyses that can be undertaken with a privacy appliance in place. Because the k-anonymity concept on which the appliance is based relies on reporting sums or averages rather than individual data fields, there is some degradation of data. Whether and in what contexts that degradation matters operationally is not known.

• Some attacks on k-anonymity are known to succeed under certain circumstances by taking advantage of background knowledge or database homogenity.[25] Background knowledge is externally provided knowledge about the variables in question (e.g., the statistical likelihood of their occurrence). Database homogeneity refers to the situation in which there is insufficient diversity in the values of sensitive attributes. Techniques have been proposed that reduce such difficulties,[26] but their compatibility with the query control approach of the privacy appliance remains to be seen.

---

[24]Stephen E. Fienberg, "Privacy and Confidentiality in an e-Commerce World: Data Mining, Data Warehousing, Matching and Disclosure Limitation," *Statistical Science* 21(2):143-154, 2006.

[25]Ashwin Machanavajjhala, Johannes Gehrke, Daniel Kifer, and Muthuramakrishnan Venkitasubramaniam, "l-Diversity: Privacy Beyond k-Anonymity," *Proceedings of the 22nd IEEE International Conference on Data Engineering* (ICDE 2006), Atlanta, Georgia, April 2006, available at http://www.cs.cornell.edu/johannes/papers/2006/2006-icde-publishing.pdf.

[26]Machanavajjhala et al., "1-Diversity," 2006.

3.8.2.2 Statistical Disclosure Limitation Techniques[27]

Other techniques can be used to reduce the likelihood that a specific individual can be identified in a data-mining application that seeks to uncover certain statistical patterns. Such techniques are useful to statistical agencies such as the Census Bureau, the Bureau of Labor Statistics, and the Centers for Disease Control and Prevention (to name only a few), which collect vast amounts of personally identifiable data and use it to produce useful data sets, summaries, and other products for the public or for research uses—most often in the form of statistical tables (i.e., tabular data). Some agencies (e.g., Census) also make available so-called microdata files—that is, files that can show (while omitting specific identifying information) the full range of responses made on individual questionnaires. Such files can show, for example, how one household or one household member answered questions on occupation, place of work, and so on.

Given the sensitive nature of much of this information and the types of analysis and comparison facilitated by modern technology, statistical agencies also can and do employ a wide range of techniques to prevent the disclosure of personally identifiable information related to specific individuals and to ensure that the data that are made available cannot be used to identify specific individuals or, in some cases, specific groups or organizations. Following are descriptions of many of those techniques.

• *Limiting details.* Both with tabular data and microdata, formal identifiers and many geographic details are often simply omitted for all respondents.

• *Adding noise.* Data can be perturbed by adding random noise (adding a random but small amount or multiplying by a random factor close to 1, most often before tabulation) to help disguise potentially identifying values. For example, imagine perturbing each individual's or household's income values by a small percentage.

• *Targeted suppression.* This method suppresses or omits extreme values or values that might be unique enough to constitute a disclosure.

• *Top-coding and bottom-coding.* These techniques are often used to limit disclosure of specific data at the high end or low end of a given range by grouping together values falling above or below a certain level. For instance, an income data table could be configured to list every income below $20,000 as simply "below $20,000."

• *Recoding.* Similar to top-coding and bottom-coding, recoding

---

[27]Additional discussion of some of these techniques can be found in National Research Council, *Private Lives and Public Policies*, National Academy Press, Washington, D.C., 1993.

involves assigning individual values to groups or ranges rather than showing exact figures. For example, an income of $54,500 could simply be represented as being within the range of "$50,000- $60,000." Such recoding could be adequate for a number of uses where detailed data are not required.

• *Rounding.* This technique involves rounding values (e.g., incomes) up or down based on a set of earlier decisions. For example, one might decide to round all incomes down to the nearest $5,000 increment. Another model involves making random decisions on whether to round a given value up or down (as opposed to conforming data according to a predetermined rounding convention).

• *Swapping and/or shuffling.* Swapping entails choosing a certain set of fields among a set of records in which values match, and then swapping all other values among the records. Records can also be compared and ranked according to a given value to allow swapping based on values that, while not identical, are close to each other (so-called rank-swapping). Data shuffling is a hybrid approach, blending perturbation and swapping techniques.

• *Sampling.* This method involves including data from only a sample of a given population.

• *Blank and impute.* In this process, values for particular fields in a selection of records are deleted and the fields are then filled either with values that have been statistically modeled or with values that are the same as those for other respondents.

• *Blurring.* This method involves replacing a given value with an average. These average values can be determined in a number of different ways—for example, one might select the records to be averaged based on the values given in another field, or one might select them at random, or vary the number of values to be averaged.

3.8.2.3 Cryptographic Techniques

The Portia project[28] is a cross-institutional research effort attempting to apply the results of cryptographic protocols to some of the problems of privacy. Such protocols theoretically allow the ability to do queries over multiple databases without revealing any information other than the answer to the particular query, thus ensuring that multi-database queries can be accomplished without the threat of privacy-threatening aggregation of the data in those databases. Although there are theoretical protocols that can be proved to give these results, implementing those protocols in a fashion that is efficient enough for common use is an open research

---

[28]See more information about the Portia project at http://crypto.stanford.edu/portia/.

problem. These investigations are in their early stages, so it is too soon to determine if the resulting techniques will be appropriate for wide use.

A similar project is attempting to develop a so-called Hippocratic database, which the researchers define as one whose owners "have responsibility for the data that they manage to prevent disclosure of private information."[29] The thrust behind this work is to develop database technology to minimize the likelihood that data stored in the database are used for purposes other than those for which the data were gathered. While this project has produced some results in the published literature, it has not resulted in any widely deployed commercial products.

3.8.2.4 User Notification

Another set of technologies focus on notification. For example, the Platform for Privacy Preferences (P3P) facilitates the development of machine-readable privacy policies.[30] Visitors to a P3P-enabled Web site can set their browsers to retrieve the Web site's privacy policy and compare it to a number of visitor-specified privacy preferences. If the Web site's policy is weaker than the visitor prefers, the visitor is notified of that fact. P3P thus seeks to automate what would otherwise be an onerous manual process for the visitor to read and comprehend the site's written privacy policy. An example of a P3P browser add-on is Privacy Bird.[31] Results of the comparison between a site's policy and the user's preferences are displayed graphically, showing a bird of different color (green and singing for a site whose policy does not violate the requirements set by the user, angry and red when the policy conflicts with the desires of the user) in the toolbar of the browser.

Systems such as Privacy Bird cannot guarantee the privacy of the individual who uses them—such guarantees can only be provided by enforcement of the stated policy. They do attempt to address the privacy issue directly, allowing the user to determine what information he or she is willing to allow to be revealed, along with what policies the recipient of the information intends to follow with regard to the use of that information or the transfer of that information to third parties. Also, the process of developing a P3P-compatible privacy policy is structured and systematic. Thus, a Web site operator may discover gaps in its existing privacy policy as it translates that policy into machine-readable form.

---

[29]Rakesh Agrawal, Jerry Kiernan, Ramakrishnan Srikant, and Yirong Xu, "Hippocratic Databases," 28th International Conference on Very Large Databases (VLDB), Hong Kong, 2002.

[30]See http://www.w3.org/P3P/.

[31]See http://www.privacybird.com/.

3.8.2.5 Information Flow Analysis

Privacy can also be protected by tools for automated privacy audits. Some companies, especially large ones, may find it difficult to know the extent to which their practices actually comply with their stated policies. The purpose of a privacy audit is to help a company determine the extent to which it is in compliance with its own policy. However, since the information flows within a large company are multiple and varied, automated tools are very helpful in identifying and monitoring such flows. When potential policy violations are identified, these tools bring the information flows in question to the attention of company officials for further attention.

Such tools often focus on information flows to and from externally visible Web sites, monitoring form submissions and cookie usage, and looking for Web pages that accidentally reveal personal information. Tools can also tag data as privacy sensitive, and when such tagged data are subsequently accessed, other software could check to ensure that the access is consistent with the company's privacy policy.

Because of the many information flows in and out of a company, a comprehensive audit of a company's privacy policy is generally quite difficult. But although it is virtually impossible to deploy automated tools everywhere within a company's information infrastructure, automated auditing tools can help a great deal in improving a company's compliance with its own stated policy.

3.8.2.6 Privacy-Sensitive System Design

Perhaps the best approach for protecting privacy is to design systems that do not require the collection or the retention of personal information in the first place.[32] For example, systems designed to detect weapons hidden underneath clothing have been challenged on privacy grounds because they display the image recorded by the relevant sensors, and what appears on the operator's display screen is an image of an unclothed body. However, the system can be designed to display instead an indicator signaling the possible presence of a weapon and its approximate location on the body. This approach protects the privacy of the subject to a much greater degree than the display of an image, although it requires a much more technically sophisticated approach (since the image detected must be analyzed to determine exactly what it indicates).

---

[32]From the standpoint of privacy advocacy, it is difficult to verify the non-retention of data since this would entail a full audit of a system as implemented. Data, once collected, often persist by default, and this may be an important reason that a privacy advocate might oppose even a system allegedly designed to discard data.

When a Web site operator needs to know only if a visitor's age is above a certain threshold (e.g., 13), rather than the visitor's age per se, collecting only an indicator of a threshold protects the visitor's privacy. More generally, systems can be designed to enable an individual to prove that he or she possesses certain attributes (e.g., is authorized to enter a building, holds a diploma, is old enough to gamble or drink) without revealing anything more about the individual. Even online purchases could, in principle, be made anonymously using electronic cash.

However, the primary impediments to the adoption of such measures appear to be based in economics and policy rather than in technology. That is, even though measures such as those described above appear to be technically feasible, they are not in widespread use. The reason seems to be that most businesses benefit from the collection of detailed personal information about their customers and thus have little motivation to deploy privacy-protecting systems. Law enforcement agencies also have concerns about electronic cash systems that might facilitate anonymous money laundering.

3.8.2.7 Information Security Tools

Finally, the various tools supporting information security—encryption, access controls, and so on—have important privacy-protecting functions. Organizations charged with protecting sensitive personal information (e.g., individual medical records, financial records) can use encryption and access controls to reduce the likelihood that such information will be inappropriately compromised by third parties. A CD-ROM with personal information that is lost in transit is a potential treasure trove for identity thieves, but if the information is encrypted on the CD, the CD is useless to anyone without the decryption key. Medical records stored electronically and protected with good access controls that allow access only to authorized parties are arguably more private than paper records to which anyone has access. Electronic medical records might also be protected by audit trails that record all accesses and prevent forwarding to unauthorized parties or even their printing in hard copy.

With appropriate authentication technologies deployed, records of queries made by specific individuals can also be kept for future analysis.[33] Retention of such records can deter individuals from making privacy-invasive queries in the course of their work—in the event that personal information is compromised, a record might exist of queries that might

---

[33]The committee is not insensitive to the irony that keeping query logs is arguably privacy-invasive with respect to the individual making the queries.

have produced that personal information and the parties that may have made those queries.

3.9 UNSOLVED PROBLEMS AS PRIVACY ENHANCERS

Although much of the discussion above involves trends in technology that can lead to privacy concerns, many technical challenges must be addressed successfully to enable truly ubiquitous surveillance. If so, one can argue that many worries about technology and privacy are therefore misplaced.

For example, the problem of data aggregation is far more than simply the problem of finding the data to be combined and using the network to bring those data to a shared location. One fundamental issue is that of interpreting data collected by different means so that their meaning is consistent. Digital data, by definition, comprises fields that are either on (represent 1) or off (represent 0). But how these 1s and 0s are grouped and interpreted to represent more complex forms of data (such as images, transaction records, sound, or temperature readings) varies from computer to computer and from program to program.

Even so simple a convention as the number of bits (values of 1 or 0) used to represent a value such as an alphanumeric character, an integer, or a floating point number varies from program to program, and the order in which the bits are to be interpreted can vary from machine to machine. The fact that data are stored on two machines that can talk to each other over the network does not mean that there is a program that can understand the data stored on the two machines, as the interpretation of that data is generally not something that is stored with the data itself.

This problem is compounded when an attempt is made to combine the contents of different databases. A database is organized around groupings of information into records and indexes of those records. The combinations and indexes, known as schema, define the information in the database. Different databases with different schema definitions cannot be combined in a straightforward way; the queries issued to one of those databases might not be understood in the other database (or, worse still, might be understood in a different way). Since the schema used in the database defines, in an important way, the meaning of the information stored in the database, two databases with different schema store information that is difficult to combine in any meaningful way.

Note that this issue is not resolved simply by searching in multiple databases of similar formats. For example, although search engines facilitate the searching of large volumes of text that can be spread among multiple databases, this is not to say that these data can be treated as belonging to a single database, for if that were the case both the format and the semantics of the words would be identical. The Semantic Web and similar research efforts seek to reduce the magnitude of the semantic problem, disambiguating syntactically identical words. But these efforts have little to do with aggregations of data in dissimilar formats, such as video clips and text or information in financial and medical databases.

This problem of interpretation is not new; it has plagued businesses trying to integrate their own data for nearly as long as there have been computers. Huge amounts of money are spent each year on attempts to merge separate databases within the same corporation, or in attempts by one company to integrate the information used by another company that it has acquired. Even when the data formats are known by the programmers attempting to do the integration, these problems are somewhere between difficult and impossible. The notion that data gathered by sensors about an individual by different sources can be easily aggregated by computers that are connected by a network presupposes, contrary to fact, that this problem of data integration and interpretation has been solved.

Similarly, the claim that increases in the capacity of storage devices will allow data to be stored forever and used to violate the privacy of the individual ignores another trend in computing, which is that the formats used to interpret the raw data contained in storage devices are program specific and tend to change rapidly. Data are now commonly lost not because they have been removed from some storage device, but because there is no program that can be run that understands the format of the data or no hardware that can even read the data.[34] In principle, maintaining documentation adequate to allow later interpretation of data stored in old formats is a straightforward task—but in practice, this rarely happens, and so data are often lost in this manner. And as new media standards emerge, it becomes more difficult to find and/or purchase systems that can read the media on which the old data are recorded.

A related issue in data degradation relates to the hardware. Many popular and readily available storage devices (CDs, DVDs, tapes, hard drives) have limited dependable lifetimes. The standards to which these devices were originally built also evolve to enable yet more data to be packed onto them, and so in several generations, any given storage device may well be an orphan, with spare parts and repair expertise difficult to find.

Data can thus be lost if—even though the data have not been destroyed—they become unreadable and thus unusable.

Finally, even with the advances in the computational power available

---

[34]National Research Council, *Building an Electronic Records Archive at the National Archives and Records Administration: Recommendations for a Long-Term Strategy*, Robert Sproull and Jon Eisenberg, eds., The National Academies Press, Washington, D.C., 2005.

on networks of modern computers, there are some tasks that will remain computationally infeasible without far greater breakthroughs in computing hardware than have been seen even in the past 10 years. Some tasks, such as those that require the comparison of all possible combinations of sets of events, have a computational cost that rises combinatorially (i.e., faster than exponentially) with the number of entities being compared. Such computations attempted over large numbers of people are far too computationally expensive to be done by any current or anticipated computing technology. Thus, such tasks will remain computationally infeasible not just now but for a long time to come.[35]

Similar arguments also apply to certain sensing technologies. For example, privacy advocates worry about the wide deployment of facial recognition technology. Today, this technology is reasonably accurate under controlled conditions where the subject is isolated, the face is exposed in a known position, and there are no other faces being scanned. Attempts to apply this technology "in the wild," however, have largely failed. The problem of recognizing an individual from a video scan in uncontrolled lighting, where the face is turned or tilted, and where the face is part of a crowd, or when the subject is using countermeasures to defeat the recognition technology, is far beyond the capabilities of current technology. Facial recognition research is quite active today, but it remains an open question how far and how fast the field will be able to progress.

3.10 OBSERVATIONS

Current trends in information technology have greatly expanded the ability of its users to gather, store, share, and analyze data. Indeed, metrics for the increasing capabilities provided by information technology hardware—storage, bandwidth, and processing speed, among others—could be regarded as surrogates for the impact of technological change on privacy. The same is true, though in a less quantitative sense, for software—better algorithms, better database management systems

---

[35]To deal with such problems, statisticians and computer scientists have developed pruning methods that systematically exclude large parts of the problem space that must be examined. Some methods are heuristic, based on domain-specific knowledge and characteristics of the data, such as knowing that men do not get cervical cancer or become pregnant. Others are built on theory and notions of model simplification. Still others are based on sampling approaches that are feasible when the subjects of interest are in some sense average rather than extreme. If a problem is such that it is necessary to identify with high probability only some subjects, rather than requiring an exhaustive search that identifies all subjects with certainty, these methods have considerable utility. But some problems—and in particular searches for terrorists who are seeking to conceal their profile within a given population—are less amenable to such treatment.

and more powerful query languages, and so on. These data can be gathered both from those who use the technology itself and from the physical world. Given the trends in the technology, it appears that there are many ways in which the privacy of the individual could be compromised, both by governments, private corporations, and individual users of the technology.

Many of these concerns echo those that arose in the 1970s, when the first databases began to be widely used. At that time, concerns over the misuse of the information stored in those databases and the accuracy of the information itself led to the creation of the Fair Information Practice guidelines in 1973 (Section 1.5.4 and Box 1.3).

Current privacy worries are not as well defined as those that originally led to the Fair Information Practice guidelines. Whereas those guidelines were a reaction to fears that the contents of databases might be inaccurate, the current worries are more concerned with the misuse of data gathered for otherwise valid reasons, or the ability to extract additional information from the aggregation of databases by using the power of networked computation. Furthermore, in some instances, technologies developed without a conscious desire for affecting privacy may—upon closer examination—have deep ramifications for privacy. As one example, digital rights management technologies have the potential to collect highly detailed information on user behavior regarding the texts they read and the music they listen to. In some instances, they have a further potential to create security vulnerabilities in the systems on which they run, exploitation of which might lead to security breaches and the consequent compromise of personal information stored on those systems. The information-collection aspect of digital rights management technologies is discussed further in Section 6.7.

At the same time, some technologies can promote and defend privacy. Cryptographic mechanisms that can ensure the confidentiality of protected data, anonymization techniques to ensure that interactions can take place without participants in the interaction revealing their identity, and database techniques that allow extraction of some information without showing so much data that the privacy of those whose data has been collected will be compromised, are all active areas of research and development. However, each of these technologies imposes costs, both social and economic, for those who use them, a fact that tends to inhibit their use. If a technology has no purpose other than to protect privacy, it is likely to be deployed only when there is pressure to protect privacy—unlike other privacy-invasive technologies, which generally invade privacy as a side-effect of some other business or operational purpose.

An important issue is the impact of data quality on any system that involves surveillance and matching. As noted in Chapter 1, data quality has a significant impact on the occurrence of false positives and false negatives. By definition, false positives subject individuals to scrutiny that is inappropriate and unnecessary given their particular circumstances—and data quality issues that result in larger numbers of false positives lead to greater invasions of privacy. By definition, false negatives do not identify individuals who should receive further scrutiny—and data quality issues that result in larger numbers of false negatives compromise mission accomplishment.

Technology also raises interesting philosophical questions regarding privacy. For example, Chapter 2 raised the distinction between the acquisition of personal information and the use of that information. The distinction is important because privacy is contextually defined—use X of certain personal information might be regarded as benign, while use Y of that same information might be regarded as a violation of privacy. But even if one assumes that the privacy violations might occur at the moment of acquisition, technology changes the meaning of "the moment." Is "the moment" the point at which the sensors register the raw information? The point after which the computers have processed the bit streams from the sensors into a meaningful image or pattern? The point at which the computer identifies an image or pattern as being worthy of further human attention? The point at which an actual human being sees the image or pattern? The point at which the human being indicates that some further action must be taken? There are no universal answers to such questions—contextual factors and value judgments shape the answers.

A real danger is that fears about what technology might be able to do, either currently or in the near future, will spur policy decisions that will limit the technology in artificial ways. Decisions made by those who do not understand the limitations of current technology may prevent the advancement of the technology in the direction feared but also limit uses of the technology that would be desirable and that do not, in fact, create a problem for those who treasure personal privacy. Consider, for example, that data-mining technologies are seen by many to be tools of those who would invade the privacy of ordinary citizens.[36] Poorly formulated limitations on the use of data mining may reduce its impact on privacy, but may also inadvertently limit its use in other applications that pose no privacy issue whatever.

Finally, it is worth noting the normative question of whether technology or policy ought to have priority as a foundation for protecting privacy. One perspective on privacy protection is that policy should come first—policy, and associated law and regulation, are the basis for the per-

---

[36]A forthcoming study by the National Research Council will address this point in more detail.

formance requirements of the technology—and that technology should be developed and deployed that conforms to the demands of policy. On the other hand, policy that is highly protective of privacy on one day can be changed to one that is less protective the next day. Thus, a second view of privacy would argue that technology should constitute the basis for privacy protection, because such a foundation is harder to change or circumvent than one based on procedural foundations.[37] Further, violations of technologically enforced privacy protections are generally much more difficult to accomplish than violations of policy-enforced protections. Whether such difficulties are seen as desirable stability (i.e., an advantage) or unnecessary rigidity (i.e., a disadvantage) depends on one's position and perspective.

In practice, of course, privacy protections are founded on a mix of technology and policy, as well as self-protective actions and cultural factors such as ethics, manners, professional codes, and a sense of propriety. In large bureaucracies, significant policy changes cannot be implemented rapidly and successfully, even putting aside questions related to the technological infrastructure. Indeed, many have observed that implementing appropriate human and organizational procedures that are aligned with high-level policy goals is often harder than implementing and deploying technology.

---

[37]Lessig argues this point in *Code*, though his argument is much broader than one relating simply to privacy. See Lawrence Lessig, *Code and Other Laws of Cyberspace*, Basic Books, New York, 2000.

4

The Legal Landscape
in the United States

Many discussions of privacy ultimately end up turning toward the law. How have legislatures and the courts defined and interpreted privacy? What are individuals' and organizations' rights and obligations under the law? Is there a constitutional right to privacy? These are the sorts of questions that have inspired hundreds of books and journal articles about the legal underpinnings of privacy. This chapter presents an overview of the legal landscape as background for discussion elsewhere in the report.

4.1 CONSTITUTIONAL FOUNDATIONS

This section addresses constitutional safeguards for a citizen's privacy against government invasion and intrusion. Although the word "privacy" does not appear expressly in the U.S. Constitution, the Supreme Court has made clear that this fundamental right is implicit from the panoply of other rights guaranteed in the First, Fourth, and Ninth Amendments.

4.1.1 The Fourth Amendment

The source of constitutional protection for privacy (now embodied most clearly in the Constitution's Fourth Amendment) lies deep in English history. Precisely four centuries ago, British courts declared in Semayne's Case that "the house of every one is to him as his castle and fortress."[1]

---

[1]Semayne's Case, 5 Co. Rep. 91a, 91b, 77 Eng. Rep. 194, 195 (K.B. 1603).

From that bold beginning developed a more specific expectation that government may search a person's house, or personal papers, only with a valid reason (later, "probable cause"), legal authority (eventually in the form of a search warrant), and only after giving adequate notice before seeking entry or access.

Prominent among the principles that the U.S. Constitution's framers felt imperative to embody in the Bill of Rights was that of privacy. The Fourth Amendment has for the past 212 years been the bulwark of such privacy protection. Most states have comparable provisions in their own constitutions, and in 1963 the U.S. Supreme Court declared that state and local governments are as fully bound to respect privacy as is the national government, since the due process clause of the Fourteenth Amendment incorporates or absorbs the basic safeguards of the Fourth and makes those safeguards fully applicable to official action at all levels.

Interpreting and applying the spare words of the Fourth Amendment have posed a major and continuing challenge for the courts. Indeed, hardly a term of the U.S. Supreme Court passes without at least one case on the docket that juxtaposes government's need for information, usually pursuant to law enforcement investigation, and a citizen's or organization's wish to withhold that information, or to prevent government from gathering the information by invading premises or conducting surveillance in other forms.

The Supreme Court's recognition of a citizen's right to be secure against unauthorized government intrusion dates at least to a batch of cases in the 1880s, beginning with *Kilbourn v. Thompson*, 103 U.S. 168, 190 (1880), noting that Congress does not "possess the general power of making inquiry into the private affairs of the citizen." Later rulings extended the same principle to inquiries by federal administrative agencies. In 1886, in *Boyd v. United States*, 116 U.S. 616, 530 (1886), the Court struck down a regulatory measure that it found unduly intrusive into "the sanctity of a man's home and the privacies of life."

The later evolution of Fourth Amendment privacy guarantees highlights several notable 20th-century decisions. While the Court ruled in *Olmstead v. United States*, 277 U.S. 438 (1928), that the use of a wiretap did not violate the Fourth Amendment because there had been no physical invasion of a citizen's home, person, or papers, later judgments importantly qualified the potential scope of that decision. Notably, the Court held in *Katz v. United States*, 389 U.S. 347 (1967), that privacy rights did extend to a telephone booth, noting that "wherever a man may be, he is entitled to know that he will remain free from unreasonable searches and seizures."

The Supreme Court has dealt extensively in the last half century with conditions and circumstances under which searches of automobiles, pedestrians, hotel rooms, and offices may or may not be deemed reasonable. These rulings have usually reflected close divisions within the Court, often by the narrowest of margins. While the prevailing principles remain constant, variations in circumstances, in the potential effect of a particular search, and in the claimed needs of law enforcement inevitably affect the outcome.

A more recent decision affecting privacy of the home may aptly illustrate the process. In 2001, the Supreme Court considered for the first time whether the use of a thermal imaging device aimed at a private home from a public street to detect relative amounts of heat within the home— to determine whether marijuana was probably being grown within— constituted a "search" for Fourth Amendment purposes. Distinguishing permissible "naked eye surveillance of a home" the Court held on a 5-4 vote that thermal-imaging surveillance was constitutionally different and did involve an unlawful search. The explanation recalls the clarity and simplicity of basic Fourth Amendment precepts: "Where, as here, the Government uses a devise that is not in general public use, to explore details of the home that would not previously have been knowable without physical intrusion, the surveillance is a 'search' and is presumptively unreasonable without a warrant."[2]

Within the ambit of protecting privacy against government action, the Supreme Court declined in *Paul v. Davis*, 424 U.S. 693 (1976), to extend privacy interests to the "stigma" created by official publication of a person's name and photo on a list of "active shoplifters" after a larceny charge filed against him had been dismissed. While renewing the broad scope of the "zone of privacy," the Court distinguished other situations in which it had recognized such interests, noting that the claim posed here was not legally analogous, but simply sought to avoid unwelcome publicity. The high Court's 2003 decisions, rejecting similar claims against the display on state Internet Web sites of the identities of past sex offenders who had served time and been released, are much in the same vein.

Finally, the Court has long held that the probable cause standard of the Fourth Amendment does not apply to individuals seeking to enter the country (as opposed to those individuals already in the United States). For example, the Supreme Court has held that "searches of persons or packages at the national border rest on different considerations and different rules of constitutional law from domestic regulations,"[3] and has thus recognized the right of Congress to grant the executive "plenary authority to conduct routine searches and seizures at the border, without probable

---

[2]*Kyllo v. United States*, 533 U.S. 27 (2001).
[3]*United States v. 12 200-Ft. Reels of Film*, 413 U.S. 123 (1973).

cause or a warrant, in order to regulate the collection of duties and to prevent the introduction of contraband into this country."[4]

4.1.2 The First Amendment

The First Amendment's recognition of free speech and press safeguards citizens' privacy in several distinct ways: Government may not compel citizens to reveal certain highly sensitive information (e.g., membership in controversial political groups) or require them to disclaim membership in such organizations as a condition of receiving public benefits such as food stamps. Nor may government require a postal patron to declare publicly a desire to continue to receive mail from Communist countries.

The Supreme Court has also found in the First Amendment rights to speak, write, or publish anonymously or pseudonymously (especially in making political statements). Beginning with its 1960 decision in *Talley v. California*, 362 U.S. 60 (1960), the Court has consistently found in freedom of expression a right to resist compelled disclosure of one's identity, especially in the context of volatile political communications. Some years later, in *McIntyre v. Ohio Elections Comm'n*, 514 U.S. 334 (1995), the justices reaffirmed their commitment to protection of anonymity, insisting that governments that had legitimate reasons to regulate political communications could use less intrusive means.

In a similar vein, the Court also struck down on First Amendment grounds a law that required citizens who wished to receive "communist political propaganda" to explicitly notify the post office. The Court's reasoning was that such notification was a limitation on the unfettered exercise of the addressee's First Amendment rights. That decision, in *Lamont v. Postmaster General*, 381 U.S. 301 (1965), retains much value to privacy law, and is indeed the touchstone of current debate about the "opt-in" provision of the federal law that requires public libraries to filter Internet access, but permits patrons wishing unfiltered access to request it.

However, the legal status of potentially intrusive government surveillance is less clear under the First Amendment; three decades ago, the Supreme Court rejected citizens' efforts to enjoin the government's Vietnam era surveillance and infiltration of controversial anti-war political groups. The high Court has never revisited this issue, although a few lower courts have been more protective—notably the California Supreme Court, a few years after the high Court ruling, in barring police departments from sending undercover agents into university classrooms, posing as students, to compile dossiers on suspected radicals.

---

[4]*U.S. v. Montoya de Hernandez*, 473 U.S. 531, 537, 105 S. Ct. 3304, 3308 (1985).

The First Amendment has also served as the basis for protecting privacy in the home. Starting with *Breard v. Alexandria*, 341 U.S. 622 (1951), the Supreme Court has shown substantial deference to local ordinances that protect privacy by forbidding door-to-door solicitation without the homeowner's permission—save when such laws unduly burden free expression, as the justices found in their most recent encounter with such privacy-protecting measures, *Watchtower Bible & Tract Soc'y v. Stratton*, 536 U.S. 150 (2002). In *Watchtower*, the Court held that a requirement to register with the mayor's office and to obtain a local permit prior to engaging in door-to-door advocacy violated the First Amendment as it applied to religious proselytizing, anonymous political speech, and the distribution of handbills.

Turning to legal protection for privacy that concerns intrusion by individuals rather than by government, the case law is more easily summarized. Publication of the truth—no matter how unwelcome or invasive of privacy—is almost invariably protected under U.S. law, though less clearly under the laws of most other nations.

The Supreme Court has stopped just short of declaring flatly that speaking truth is categorically protected. What the justices have consistently said on this subject is that a publisher may not be held criminally or civilly liable if the challenged information meets three conditions, spelled out in cases like *Cox Broadcasting Corp. v. Cohn*, 420 U.S. 469 (1975), and *The Florida Star v. B.J.F.*, 491 U.S. 524 (1989). The statements must be accurate, else they would be subject to a legal claim for defamation. They must hold public interest—which means little more than that someone wishes to read or hear them. Finally, the information or images must not have been unlawfully obtained. This last criterion created substantial confusion over the issue of whose unlawful conduct would taint the information. That issue has now been largely resolved by the Supreme Court's 2001 ruling in *Bartnicki v. Vopper*, 532 U.S. 514 (2001), that even if a tape recording that was eventually broadcast on the defendant's radio station resulted from a clearly illegal wiretap, the station would not be liable if the evidence showed no complicity on its part in the unlawful taping. The case did involve, beyond a finding for the station's innocence, subject matter of great public interest and value to the community, and a privacy interest on the part of the illegally taped parties, which—given the illegality of the activities they were plotting on the phone—the Court characterized as "attenuated."

The Supreme Court's reluctance ever to declare unambiguously that truth trumps privacy may give pause to some publishers, and might imply that the ghost of Warren and Brandeis survives. Indeed, there are several situations in which truthful publications might generate liability. Clearly if the information was unlawfully obtained by the publisher or by someone for whose conduct the publisher bears responsibility—by hacking into an electronic database or breaching a legal privilege such as that between physician and patient, the legal immunity no longer applies. If truthful information is presented in a damaging "false light," the law of some states affords redress, which the Supreme Court seems to have condoned. Conceivably an intrusive publication could be deemed to lack public interest, and forfeit protection on that basis.

The ultimate question remains: If information has clear public interest, is accurate, and was not unlawfully obtained, can there ever be liability? The short answer seems to be no, and perhaps the longer answer as well. Yet one can imagine two cases in which such a negative answer would at least compel reflection. One would be the widespread dissemination—through a popular Web site, for example, of a photograph taken on a public street by a concealed camera of a female pedestrian's intimate apparel and private features. Since the site was public—a place where there is no expectation of privacy (unlike a bathroom, dressing room, etc.)—the general policy is that anyone walking there is fair game for potentially embarrassing images. (As close as Canada, the law differs on just this point; a Canadian may be photographed with impunity at a rally or athletic event, but not without consent when sitting on a doorstep, even in clear public view.) There have been persistent suggestions that U.S. law should recognize some exception to the publisher's immunity in such a situation.

The other poignant case involves a person whose HIV-positive status is unknown to friends, family, employer, and neighbors but is disclosed to the world by someone who obtained this highly sensitive information "not unlawfully" (an estranged ex-spouse, for example). Here again, the revelation may not be actionable for a violation of a federal right of privacy, although it may be actionable under state constitutional privacy jurisprudence, for a variety of torts (e.g., tortuous interference with business relations), state or federal statutes, or for violation of contractual rights (e.g., divorce settlement agreements often have gag provisions). Yet there is something about such a case that gives even the most ardent free-press advocate some pause. For the moment, the short answer—"the truth shall set you free"—remains the long answer as well.

4.1.3 The Ninth Amendment

Finally among constitutional safeguards for privacy (though not for informational privacy), a "penumbral" protection derived in part from the Ninth Amendment has recently joined more traditional sources. Among the most prominent cases in this regard is *Griswold v. Connecticut*, 381 U.S. 479 (1965). In this case, the Supreme Court held unconstitutional a Connecticut law banning the use even by married couples of contraceptives, stating that the ban violated basic privacy precepts since it invaded "a zone of privacy created by several fundamental constitutional guarantees." In that case, Justice William O. Douglas concluded his opinion for the Court with a reminder that is useful here: "We deal with a right of privacy older than the Bill of Rights—older than our political parties, older than our school system." Such statements remind us that the framers of the Constitution and of the Bill of Rights were not creating protection for privacy against government, but codifying ancient precepts in new language, and with new force behind those words.

On the other hand, a sharply split Court failed in *Bowers v. Hardwick*, 478 U.S. 186 (1986), to find in the right of privacy a constitutional basis for protection against state laws criminalizing homosexual sodomy. The status of that case had become increasingly problematic. Before his death, one justice who had voted in the majority declared he had been wrong in so doing. At least five states declined to follow *Hardwick*, granting protection to private homosexual activity under their own constitutions—as states are free to do, since the national Bill of Rights sets only a floor and not a ceiling. Thus when the issue returned to the Supreme Court during the 2002-2003 term, the likelihood of an overruling seemed substantial. Only the margin was in doubt, as well as the precise rationale a differently disposed majority would adopt.

On June 26, 2003, the final day of its term, the justices by a decisive 6-3 vote overruled *Bowers v. Hardwick*, in *Lawrence v. Texas*, 539 U.S. 558 (2003). Justice Anthony M. Kennedy, writing for the majority, posed in this way the central question of the case: "whether [the defendants] were free as adults to engage in the private conduct in the exercise of their liberty under the Due Process Clause . . . ." After reviewing the high Court's own post-*Hardwick* privacy rulings, and taking an unprecedented account of foreign judgments, the majority concluded that the Constitution did and should protect such activity among consenting adults. Though primary emphasis rested on due process and equal protection, the Court did stress a strong privacy interest as well: "The [defendants] are entitled to respect for their private lives. The State cannot demean their existence or control their destiny by making their private sexual conduct a crime." The majority quoted a passage from one of the earlier abortion-rights cases, recognizing "that there is a realm of personal liberty which the government may not enter," and concluded that "the Texas statute furthers no legitimate state interest which can justify its intrusion into the personal and private life of the individual."

Not every recent ruling has favored privacy claims, however. A few years ago, the Court declined in *Washington v. Glucksberg*, 521 U.S. 702 (1997), to find in the due process clause a privacy interest sufficient to invalidate state laws that ban assisted suicide—a ruling that was actually consistent with the high Court's earlier refusal in *Cruzan v. Missouri Health Dep't*, 497 U.S. 261 (1990), to order the removal (pursuant to parental pleas) of life support from a vegetative accident victim.

4.2 COMMON LAW AND PRIVACY TORTS

The modern quest for recognition of such a right of privacy is often traced to a seminal *Harvard Law Review* article, published in 1890 by a young Louis D. Brandeis and his senior partner Samuel Warren.[5] The article reflected growing concern about unwelcome and intrusive media publicity about the private lives of the rich and famous (notably the newspaper publication of sensitive guest lists for social events hosted by the Warrens). The thesis of the piece was that courts should be more receptive to claims of privacy, and should develop "a right to an inviolate personality."

Today, common law regarding privacy is formulated in terms of a set of four privacy torts for which legal recourse may be appropriate—although when the threat is created by a publisher, broadcaster, or other entity protected by the First Amendment, courts will not always grant relief to the person whose privacy has been compromised. First articulated by William Prosser,[6] these torts include:

- *Intrusion*—Objectionable intrusion into the private affairs or seclusion of an individual. The intrusion may be physical or electronic and is oriented toward improper information gathering. For example, watching someone urinating in a bathroom stall—whether through a peephole or using a video camera—is likely such an intrusion. Intrusion would generally not be applicable when someone is seen or photographed in public, although certain exceptions can be easily imagined (e.g., an out-of-visual-band camera that could generate realistic images of human bodies underneath clothing or "up-skirt" cameras embedded in the sidewalk.

- *Public disclosure of private facts*—Publication of personal information

[5]Samuel Warren and Louis D. Brandeis, "The Right to Privacy," *Harvard Law Review* 4(5):193, 1890.

[6]William L. Prosser, "Privacy," *California Law Review* 48:383, 1960. The discussion in this section draws on Joey Senat, "4 Common Law Privacy Torts," 2000, an online study reference, available at http://www.cas.okstate.edu/jb/faculty/senat/jb3163/privacytorts.html; "The Privacy Torts: How U.S. State Law Quietly Leads the Way in Privacy Protection," a special report issued by Privacilla.org, July 2002, available at http://www.privacilla.org/releases/Torts_Report.html; and National Research Council, *Who Goes There? Authentication Through the Lens of Privacy*, Stephen T. Kent and Lynette I. Millett, eds., The National Academies Press, Washington, D.C., 2003.

that a reasonable person would object to having made public. The information must be both true and reasonably construable as private (e.g., a person's height would be less private than an account of his sexual past). In addition, the disclosure must be public—disclosure to a small number of people or those with a legitimate need to know does not count as public. Disclosure in the form of a movie that reveals someone by name is public; discussion among a group of acquaintances is not. Finally, the disclosure must not be newsworthy—thus making publication about the private lives of celebrities fair game. In an information age context, publication of a non-celebrity's personal information on a publicly accessible Web page is largely uncharted territory.

• *Misappropriation of name or likeness*—Unauthorized use of an individual's picture or name for commercial advantage. The misappropriation tort applies if and when a person's name, likeness, or identity is used without his or her permission for trade or advertising purposes. The misappropriation tort relates to information privacy, but only insofar as it deals with a particular kind of use of a certain kind of personal information.

• *False light*—Publication of objectionable, false information about an individual. The intent of this tort is to protect people against being cast in a false light in the public eye. For example, this tort would apply when someone's photograph is publicly exhibited in a way or a context that creates negative inferences about him. The false light tort has been found applicable when people have been wrongly associated with juvenile delinquents or drug dealing, for example. Of the four privacy torts, the false light tort is least applicable to informational privacy, since it deals with false information.

The 1964 *Restatement of the Law of Torts* (a clarification and compilation of the law by the American Law Institute) adopted the Prosser framework.[7] Together, these torts provide a basis for privacy suits against the disclosure, without consent, of embarrassing false information about a person, or of intimate details or images from a person's private life, or unauthorized use for profit or commercial gain of an individual's image, likeness, voice, or reputation.

As a matter of practice, these privacy torts have not been used much to protect the information-age privacy of individuals. However, the principles behind these torts are useful reminders of some of the interests that privacy is designed to protect against—intrusion into personal affairs and disclosure of sensitive personal information, among others.

As a historical matter, the Warren-Brandeis article may not fully

---

[7]American Law Institute, *Restatement of the Law of Torts*, Philadelphia, 1964.

deserve the credit it usually draws. Fully a decade earlier, Judge Thomas Cooley had written in his *Treatise on the Law of Torts* that "the right to one's person may be said to be a right of complete immunity: to be let alone."[8] Although Cooley seems to have been more focused on physical than psychological intrusion, the phrase that he used first gave momentum to the quest for broader protection. Warren and Brandeis, in fact, fashioned an analogy between the legal basis for physical privacy (well established in British case law) and the emerging and more subtle value of protection for feelings, personal dignity and the like, for which they would invoke the new doctrine championed in their article.

The impact of the Warren-Brandeis thesis, well over a century later, is still not easily assessed. On the one hand, nearly every state has adopted statutory protection for privacy claims that extend well beyond the physical sanctity of the home and office; at last count, North Dakota and Wyoming were the only holdouts. On the other hand, the degree to which the Warren-Brandeis view really has gained legal acceptance remains far less uniform.

The most recent *Restatement of the Law of Torts*, issued in 1977, recognized a cause of action for unconsented "public disclosure of private facts" but qualified that recognition by noting, for example, that "while [a person] is walking on the public highway, there can be no liability for observing him or even taking his photograph."[9]

Nonetheless, another comment to the 1977 *Restatement* posits that publishing "without consent, a picture of [the subject nursing her child]" would be actionable even if taken in a public place. In short, there is uncertainty and substantial ambivalence on the precise contours of this legal claim. Scholars, too, have remained ambivalent. In the mid-1960s, Harry Kalven asked rhetorically (in the title of an article on just this subject), "Were Warren and Brandeis Wrong?," concluding that we are probably better off today because their plea for broad protection of privacy never has been fully embraced by the courts.

4.3 FREEDOM OF INFORMATION/OPEN GOVERNMENT

Freedom of information has been and remains in this country a creature of statute and not of constitutional right. Save for a few situations (notably the criminal trial) where courts have recognized a First Amendment claim of access, obtaining government information or covering sen-

---

[8]Thomas Cooley, *A Treatise on the Law of Torts or the Wrongs Which Arise Independent of Contract*, Callaghan, Chicago, 1879.
[9]American Law Institute, *Restatement of the Law of Torts*, 2nd Edition, Philadelphia, 1977, pp. 379-380.

sitive proceedings remains subject to the will of that government which controls the data or the site. Since 1965, at the federal level, the Freedom of Information Act (FOIA) has been the vital basis for access claims, many of which have been litigated with varying results.

Among the nine statutory exemptions to a citizen's right of access under FOIA, those most likely to precipitate privacy tensions are Exemptions 6 and 7c. The first of these relates to information such as personnel and medical files, the disclosure of which would "constitute a clearly unwarranted invasion of personal privacy." Exemption 7c excludes records or information compiled for law enforcement purposes, "but only to the extent that the production of such [materials] . . . could reasonably be expected to constitute an unwarranted invasion of personal privacy."

In the major decision construing and applying Exemption 7c, *United States Department of Justice v. Reporters Committee for Freedom of the Press*, 489 U.S. 749 (1989), the Supreme Court noted the need, under the statute, to balance the interests of openness and accountability against the statutory recognition of individual privacy. The justices unanimously rejected claims of access to a suspect's rap sheet, noting the vital distinction (in FOIA) between the statute's "purpose to ensure that the Government's activities be opened to the sharp eye of public scrutiny" and the contrasting claim that "information about private citizens that happens to be in the warehouse of the Government be so disclosed."

But in a case that eventually led to extensive revelations of truly chilling law enforcement activity in the 1960s, a federal appeals court ruled in *Rosenfeld v. Department of Justice*, 57 F.3d 803 (9th Cir. 1995), that Exemption 7 would not justify withholding FBI documents pertaining to investigations of faculty and students at Berkeley during the Vietnam War era, the court noting that the FBI had no legitimate law enforcement interest in its probe of the Free Speech Movement and thus could not invoke a valid privacy interest to resist disclosure.

Tensions between privacy and access arise occasionally in a very different context. The Supreme Court has twice in recent years resolved those debates in favor of the privacy interest. California law, in the interests of privacy, limited to certain groups ready access to records including the addresses of persons arrested on driving charges. Commercial enterprises were excluded from the access pathway and challenged the restriction through the state courts to the U.S. Supreme Court. The justices, in *Los Angeles Police Department v. United Reporting Publishing Co.*, 528 U.S. 32 (1999), rejected, at the least, the challenge brought forward by the proprietary data seekers, leaving open the possibility of a future attack on the statute as it had been applied.

Finally, in the aftermath of the September 11, 2001, attacks, regulations binding on federal agencies have been promulgated to reduce the amount of information available through the Freedom of Information Act. Specifically, in October 2001, Attorney General John Ashcroft promulgated a memorandum throughout the executive branch that established a "sound legal basis" standard for governing the Department of Justice's decisions on whether to defend agency actions under FOIA when they are challenged in court. That is, the Department of Justice would defend all decisions to withhold information under FOIA "unless they lack a sound legal basis or present an unwarranted risk of adverse impact on the ability of other agencies to protect other important records." This new standard changed the previously operative "foreseeable harm" standard that was employed under previous guidance, which would defend a decision to withhold information only in those cases where the agency reasonably foresees that disclosure would be harmful to an interest protected by that exemption.

4.3.1 Federal Laws Relevant to Individual Privacy

Over the past three decades, many federal laws have been enacted to protect individual privacy.[10] Often they have responded to growing public awareness of privacy invasions made possible by technology developments.

In commerce, one of the most important pieces of legislation with privacy impact is the FTC Act (15 U.S.C. 41-58, as amended), enacted by the U.S. Congress in 1914. The FTC Act established the Federal Trade Commission and charges it with, among other things, protecting the public from unfair and deceptive trade practices.

In recent years, the FTC has brought a number of cases to enforce the promises in statements of privacy policy, including promises about the security of consumers' personal information, and to challenge practices that cause substantial consumer injury. These cases include actions against companies with faulty information security practices that allow sensitive customer data to be exposed to unauthorized parties (a typical settlement might require the offending company to implement a comprehensive information security program and to obtain audits by independent third-party security professionals every other year for 20 years) and companies that use collected data in a manner inconsistent with their stated policies (a typical settlement agreement might require the offending company to

---

[10]Many of the thumbnail descriptions of the laws in this section draw heavily on a description of laws related to information law and privacy prepared by the John Marshall Law School, "Information Law and Policy: Existing U.S. Information-related Law," 2000, available at http://www.citpl.org/infolaw/spring2000/law.html.

forego monetary gains from its improper use and to agree to not engage in such improper use in the future).

In addition, in late 2005 and early 2006, the FTC has also used its authority to hold companies liable for insufficient security measures in place to protect customer information, and at least two cases have been brought against companies on this basis, both of which resulted in consent agreements to obtain security audits and be subject to FTC oversight of their security practices.[11] A complete listing of cases undertaken by the FTC can be found on the FTC Web site.[12]

In the financial area, Congress has enacted several bills that relate to privacy. Some are intended to enhance individual privacy, and some detract from it.

- The Fair Credit Reporting Act (FCRA), 15 U.S.C. 1681 (1970), broadly regulates the consumer reporting agencies in the interest of protecting the confidentiality and privacy rights of the consumer. The FCRA requires credit investigations and reporting agencies to make their records available to the subjects of the records, provides procedures for correcting information, and permits disclosure only to authorized customers.
- The Bank Secrecy Act, 31 U.S.C. 5311-5355 (1970), was designed to aid the federal government in detecting illegal activity through tracking certain monetary transactions, and it requires financial institutions to file reports of certain kinds of cash transactions and to keep records on other kinds of transactions for which no record-keeping or filing requirements previously existed.
- The Right to Financial Privacy Act (RFPA), 12 U.S.C. 3401 et seq. (1978), provides some confidentiality for the financial records of depositors by governing the transfer of financial records. In general, the act prohibits banks from disclosing client payment information to the government without a court order or other formal request. In some instances, the consumer has the right to challenge the request.
- The Consumer Credit Reporting Reform Act, 15 U.S.C. 1681-1681t (1997), helps to close some of the loopholes found in the FCRA. The act

---

[11]The FTC identified six practices that contribute to a judgment that security practices were insufficient: storing sensitive information in multiple files when the company no longer had a business need to keep the information; failure to encrypt consumer information when it was transmitted or stored on computers in company stores; failure to use readily available security measures to limit access to its computer networks through wireless access points on the networks; storing the information in files that could be easily accessed using a commonly known or default user ID and password; failure to limit sufficiently the ability of computers on one in-store network to connect to computers on other in-store and corporate networks; and failure to employ sufficient measures to detect unauthorized access.

[12]See http://www.ftc.gov/privacy/privacyinitiatives/promises_enf.html.

narrows the broad "legitimate need" purpose for which credit reports can be disseminated. Consumer credit reports cannot be furnished for employment purposes except if the employer certifies that the employee has consented in writing.

• The Gramm-Leach-Bliley Act (1999) requires financial institutions to notify consumers of their privacy policies and gives them the opportunity to prevent disclosure of nonpublic personal information about them to nonaffiliated third parties. It also makes the practice of "pretexting" unlawful (i.e., seeking financial information under the pretext of being the customer). See Section 6.3 for more on the Gramm-Leach-Bliley Act.

In the area of electronic communications (including telephone, pager, and computer-based communications), Congress has passed several acts.

• The Omnibus Crime Control and Safe Street Act (1968) in Title III sets forth specific requirements for conducting telephone wiretaps. The legislation today is typically known as the Title III Wiretap Act. Under Title III legislation, law enforcement authorities must usually obtain a warrant based on a court's finding that "there is probable cause [to believe] that an individual is committing, has committed, or is about to commit a particular offense . . . [and that] normal investigative procedures have been tried and have failed or reasonably appear to be unlikely to succeed if tried or to be too dangerous." Only certain federal crimes may be investigated under Title III authority (e.g., murder, kidnapping, child molestation, racketeering, narcotics offenses), and Title III also has a variety of provisions that minimize the intrusiveness of the wiretap on telephonic communications that are unrelated to the offense being investigated, provide for civil and criminal penalties for law enforcement officials or private citizens who violate its provisions, and allow the suppression of evidence obtained in violation of the central features of Title III requirements, even if such evidence meets the relevant Fourth Amendment tests.

• The Foreign Intelligence Surveillance Act (1978), enacted as a reaction to an asserted executive branch authority to conduct wiretaps without restriction in intelligence matters, establishes mechanisms through which court-approved legal authority for obtaining a wiretap can be granted. Passed at the time with strong support from the American Civil Liberties Union, this extent of this law's reach is now being challenged, as discussed in Chapter 9.

• The Cable Communications Policy Act, 47 U.S.C. 551 (1984), requires cable services to inform their customers of the nature of personally identifiable information and the use of that information, and also places restrictions on the cable services' collection and disclosure of information. Significantly, it requires that cable operators utilize fair information procedures and that they not disclose identifiable information, including viewer choices or retail transactions, without written or electronic consent. Subscribers are given the right to limit disclosure of name and address for mail solicitation purposes and have a right of accuracy and correction. However, restrictions in this act on disclosure of information related to the cable provision of communications services such as voice-over-IP phone service were substantially relaxed by the USA PATRIOT Act in response to law enforcement requests for information.

• The Electronic Communications Privacy Act (ECPA), 18 U.S.C. 2510-2520, 2701-2709 (1986), amends the Title III Wiretap Act. ECPA extends the coverage of Title III to new forms of voice, data, and video communications including cellular phones, electronic mail, computer transmissions, and voice and display pagers.

• The Telephone Consumer Protection Act (1991) protects the consumer's right to be left alone by authorizing the FCC to require telemarketers to create and maintain lists of consumers who do not wish to be called (do not call lists). The law also protects consumers from some forms of marketing by banning the use of unsolicited prerecorded telephone calls, and unsolicited advertisements by fax.

• The Communications Assistance for Law Enforcement Act (CALEA; 1994) requires telecommunications carriers to expeditiously isolate and enable the government to surreptitiously intercept all wire and electronic communications in the carrier's control to or from the equipment, facilities, or services of a subscriber, in real time or at any later time acceptable to the government. CALEA covers telephone communications carried over traditional circuit-switched networks, but it provides an exemption for "information service providers" unless they are providing services that are "a replacement for a substantial portion of the local telephone exchange service" as determined by the FCC. In May 2006, the FCC determined that voice-over-IP providers were indeed subject to the requirements of CALEA.[13]

• The Telemarketing and Consumer Fraud and Abuse Prevention Act, 15 U.S.C. 6101-6108 (1994), places constraints on telemarketing calls, especially those made by autodialers, and also forbids telemarketing conducted in a pattern that is abusive of consumers' privacy.

• The Telecommunications Act, 47 U.S.C. 222 (1996), was a major overhaul of telecommunications law. Certain provisions impose restrictions on the use of automated phone dialing systems, artificial or prerecorded voice messages, and fax machines to send unsolicited advertise-

---

[13]See http://www.askcalea.net/docs/20060503_2nd-memorandum.pdf.

ments. Where calling information (which might be regarded as sensitive personal information) is obtained by one telecommunications carrier from another, the Telecommunications Act stipulates that the sole purpose must be the provision of communications service or ancillary purposes necessary to or used in the provision of such services, including the publishing of directories.

In the area of information contained in government records, Congress has passed several acts.

• The Freedom of Information Act (1996) establishes a presumption that records in the possession of agencies and departments of the executive branch of the U.S. government are accessible to the people. Federal agencies are required to disclose records upon receiving a written request for them, except for those records that are protected from disclosure by any of the nine exemptions or three exclusions of FOIA. This right of access is enforceable in court. In 1996, Congress passed the Electronic Freedom of Information Act (E-FOIA) Amendments, which provided for public access to information in an electronic format and for the establishment of electronic FOIA reading rooms through agency FOIA sites on the Internet.

• The Privacy Act of 1974, 5 U.S.C. 552a, provides safeguards against an invasion of privacy through the misuse of records by federal agencies. In general, the act allows a citizen to learn how records are collected, maintained, used, and disseminated by the federal government. The act also permits an individual to gain access to most personal information maintained by federal agencies and to seek amendment of any inaccurate, incomplete, untimely, or irrelevant information. Note that the Privacy Act is concerned primarily with systems of records rather than data accrued from networks.

• The Driver's Privacy Protection Act of 1994, 18 U.S.C. 2721, was passed subsequent to the stalking and murder of actress Rebecca Schaeffer by a fan who allegedly retrieved her name and address from a motor vehicle department. The act, which became effective in 1997, prohibits state Departments of Motor Vehicles and their employees from releasing "personal information" from a driver's record unless the request fits within 1 of 14 exemptions. As originally passed, it also required state motor vehicle departments to provide a citizen an opt-out means of prohibiting the disclosure of certain personal information to other individuals, although businesses could still receive such information for certain specified purposes. The act was subsequently amended to require opt-in consent for disclosure of personal information to other individuals, and also for the disclosure of "highly restricted personal information" (an individual's photograph or image, Social Security number, or medical or disability information) for almost all purposes.

• Megan's Law, 42 U.S.C. 14071 (1999), obligates states to require prison officials or courts to inform convicted sex offenders of their obligation to register with state law enforcement authorities and to re-register if they move to another state. The state agencies in turn are to inform local law enforcement authorities, typically the local police department, of convicted sex offenders who reside in their jurisdiction. The state law enforcement agencies are also required to inform the FBI about the whereabouts of convicted sex offenders. (In many cases, states have gone farther in requiring the publishing of the addresses of sex offenders so that the communities in which they reside will be alerted to their presence.)

Also, a number of federal laws require the attorney general to promulgate regulations for access to criminal history and incarceration records of individuals. These regulations, 28 C.F.R. 20, are intended to ensure the accuracy, completeness, currency, integrity, and security of such information and to protect individual privacy.

In 1996 Congress passed a major piece of health care legislation called the Health Insurance Portability and Accountability Act (HIPAA). Among its privacy provisions, it mandates regulations to protect the confidentiality of individually identifiable health information and is further discussed in Chapter 7.

In 2001, Congress passed the Uniting and Strengthening America by Providing Appropriate Tools Required to Intercept and Obstruct Terrorism (USA PATRIOT) Act, and in 2006, a number of amendments to the act. In general, the USA PATRIOT Act and subsequent amendments lower some of the barriers to conducting surveillance in the United States for national security or foreign intelligence purposes, provide the U.S. intelligence community with greater access to information uncovered during criminal investigations, and encourage cooperation between law enforcement and foreign intelligence investigators. The USA PATRIOT Act also lessens certain restrictions on criminal investigations, such as delayed notification of physical searches executed pursuant to a search warrant under some circumstances and court-enabled access to otherwise-protected educational records in terrorism cases. Finally, the USA PATRIOT Act creates judicial oversight for e-mail monitoring and grand jury disclosures.[14]

---

[14]This discussion is based on Charles Doyle, *The USA PATRIOT Act: A Legal Analysis*, Order Code RL31377, Congressional Research Service, Washington, D.C., April 15, 2002, available at http://www.fas.org/irp/crs/RL31377.pdf; and Brian T. Yeh and Charles Doyle, *USA PATRIOT Improvement and Reauthorization Act of 2005: A Legal Analysis*, Order Code RL33332, Congressional Research Service, Washington, D.C., March 24, 2006, available at http://www.fas.org/sgp/crs/intel/RL33332.pdf.

A host of miscellaneous privacy protection acts have also been passed in the last 30 years.

- The Family Educational Rights and Privacy Act (FERPA), 20 U.S.C. 1232g (1974), regulates institutions that receive public funds. The act requires educational institutions to grant students, or parents of students, access to student records, establishes procedures to challenge and correct information, and limits disclosure to third parties. Section 6.2 discusses the impact of this legislation. Section 5.1 addresses FERPA's origins.
- The Computer Fraud and Abuse Act, 18 U.S.C. 1030, was originally passed in 1986 and subsequently amended in 1994, 1996, and 2001 to criminalize certain computer "hacking" activities, such as intentionally accessing a computer without authorization to obtain information contained in a financial record of a financial institution, information from any department or agency of the United States, or information from any protected computer if the conduct involves an interstate or foreign communication and knowingly causing damage through the use of a computer. Authorities under this act have been used to protect the privacy and confidentiality of computer-resident information.
- The Video Privacy Protection Act, 18 U.S.C. 2710, was passed in 1988 in response to actions taken by reporters covering the hearings for Judge Robert Bork's nomination to the Supreme Court. Reporters were able to gain access to records of the Bork family's video rentals. Congress deemed this an invasion of privacy and reacted by enacting the Video Privacy Protection Act.
- The Children's Online Privacy Protection Act, 15 U.S.C. 6501-6506 (1998), requires the FTC to prescribe regulations to protect the privacy of personal information collected from and about children on the Internet and to provide greater parental control over the collection and use of that information.
- The Identity Theft and Assumption Deterrence Act, 18 U.S.C. 1028 (1998), addresses the problem of identity theft (Box 4.1). It stipulates that the person whose identity was stolen is a true victim (whereas previously only the credit grantors who suffered monetary losses were considered victims); enables the Secret Service, the FBI, and other law enforcement agencies the authority to investigate this crime; allows the identity theft victim to seek restitution if there is a conviction; and establishes the FTC as a central agency to act as a clearinghouse for complaints, referrals, and resources for assistance for victims of identity theft.
- The CAN-SPAM Act (Controlling the Assault of Non-Solicited Pornography and Marketing Act), 15 U.S.C. 7701-7713 (2003), applies to unsolicited commercial e-mail. In such e-mails, the act bans false or misleading header information (e.g., false "From" information) and deceptive subject lines, requires that recipients be given a method for opting out of receiv-

---

BOX 4.1
Identity Theft

Identity theft or fraud is a major and growing concern in the information age. In 1998, it was made a federal crime under the Identity Theft and Assumption Deterrence Act. The crime consists of stealing key pieces of another's personal information such as Social Security, credit card, or bank account numbers, and using that information to obtain credit or purchase goods or services.

In the typical case, the thief uses the personal information to open a new credit card account, cellular phone service, or new checking account (with new blank checks). Or the thief uses a stolen account number to gain access to the account, and then changes the address on the account and runs up a huge bill before the account owner discovers what has happened.

The injury to consumers is considerable, even though much of the ultimate financial loss falls on financial institutions. The injury to consumer victims takes many forms, including the significant amount of time and frustration involved in tracking down the extent of the theft, and reporting it to all the various institutions that must be notified, such as credit card issuers, banks, lenders, credit reporting agencies, and so on. Injury can also take the form of lost credit, insurance, and even jobs and driver's licenses, before victims are able to correct their financial records.

Identity theft also has implications for national security. For example, Dennis M. Lormel, chief of the FBI's Terrorist Financial Review Group, testified on July 9, 2002, before the Senate Judiciary Committee Subcommittee on Technology, Terrorism and Government Information:[1]

> The threat [of identity theft] is made graver by the fact that terrorists have long utilized identity theft as well as Social Security Number fraud to enable them to obtain such things as cover employment and access to secure locations. These and similar means can be utilized by terrorists to obtain Driver's Licenses, and bank and credit card accounts through which terrorism financing is facilitated. Terrorists and terrorist groups require funding to perpetrate their terrorist agendas. The methods used to finance terrorism range from the highly sophisticated to the most basic. There is virtually no financing method that has not at some level been exploited by these groups. Identity theft is a key catalyst fueling many of these methods.
>
> For example, an Al-Qaeda terrorist cell in Spain used stolen credit cards in fictitious sales scams and for numerous other purchases for the cell. They kept purchases below amounts where identification would be presented. They also used stolen telephone and credit cards for communications back to Pakistan, Afghanistan, Lebanon, etc. Extensive use of false passports and travel documents were used to open bank accounts where money for the Mujahadin movement was sent to and from countries such as Pakistan, Afghanistan, etc.

Identity thieves obtain information in a variety of ways. Often old-fashioned techniques are used, e.g., retrieving numbers from paperwork in trash bins ("dumpster diving") and observing numbers entered by consumers at ATMs, pay telephones, or on forms at bank counters ("shoulder surfing"). These techniques seem more common than more sophisticated methods, such as hacking into databases on the Internet.

---

[1]Testimony available at http://www.fbi.gov/congress/congress02/idtheft.htm.

But modern information technology facilitates identity theft on a large scale. For example, 8 of the 36 incidents of large-scale compromise of personal information reported by the Identity Theft Resource Center[2] involved the theft of computers containing personal information. In other cases, the compromise of personal information arises from unauthorized break-ins into databases containing such information or the loss or theft of tapes and other storage media with such information in unencrypted form.[3]

The Internet is also increasingly important in facilitating the use of illicitly acquired information, since online transactions require no personal interaction. The speed of the Internet also allows thieves to engage in large numbers of transactions in a very short period of time, thus increasing the losses that result from identity theft. For example, in November 2005 six men who administered and operated the "Shadowcrew.com" Web site—one of the largest online centers for trafficking in stolen credit and bank card numbers and identity information—pleaded guilty to charges of conspiracy to commit credit and bank card fraud, as well as identification document fraud.

Some have argued that identity theft is more accurately described as a financial crime than as a privacy problem. They argue that solutions should focus on stopping the behavior of wrongdoers, and express concern about solutions that might have the effect of limiting the availability of information.

But stopping wrongdoers is a real challenge. The thieves are difficult to identify and locate; often consumers do not know how their information was stolen and remain unaware of the theft for some time (on average from 6 months to a year). Notification of consumers does help, but in some instances, the notification is accompanied by an offer of a year of free credit monitoring, and to obtain this service consumers have to provide personal information as an authenticating mechanism to prove who they are. This approach thus opens yet another mechanism for identity theft—a forged letter or e-mail from identity thieves notifying consumers of a purported compromise of personal information. Finally, such crimes may not be a high priority for federal or local prosecutors. While the Federal Trade Commission (which receives the complaints and refers cases to law enforcement agencies) reports that prosecutions have increased, criminal law enforcement can never be expected to address more than a small percentage of the cases.

Private sector solutions offer an alternative to law and regulation for reducing the impact of identification theft. Financial institutions, which bear the considerable financial loss from identity theft, have considerable incentive and capacity to find effective tools for detecting fraud and preventing the misuse of stolen information.

Consumer education is also part of the solution. And increasingly, word is getting out through government and private sector initiatives on how consumers can prevent their information from being stolen.

It is too soon to tell whether all these efforts will put a real dent in identity theft. The Federal Trade Commission's call center reports continuing increases in the number of complaints. While these numbers no doubt reflect greater consumer awareness of the problem and the toll free number, they also suggest a growing problem and the considerable challenge ahead.

---

[2] See http://www.idtheftcenter.org/breaches.pdf.
[3] See, for example, http://www.consumersunion.org/campaigns//learn_more/002232indiv.html. In a quite recent—and large-scale—incident, Social Security numbers and other personal information for as much as 80 percent of the U.S. active-duty military force were among the unencrypted data stolen from the home of a Department of Veterans Affairs analyst in May 2006. See Ann Scott Tyson and Christopher Lee, "Data Theft Affected Most in Military: National Security Concerns Raised," *Washington Post*, June 7, 2006, p. A01.

ing further communications, and requires that the e-mail is identified as an advertisement and includes the sender's valid physical postal address. The act also gives the FTC the authority to enforce it, and the Department of Justice the authority to enforce its criminal sanctions.

• The Real ID Act (2005) requires federal agencies to accept drivers' licenses or personal identification cards as identification after May 11, 2008, only if these documents meet certain federal standards. These documents must include, at a minimum, a person's full legal name, date of birth, gender, driver's license or personal ID card number, digital photograph, address of legal residence, and signature; physical security features designed to prevent tampering, counterfeiting, or duplication for fraudulent purposes; and a common machine-readable format for defined data elements. In addition, states must require the presentation and verification of a photo identity document (except that a non-photo identity document is acceptable if it includes both the person's full legal name and date of birth), documentation showing the person's date of birth, proof of the person's Social Security number (SSN) or verification that the person is not eligible for an SSN, and documentation showing the person's name and address of principal residence. States are also required to provide to all other states electronic access to information contained in the motor vehicle database of the state.

4.3.2 Federal Laws Relevant to Confidentiality

A number of federal laws protect the confidentiality of personal information collected by the statistical agencies of the United States. For example, the Census Bureau collects detailed personal information on most Americans every decade. Such information includes but is not limited to income, housing situation and living arrangements, employment, and ethnicity. These data, collected via survey, are protected by the provisions of Title 13, Section 9, which prohibits dissemination of such data in a manner that allows identification of the respondent. This prohibition applies to individuals who have not been sworn as agents of the census. In addition, the Census Bureau is explicitly prohibited from using survey information in any way apart from statistical purposes. Survey information may also not be used as legal evidence.

A second relevant law is the Confidential Information Protection and Statistical Efficiency Act (CIPSEA), passed as Title V of the E-Government Act of 2002. CIPSEA strengthens and extends confidentiality protection for all statistical data collections of the U.S. government. If data are furnished by individuals or organizations to an agency under a pledge of confidentiality for exclusively statistical purposes, CIPSEA provides that the data will be used only for statistical purposes and will not be disclosed in identifiable form to anyone not authorized by the title. Data covered under CIPSEA are also not subject to release under a Freedom of Information Act request.

A third example (and there are still others) is the confidentiality of information collected for public health purposes, specified by Section 308(d) of the Public Health Service Act (42 U.S.C. 242m). This section requires that the information collected can be used only for the stated purposes unless consent for another purpose is obtained.

Note also that laws protecting the confidentiality of personal information can be, and have been, altered to allow uses other than the one for which such information was originally collected. For example, the USA PATRIOT Act amended the National Education Statistics Act of 1994 to allow the U.S. attorney general or assistant attorney general to submit a written application to a court of competent jurisdiction for an ex parte order to collect reports, records, and information from the National Center for Education Statistics (NCES), all of which may have been collected under the confidentiality guarantee, if they are related to investigations and prosecutions of terrorism.

4.3.3 Regulation

Regulations related to privacy are extensive and too voluminous to recap fully in this report. At the federal level, most privacy statutes are implemented through rule making. The U.S. Congress passes legislation that lays out the general issues and principles in question, but leaves to a regulating agency the responsibility of working out the details of how that legislation will be implemented. The agency proposes the regulations, invites public comment on the proposal, and issues the final regulation, which can be challenged in court. Once promulgated, regulation has the force of law. Enforcement actions may be taken for violations of regulations, often resulting in a consent decree, in which a company agrees to take actions to ensure that the offending behavior will not be repeated. Typically, consent decrees are enforceable in federal courts.

Although many agencies have regulatory authority, the Federal Trade Commission has played a key role in enforcing regulations related to information-age privacy and has some authority to promulgate regulations as well. For example, the FTC states,

> Privacy is a central element of the FTC's consumer protection mission. In recent years, advances in computer technology have made it possible for detailed information about people to be compiled and shared more easily and cheaply than ever. . . . At the same time, as personal information becomes more accessible, each of us—companies, associations, government agencies, and consumers—must take precautions to protect against the misuse of our information.

Under a number of statutory provisions (including the Gramm-Leach-Bliley Act, the Fair Credit Reporting Act, the Fair and Accurate Credit Transactions Act, and the Children's Online Privacy Protection Act), the FTC—often jointly with other regulatory agencies—has issued a variety of regulations that relate to privacy.

- Under the Gramm-Leach-Bliley Act (also known as the Financial Modernization Act of 1999 and codified at 15 U.S.C. 6801-6809 and 6821-6827), the FTC has issued regulations (16 C.F.R. Part 313) to ensure that financial institutions protect the privacy of consumers' personal financial information.[15] The main privacy protection provision is the Financial Privacy Rule, which governs the collection and disclosure of customers' personal financial information by financial institutions.[16] In brief, the Financial Privacy Rule requires covered institutions to give consumers privacy notices that explain the institutions' information-sharing practices, gives consumers the right to limit certain types of sharing of their financial information on an opt-out basis, and puts some limits on how anyone receiving nonpublic personal information from a financial institution can use or re-disclose the information.

In addition, the FTC has also promulgated the Safeguards Rule, which requires financial institutions to have a security plan to protect the confidentiality and integrity of personal consumer information. Such a plan has administrative, technical, and physical information safeguards, and is intended to protect against any unauthorized access that might harm the consumer. Finally, other provisions of the Gramm-Leach-Bliley Act also affect how a company conducts business, such as a prohibition on financial institutions disclosing customers' account numbers to non-affiliated companies for marketing purposes.

- Under Section 114 of the Fair and Accurate Credit Transactions Act of 2003, the FTC (in cooperation with the federal agencies regulating financial services, such as the Securities and Exchange Commission and the Commodity Futures Trading Commission, and the National Credit Union Administration) promulgated regulations specifying procedures under which financial institutions would protect account holders from

---

[15]"Financial institutions" include banks, securities firms, insurance companies, and other companies providing certain types of financial products and services to consumers, including lending, brokering, or servicing any type of consumer loan, transferring or safeguarding money, preparing individual tax returns, providing financial advice or credit counseling, providing residential real estate settlement services, collecting consumer debts, and an array of other activities.

[16]See Federal Trade Commission, "In Brief: The Financial Privacy Requirements of the Gramm-Leach-Bliley Act," available at http://www.ftc.gov/bcp/conline/pubs/buspubs/glbshort.htm.

identity theft. Section 151 directed these agencies to jointly develop a summary of the rights of identity theft victims that would be made available to all such victims. Regulations issued under Section 211 established a single source through which a consumer could obtain a free credit report. Section 216 directed these agencies and the Securities and Exchange Commission to promulgate regulations for the disposal of consumer report information and records, whether they are stored in electronic or paper form. Examples of consumer reports include credit reports, credit scores, reports businesses or individuals receive with information relating to employment background, check writing history, insurance claims, residential or tenant history, and medical history.

• Under the Children's Online Privacy Protection Act (15 U.S.C. 6501-6506), the FTC is responsible for promulgating regulations (16 C.F.R. Part 312) implementing the protections of the act. These protections require that operators of commercial Web sites and online services directed to collect or knowingly collecting personal information from children under 13 must (1) notify parents of their information practices; (2) obtain verifiable parental consent before collecting a child's personal information; (3) give parents a choice as to whether their child's information will be disclosed to third parties; (4) provide parents access to their child's information; (5) let parents prevent further use of collected information; (6) not require a child to provide more information than is reasonably necessary to participate in an activity; and (7) maintain the confidentiality, security, and integrity of the information.

The rule-making authority of the FTC described above illustrates a common relationship between statutory authority and regulation. The U.S. Congress passes legislation that lays out the general issues and principles in question, but leaves it to a regulating agency to work out the details of how that legislation should be implemented. But this relationship is not the only possible one, and in some instances, Congress has delegated extremely broad regulatory authority to an agency, thus making it the primary source of guidance on a major privacy-related topic.

A good example of this phenomenon is apparent in the privacy-protecting regulations of the Health Insurance Portability and Accountability Act of 1996. Legislators understood very well that the privacy of personal health information was a central issue for health insurance portability, but they were unable to reach agreement on the nature and scope of the appropriate privacy protections. Thus, Section 264 of HIPAA directed the secretary of the Department of Health and Human Services (DHHS) to promulgate regulations on appropriate privacy standards (covering at least the rights that an individual who is a subject of individually identifiable health information should have, the procedures that should be established for the exercise of such rights, and the uses and disclosures of such information that should be authorized or required) if the U.S. Congress did not pass appropriate privacy legislation within 3 years of HIPAA's enactment. This is indeed what happened, and the final privacy rule was published in the Federal Register (65 FR 82462) on December 28, 2000. On August 14, 2002, the Final Modifications to the Privacy Rule were published in the Federal Register.[17]

In short, Congress anticipated its possible inability to reach agreement on the contentious issue of health care privacy, and delegated to the DHHS secretary the regulatory authority to act in its stead.

4.4 EXECUTIVE ORDERS AND PRESIDENTIAL DIRECTIVES

As the chief executive, the president of the United States has considerable latitude to direct the activities of various executive branch agencies. Some directives or executive orders have a bearing on privacy, as illustrated below.

One example is Executive Order 13145, issued on February 8, 2000. This executive order prohibited the federal government and its agencies from using genetic testing in any employment decision, and specifically forbids federal employers from requesting or requiring that employees undergo genetic tests of any kind. In addition, it forbids federal employers from using genetic information to classify employees in such a way that deprives them of advancement opportunities, such as promotion for overseas posts.

A second example is Executive Order 13181, issued on December 20, 2000. This executive order declared as the policy of the government of the United States that law enforcement may not use protected health information concerning an individual that is discovered during the course of health oversight activities for unrelated civil, administrative, or criminal investigations of a non-health oversight matter, except when the balance of relevant factors weighs clearly in favor of its use.

A third example is a presidential order issued in 2002 that authorized the U.S. National Security Agency to eavesdrop on Americans and others inside the United States to search for evidence of terrorist activity under certain circumstances without the court-approved warrants ordi-

---

[17]For more information, see U.S. Department of Health and Human Services, "Medical Privacy—National Standards to Protect the Privacy of Personal Health Information: Background and General Information," available at http://www.hhs.gov/ocr/hipaa/bkgrnd.html.

narily required for domestic wiretapping.[18] This presidential order is still classified.

Orders and directives such as these clearly have a potential for affecting the privacy interests of Americans. But it is important to note that they are limited in at least three important ways.

- Though they are authoritative statements of presidential direction, their implementation must be consistent with existing statutory law.
- Executive orders have the force of law, but only with respect to executive branch agencies.
- Executive orders have no direct impact or force on private sector entities, although because they change the behavior of government, they can have considerable indirect impact.

Upon signing a law, presidents often issue a signing statement that is published in the Federal Register and that documents the presidential interpretation of how the law should be construed. Signing statements do not have the force of law, but if a president directs an agency to behave in a manner that is allegedly contravened by the law, or by some other law, only court action can force the agency to cease and desist.

4.5 STATE PERSPECTIVES

As one might expect within a federal system such as the U.S. system, legal protection of privacy varies vastly from state to state—reflecting what are often little more than anecdotal experiences that have triggered legislative safeguards. Table 4.1 indicates the variation in state laws regarding privacy for the first 16 states, listed alphabetically.

Such diversity is not inherently problematic; one recalls Justice Louis Brandeis's commendation for the role that unusually progressive states might play as "laboratories" for reform and innovation. The problem in regard to privacy protection, however, is the inevitably broad reach across much (if not all) of the nation of especially restrictive measures, and the potentially heavy burdens of compliance for those business entities that serve clients and customers in many states.

Efforts to protect the privacy of sensitive (and even not-so-sensitive) financial data illustrate the problem extremely well. In the mid to late 1990s, North Dakota and Minnesota each enacted uniquely protective measures, ostensibly to shield its own citizens from unwelcome sharing or disclosure of financial information. It soon became apparent to insur-

---

[18]James Risen and Eric Lichtblau, "Bush Lets U.S. Spy on Callers Without Courts," *New York Times*, December 16, 2005.

TABLE 4.1 Privacy Laws by State

Category	US	AL	AK	AZ	AR	CA	CO	CT	DE	DC	FL	GA	HI	IL	IN	IA	KS
Arrest records	O	X	O	X	O	X	X	X	X	X	X	X	X	X	X	O	O
Bank records	X	X	X	O	O	X	O	X	O	O	X	O	O	X	O	X	O
Cable TV	X	O	O	O	O	X	O	X	O	X	O	O	O	X	O	O	O
Computer crime	X	X	X	X	X	X	X	X	X	O	X	X	X	X	X	X	X
Credit	X	O	O	X	O	X	O	X	X	O	X	X	O	O	O	X	X
Criminal justice	X	X	X	X	X	X	X	X	X	O	X	X	X	X	X	X	X
Government data banks	X	X	X	X	O	X	X	X	X	X	X	O	X	X	X	X	X
Employment	X	O	X	O	O	X	O	X	X	X	X	O	O	X	O	O	O
Insurance	X	O	O	X	O	X	O	X	O	O	X	X	O	X	O	X	X
Mailing lists	X	O	O	X	O	X	X	X	X	O	X	O	X	X	X	X	X
Medical	X	O	X	X	X	X	O	X	X	X	X	X	X	X	X	X	X
Miscellaneous	X	O	O	O	O	X	O	X	O	O	X	O	X	X	X	O	O
Polygraph results	X	X	X	X	X	X	O	X	X	X	O	X	X	X	O	X	O
Privacy statutes	X	O	X	X	O	X	O	X	X	O	X	X	X	X	O	O	O
Privileges	O	X	X	O	O	O	X	X	X	O	O	X	O	O	X	O	O
School records	X	O	O	X	O	X	X	X	X	O	X	O	O	X	O	X	O
Social Security numbers	O	O	O	O	O	O	O	O	O	O	O	O	O	O	O	O	O
Tax records	X	O	X	X	O	O	X	O	X	O	X	X	X	X	O	O	X
Telephone solicitation	X	O	X	X	X	X	X	X	O	O	X	X	X	X	X	X	X
Testing	O	O	O	O	O	O	O	X	O	O	X	O	X	O	O	X	O
Wiretaps	X	X	X	X	X	X	X	X	X	X	X	X	X	X	X	X	X

[a] An X in indicates that the state has a privacy law relevant to the category indicated, although it does not indicate how effective or strong the law is. Only the first 16 states (in alphabetical order) are listed.

SOURCE: Data from http://www.epic.org/privacy/consumer/states.html.

ance and financial service providers that the need for compliance with this exceptionally protective law went well beyond the state of its origin and initial reach. Since North Dakotans and Minnesotans might well move to other states, while policy holders or customers from elsewhere would move to North Dakota and Minnesota, the costs of bringing the entire national business enterprise into compliance with the strictest standard eventually seemed less onerous than the incalculable costs of confining compliance to residents of the target state. What ensued was a novel kind of reverse Gresham's law, in which the most rigorous standard eventually shaped the norm, effectively forcing divergent standards to yield by default.

Congress could, of course, achieve uniformity in several ways. In a very few areas—patent, copyright, and admiralty being the most familiar—the Constitution itself makes federal law exclusive and thus completely forestalls any possibility of variant regulation at other levels. But the exclusively federal field is the rarity, and in most regulatory realms power is shared between national and state government until and unless Congress or the federal courts declare otherwise.

The most obvious means of setting a single national standard would be for Congress itself to regulate the activity in question, and in so doing either declare that inconsistent state and local standards were being preempted, or establish that the federal norm was the exclusive mode of regulation, thus precluding even consistent action by state and local government. A less obvious but theoretically possible approach would be for Congress to enter a regulatory area only to the extent necessary to limit or ensure uniformity in the standards that states and localities may set, but without creating its own federal regulatory system—in other words, leaving the actual regulation to other levels of government, but at the same time ensuring a degree of uniformity by setting parameters and boundaries for the exercise of that authority by states and localities.

There is one precedent for such action. In 1999, Congress amended the Driver's Privacy Protection Act (DPPA) to forbid state departments of motor vehicles and law enforcement officials to sell or otherwise release personal information obtained in connection with any motor vehicle or license record without affirmative opt-in consent. The constitutionality of this law was challenged by a group of states that apparently wished to retain the revenue streams associated with the sale of such data.

In 2000, the U.S. Supreme Court unanimously sustained the constitutionality of this act in *Reno v. Condon*, 528 U.S. 141 (2000). The DPPA was found to be not only an appropriate exercise of Congress's power over interstate commerce, but also one that invaded no state powers protected by the Ninth and Tenth Amendments.

The *Condon* decision was unusual and stands as one among a very few decisions in the Rehnquist Court that sustains an act of Congress imposing obligations on the states or limiting state power. By contrast, during the late 1980s and much of the 1990s the Supreme Court was generally unsympathetic to congressional initiatives in areas of state and local interest and authority. Whereas previous Courts would likely have had little trouble finding federal power under the commerce (or other) clause, the Rehnquist Court rejected on constitutional grounds a number of acts that seemed to be perfectly reasonable and appropriate exercises of federal power. Two such decisions were one striking down federal laws that sought to ensure public school safety by requiring installation of metal detectors, and another that granted relief to women who had been victims of sexual assaults and wished to seek redress in federal courts. In these and a host of other situations in which the Warren Court and even the Burger Court would almost routinely have sustained the power of Congress to act, the Rehnquist Court found federal power lacking under its view of Article I of the Constitution, and deferred to state power under the Ninth and Tenth Amendments. Although the justices were sharply divided in these cases, a clear majority consistently sided with the states throughout this decade.

Thus, the extent to which the *Condon* decision indicates a willingness of the Supreme Court to uphold congressional preemption of state laws regarding privacy is unknown. And a new chief justice—John Roberts— has been recently sworn in, making predictions about future court action in this domain much more uncertain than they already were.

Finally, it should be noted that state laws can have national impact. The best such example is California's SB-1386 (sometimes known as the California Security Breach Information Act), which mandated the disclosure of compromises in the security of certain types of personal information. Even though the law ostensibly affected only enterprises operating in California, that many businesses affected by the law have multistate operations has meant that residents of other states have also sometimes been notified when their personal information has been compromised. In addition, the passage of this law has spurred a number of other states to attempt the passage of similar legislation.[19] (As this report is being written, Congress is considering a law (H.R. 4127, the Data Accountability and Trust Act) to set uniform standards across the states for disclosure in the event of such breaches; as written, some proposals for this law would reduce notification and disclosure requirements for some states.)

---

[19]For additional discussion, see Eric M. Friedberg and Michael F. McGowan, *Lost Backup Tapes, Stolen Laptops and Other Tales of Data Breach Woe*, white paper from Stroz Friedberg, LLC, Washington, D.C., June 26, 2006.

4.6 INTERNATIONAL PERSPECTIVES ON PRIVACY POLICY

Interest in and concern about privacy as a legal and a policy matter are certainly not limited to the United States. A review of perspectives on privacy around the world (Appendix B) suggests that the issues usually covered under the rubric of privacy in the United States are also evident in other Western nations, although they tend to be couched in a language that avoids explicit reference to "privacy" or closely related terms. Instead, the term "data protection" seems to have gained broad popularity, especially in Europe and, to a lesser extent, elsewhere, although the term "data privacy" is becoming more prominent. A number of other nations also use terms such as "personal integrity" or "information self-determination."

U.S. perspectives on privacy rights are shaped by a view that tends to focus primarily on the benefits of such rights for individuals as individuals: individuality, autonomy, dignity, emotional release, self-evaluation, and so on. Although such concerns also characterize the debate in many other nations, the balance and emphases of these other debates are often different. For example, the German jurisprudential perspective emphasizes that the value of data privacy norms lies in their ability to secure the necessary conditions for active citizen participation in public life, in other words, to secure a flourishing democracy, whereas this perspective is arguably underdeveloped in U.S. jurisprudence.

Finally, it is important to note that the United States does not protect privacy as extensively or as comprehensively as some other nations, notably the member states of the European Union. This is best illustrated by the absence of comprehensive data privacy legislation regulating the U.S. private sector and the absence of an independent agency (data protection authority or privacy commissioner) to specifically oversee regulation of data privacy matters. Whether this absence reflects differences in the popular support for privacy in various nations is much less clear. For example, it can be attributable to differences in perceptions of the degree to which privacy is or will be threatened—one might easily argue that the comprehensive nature of European data privacy regulation reflects traumas induced by relatively recent, firsthand experience of totalitarian oppression. Or the U.S. approach might be due to skepticism about the value and appropriateness of government involvement in the social sphere.

4.7 THE IMPACT OF NON-U.S. LAW ON PRIVACY

In an increasingly globalized economy, it might be expected that the laws of foreign nations might have a privacy impact on U.S. citizens and businesses—and this is indeed the case. Two examples will illustrate:

• In 1998, the European Commission's Directive on Data Protection went into effect. This directive was intended to prohibit the transfer of personal data to non-European Union nations that do not meet the European "adequacy" standard for privacy protection. However, differing approaches of the United States and the European Union to protecting privacy might have hampered the ability of U.S. companies to engage in many trans-Atlantic transactions.[20] While some privacy advocates at the time had hoped that the directive would force the United States to move significantly in the direction of the European approach to protecting privacy (i.e., in the direction of comprehensive privacy protection), the United States and the European Union agreed on a "safe harbor" approach.[21] Under this approach, any U.S. company may self-certify that it agrees to adhere to the safe harbor's requirements, which are based in large measure on the fair information practices described in Chapter 1. Enforcement of the safe harbor takes place in the United States in accordance with U.S. law and is carried out primarily by the private sector, backed up as needed by government enforcement of the federal and state statutes prohibiting "unfair and deceptive" trade practices. Companies in certifiable compliance with safe harbor requirements are deemed to meet the European "adequacy" standard.

• In 2004, Yahoo! (more specifically, its Chinese subsidiary) provided Chinese government authorities the computer IP address and other information that was used to link specific e-mail messages to the e-mail account of Shi Tao, a former Chinese journalist. The information—generally regarded as non-public—was used to convict and sentence Tao to 10 years in prison in 2004, for e-mailing groups in the United States about the return of Chinese emigrants for the 15th anniversary of the Tiananmen Square incident.[22] More recently, Yahoo! has been accused of releasing information generally regarded as non-public from an online discussion group that led to the conviction of Li Zhi, a former civil servant, in December 2003, who is serving 8 years in prison for the charge of "inciting sub-

---

[20]As discussed in Appendix B, the United States protects privacy by relying on a sectoral approach based on a mix of legislation, regulation, and self-regulation. The European Union relies on comprehensive legislation that is, in part, based on the use of government data protection agencies, registration of databases containing personal information with those agencies, and in some instances prior approval of the data subject before any processing of that data may begin.

[21]For more information, see http://www.export.gov/safeharbor.

[22]Court documents, released by Reporters Without Borders, reveal that the Yahoo! subsidiary in Hong Kong supplied the information to the Chinese authorities revealing the user's identity. For a translated copy of the court verdict, see http://www.rsf.org/article.php3?id_article=14884.

version."[23] Yahoo! has declined to comment on these cases or to disclose how often it provides user information to Chinese authorities. However, Yahoo! has acknowledged that it lacks control over some operations since Yahoo! China merged with Alibaba.com, a Chinese company that holds 60 percent of the company.[24]

These examples barely scratch the surface of an extraordinarily complex and ill-defined international policy environment in which non-U.S. organizations and institutions have an impact on U.S. companies and policy. For many years, the Organisation for Economic Co-operation and Development was actively involved in the negotiation of guidelines for the management and protection of personal information that had become a substantial part of the trans-border data flows essential to international trade in information goods and services. Although debates about trade became tangled up within fierce ideological struggles about "cultural imperialism" and the New World Information and Communication Order,[25] ideological concerns were replaced to some degree by concerns about market power as the development of a more closely integrated European marketplace was thought to depend on more uniform policies regarding the treatment of personal information.

In order to understand the development of privacy policies at the international level, it is important to understand the interests, strategies, and resources of different sorts of participants in the policy process. Although traditional sources of power and influence such as national governments and representatives from key missions and administrative agencies with interests and responsibility for national security and foreign trade have to be considered along with the more complex interests of transnational firms, it is also important to consider the role of the epistemic community of policy experts who are engaged in the elaboration of new ways of thinking about the international arena.[26]

Policy formation at the international level is also characterized by a considerable amount of negotiation, bargaining, and compromise among

---

[23]Hiawatha Bray, "Yahoo Said to Aid China in 2003 Subversion Trial," *Boston Globe*, February 9, 2006, available at http://www.boston.com/business/technology/articles/2006/02/09/yahoo_said_to_aid_china_in_2003_subversion_trial/.

[24]Eric Schonfeld, "Analysis: Yahoo's China Problem," *CNNMoney.com*, February 8, 2006, available at http://money.cnn.com/2006/02/08/technology/yahoo_china_b20/.

[25]Thomas L. McPhail, "Electronic Colonialism: The Future of International Broadcasting and Communication," *Sage Library of Social Research*, Revised Second Edition, Vol. 126, Sage Publications, 1987.

[26]Jonathan D. Aronson, "The Evolution of Global Networks: The Precarious Balance Between Governments and Markets," pp. 241-255 in Eli Noam and Alex Wolfson, eds., *Globalism and Localism in Telecommunications*, Elsevier Science, 1997.

different stakeholders. Coalitions among business leaders facing similar limitations on their ability to make use of personal information for marketing purposes pooled their resources to support intensive lobbying efforts against the opt-in requirements that seemed likely in the European Union in 1990.[27] These business coalitions also sought and received support from their nations' trade commissions because of a well-placed concern about regulatory threats to the market in data-processing services. Coalitions among regulators were also common.[28] Privacy and data protection commissioners met to develop strategies for preserving what they saw as important progress in the protection of privacy.

One result of the participation of so many actors with such varied interests and resources was the development of highly complex policy instruments. Unique and often contradictory policy perspectives continue to challenge policy advocates largely dependent on grants from foundations. Global policies regulating the treatment of personal information as it moves across virtual borders raise important questions about national sovereignty and respect for policies reflecting cultural values and social history.[29] The presumed need to identify the location of the jurisdiction from which an order is placed, or is to be delivered, in order to determine whether a particular transaction can be completed within the laws of that region raises a complex set of issues for supporters of autonomous choice.[30]

---

[27]Priscilla M. Regan, "American Business and the European Data Protection Directive: Lobbying Strategies and Tactics," pp. 199-216 in Colin Bennett and Rebecca Grant, eds., *Visions of Privacy: Policy Choices for the Digital Age*, University of Toronto Press, 1999.

[28]Colin J. Bennett and Charles D. Raab, *The Governance of Privacy: Policy Instruments in Global Perspective*, Ashgate Publishing, 2003.

[29]National Research Council, *Global Networks and Local Values: A Comparative Look at Germany and the United States*, National Academy Press, Washington, D.C., 2001.

[30]Priscilla M. Regan, "'Dry Counties' in Cyberspace: Governance and Enforcement Without Geographic Borders," pp. 257-276 in Thomas Leinbach and Stanley Brunn, eds., *Worlds of E-Commerce: Economic, Geographical and Social Dimensions*, John Wiley & Sons, 2001.

5

The Politics of Privacy Policy
in the United States

Privacy policies are formulated in response to problems in the management of access to information about persons or their effects, or to images or impressions of people as may be derived from the analysis of data. But many factors affect the formulation of policy.

5.1 THE FORMULATION OF PUBLIC POLICY

Protection of privacy has been an objective of public policy for at least a century, especially for the legislative branch. When New York state's highest court declined, in 1902, to create a cause of action for invasions of privacy, the legislature promptly intervened. The result of that intervention was, at that time, the most rigorous and far-reaching of state privacy statutes, and remains among the strongest even to this day. New York has hardly been alone in responding to concerns about the status of personal privacy, and nearly all states provide such protection today, either by statute or by court decision. By the 1920s, protecting privacy had become a matter of federal policy as Congress focused first on making wiretapping unlawful.[1]

Although legislators have addressed privacy to a considerable extent, it is less clear that the legal safeguards for privacy that they have enacted

---

[1]It is unclear today whether the legislation of the time reflected more a concern about the integrity of the burgeoning telecommunications system rather than a fear that wiretapping would imperil the privacy of individual conversations.

reflect political pressure from a public distressed in general about unwelcome exposure of their private lives. Public concerns about privacy, and pressures for its protection, seem closely related to episodic "horror stories" about violations of privacy (at least violations perceived to be egregious). On an ongoing basis, scholars of public policy often view the development of policy as a struggle between interests, and the history of policy regarding privacy illustrates this point clearly. Privacy is not pursued or defended by public policy makers in the United States as a fundamental right to be protected. Instead it is framed as one of a number of interests that have to be weighed on the scales of social worth. As a result, the scope of privacy concerns has been narrowed to a limited array of individual and personal interests.

For example, Priscilla Regan notes that public policy regulation can serve the interests of the nation or the society for the collective good. She underscores the distinction between privacy policy as a struggle over ideas and privacy policy as a struggle between interests.[2] Because the idea of privacy is so broad and complex as to defy specification, privacy policy has rarely been pursued on the basis of privacy as a fundamental value. Unlike the values of "competition" and "efficiency" that have emerged as compelling rationales for the pursuit of a broad range of policy outcomes, privacy policies have been far more narrowly drawn. Some of those opposed to the extension or reinforcement of privacy rights have tended to argue that privacy was the enemy of efficiency; respecting privacy imposed costs on actors and agents in ways that could not be justified in economic terms. This was nearly always the case when opponents of privacy restraint sought to justify the use of some new technology of surveillance that was supposed to enhance security and reduce fraud, waste, and abuse in the delivery of goods and services.[3] From the perspective of business, opposition to measures to enhance individual privacy was often cast in terms of unnecessarily increasing the regulatory burden of compliance. Because the value of economic efficiency had emerged as the dominant rationale for policy choice in the decade between 1974 and 1984,[4] much of the legislation that was presented as preserving privacy interests actually helped to normalize a set of routine institutional practices that narrowed the scope of privacy's reach.[5]

One way of framing the interests at stake is according to the distribu-

---

[2]Priscilla M. Regan, *Legislating Privacy: Technology, Social Values, and Public Policy*, University of North Carolina Press, 1995.

[3]David Lyon, *Surveillance Society: Monitoring Everyday Life*, Open University Press, 2001.

[4]Regan identified seven bills passed in this decade that explicitly traded privacy interests against expected gains in efficiency. See Regan, *Legislating Privacy*, 1995, p. 88.

[5]See Oscar H. Gandy, Jr., *The Panoptic Sort: A Political Economy of Personal Information*, Westview Press, 1994, pp. 209-211, for a discussion of the Video Privacy Protection Act of 1998.

tions of costs and benefits among the stakeholders involved in any policy issue. For example, James Q. Wilson distinguishes between "majoritarian," "entrepreneurial," "client," and "interest group" politics in terms of whether the costs and benefits are broadly or narrowly distributed.[6] In this framework, majoritarian politics describes outcomes in which both the costs and the benefits are widely distributed. Entrepreneurial politics describes outcomes in which the costs are concentrated, while the benefits are widely distributed. In the case of client politics, the benefits are concentrated while the costs are widely distributed. Finally, in the case of interest group politics, both the costs and the benefits are narrowly concentrated.[7] Expectations regarding the distribution of costs and benefits help to determine the level of interest and involvement of stakeholders in the policy process. The mass media play a critical role in shaping the expectations of the general public about the ways in which the policies will affect their well-being. It is only in the case of interest group politics, where the benefits and the costs are narrowly distributed, that public concerns about a particular policy outcome are dormant.

Theorists of policy change such as Baumgartner and Jones associate changes in U.S. political agendas within shifts in the legislative venues and evaluative orientations of policy entrepreneurs concerned about emergent and maturing technologies.[8] Understanding cyclical and even irregular patterns of change in public policy requires considerable attention to the role of organized interests that are able to focus their resources on committees and in other venues where their chance of success is higher. Organized interests, especially those with a long-standing institutional claim on resources derived from existing government practice, tend to prefer to keep the discussion private, or limited to a manageable group of insiders.

Multiple jurisdictions also provide many venues for different stakeholders to pursue their interests. Government policies affecting privacy are established at the administrative, legislative, and judicial levels in states, nations, and economic regions like the European Union, as well as at the international level.[9] The fact that these policies can vary quite substantially from jurisdiction to jurisdiction means that information-inten-

[6]James Q. Wilson, "The Politics of Regulation," pp. 357-94 in James Q. Wilson, ed., *The Politics of Regulation*, Basic Books, New York, 1980.

[7]Elizabeth E. Bailey, "The Evolving Politics of Telecommunications Regulation," pp. 379-399 in Roger Noll and Monroe Price, eds., *A Communications Cornucopia*, Brookings Institution Press, Washington, D.C., 1998.

[8]Frank Baumgartner and Bryan Jones, *Agendas and Instability in American Politics*, University of Chicago Press, 1993.

[9]Colin J. Bennett and Charles D. Raab, *The Governance of Privacy: Policy Instruments in Global Perspective*, Ashgate Publishing, 2003.

sive businesses and their trade associations have to invest considerable time, effort, and economic resources to ensure that their standards and practices conform to local regulations. They are also likely to be involved in coordinated attempts at modifying those policies, or negotiating special exceptions.[10]

The large number of stakeholders leads to a proliferation of voices speaking on privacy issues in national and state councils. Lawmakers not only hear from both sides of almost any privacy proposal but also receive potentially conflicting counsel from organizations with nearly indistinguishable titles. While such a cacophony complicates the lawmaking process in almost any contentious area of public policy, the range of the dissonance in the privacy area adds a new dimension to the process.

Consistent with the view of privacy policy as a struggle between competing interests, efforts to protect privacy have not had much resonance with lawmakers seeking to broaden their electoral appeal. As recently as 1995, Priscilla Regan, drawing on her Capitol Hill experience as well as her extensive scholarship, concluded that "privacy issues do not provoke great electoral support" and so members of Congress are "unlikely to champion or adopt these issues because they believe there will be an electoral payoff."[11] Indeed, noting that "privacy has not been an issue in the electoral arena at either the national or the state level," Regan finds no obvious "explanation for why a member of Congress chooses to champion privacy issues."

Politicians, especially members of the House of Representatives, who are almost continually in search of support for re-election, are careful to select issues that can attract press coverage. As an issue, privacy does not usually generate support and opposition along party lines, but instead finds bipartisan agreement through compromise and negotiation after extended periods of debate.[12] Indeed, in her review of the legislative history of major privacy bills passed before 1992, Regan suggests that these issues were "on the congressional agenda for years, if not decades, before Congress passed legislation."[13] Indeed, the candidate who runs on a privacy protection platform is a rarity, and the evidence is scarce at best that voters care enough to make elections turn on which candidate offers the boldest privacy-protective platform.

---

[10]Priscilla M. Regan, "American Business and the European Data Protection Directorate: Lobbying Strategies and Tactics," pp. 217-228 in C.J. Bennett and R. Grant, eds., *Visions of Privacy: Policy Choices for the Digital Age*, University of Toronto Press, 1999.

[11]Regan, *Legislating Privacy*, 1995.

[12]Bipartisanship, of course, does not mean that support is unanimous throughout the membership of each party. Rather, it means that any given measure can appeal to a substantial number of members from both sides of the aisle.

[13]Regan, *Legislating Privacy*, 1995.

This is not to say that legislators have never taken the lead in fighting for privacy protection. For example, a number of such leaders can be identified, including former Senator Sam Ervin and former Representative Robert Kastenmeier. Senator Ervin was especially dogged in his pursuit of the kind of statutory restraints on government data gathering that eventually became the Privacy Act of 1974.[14] Concerns about the excesses of the McCarthy era and the emergence of a "national security state" attracted the interest of Representative Kastenmeier to problems of surveillance.[15] More recently, Representatives Ed Markey (D-Mass.) and Joe Barton (R-Tex.) cooperated in 2001 to provide privacy protections in the Gramm-Leach-Bliley Act, discussed further in Chapter 6.

The lack of abiding electoral concern about privacy can be explained in part by a deep-seated popular ambivalence about just how—and how far—privacy should be protected. David Brin aptly observes that "whenever a conflict arises between privacy and accountability, people demand the former for themselves and the latter for everybody else."[16] Such paradoxical views exist "in almost every realm of modern life, from special prosecutors investigating the finances of political figures to worried parents demanding that lists of sex offenders be made public." The framing and passage of broadly acceptable privacy-enabling legislation have undoubtedly been impeded by the existence of such ambivalent views, and by the imposition of irreconcilable demands by constituents who are often unaware of the conflict they create by insisting that privacy be protected as far, but only as far, as necessary to serve subjective needs and interests.

When privacy concerns do emerge on the public agenda, the development of privacy policy almost inevitably involves some conflict over the "balancing" of competing interests and values.[17] While privacy is not weightless, considerations of efficiency, security, and global competitiveness hold considerable sway in the policy debate.

Moreover, contemporaneously with the rise of the Internet as a pervasive technological substrate for much of society, policy makers have demonstrated in recent years an increasing tendency to think about pri-

---

[14]David F. Linowes, *Privacy in America: Is Your Private Life in the Public Eye?*, University of Illinois Press, 1989, p. 2. Regan suggests that Ervin actually resisted labeling his concerns about government surveillance as "privacy" concerns, preferring instead to emphasize the value of "due process."

[15]Regan, *Legislating Privacy*, 1995, p. 202.

[16]David Brin, *The Transparent Society: Will Technology Force Us to Choose Between Privacy and Freedom?*, Addison-Wesley, 1998.

[17]Charles D. Raab, "From Balancing to Steering: New Directions for Data Protection," pp. 68-93 in Colin Bennett and Rebecca Grant, eds., *Visions of Privacy: Policy Choices in the Digital Age*, University of Toronto Press, 1999.

vacy in terms of technological systems, marketplace incentives, and even self-regulation rather than government regulation. Such perspectives are consistent with growing skepticism among many elected representatives about government as a meaningful and positive influence on the lives of citizens.

Among the most common criticisms of U.S. privacy policy making is its eclectic and piecemeal quality. Instead of regulating from the top down after a comprehensive overview of privacy needs and concerns, as do most other Western nations, the United States tends to address particular problems as they arise, thus moving from the bottom up.[18] The resulting patchwork reflects little broad policy making, and much intuitive response to momentary concerns. There is little correlation, in consequence, between the importance or value of protecting certain elements of privacy (as might be determined with the benefit of a comprehensive framework to prioritize different privacy concerns) and the degree to which U.S. laws do in fact protect those interests.

A classic example of this patchwork is the Video Privacy Protection Act of 1998. During confirmation hearings over the eventually thwarted Supreme Court nomination of appeals court judge Robert H. Bork, a Washington, D.C., weekly (*The City Paper*) published a list of videotape titles the judge had recently borrowed from video rental stores. In the wave of popular indignation that followed the defeat of the nomination, Congress easily enacted the Video Privacy Protection Act (VPPA) of 1988, which bars retailers from selling or disclosing video rental records without a customer's permission or a court order. As a result of this eclectic and selective response to a special perceived need, video borrower records have for nearly a decade been better protected than a wide range of arguably more sensitive and vital data, such as personal medical information.

Much the same could be said of the so-called Buckley Amendment (more formally the Family Educational Rights and Privacy Act), adopted in the mid-1970s in response to similar pressure. In that case, a few less-than-fully-satisfied recent university graduates found themselves in powerful staff positions on Capitol Hill and seized an opportunity to bar forever any dissemination of all but minimal information about college students to the news media, or for that matter to any but a tiny group of academic officials with an urgent need for access to such data.

The result of legislative forays like those that produced the Buckley

---

[18]Appendix B addresses the point from a comparative perspective. In addition, the National Research Council report *Global Networks and Local Values* (National Academy Press, Washington, D.C., 2001) elaborates on the difference between U.S. and German perspectives on privacy regulation.

Amendment and VPPA is that certain types of information—specifically college student records and video rental profiles—enjoy a highly elevated, though not altogether logical, level of protection, whereas much highly sensitive information remains far more vulnerable. Regardless of the desirability or undesirability of these specific statutes, few features of the U.S. network of privacy protection could more fairly be faulted than its patchwork or piecemeal quality.

As noted in the National Research Council report *Global Networks and Local Values*, "In practice, the U.S. norm [of privacy protection] is a patchwork of legislation and court decisions arising from episodic scandals and political pressures from both industry and privacy advocates."[19] As a result, the report continues, "highly specialized solutions have been crafted for different technologies (e.g., statutory regimes specific to the protection of postal mail, e-mail, and other Internet communications) and for different subject areas." Although the United States might be credited with the development of privacy as an individual right,[20] the legislative approach to the specification of this right, especially as it relates to the behavior of private firms, has been sectoral and piecemeal, rather than comprehensive.[21] Critics suggest that as a result of this sectoral emphasis, the interests of data users will be more clearly understood and appreciated than the interests of individuals or groups of data subjects.[22]

The patchwork is further complicated by the fact that states are allowed to set higher standards for protecting privacy and may be more protective than national policy requires—at least as long as doing so does not abridge due process or equal protection or violate any other federal constitutional guarantee. To phrase the point quite simply, the U.S. constitution and federal laws generally set a floor but not a ceiling, so that state actions cannot fall below the floor but may surpass the ceiling.

A recent and quite apt example of this dynamic comes from the regulation of the ways in which financial service providers secure the consent of their customers for the use and possible dissemination of certain personal information. Federal law, for the most part, adopts an "opt-out" approach, under which banks and other providers must inform their customers of potential data-sharing practices and can assume acquiescence from a customer's silence—that is, from the customer's refusal to

---

[19]National Research Council, *Global Networks and Local Values*, National Academy Press, Washington, D.C., 2001, p. 141.

[20]Irwin R. Kramer, "The Birth of Privacy Law: A Century Since Warren and Brandeis," *Catholic University Law Review* 39:703-724, 1990.

[21]David H. Flaherty, *Protecting Privacy in Surveillance Societies*, University of North Carolina Press, 1989.

[22]Charles D. Raab and Colin J. Bennett, "The Distribution of Privacy Risks: Who Needs Protection?," *The Information Society* 14:263-274, 1998.

opt out by so informing the provider, as only 2 or 3 percent of customers have in fact done in response to such an invitation. If a single state wishes, however, to empower customers to a higher degree by requiring that they must affirmatively opt in before their consent to data sharing may be inferred, that is an option open to any state.

To date, a number of states (Alaska, California, Vermont, Connecticut, Florida, Illinois, North Dakota) have required that banking and financial services customers be invited to opt in. But even if only one state takes such a position, it effectively requires financial service providers to treat their customers in that state very differently, and to make certain that they have evidence of opting in before any personal data are shared. Such state action may, of course, be challenged on grounds other than due process—for example, as a burden on interstate commerce or invasion of an area in which uniformity is essential even though Congress has not so mandated—but such challenges rarely succeed, since the federal courts often (or even mostly) defer to the judgment of state legislatures on the needs of their citizens.

5.2 PUBLIC OPINION AND THE ROLE OF PRIVACY ADVOCATES

Public opinion is one obvious and important influence on the legislative formulation of many aspects of public policy, and privacy is no exception. A review of public opinion over the last decade performed for the committee suggests the following generalizations:[23]

• The public expresses considerable concern over privacy; this concern appears to have increased over time. Moreover, much of the U.S. public appears to believe that privacy is a fundamental right that they ought to enjoy, and this belief seems to be independent of perceptions of threat.

• People are not concerned about privacy in general; they are concerned about protecting the privacy of sensitive information about themselves. Thus, for example, they are quite willing to agree to contact tracing in the case of AIDS patients, and they are ready to define AIDS as a community health rather than a privacy issue. Most people are not HIV-positive, and they are more concerned about the risks of being infected than about the privacy interests of patients. At the same time, most people are unwilling to have medical information about themselves disclosed without their permission, even when the information does not identify them

---

[23]Amy Corning and Eleanor Singer, "Survey of U.S. Privacy Attitudes," Survey Research Center, University of Michigan, 2003, a paper written under contract to the National Research Council for this project.

by name. In that situation, the privacy value of the information outweighs the juxtaposed social value of "research."

• Public opinion about privacy is not well crystallized; people tend to be highly responsive to the way questions are framed. For example, public support for individual monitoring or surveillance measures can be very high, particularly when questions emphasize the need to combat terrorism. Respondents also generally believe that government will use its powers appropriately. Yet when respondents are reminded that government powers may be abused, or that even properly used powers may reduce the rights and freedoms people enjoy, they appear to be quite concerned about such possibilities.

• Public opinion is responsive to salient events. For example, Alan Westin and others have explored the ways in which public attention to privacy concerns has tended to rise and fall in response to a number of changes in the policy environment.[24] These changes included both long-term trends in the organization of the economy as well as short-term disruptions marked by critical events, such as those on September 11, 2001. Immediately after the September 11 attacks, the U.S. public expressed an increase in support for public policy measures with negative implications for privacy. However, this support has gradually waned in the attack-free years afterward. Similarly, public concerns about privacy jumped in the mid-1970s in the wake of the Watergate scandal and the Church Committee report, but tended downward in subsequent years.[25]

• Public opinion is also responsive to technological developments. For example, concerns have risen with technology developments that make it easier, faster, and cheaper to store, process, and exchange vast amounts of individual-level data, and with the advent of new and expanding techniques for acquiring information about individuals such as data mining to link consumer purchases with demographic information and new techniques of surveillance.

• Despite manifest concerns about privacy, public opinion about privacy is generally not well informed. Because of this, and perhaps for other reasons, individuals do not generally take actions to protect their privacy even though they are highly concerned about personal privacy (e.g., they return warranty cards filled out with personal information even though such information is not needed to validate the warranty). Nevertheless,

---

[24]Alan Westin, "Social and Political Dimensions of Privacy," *Journal of Social Issues* 59(1):431-453, 2003.

[25]*Warrantless FBI Electronic Surveillance*, Book III of the Final Report of the Select Committee to Study Governmental Operations with Respect to Intelligence Activities, United States Senate, U.S. Government Printing Office, Washington, D.C., April 23, 1976. (The Select Committee is popularly known as the Church Committee, after its chair, Frank Church, senator from Idaho.)

their perspectives on privacy may well influence their opinions in other domains and even possibly their behavior. Concerns about privacy and confidentiality do affect people's participation in surveys, and in particular the U.S. decennial census. Specifically, Singer et al. found that concerns about privacy and confidentiality have a small but statistically significant effect on response rates.[26]

• Consumers are often willing to trade away their control over their personal information in return for some benefit, which may be small in absolute terms. Some analysts believe that such behavior is the result of a rational approach on the part of the public to privacy issues, which allegedly weighs the privacy risks against the potential benefits of providing information. Others believe that such behavior results from the average consumer being simply unaware of the ways in which transaction-generated information is gathered and used by businesses on the Web and in other places.[27]

Although public opinion about privacy is shaped by myriad actors that affect the policy-making process (including in particular organized interest groups and policy entrepreneurs),[28] privacy advocacy groups and the mass media are among the most important. Westin's analysis of change in the privacy agenda notes the very important role that publicity or media coverage has played in the policy process, and emergent theory suggests that it is when the policy debate moves into the public sphere that the outcomes of the process are less certain.[29]

Public concern and a legislative response are often activated in response to the efforts of activist organizations concerned with technology, media, and civil liberties more generally.[30] The press and these activist organizations help to raise public awareness about the extent to which many of the business practices that the public assumed were against the

---

[26]Eleanor Singer, Nancy A. Mathiowetz, and Mick P. Couper, "The Role of Privacy and Confidentiality as Factors in Response to the 1990 Census," *Public Opinion Quarterly* 57(4):465-482; and Corning and Singer, "Survey of U.S. Privacy Attitudes," 2003.

[27]Oscar H. Gandy, "Public Opinion Surveys and the Formation of Privacy Policy," *Journal of Social Issues* 59(2):283-299, 2003; Priscilla M. Regan, "From Privacy Rights to Privacy Protection: Congressional Formulation of Online Privacy Policy," in C.C. Campbell and J.F. Stack, Jr., eds., *Congress and the Politics of Emerging Rights*, Blackwell Publishing, Lanham, Md., 2002; and Corning and Singer, "Survey of U.S. Privacy Attitudes," 2003.

[28]Bennett and Raab, *The Governance of Privacy*, 2003, pp. 171-183.

[29]Bruce Berger, "Private Issues and Public Policy: Locating the Corporate Agenda in Agenda-Setting Theory," *Journal of Public Relations Research* 13(2):91-126, 2001.

[30]Alan F. Westin, "Social and Political Dimensions of Privacy," *Journal of Social Issues* 59(2):431-453, 2003; see also Gandy, "Public Opinion Surveys and the Formation of Privacy Policy," 2003.

law are in fact the behavioral norm[31] and alert citizens to the fact that their privacy rights (e.g., those granted under the Privacy Act) may have been infringed. Members of public interest groups, or outsiders to the debate, play a key role in "taking the discussion public" by amplifying public concerns about institutional practices that they oppose.

A number of public interest organizations have established a significant presence within the policy environment as supporters of what they define as the public interest in privacy, and a reasonable argument can be made to suggest that very little in the way of regulatory pro-privacy policy would exist if it were not for the efforts of privacy advocates.[32]

General organizations like the American Civil Liberties Union (ACLU) have long been active in pressing both in court and in lawmaking and regulatory bodies for protection of a range of personal freedoms, privacy among them. The ACLU's concerns continue unabated, indeed intensified, especially in the period after September 11, 2001, and other broad mission organizations have now entered the fray, including some that have found common ground with the ACLU on privacy issues regarding government access to personal information despite being in opposite corners in many other areas.

The most dramatic change in public advocacy groups is that, within the past decade or less, the field has now become far more crowded by the entry of a host of influential specialized groups, such as the Electronic Frontier Foundation, the Electronic Privacy Information Center, Americans for Computer Privacy, the Online Privacy Alliance, the Center for Democracy and Technology, and the Privacy Rights Clearinghouse. A number of these organizations emerged into prominence during what Alan Westin identifies as the "third era of privacy development."

These organizations attempt to influence the policy process through a variety of means, including the mobilization of public opinion. Policy advocates attempt to raise public awareness and concern about privacy by supplying sympathetic reporters and columnists with examples of corporate or government malfeasance, or with references to the "horror stories" of individuals who have been the direct or indirect victims of privacy invasion.[33] These stories help to raise the level of concern that is then reflected in the periodic surveys of public opinion that get reported

---

[31]Joseph Turow, "Americans and Online Privacy: The System Is Broken," a report from the Annenberg Public Policy Center of the University of Pennsylvania, Philadelphia, 2003.

[32]Bennett and Raab, *The Governance of Privacy*, 2003, pp. 42-43.

[33]Timothy E. Cook, *Making Laws and Making News: Media Strategies in the U.S. House of Representatives*, Brookings Institution, Washington, D.C., 1989.

in the press[34] and referred to in testimony in legislative hearings on privacy policy.[35]

Privacy advocates play an important role in the framing of privacy issues. This framing is a strategic activity oriented toward finding the best way to mobilize support or opposition. Privacy advocates have followed the general trend in policy rhetoric away from a discourse of "rights" toward a more instrumentalist framework in support of developing protections for valued interests, and the avoidance of measurable harm.[36] Some argue that this shift from rights to interests reflects a larger shift in policy discourse from talk about citizens and moral rights to talk about consumers and the performance of markets.[37]

Corporate strategies for addressing public opinion differ somewhat from those of public interest organizations in that firms within information-intensive industries can afford to sponsor opinion surveys that are directly relevant to emerging policy deliberations. For example, privacy-related surveys sponsored by Equifax not only enjoyed a high degree of visibility in the press but also were cited in legislative testimony more often than surveys by any other sources.[38]

Finally, surveys by independent sources, such as the Pew Internet and American Life Project, reinforce the general conclusion that the public would prefer the presumption of privacy online at the same time that they express a concern about business practices that challenge that presumption.[39]

5.3 THE ROLE OF REPORTS

The position of privacy on the legislative agenda is often established in response to the release of a special investigative report by a government

---

[34]Timothy E. Cook, *Governing with the News: The News Media as a Political Institution*, University of Chicago Press, 1998.

[35]Gandy, "Public Opinion Surveys and the Formation of Privacy Policy," 2003.

[36]Priscilla M. Regan, "From Privacy Rights to Privacy Protection: Congressional Formulation of Online Privacy Policy," pp. 45-63 in Colton Campbell and John Stack, eds., *Congress and the Politics of Emerging Rights*, Rowman and Littlefield Publishers, 2002.

[37]Oscar H. Gandy, Jr., with the assistance of Francesca Wellings, "The Great Frame Robbery: The Strategic Use of Public Opinion in the Formation of Media Policy," report to the Ford Foundation, 2003. See also Simon G. Davies, "Re-engineering the Right to Privacy: How Privacy Has Been Transformed from a Right to a Commodity," pp. 143-165 in Philip Agre and Marc Rotenberg, eds., *Technology and Privacy: The New Landscape*, MIT Press, Cambridge, Mass.,1997.

[38]Gandy, "Public Opinion Surveys and the Formation of Privacy Policy," 2003, p. 292.

[39]Gandy, "Public Opinion Surveys and the Formation of Privacy Policy," 2003; Regan, "From Privacy Rights to Privacy Protection," 2002; and Corning and Singer, "Survey of U.S. Privacy Attitudes," 2003.

agency, a special task force, a policy center, or an independent commission established with support from foundations or private sector coalitions. A substantial increase in apparent public concern occurred during the 1960s, driven in part by the appearance of such ominous studies as Alan Westin's *Privacy and Freedom* (1969), Jerry Rosenberg's *The Death of Privacy* (1969), and Arthur Miller's *The Assault on Privacy* (1971).

Reports can lay the groundwork for the passage of legislation. In each of the three policy phases identified by Westin, an influential report established the basis for a significant policy response. In the first phase, between 1960 and 1980, a report from the National Academy of Sciences titled *Databanks in a Free Society: Computers, Record-Keeping and Privacy* (Box 5.1) was followed by a report from an advisory committee to the Department of Health, Education, and Welfare that proposed the very influential framework on Fair Information Practices (FIP) that was later adopted by the Organisation for Economic Co-operation and Development.[40] The Watergate scandal and related concerns about the abuses of civil liberties by elements within the intelligence community led to the establishment of a special Senate committee headed by Frank Church. The report generated by the far-ranging investigation of this committee[41] helped to support the passage of the Foreign Intelligence Surveillance Act (1978),[42] the Right to Financial Privacy Act (1978), and the Privacy Protection Act (1980) as an effort to establish more meaningful boundaries around the government's intelligence activities.

Although Westin describes the years between 1980 and 1989 as a period of relative calm, a series of reports by the Office of Technology Assessment and the General Accounting Office focused on the use of computers and information technology within the federal government that raised important privacy concerns. The Computer Matching and Privacy Protection Act and the Employee Polygraph Protection Act of 1988 were the results of those studies.[43]

In the third phase (1990-2002) described by Westin it was not a single investigation or comprehensive report that sparked a legislative response but instead what Westin characterizes as a "stream of national surveys" that focused on a rise in privacy concerns among the public.[44] For example, content analyses designed to assess the presence and quality of the privacy notices of firms engaged in e-commerce were the result of a

[40]Regan, *Legislating Privacy*, 1995.

[41]*Warrantless FBI Electronic Surveillance*, Select Committee to Study Governmental Operations with Respect to Intelligence Activities, 1976.

[42]Whitfield Diffie and Susan Landau, *Privacy on the Line: The Politics of Wiretapping and Encryption*, MIT Press, Cambridge, Mass., 1998.

[43]Regan, *Legislating Privacy*, 1995.

[44]Westin, "Social and Political Dimensions of Privacy," 2003, p. 444.

BOX 5.1
Databanks in a Free Society

In the early 1970s, professors Alan Westin and Michael Baker directed a study investigating how the increasing use of computers was affecting U.S. record-keeping processes and what impact the resulting large-scale collections of data (or databanks) might have on privacy, civil liberties, and due process. Conducted under the aegis of the National Academy of Sciences' Computer Science and Engineering Board, the study was prompted by—among other things—growing concerns about the increasing feasibility and efficiency of collecting and sharing large volumes of personal information, things made much simpler by the use of computer technology.

The study, which included more than 50 project staff site visits to organizations with record-keeping operations, culminated in a final report written by Westin and Baker, *Databanks in a Free Society: Computers, Record-Keeping and Privacy.*[1] The report had five major sections: (1) a brief context-setting discussion of computers and privacy concepts; (2) profiles of the record-keeping practices of 14 organizations from both the public and the private sector, including descriptions of organizational record-keeping practices before the application of computer technology, as well as information on the ways that computers were affecting or changing their record-keeping practices at that time; (3) presentation of the principal findings from the site visits; (4) a discussion of how organizational, legal, and socio-political factors affect the deployment of computer technology; and (5) a discussion of public policy issues in light of the report's findings and forecasts, including several priority areas for civic action.

The report described a "profound public misunderstanding" about the effects of using computers in large-scale record-keeping systems and suggested that U.S. public policy, legislation, and regulation (at that time) had not kept pace with the rapid spread of computer technology and growing public concern. The report also identified a number of policy areas deserving of higher priority by courts and legislatures—for example, citizens' rights to see and contest the contents of their own records; rules for confidentiality and data sharing; limitations on the unnecessary collection of data; technological safeguards for information systems; and the use of Social Security numbers as universal identifiers. The report went on to suggest that the then-present 1970s was the right time for lawmakers to address many of the public policy, civil liberties, and due process issues being brought to light by changing record-keeping technology.

The report has influenced much of the privacy work that has followed it and has been cited extensively, no doubt also informing the policy debate leading up to the passage of the Privacy Act of 1974 (5 U.S.C. Section 552a).

---

[1]Alan F. Westin and Michael A. Baker, *Databanks in a Free Society: Computers, Record-Keeping and Privacy,* Quadrangle Books, New York, 1972. Additional commentary can be found in Alan F. Westin and Michael A. Baker, "Databanks in a Free Society," *ACM SIGCAS Computers and Society* 4(1):25-29, 1973.

renewed activism at the Federal Trade Commission (FTC). The Children's Online Privacy Protection Act of 1998 was the major legislative result of this assessment. Regan suggests that the bill received overwhelming legislative support because of the unusual strength of a broad-based privacy coalition, sustained attention to the issue in the press, and a well-received report from the FTC on the inadequacy of business efforts at self-regulation.[45]

Finally, the discontinuity in the privacy policy environment since September 11, 2001, has been evident in the nature and tone of a number of influential reports released in the aftermath. A primary focus of these reports has been the inability of the U.S. government to "connect the dots" that might indicate a terrorist operation in planning or preparation, and it is not surprising that they have emphasized the importance of improving the government's information collection and analytic capabilities. For example, a special task force organized by the Markle Foundation argued forcefully for the accelerated development of the government's capacity to gather, process, and interpret information from sources and with means that had previously been barred by law.[46] The 9-11 Commission emphasized the key role of information and intelligence in preventing future terrorist actions in the United States and the importance of sharing information among appropriate agencies.[47]

Though the ultimate outcomes remain to be seen, reports cast in such terms may well help to tip the scales toward greater collection, consolidation, and sharing of personal information than had been considered reasonable, appropriate, or just in the past. Indeed, the core fundamentals of the fair information practices that emphasize the minimization of information gathering and limitation of the use of information to the purposes for which it was originally gathered are largely incompatible with the fundamental principles of intelligence analysis, which include notions of collecting everything just in case something might be useful and using any information that might be available.

---

[45]Regan, "From Privacy Rights to Privacy Protection," 2002, p. 58.

[46]*Freedom in the Information Age*, a Report of the Markle Foundation Task Force, October 2002; *Creating a Trusted Network for Homeland Security*, Second Report of the Markle Foundation Task Force, December 2003; *Mobilizing Information to Prevent Terrorism: Accelerating Development of a Trusted Information Sharing Environment*, third report of the Markle Foundation Task Force, July 2006.

[47]National Commission on Terrorist Attacks Upon the United States, *The 9/11 Commission Report*, 2004, available at http://www.9-11commission.gov/report/911Report.pdf.

5.4 JUDICIAL DECISIONS

Periodically we are reminded of the special benefit we expect to derive from the separation of legislative, administrative, and judicial powers.[48] Yet it is clear that the independent decisions and pronouncements of jurists have an enormous influence on the nature of statutory bars and constitutional limits on the actions of public and private actors.

It is difficult to characterize the development of privacy policies through the courts as the same sort of process that is seen with regard to federal and state legislatures. Still, the courts have been the focus of political action involving privacy advocates as well as organized interests in search of relief from a statutorily enforced constraint. Public opinion can be expressed in many different ways, ranging from demonstrations in front of the Supreme Court to "friends of the court" amicus briefs, although the U.S. judiciary has long enjoyed relative independence from the vagaries of public opinion. Nevertheless, some believe that public opinion can at the very least pressure members of the judiciary to provide extended rationales for decisions that appear to conflict with popular views.[49]

It is also difficult to characterize the interactions between legal scholars who engage in extended debates over the meaning and importance of legislative and judicial activities that help to determine the legal status of privacy as a right and abuses as actionable torts. This difficulty extends to the efforts of authoritative bodies, such as the American Law Institute, that have codified the "right of privacy" in successive Restatement(s) of Torts.[50]

The action of the courts is also important to consider because of their corrective function in the face of executive branch opposition or indifference to the privacy agenda. Such opposition or indifference is rarely manifested in declaratory policy by responsible administration officials but can be seen in a lack of compliance with fair information practices. Under such circumstances, it is generally only the courts that can induce the agency or agencies involved to comply, and individual citizens and privacy advocates have had to sue government agencies in order to ensure that the rights of privacy established under the Privacy Act have meaning in practice.[51]

---

[48]Jurgen Habermas, *Between Facts and Norms: Contributions to a Discourse Theory of Law and Democracy*, translated by William Rehg, MIT Press, Cambridge, Mass., 1998.

[49]Habermas, *Between Facts and Norms*, 1998, p. 442.

[50]An initial *Restatement* was published in 1937, but the identification of four separate but ultimately unequal torts was published in 1977, adding weight to the suggestions along these lines offered by William Prosser in 1960 (*Cal. L. Rev.* 48:383).

[51]Flaherty, *Protecting Privacy in Surveillance Societies*, 1989, p. 315.

Individual petitioners in search of relief or compensation for the harms visited upon them by others contribute to the development of the body of laws that are recognized as the torts of privacy. Individuals in pursuit of their own interests have been joined from time to time by "friends of the court" who argue in support of more general principles of law. These advocates may also intervene in the development of case law through their active pursuit of the interests of a broad class of citizens whom they claim to represent. They may act as members of a special interest coalition to challenge the actions of an administrative agency.

It is when those decisions reach the Supreme Court that the political nature of the process becomes more clear. Because there are few restraints on the power of the justices to pursue their own ideological perspectives in supporting or opposing the decisions of their colleagues on the Court, the appointment of judges to the Supreme Court is a highly political act. For example, privacy advocate Robert Ellis Smith has argued that the appointment of William Rehnquist to the Court came just in time for him to demonstrate the extent of his opposition to a privacy agenda that had only been hinted at by his testimony before the Senate on presidential powers.[52] Somewhat ironically, concerns about the private lives of some nominees to the Court have figured prominently in their review.[53]

Although political debate addresses one or another competing values, it is rare that the political debate explicitly addresses tradeoffs. Explicit discussion of tradeoffs does often take place during judicial review, where tensions between competing values, such as those between privacy and the freedom of speech, can be made explicit. It is also here that the almost metaphysical "balancing" among incommensurable values is thought to take place.[54]

5.5 THE FORMULATION OF CORPORATE POLICY

While administrative, legislative, and judicial processes are largely open to public scrutiny, the deliberations of business and other private organizations tend to be more hidden behind a wall of proprietary interest.[55] As a result, most individuals are relatively uninformed about the

---

[52]Rehnquist's testimony before the Senate Judiciary Subcommittee on Constitutional Rights is discussed by Robert Ellis Smith, *Ben Franklin's Web Site: Privacy and Curiosity from Plymouth Rock to the Internet*, Privacy Journal, Providence, R.I., 2000, pp. 263-275.

[53]The cases of Robert Bork and Clarence Thomas are especially relevant because of the privacy concerns that were raised during their consideration.

[54]Cass Sunstein, "Incommensurability and Valuation in Law," pp. 70-107 in C. Sunstein, ed., *Free Markets and Social Justice*, Oxford University Press, 1997.

[55]H. Jeff Smith, *Managing Privacy: Information Technology and Corporate America*, University of North Carolina Press, 1994.

ways in which corporate policies affecting privacy are brought into being.

Private firms, especially those that do business with individual consumers, have always had a privacy policy of one sort or another, even if the policy was implied by routine practice rather than explicitly stated. However, in recent years more firms are establishing formal policies and informing consumers of the nature of those policies than was common in the past. Firms within information-intensive (and therefore privacy-sensitive) businesses such as insurance, health care, finance, telecommunications, and direct marketing to consumers are more likely than other firms to establish a set of formal policies governing the collection and use of personal information.[56] The establishment and posting of privacy policies by firms doing business over the Internet has become a standard business practice, and the lack of a published policy has become an exception.

These policies are often based on guidelines developed by membership associations representing the sectoral interests of firms within a particular industry. Trade associations, such as the Direct Marketing Association, often develop and publish a set of standard practices or codes of ethics that members are expected to honor.

Two privacy-related organizations are also influential in shaping corporate privacy policies. One organization is Privacy & American Business, which is an activity of the non-profit Center for Social & Legal Research, a non-profit, non-partisan public policy think tank exploring U.S. and global issues of consumer and employee privacy and data protection. Launched by Alan Westin in 1993 as a "privacy-sensitive but business-friendly" organization to provide information useful to businesses about privacy,[57] it began training and certifying corporate privacy officers in 2000. A second organization, the International Association of Privacy Professionals, offers the Certified Information Privacy Professional credentialing program and a variety of information resources (newsletters, conferences, discussion forums, and so on).[58]

Firms within industrial sectors that have traditionally been the target of government oversight are more likely than firms in other sectors to have established their own privacy policies—financial services and health care are two of the most obvious, and privacy efforts in these areas have been driven legislatively with the Gramm-Leach-Bliley Act of 1999 for the former and the Health Insurance Portability and Accountability Act of 1996 for the latter. Firms in other business sectors tend not to develop

---

[56]Gandy, *The Panoptic Sort*, 1993.

[57]Westin, "Social and Political Dimensions of Privacy," 2003, p. 443. More information on privacy and U.S. business can be found at http://www.pandab.org/.

[58]For more information on the IAPP, see http://www.privacyassociation.org.

privacy policies until the weight of public opinion demands a response, either from them or from the government.[59] The threat of government regulation of information practices that have aroused public anger and concern often provides an especially powerful incentive for firms to develop their own versions of "fair information practices."

On the basis of his study of a number of firms within privacy-intensive lines of business, Smith identified a characteristic "policy-making cycle" that moves through a period of rudderless "drift" that is disrupted by some form of "external threat" that activates a number of "reactive responses" at different levels of the organization.[60]

On occasion, the external threat that an information-intensive firm is forced to respond to is a class action suit, such as the one filed against DoubleClick for its use of cookies to develop profiles of individuals' navigation of the Web.[61] On other occasions the threat to current or proposed business practices comes from competitors that claim proprietary rights to customer information. On a number of occasions retailers and direct marketers have challenged the right of telephone companies or credit card firms to make use of transaction-generated customer information for their own business purposes.[62]

Conflicts within the corporate policy environment reflect both strategic interests as well as concerns about ethical standards of good business practice. These conflicts represent constraints on the ability of corporate actors to develop a comprehensive position on the privacy rights of employees, consumers, and members of the public at large.[63]

---

[59]Smith, *Managing Privacy*, 1994.

[60]Smith, *Managing Privacy*, 1994, pp. 83-85.

[61]DoubleClick Inc. Privacy Litigation, Case No. 00-CIV-0641, 154 F. Supp. 2d 497 (S.D. N.Y. 2001).

[62]Smith, *Managing Privacy*, 1994, pp. 184-204.

[63]Oscar H. Gandy, Jr., "Dividing Practices: Segmentation and Targeting in the Emerging Public Sphere," pp. 141-159 in W. Bennett and R. Entman, eds., *Mediated Politics: Communication in the Future of Democracy*, Cambridge University Press, 2001.

Part III

Privacy in Context

Chapters 2-5 sketch out the intellectual tools with which the committee addresses privacy in specific contexts. As noted in Chapter 1, privacy in the abstract is an ill-defined concept. However, privacy in specific contexts is much easier to define and talk about.

Chapter 6 ("Privacy and Organizations") discusses how organizations of various kinds use personal information and looks at some of the implications for privacy of such use. In particular, Chapter 6 focuses on the education sector (both K-12 and university), financial institutions, retail establishments, data brokers and aggregators, nonprofit institutions and charities, mass media and publishing companies, and statistical and research agencies. The diversity of these sectors suggests that the interaction of technology and privacy is not an issue that can be limited to only some isolated areas of our society. What this quick look at various sectors of society makes clear is that it is often not the gathering of information itself that is perceived as a violation of privacy, but rather a specific use of that information. In addition, a number of generic questions are suggested by the privacy issues these domains raise, questions that set the stage for a more detailed analysis of three important sectors: health care, libraries, and law enforcement and national security.

Chapter 7 ("Health and Medical Privacy") notes the importance of personal information for providing effective health care, and it describes four approaches for protecting such information: industry self-regulation, legislation and regulation, consumer/patient awareness and self-help, and official advocacy. The chapter also notes that issues related to the privacy of health information will become more salient and important as electronic medical records become more widely deployed.

Chapter 8 ("Libraries and Privacy") addresses the long tradition of sensitivity to privacy issues in the library community. In addition, the library community has been an early adopter of information technology as a way of furthering its mission, and thus the impacts of technological change have manifested themselves very clearly in the library context. Thus, many of the most basic questions about policy can be seen in libraries and among librarians.

Chapter 9 ("Privacy, Law Enforcement, and National Security") addresses some of the starkest polarities in the privacy debate. Since the terrorist attacks on September 11, 2001, some of the loudest arguments have been heard about the appropriate balance between counterterrorism efforts and privacy. Although this is not a new tension, new information technologies make it possible for privacy to be eroded far more extensively than ever before. Chapter 9 identifies a number of reasons that citizens might be concerned about privacy in a law enforcement/national security context. First, these individuals may be concerned that such information might be abused. Second, government knowledge about certain activities often has a chilling effect on individuals' participation in such activities, even if such activities are entirely legal. Third, many individuals do not want government authorities to collect personal information simply on the theory that such collection raises their profiles and makes it more likely that they might be erroneously singled out in some manner to their detriment even if they have done nothing illegal.

6

Privacy and Organizations

Privacy is an issue in many sectors of society. This report addresses privacy concerns in depth in the areas of health care (Chapter 7), libraries (Chapter 8), and law enforcement and national security (Chapter 9). However, tensions between the access to information that technology makes possible and the privacy of the individual are not restricted to those clearly sensitive areas. In recent years, technology has transformed organizations and institutional practice across the board. Our lives are intimately tied to organizations and institutions that gather, collate, and use information about us. Whether those organizations are for-profit corporations, educational institutions, media and content providers, or not-for-profit organizations, they all gather, store, and use information about their customers, users, and clients.

This chapter presents a brief overview of several institutional sectors and their use of information and information technology particularly as that use relates to the privacy of the individuals involved. It points out some of the difficult tradeoffs required in applying the technology and shows how concerns about privacy can arise even when the technology user's intent is to help the customer or client. The purpose of this chapter is not to examine any of the areas in depth or to solve any of the problems being discussed, but rather to indicate the difficulty of sorting them out and addressing them even when it would seem that answers should be easy to find.

6.1 INSTITUTIONAL USE OF INFORMATION

Information is an enabler for modern businesses and other institutions. That technology allows increasing amounts of information to be brought to bear raises the possibility that decision making can be improved.[1] For example, an insurance company can use more and better information about customers as a basis for improving the judgments it makes about risks. A retail firm can use more and better information about customers to target advertising to those who are most likely to respond to it. Businesses and organizations that know more about their customers are better able to offer enhanced services, or even completely new services.

At the same time, the personal information collected about customers can be used for many different purposes, and information that was initially gathered for a benign purpose can be used in different ways for other purposes—sometimes with undesirable or inappropriate results. For example, information gathered to study the correlations between the financial well-being of residents and their place of residence can be used for redlining by lenders, that is, denying financial services to people based solely on the shared attribute of where they live, rather than a full consideration of their individual situation. Information gathered to allow updating people on new therapies can be misused in the marketing of antidepressants. The same techniques that can be used to offer higher levels of service can also be used to target products to particularly susceptible individuals, to generate and send larger quantities of both electronic and physical junk mail, or to inappropriately deny financial or other kinds of services to individuals based on their place of residence, their ethnicity, or a host of other factors that are only weakly correlated, if at all, with increased risk.

A key aspect of the use of information by businesses involves the practice of record linkage, or in other words linking databases on individuals collected for apparently unrelated purposes. For example, a small amount of information collected at the drugstore about your purchase can become quite valuable to businesses if linked to your medical records, which contain much more information.

As a point of departure, consider the issue of privacy as it relates

---

[1]Of course, technology-based presentations of information can hide inadequacies in that information. Beyond the dangers of drowning in the data, the information age offers an abundance of unsubstantiated theories and bogus data, and unquestioning faith in "the computer that said so" has been the downfall of many a decision maker. Data entries and means of analyzing these are not given in nature but reflect human decisions at a multitude of levels. Interesting though these considerations are, they are unfortunately outside the scope of this report.

to businesses linking records on their customers. Using the anchoring vignette approach described in Section 2.4 (see Box 2.2), a possible survey question might be, *How much do businesses respect [your/"Name's"] privacy?* Here are a number of possible vignettes:

1. [Jerry] signs up for an account at the local video store. The rental record is shared with the affiliated video store in a neighboring city.

2. [Suzanne] signs up for an account at the local video store. The store shares her rental record with the affiliated local music store, which begins to send [Suzanne] coupons for soundtrack CDs of movies that she has rented.

3. [Roderick] sees a doctor to treat an illness. The doctor calls in the prescription to the pharmacy via a shared database. [Roderick] begins to receive advertisements from the pharmacy for drugs that treat his illness.

4. [Anne's] bank shares information about its customers' income and spending habits, including those of [Anne], with its investment division. [Anne] now regularly receives investment advertisements related to her recent purchases.

5. A parent company creates a database with consumer information obtained from its subsidiary companies. The database contains information on people's spending habits at grocery stores, cable TV usage, telephone calls, and the Internet surfing of many consumers, including [Marie]. The company offers this information for free on its Web site, although in a de-identified form.

As indicated in the above vignette, information originally collected for one reason can be used for many different reasons—a practice known as repurposing. Individuals may be unaware of how their information is used or what the fine print they supposedly have agreed to actually means.[2] The information collector may be disingenuous in describing how information will be used. Information may be fraudulently obtained (as in cases of identity theft) and used for purposes clearly unanticipated by its original provider. And, in many instances, a new use for information occurs simply because a clever individual or an innovative organization discovers or invents a way that information already collected and on

---

[2]The "fine print" of published privacy policies is a well-known issue. Many privacy policies are written in a way that requires college-level reading scores to interpret. See, for example, Mark Hochhauser, "Lost in the Fine Print: Readability of Financial Privacy Notices," Privacy Rights Clearinghouse, July 2001, available at http://www.privacyrights.org/ar/GLB-Reading.htm.

file can be used in some novel way to solve some problem or to advance some interest.[3]

"Repurposing" of information is not by definition wrong, at least not always. But it often happens that information collected and used in one domain, and expected by the individual to be used in that domain, turns up in another. Even if such use is entirely legal, the surprise and sometimes shock individuals feel as a result of learning about this use of information about them can generate not only personal angst, but also political issues in our system of democratic elections, judicial litigation, and public debate.

Similar issues arise in an Internet context. Consider the issue of privacy as it relates to businesses and the behavior of their Internet customers. Using the anchoring vignette approach, a possible survey question might be, *How much privacy [do you/does "Name"] have about information that [you/he/she] disclose[s] while surfing the Internet?* Here are a number of possible vignettes:

1. [Sandra] is diagnosed with diabetes and consults the Web for related information. She begins to receive e-mail advertisements offering diabetes supplies.

2. [Jamie] is diagnosed with diabetes and consults the Web for related information. He begins to receive catalogs for products related to diabetes.

3. [Ricardo] is diagnosed with diabetes and consults the Web for related information. He begins to receive catalogs for products related to diabetes. Some of the catalogs are too big to fit into his mailbox, and his neighbors see them.

4. [Alicia] is diagnosed with diabetes and participates in an online diabetes support group. She reads and posts anonymous e-mail to the support group from her computer at work. Her employer monitors all Web usage from work computers and learns that she has diabetes.

A broader though related issue is how businesses advertise their goods and services to prospective customers. Consumers often find advertising, particularly targeted advertising based on personal information, infuriating, but they also find some advertisements, catalogues, and so on to be of

---

[3]For example, the use of the SWIFT banking communications network as a tool for tracing international banking system transfers of funds to and from terrorists was an innovative way to use existing information for a new purpose. For more information, see Jennifer K. Elsea and M. Maureen Murphy, *Treasury's Terrorist Finance Program's Access to Information Held by the Society for Worldwide Interbank Financial Telecommunication (SWIFT)*, Congressional Research Service, Report Code RS22469, July 7, 2006, available at http://www.fas.org/sgp/crs/natsec/RS22469.pdf.

considerable information value. Businesses normally want more information to reduce the costs of advertising by better targeting, but they do not want a backlash from consumers. A different set of vignettes might pose the following survey question: *How much privacy [do you/does "Name"] have from business solicitations?*

1. [Elizabeth] has an unlisted telephone number and address. She never receives any advertisements or telemarketing calls.
2. [Jasper] occasionally receives "pop-up" advertisements while browsing the Web.
3. [George] occasionally receives e-mail advertisements.
4. [Mark] occasionally receives catalogues from department stores that he has shopped at.
5. [Grace] frequently receives phone calls from telemarketers asking her to purchase various household items.
6. Door-to-door salesmen frequently come to [Derek's] home and attempt to sell household items to him.

These vignettes suggest some of the variability in this issue and leave room for consumers, businesses, public policy makers, and others to identify scenarios that they find appropriate and inappropriate.

Yet another dimension of organizational conduct involves the relationship between the supervision of employees in the workplace and the nature and extent of surveillance of those employees.[4] It is broadly accepted that employers have rights and even obligations to supervise employees. In one sense, any kind of employee supervision might be regarded as surveillance. As a point of departure, consider the possible survey question, *How much privacy [do you/does "Name"] have at work from [your/his/her] employer?* Here are a number of possible vignettes:

1. [Alex] works without supervision. He sets his own schedule and takes breaks whenever he wants.
2. [Bob] submits a time sheet summarizing how he has spent his day. He may take breaks as long as they are listed.
3. [Carol] punches a clock to check in and out of work. Her boss checks in on her frequently and uses a monitoring system to record how many keystrokes she types per minute.
4. [Jane's] employer keeps lists of every Web site visited by each

---

[4]Additional discussion of privacy issues related to worker surveillance can be found in Mark Jeffery, ed., "Information Technology and Workers' Privacy," *Comparative Labor Law and Policy Journal* 23(4):251-280, 2002.

employee who uses a computer at work. Her boss occasionally reviews the lists.

5. [Gordon's] employer hires a company to search the Web for information about all employees, including their posts to Web boards and chat rooms. The employer reviews this information to see if employees are criticizing the company.

6. [Debbie's] boss frequently listens in on her phone conversations at work and reads her e-mail, whether work-related or not.

7. [Ed's] boss monitors all forms of communications in the office, whether work-related or not, and uses a video camera system to track work activity. [Ed] must bring a letter from his doctor to be paid for his sick leaves, and breaks are timed to the minute.

Government collection of personal information presents special issues by virtue of government's unique status without competitors, its coercive capabilities, and the mandatory character of many of its data requests. Governments are involved in many activities of daily life, and they collect a great deal of personal information pursuant to such involvement. This provides many opportunities for repurposing. For example, states issue drivers' licenses, for which they collect personal information. Such information is manifestly necessary for the purpose of enforcing state laws about driving—but states have also sold driver's license information, including names and addresses, to obtain additional revenue. Such actions have had tragic consequences, as in the 1987 Rebecca Schaeffer shooting discussed in Section 4.3.1. Government agencies also collect large amounts of personal information for statistical purposes, such as the Census.

The scenarios discussed above and below are not necessarily instances of "good" technology or information being misappropriated by "bad" people, or of "bad" technology that is being used only for the invasion of privacy. Looking at particular cases shows the range of purposes and motives for both the technology and the institutions using that technology. There is often a difference in perception about whether a given application of technology offers more or less privacy and whether the outcome of the use is good or bad. Indeed, there are conflicting desires by both the targets of the information gathering and those who are doing the gathering. Understanding these issues gives a picture of a privacy landscape that is painted not in black and white but in multiple shades of gray.

To the extent that businesses and other organizations see fit to develop and implement privacy policies, these policies to varying degrees are informed by the principles of fair information practice described in Section 1.5.4. Fair information practices were originally developed in a context of government use of information, but over the past 30 years, they have proven relevant to private sector use of information as well. This is not to say that businesses and other organizations have fully embraced them in practice—only that they are an important point of departure for these organizations in formulating relevant privacy policies.

6.2 EDUCATION AND ACADEMIC RESEARCH INSTITUTIONS

6.2.1 Student Information Collected for Administrative Purposes

Educational institutions at all levels maintain enormous quantities of information about their students. Indeed, school children often learn that information about them is being kept and accumulated in a "permanent record" that potentially follows them throughout life. This record contains not only grades but also standardized testing scores, comments from teachers, and a record of behavioral and developmental changes, challenges, and observations. Although all educational institutions at all levels collect a rich store of information about the students who have attended the institution, the amount of information increases with the level of education. Elementary and secondary schools have considerable information about the grades, behaviors, and capabilities of their current and former students. Colleges and universities usually have richer (although, perhaps, less centrally aggregated) stores of information about their students. Indeed, colleges and universities could be regarded as conglomerates of different "businesses" that need personal information for different purposes (e.g., student health services, registration, management of facilities such as dormitories, issuing transcripts and parking permits, providing food service, and so on) in addition to the primary purposes of educating students and performing research. In the course of their everyday functioning, they may collect information on students' movements on campus (as ID cards are used to unlock doors electronically), library use (as they check out books), and even some forms of consumption (as their ID card is used to debit their account when they purchase a meal at the cafeteria or condoms at the campus book store).

Much of this information is gathered to chart the progress of the individual student. Grades, standardized test scores, and various evaluations are used to track the progress of the individual student and to determine future placements and admissions as well as past accomplishments. Most of this information is considered confidential—it is available only to the student and possibly that student's parents, teachers who can demonstrate a need to see the information, and the administrators and counselors in the school itself. Some information, such as scores on diagnostic or capabilities testing, may not even be available to the student or parents of the student.

While the original goal of gathering information about students was to aid in the education of the student, much of that information is now being used for secondary purposes. Standardized test scores are now often aggregated and used to evaluate the effectiveness of teachers, the curriculum, or the school itself. Demographic information about students is gathered and used to show compliance with federal regulations concerning equal opportunity. Information about students—sometimes individually and sometimes in the aggregate—is used internally and externally by schools for fund-raising purposes and for marketing of the school itself.

Colleges and universities also gather large amounts of information about students as a by-product of the educational process. Such information ranges from the mundane (e.g., student telephone listings and class schedules) to the potentially quite intrusive (e.g., records of e-mail and chat sessions conducted via school computer networks, records of Web browsing activities). In a desire to exploit the full educational potential of computer networks, many institutions now provide "wired" dormitories, classrooms, and even campuses. Information collected within such systems may include records of whereabouts on campus generated by networked ID cards or laptop Ethernet access logs, purchase records generated by multipurpose student ID/debit cards, and so on. University libraries contain records of varying degrees of completeness of what students have borrowed or checked out or used online. Meal plan records may contain detailed information on the eating habits of individual students. Student health services collect detailed medical histories. As more and more educational institutions begin using access control mechanisms for entry to their facilities, even the location of individual students will become more traceable at various levels of granularity—and information about who entered and left a given location in a given time window could facilitate the identification of social networks.

Much of the academic information about students is subject to the protection of the Family Educational Rights and Privacy Act (FERPA), sometimes known as the Buckley Amendment, which drastically limits the range of information that schools and colleges can release about their students. This act bars nonconsensual release of student records, and little beyond a student's enrolled status and (if it appears in a published source like a campus directory) address and phone number can be revealed, except to persons within the institution who have a demonstrable "need to know." It also ensures that students (and the parents of students who are minors) will have access to those records and a right to correct or amend those records. Other information, such as medical records generated in university hospitals, is often subject to other legal protections, such as those mandated by the Health Insurance Portability and Accountability Act (HIPAA) of 1996 (as discussed in Chapter 7).

The implementation of appropriate data management and security procedures to fulfill external and internal privacy requirements would be a challenge in the best of cases, and is doubly so in many educational contexts where the network of computers storing personal information tends to develop out of systems that were originally self-contained and unavailable over a network. Adding appropriate security to such applications is difficult on a case-by-case basis. Ensuring that all of the applications containing confidential information are appropriately protected is far more difficult.

This is especially so as these institutions try to use the Internet to allow easy access for staff, faculty, and students. Simply designing appropriate authentication procedures is a challenge; coupling those with the correct authorization and auditing mechanisms is an additional technical challenge.[5] Media accounts frequently report on weaknesses in such systems, whether it be the inappropriate use of Social Security numbers for identification (as was done at Princeton University in 2002[6]) or the hacking in to a third-party admissions records site for the MBA programs of such schools as Harvard University, MIT, and Carnegie Mellon University (Box 6.1).

If nothing else, these cases illustrate the fact that implementing appropriate data management procedures has always been a challenge; doing so securely in a digital networked environment is even more difficult. The desire to provide secure but accessible online services that would simplify the application process for students and allow ready access for those within the educational institutions to the submitted material led to a situation in which the security of the overall system could be compromised. Similar worries have arisen over other systems used by educational institutions, whether they have to do with applications, current students, or alumni. In all cases, allowing anyone access to these online repositories raises additional security concerns that those who are not to have access will somehow gain it, violating the privacy of the individuals involved. The issues range from the proper design of authentication procedures to parameters for enabling access from publicly accessible terminals.

This case also points to disagreements about the proper balance between technical and non-technical approaches to guaranteeing security and privacy. Those who argue that the applicants should not be penalized since they only exploited a hole in the system advance a position that anything that can be done in such systems is permissible. The schools,

---

[5]See National Research Council, *Who Goes There? Authentication Through the Lens of Privacy*, Stephen T. Kent and Lynette I. Millett, eds., The National Academies Press, Washington, D.C., 2003.

[6]"Cybercrime? Princeton Spies on Yale," CBS News, July 26, 2002, available at http://www.cbsnews.com/stories/2002/07/27/tech/main516598.shtml.

BOX 6.1
A Case Study in the Ethics of Privacy

The discovery, reaction, and counter-reaction to the 2005 compromise of information in records for several universities' business-school admissions add up to an interesting case study in the area of privacy, technology, and education. A number of business schools subscribed to a service that allowed a single admissions dossier to be shared among the schools, which is a convenience for the students applying to these schools. The service also allowed the schools to manage their own admissions procedure, which is a way for the schools to gain efficiency. However, the security of the service was compromised by a person who published a way for those who had used the service to get access to their own records (which could in principle contain information about the disposition of their applications). A number of the applicants did so. However, using an audit procedure, the schools were able to determine which records had been observed in this way, and a number of those schools decided that anyone who had accessed the records would be denied admission to the program on the basis of a lack of ethics. A privacy issue arises because applicants could also, in principle, gain access to the records of other applicants, although none were known to do so in this case.

This decision by the schools caused considerable controversy. There were some who agreed with the schools, pointing out that such a lapse was just the sort of bending of the rules that had led to scandals such as those surrounding Enron and WorldCom. Others claimed that the schools had acted far too harshly, arguing that the breach of security was the fault of the service used by the schools, and the use of the mechanism by the applicants was no worse than looking at their records if those records had been left out in public.

SOURCE: Geoff Gloeckler and Jennifer Merritt, "An Ethics Lesson for MBA Wannabes," *Business Week*, March 9, 2005, available at http://www.businessweek.com/bschools/content/mar2005/bs2005039_7827_bs001.htm.

---

on the other hand, took the position that even though looking at the sites was technically feasible, actually looking shows a flaw in character that counts against the applicant. They are enforcing the security by other than technical means—by showing that violation of the integrity of the admissions process will entail a penalty, they hope to deter such actions in the future. This case also raises the question of when individuals should have access to information about themselves and just whose information it is. The schools maintain that the information about the applicants was properly withheld, while others argued that the information (including admissions status), being about a given student, should properly be accessible to that student.

As a condition for the use of campus IT resources, many institutions require students to sign and abide by acceptable use policies under which students agree that their Internet activities are subject to monitoring under certain circumstances. Although students sign these agreements routinely, 6 months later they often have no memory of having signed them, let alone what the agreement actually said.[7] As a result, these institutions find themselves in the forefront of debates about the values and costs of surveillance, and must develop policies about handling the vast amounts of information they cause to be generated.

6.2.2 Personal Information Collected for Research Purposes

Along with all of the information gathered and stored concerning potential, current, and future students, educational institutions involved in research gather and store large amounts of data as part of that research. Some of this information (especially in the social sciences) may be confidential but not refer to any person actually associated with the educational institution (e.g., data on public responses to a questionnaire). Other information can have considerable worth in terms of intellectual property.

Unlike information about the students that attend such institutions, information gathered in the course of research is not clearly covered by the general laws and regulations regarding the privacy of student records. However, there are extensive federal and international statues, policies, and guidelines that govern the use of human subjects in research. These regulations, many of which trace their heritage back to the Nuremberg Code,[8] govern not only what information can be gathered as part of research but when and how that information can be released to ensure the privacy of the individuals who were the subjects of the study.

However, there are competing interests in such information, given that the institution holding the information needs to weigh the cost of releasing the information, both in terms of the privacy of the subjects and in terms of possible lost revenues in terms of patent rights and other intellectual property fees, against the value of having open research results based on repeatable experimentation.

The tradeoff between the value of privacy to an individual and the

---

[7]Janet W. Schofield and Ann L. Davidson, *Bringing the Internet to School: Lessons from an Urban District*, Jossey-Bass, New York, 2002, pp. 319-320.

[8]The Nuremberg Code was developed in the wake of the Nuremberg Tribunals after World War II. Briefly, the Nuremberg Code articulates 10 points that define legitimate and permissible medical research. Prior to the Nuremberg Tribunals, no international law or informal statement differentiated between legal and illegal human experimentation. See *Trials of War Criminals Before the Nuremberg Military Tribunals Under Control Council Law No. 10*, Vol. 2, pp. 181-182, U.S. Government Printing Office, Washington, D.C., 1949, available at http://www.hhs.gov/ohrp/references/nurcode.htm.

value of the individual's information to the researcher and ultimately to society is real, substantial, and not resolvable in any final sense. It will always remain an important tension, no matter how society's rules govern any particular research project, at any one time, in any one institution, under any one set of policies, and as governed by any given granting institution. The benefits here are so contextual and dependent on the type of privacy and the value of the information to the individual and society that there will be a continuing need to make decisions about the tradeoff in each research situation.

6.3 FINANCIAL INSTITUTIONS

Financial organizations (including insurance companies) gather and maintain enormous amounts of sensitive information about individual adults. Financial organizations such as banks, credit card issuers, investment houses, and loan originators (all of which may be part of the same organization) know how much we make, how much we save, what investments we make, and how much (and to whom and for what) we owe money. Such organizations seek information about their customers and potential customers, both so that the organizations can offer new services to those customers and so that the organizations can more completely manage the risks involved in a customer's use of those services (such as the use of credit). Insurance companies seek and maintain information on the health, possessions, security provisions, and other habits of their customers, both to keep track of what is insured and to determine the prices they will charge based on the actuarial information that can be derived from such information.

The amount, sensitivity, and importance of this information have long been known. The financial sector was one of the first to be subject to broad-ranging privacy legislation with the passage of the Fair Credit Reporting Act of 1970, and many of the considerations cited in the landmark study *Records, Computers, and the Rights of Citizens* originated in concerns regarding the gathering and use of financial information.[9] Many of these regulations have as their main goal ensuring that the information gathered and used by these institutions is accurate. However, recent worries have also centered on how that information is used and shared between various parts of the financial institution.

The need for accuracy is clear; inaccurate information that makes a person appear to be a higher risk than would otherwise be the case can

---

[9]U.S. Department of Health, Education, and Welfare, *Records, Computers, and the Rights of Citizens*, Report of the Secretary's Advisory Committee on Automated Personal Data Systems, MIT Press, Cambridge, Mass., 1973.

slow the delivery of financial services, increase the cost to the person of those services, or even keep the person from receiving those services at all.[10] The Fair Credit Reporting Act allows consumers to see the information on which financial institutions base their decisions concerning lending or the offer of other services, and provides mechanisms by which those credit records can be corrected or amended.

In 1978, the U.S. Congress passed the Right to Financial Privacy Act, which is intended to protect the confidentiality of personal financial records. Today, the act covers financial records held by covered institutions, including banks, credit card issuing institutions, credit unions, and securities firms, among others. The act forbids most federal authorities from obtaining access to these records unless the individual(s) in question has granted access or an appropriate legal authorization has been explicitly sought. In addition, under most circumstances, the individual in question has the right to challenge the government's request before the access occurs.

However, the act also immunizes covered institutions and their employees against civil liability for the voluntary filing of suspicious activity reports (SARs) with the Financial Crimes Enforcement Network of the Department of Treasury. The USA PATRIOT Act, passed in 2001, also expanded the circumstances under which covered institutions must file an SAR and established identification requirements for customers. The Right to Financial Privacy Act also does not apply to state or local governments, private organizations, or individuals—and to the extent that covered institutions do not comply with requests for such records originating from these entities, their refusal is based on constraints other than the act (e.g., rules of business practice, auditing requirements, state or local law, and so on).

More recent worries about such information center on the use of the information gathered for one purpose and then used for a completely different purpose. For example, information gathered to determine the risk of offering loan or credit services could be used to market other, unrelated services to particularly creditworthy customers, such as additional credit cards or lines of credit. Payment records indicating international travel could be used to market travel insurance or loss protection. Such repurposing of information has led many consumers to feel that their privacy is being violated, and led to the passage of the privacy protections contained

---

[10]The Sarbanes-Oxley Act, also known as the Public Company Accounting Reform and Investor Protection Act of 2002, was intended to increase management accountability in private firms, and has had the effect of increasing the need for high-quality personal information before it is aggregated or de-identified and transformed into "financial data."

in the Gramm-Leach-Bliley Act (also known as the Financial Services Modernization Act) of 1999.

The primary purpose of the Gramm-Leach-Bliley Act was to eliminate distinctions between commercial banking and investment banking. It allowed the creation of financial service companies that could hold commercial banks, investment banks, and insurance companies as affiliated subsidiaries, and it permitted those subsidiaries to sell each other's products where such sales had not been permitted in the previous regulatory regime established by the 1933 Banking Act (also known as the Glass-Steagall Act). More important from a privacy standpoint, financial service companies were allowed to use personal information obtained from one subsidiary to further the sales of another subsidiary's products. For this reason, the Gramm-Leach-Bliley Act required financial service companies to state their policies having to do with privacy, especially with respect to sharing information among subsidiaries and selling that information to third parties. The act also gave consumers the right to opt out of various forms of information sharing that would result in the use of that information for purposes other than the originally intended purpose.

The success of the Gramm-Leach-Bliley Act is uncertain, at best. From the consumer standpoint, the privacy statements that are required by the law are detailed and technical. They are hard to understand, and as a result there are a number of public Web sites that attempt to explain to consumers what the privacy statements mean,[11] and some regulators are pushing to rationalize privacy notices in order to increase their clarity and usefulness to customers. While the law allows consumers to choose not to allow sharing of certain kinds of information, some studies have shown that relatively few consumers who could make such a choice have actually done so. This could be an indication of a lack of interest in blocking such sharing, or it could be an indication of the complexity of the mechanism created by the law for making such a choice. The exercise of formulating these notices, however, has arguably forced financial institutions to review their privacy policies and data-handling practices in a way that they otherwise would not have done, and thus reduced the likelihood of egregious privacy practices that might have slipped through the cracks.

Even if opting out were easier, it is not clear that making use of the mechanism would have the intended effect. The worry of the privacy advocates is that by sharing this information across divisions, subsidiaries, and with partners, the companies doing the marketing are adding to the number of useless catalogs, mass mailings, and solicitations received by consumers. However, those within the industry argue that such shar-

---

[11]See, for example, "Fact Sheet 24(a): How to Read Your 'Opt-Out' Notices," Privacy Rights Clearinghouse, available at http://www.privacyrights.org/fs/fs24a-optout.htm.

ing actually reduces the amount of extraneous marketing received by a consumer by enabling solicitation that can be targeted to only those more likely to respond to it as determined by the interests shown in the shared information. The alternative is to ensure that the solicitations are sent to everyone, rather than a targeted set.

Finally, the financial sector presents a number of good examples to illustrate the need for tradeoffs. The discussion above makes clear at least a rough societal consensus that financial information is sensitive and is deserving of considerable privacy protection. At the same time, criminal elements often interact with financial institutions, and law enforcement authorities have found financial information to be of enormous value in apprehending and prosecuting criminals. Thus, a number of laws enable law enforcement agencies to obtain personal financial information under appropriately authorized circumstances. Laws related to the reporting of large cash transactions (in excess of $10,000) are also intended to discourage money laundering, even though a privacy interest might well be asserted in such transactions.

6.4 RETAIL BUSINESSES

The attempts by financial institutions to provide better service (and to cut their own costs) through the gathering and mining of information about their customers have been mirrored by similar efforts in the retail industry. Whether in online e-commerce or the bricks-and-mortar retail trade, the gathering of information about the buying habits and past histories of customers has led to efficiencies in retail businesses, but also to concerns about the privacy of the individuals about whom the information is gathered.

Although many different schemes have been used to collect information about consumers, the dimension of privacy that these affect is fairly straightforward to understand. As a point of departure, consider the issue of privacy as it relates to merchants collecting information from shoppers. Using the anchoring vignette approach, a possible survey question might be, *How much privacy [do you/does "Name"] have from merchants while shopping?* Here are a number of possible vignettes:

1. [Susan] pays cash at a large, crowded department store and provides no information about herself to the cashier.
2. [Mary] pays with cash at a convenience store. The clerk insists on recording her zip code on the computer-generated receipt.
3. [Carmen] pays with her credit card at the convenience store. The clerk insists that she provide picture identification, as well as her telephone number to record on the transaction slip.

4. [Horace] goes to a drugstore to buy film, which was advertised to be on sale. He finds out at the store that in order to receive the discount, he must apply for a courtesy card, which entails an application requiring home address, work, and marital status.

5. [Julio] applied for a courtesy card at the drugstore, which entailed an application requiring home address, work, and marital status. Whenever he shops he receives by mail advertisements and coupons for alternatives to the drugs that he usually purchases.

6. [Evelyn] applied for a courtesy card at the drugstore, which entailed an application requiring home address, work, and marital status. Evelyn used the middle initial "Q" on her application, even though that is not her real middle initial. She now receives catalogs in the mail from businesses that she has never patronized, all with mailing labels that include the middle initial "Q."

7. [Rosco] applies to join a local gym. The membership application includes questions about his health, income, and criminal background. In addition, he is required to grant permission for the search of public records and undergo a credit check.

Of course, although one dimension can be defined by example through these vignettes, consumers and different businesses have markedly different preferences about what level of privacy, as indicated by one of these seven vignettes listed from most privacy preserving to least, is acceptable or even should be legal.

One such information-enabled marketing effort to come to the attention of consumers is the use of historical information by the online bookstore Amazon.com to make suggestions to visitors on items that might interest them. When customers log in to the Amazon.com Web site, they are greeted with a series of recommendations on items they might like. These recommendations are based on the purchase history of the customer and the purchase history of other customers who resemble the one logging on. Many people find the recommendations helpful, and Amazon.com finds that it helps their business. Nevertheless, there are some who find this an indication of how much information has been gathered about them and wonder what else this customer database reveals about them.

A similar trend can be seen in bricks-and-mortar retail businesses such as grocery stores and pharmacies that use customer loyalty cards. These cards are used to identify customers, allowing the purchases made by those customers to be tracked and aggregated. Some stores use the information to give out discount coupons differentially depending on the interests and history of different customers, which can be thought of as a variation on the recommendations made by the online retail sites. In addition to the accumulation of information that these cards allow, there have been some who are troubled by the fact that the use of such cards can be a condition for a discount on certain purchases, meaning that those who do not want this information gathered about them are forced to pay higher prices than those who allow the information to be gathered.[12]

The change, in both the online and the bricks-and-mortar retail case, is not necessarily in the information that is being gathered. For some time now, individual merchants have had their own credit cards, and all purchases by customers using such cards were thus recorded and the records made available to those merchants. What has changed is the use of that information. With new data-mining software, this information has become an important input for decisions about what suggestions to make to particular customers to how to lay out a retail store to what items to put on sale.

As the above discussion suggests, retailers, credit card companies, and manufacturers often collect and make subsequent use of purchase information, and because they do not go out of their way to remind consumers that they are doing so, such collection and use are unlikely to be foremost in a consumer's mind. To the extent that individual consumers are not aware of information-based marketing, they may find such marketing helpful and benign or intrusive and inappropriate.

In the helpful and benign category are marketing offers that consumers value, such as a discount on the next purchase of an item previously purchased, a coupon for a competitor's product, a more convenient online shopping experience, or a suggestion for a different purchase that the customer might find useful and of interest. Indeed, some consumers seek out information-based marketing services and knowingly provide information about themselves to improve the operation of recommendation systems.

In the intrusive and inappropriate category are sales techniques that make individuals feel that their privacy has been violated, such as advertisements for undesired sexually oriented material or drugs for socially stigmatizing diseases. More troubling is the use of information-based marketing to avoid certain demographic groups in offering an advantageous deal or to target certain groups with fraudulent intentions in mind.

---

[12]In some cases, a customer without an individual loyalty card is supplied with a "register" card upon checking out, thereby enabling the customer to receive the discount. However, the existence of this practice does not negate the potential privacy concerns raised by customer loyalty cards in the first place. Although even a customer with a loyalty card can request that the register card be used, the customer must know about that option to exercise it, and it is not accidental that there is generally no sign at the register indicating that customers may use the register card. In addition, the customer may lose any benefits associated with aggregate purchases over a period of time (e.g., a coupon for a 10 percent savings after $500 in purchases).

Some have asserted that one way to solve, or at least substantially mitigate, the intrusive aspects of information-based marketing is to collect even more personal information so that offers can be targeted more precisely to those who are likely to appreciate getting them, and other customers can then be left alone. But the notion that preserving privacy could depend on providing even more personal information is ironic and counter-intuitive at best. Indeed, much of the objection to marketing uses of personal and transactional information is based in the fact that many people simply do not believe that marketers are their agents working in their interest. By contrast, sharing personal and sensitive information with someone known to have the information provider's interests at heart is likely to be undertaken with much greater comfort and ease.

The latest extension to worries in a retail privacy context is the introduction of radio-frequency identification (RFID) tags that carry an identifier able to differentiate retail goods at the item level (as opposed to just the kind of item, which is the case with barcodes). RFID tags respond to transmissions in the radio frequency range by sending a reply that is their unique identifier. Their use is not currently widespread, but both the Department of Defense and WalMart have active plans for deploying the technology in the near future.

Privacy advocates have argued that RFID tags will allow anyone with a reader to determine all of the items carried or worn by an individual, and would allow someone with a reader to take a complete inventory of the contents of a house from outside the house. Correlating the items being worn by an individual could enable determining the identity of that individual. Moreover, a tag wearer/holder's movements and personal contacts might become more traceable.[13] Tags placed in books could allow inferences to be made about the reading habits of the individual.

To date, the use of RFID technology in retail applications has, in almost all cases, been confined to the supply chain, in keeping with RFID's original purpose to ensure a smooth movement from the manufacturer, through the warehouse, and to the final retail space. It is believed that the automation of the identification of palettes and items through this process will save considerable cost and improve the detection of lost, misplaced, and stolen items. Even in the retail store, the main use of RFID technology is intended to be the reduction of the inventory that the store must carry—pilot programs (such as that done in the United Kingdom by

---

[13]Once an individual is identified and associated with the serial numbers of tagged items possessed, the individual is subject to identification when he or she passes an RFID-monitoring point. If two such people meet—deliberately or by chance—nearby a monitoring point, a de facto record of their meeting can made.

Marks and Spencer[14]) show considerable cost savings in the use of this technology.

RFIDs also have marketing significance. For example, it is relatively straightforward to embed a different product serial number in each product, so that every shirt sold by any store has its own serial number. A consumer who bought an RFID-tagged shirt at Store A could then be identified every time she wore that shirt in Store A. Since the array of personal items she would be carrying on each visit would vary, it would be possible over time to develop an inventory of many of the personal items that she owned. Furthermore, it is possible that the databases of different stores could be networked together, which means that every store in the network would have such information available. With an inventory of personal items in hand, albeit incomplete, stores could deploy recommender systems to suggest other items that an individual might be likely to purchase, with suggestions transmitted to the consumer as text messages on a cell phone.

To date, no retailer has announced any such plans and would receive abundant negative press if it did. This subject has become "radioactive" because of privacy concerns, and retailers are currently using RFID technology only for inventory, supply chain management, and theft control. An individual retailer might be reluctant to expose itself to such risk, and it is even less likely that retailers would do this en masse, an action that would be required for the network scheme described above. But as privacy advocates point out, it could someday be possible.

Although few people object to the use of RFID tags in retail stores before an item becomes the property of the consumer, post-sale privacy concerns have been raised regarding just such scenarios. As in the case of the Amazon.com book recommender systems, targeted marketing can be considered a benefit to the willing consumer or an intrusion to the unwilling consumer. One technical approach to address post-sale privacy concerns involves deactivating the tags at the point of sale.[15] Such an operation would make the tags permanently unresponsive to any request; in effect the tag would become inoperable.

Most of the controversy around the collection of information at the retail level seems to stem, on analysis, from a concern about the amount of information that could be gathered about everyone during even the most mundane of tasks. Today, even the seemingly anonymous shopping over

---

[14]See generally, Simson Garfinkel and Beth Rosenberg, eds., *RFID Applications, Security and Privacy*, Addison Wesley, 2006. See especially Chapters 4-6.

[15]Some RFID tags can also be deactivated by microwaving them for several seconds. Consumer deactivation of an RFID tag has the advantage of verification, as vendors themselves have little inherent economic incentive to kill the tag.

the Internet results in enough information to allow merchants to make suggestions that seem uncomfortably accurate to some. New technologies seem to allow ever greater collections of information about what we buy, wear, and do, and about our associates as well. The information can be gathered at a distance (and thus without our knowledge) and might even be gathered well after the action that led to the acquisition of the item giving out the information (as would be the case with RFID tags being read in the clothing we were wearing instead of buying). Multiple worries arise from the volume and variety of information being gathered, the known uses to which that information is being put, and the unknowns about what other uses there are now or may be in the future.

6.5 DATA AGGREGATION ORGANIZATIONS

In addition to allowing the collection, retention, and analysis of information by existing organizations, advances in technology have led to the creation of the data aggregation business. This business might be thought of as the networked-world's equivalent to the traditional private detective agency of the past, in that it is built around being able to supply information to those who need it. Unlike the detective agencies of the past, however, these new-age businesses attempt to aggregate and repackage already-available information.

Data aggregation services obtain their information in a number of ways. Much of the information is gathered from public sources, such as the records held by various governmental bodies. These records are public by law, and many of these records are now available in digital form, either by request or directly over the Internet. Other forms of information come from partner businesses, or from businesses that want to use the information supplied by the data aggregation service. Such information can include the history of insurance claims made or the jobs held by an individual. In addition, customers of a data aggregation service supply it with some information about an individual of interest, which can then be used to find still more information about that individual. When the work for the client who has supplied the "seed" information is done, the seed data are added to the aggregator's store of information.

Unlike search engine companies, which index information about individual users as a by-product of the overall indexing of the World Wide Web, the main business of data aggregation companies is the gathering and indexing of information about individuals, and the amount of information that can be gathered in the ways described above is staggering. And the more information acquired concerning an individual, the more valuable the services data aggregators can provide.

Data aggregation services are businesses—one must pay for and must be credentialed by the data aggregation company to use, those services.[16] The services offered by data aggregators are used by businesses for pre-employment background checks, by law enforcement agencies for investigations, and by financial and insurance and other companies to check the backgrounds of potential customers and associates. However, the quality of the data available through these services is variable. In a 2005 study, Pierce and Ackerman found that 67 to 73 percent of data records on individuals obtained from two data aggregation services contained incorrect biographical data, and between 13 and 25 percent contained errors in basic biographical data (name, date of birth, Social Security number, current address, phone number).[17]

In a sense, data aggregators can be seen as an extension of companies such as Equifax, Experian, and Trans Union Corporation—credit bureaus that have made a business of amassing financial information about individuals and businesses for years. But data aggregators are made possible by the advances in technology over the past decade. Only because of the amount of information that is available on the network, the amount that can be easily stored, and the advances in hardware and software that allow analysis of that information can data aggregators offer information services that cover almost everyone in the United States.

That these companies can collect enough information that they can "know" a person well is noteworthy to many and troubling to some. Perhaps a greater concern is the fact that many of the activities of these companies are not clearly covered by the laws and regulations that cover financial institutions, such as the Fair Credit Reporting Act. Unless they are in fact covered by such laws and regulations, there is no requirement that the companies make known to individuals information gathered about them, nor are individuals guaranteed by law a means for challenging, changing, correcting, or amending that information.

Indeed, the public was generally uninformed about the existence of data aggregation services until one company (ChoicePoint) disclosed that it had provided large amounts of personal information on many individuals to fraudulently constituted businesses. ChoicePoint has always marketed itself to business and the government rather than consumers, thereby escaping much public notice. In February 2005, ChoicePoint reported, most likely as the result of California law mandating such notice

---

[16]Some data aggregation services are free, although the amounts of data made available for free are quite limited. For example, Zabasearch (www.zabasearch.com) makes available for free personal information regarding name, address, phone number, and year of birth.

[17]Deborah Pierce and Linda Ackerman, *Data Aggregators: A Study of Data Quality and Responsiveness*, May 19, 2005, available at http://www.privacyactivism.org/docs/DataAggregatorsStudy.pdf#search=%22data%20brokers%20choicepoint%20acxiom%22.

in the event of improper disclosures of personal information, that it had sold information about individuals to fraudulent front companies.[18]

ChoicePoint's response to this breach was to tighten its mechanisms for credentialing a company; from its point of view the problem was one of fraud in obtaining the services it offered. But many observers argued that the incident showed a basic problem with the relatively unregulated and unrestrained companies that collect and store personal information about individuals without their knowledge and without direct benefit to them. These observers argued that the appropriate response was greater regulation of the data aggregation industry along the lines of how the financial and health sectors are now regulated.

It is not known at this writing what the ultimate reaction will be to the disclosure of the loss of this information. Calls have been made for new legislation and regulation of data aggregators. Many people have expressed shock that these kinds of businesses even exist. However, without such services it would be more difficult for businesses to do the required checks on potential employees to validate claims regarding educational background or the absence of prior criminal records, although data aggregation companies have much more personal information on individuals than just what is needed for background checks regarding criminal records and educational history.

What and how much information should be collected about citizens by private businesses has generally not been the subject of regulation in the United States, where worries have generally focused on the potential for privacy violations by the government. Knowledge of the existence of data aggregation services, and the dangers posed by the compromise of the information held by such services, potentially changes that, and concerns may increase about the possibility of privacy violations by private firms, especially as the data aggregation industry grows. In addition, an increasing tendency for government agencies to contract with data aggregation companies to provide otherwise unavailable data could easily lead to more intense concern as the line between the public and private sector becomes more blurred.[19] Box 6.2 lists the data that are easily accessible to

---

[18]"Consumer Data Company Warns 145,000 of Possible Identity Theft," *AP News*, February 17, 2005, available at http://sfgate.com/cgi-bin/article.cgi?f=/n/a/2005/02/17/state/n041832S59.DTL.

[19]For example, Hoofnagle found that law enforcement authorities can quickly obtain a broad array of personal information about individuals from data aggregation companies. Indeed, in 2004, ChoicePoint had designed a Web site, www.cpgov.com, as a one-stop shopping point for obtaining a compilation of personal information on almost any adult (Chris Jay Hoofnagle, "Big Brother's Little Helpers: How ChoicePoint and Other Commercial Data Brokers Collect, Process, and Package Your Data for Law Enforcement," *University of North Carolina Journal of International Law & Commercial Regulation* 29:595, 2004). At this writing, this site has been replaced by another site, www.atxp.com, which is the entry point for a

---

BOX 6.2
The AutoTrackXP Service of ChoicePoint

A typical information set (AutoTrackXP) from ChoicePoint offers the following information on a given individual subject:

- Aliases for the subject
- Social Security numbers associated with the subject
- Other names and associated Social Security numbers linked with the subject
- Driver licenses held
- Addresses associated with the subject
- Risk classification for the subject's address
- Infractions
- Phone listings for the subject's addresses
- Sexual predator status
- Felony/probation/parole status
- Real-property ownership and deed transfers
- Property owners of subject's addresses
- Deed transfers
- Vehicles registered at subject's addresses
- Real-time vehicle registrations
- Criminal offenses
- Watercraft owned
- Federal Aviation Administration (FAA) aircraft registrations
- Uniform Commerical Code (UCC) filings
- Bankruptcies, liens, and judgments
- Professional licenses
- FAA pilot licenses
- Drug Enforcement Administration controlled-substance licenses
- Hunting and fishing licenses
- Business affiliations (including officer name match)
- Fictitious business names (doing business as, or dba)
- Names of relatives
- Other people who have used the same addresses as the subject
- Licensed drivers at the subject's addresses
- Neighbor listings for the subject's addresses

ChoicePoint customers, and although most of the information is available from public sources, the service provided is that of one-stop shopping on a relatively short time scale.

---

new service known as AutoTrackXP (see Box 6.2). The www.cpgov.com Web site notes that the ChoicePoint Online public records interface is no longer available and directs users to the new site, www.atxp.com, with instant access to "ChoicePoint's Premier Web-based investigative information solution, AutoTrackXP®." The site further notes that AutoTrackXP "provides the extensive public record content you are accustomed to obtaining through ChoicePoint Online."

Observers critical of data aggregators are specifically concerned about the ways in which private firms in the business of collecting, aggregating, and aggressively marketing services that depend on the secondary use of information about individuals have managed to avoid compliance with fair information principles.[20] They suggest that implementing fair information practices in a way that would protect legitimate privacy interests in this growing sphere of activity would require the following:

1. Some mechanism for providing notice to the general public about the kinds of information gathered for use by organizations that are the clients and customers of these firms;

2. A centralized resource that would allow individuals to consent to, or at the very least opt out of, particular kinds of secondary uses of their personal information; and

3. Reduction of the government's reliance on private firms as adjuncts that enable agencies to bypass statutory limitations on access to personal information. Of particular importance would be the development of rules governing the kinds of contracts that can be let by agencies for data-mining efforts.

6.6 NONPROFITS AND CHARITIES

Nonprofit organizations and charities have become increasingly sophisticated in the information that they gather about their contributors, members, and potential contributors and members. Many of these organizations use some of the techniques of for-profit businesses, such as keeping track of those who visit their Web sites or make use of the services they offer. In many respects, the personal information stored by noncommercial entities is much the same as the information stored by for-profit enterprises. Credit card information, for example, is often stored to allow ease of contribution in the future, or private financial information is stored over time to enable automatic payments from bank accounts.

At times the information acquired by noncommercial entities about their members or contributors is even more sensitive than that kept by for-profit businesses. While tracking clothing stores patronized and the purchases made at those stores can generate information about an individual's taste and style, knowing the charities to which an individual contributes and the nonprofit organizations of which one is a member can reveal political or religious views, intellectual interests, and personal

---

[20]Daniel J. Solove and Chris Jay Hoofnagle, "A Model Regime of Privacy Protection (Version 2.0)," GWU Law School Public Law Research Paper No. 132, GWU Legal Studies Research Paper No. 132, April 5, 2005, available at http://ssrn.com/abstract=699701.

opinions that are far more telling and private. The Supreme Court recognized the connection between the privacy of organizational membership and the right to free association in *NAACP v. Alabama* (357 U.S. 449 (1958)), holding that public identification could not be forced for members of an organization engaged in the dissemination of ideas as such identification could be a limit on the right of free association. Some nonprofit organizations also seek to raise money from wealthy individuals, and they often compile information relevant to estimating a potential donor's net worth. Such information also may be regarded as sensitive in many contexts.

Unlike for-profit entities such as financial institutions, noncommercial collectors of information are not governed by laws concerning either the privacy of those about whom they collect information, or the uses to which they can put the information. They are exempt from the Do Not Call Registry on First Amendment grounds. Further, such organizations are often resource constrained, and thus unable or unwilling to invest in a security infrastructure that will protect from acquisition by third parties the information they have gathered. The combination of the information gathered and the weaker security found in many noncommercial undertakings makes them lucrative targets for those gathering information needed for identity theft, or for observation for political purposes, although to the committee's knowledge such things have happened only rarely, if at all.

6.7 MASS MEDIA AND CONTENT DISTRIBUTION INDUSTRIES

Whether they distribute information through the printed page or broadcast media or the Internet, mass media and content distribution companies gather information about their customers both to hone the content they offer and to determine the rates that they charge the advertisers that are often their main source of revenue.

Customer databases maintained by providers of subscription- or membership-based content to ensure delivery to and billing of the customers have evolved to often include information on the age, sex, income levels, and other demographic and personal details of the subscriber—information that the content providers keep and use to determine how best to serve their customers, and also to determine the size and the demographics of their audience, which in turn allows them to attract advertisers and set rates. The more information that can be gathered, the better the information that can be used to plan the content provided in the future.

Newpapers, radio and television news, and Internet sites all try to provide content of interest to subscribers, viewers, and readers that often includes information of a personal nature about individuals and that might be considered private. Although libel laws provide some protections against the publication of untrue information, it is difficult to claim invasion of privacy when the information is truthful (as discussed in Section 4.2).

For many people, privacy from the media is important. Of concern to them is the surprise factor, that unbeknownst to individuals, and without their permission, they are suddenly in the public view more than they had realized would be possible. As a point of departure, consider the issue of privacy as it relates to the media collecting personal information about individuals. Using the anchoring vignette approach, a possible survey question might be, *How much privacy [do you/does "Name"] have from the media?* Here are a number of possible vignettes:

1. [Claudio] just got divorced from his spouse. He calls his close friends to tell them and they keep this confidential.

2. [Pamela] just got divorced from her spouse. The local newspaper publishes a list of all civil divorce filings, including [Pamela's], in its back section.

3. [Mary] just got divorced from her spouse. Her college alumni magazine publishes an article about her divorce, speculating what the disagreement was about.

4. [Christopher] just got divorced from his spouse. Without his permission, CNN runs a feature story on divorce in America, which includes interviews with his ex-spouse and friends about his divorce.

The range here is quite clear, and the diverse interested parties involved will often have different preferences about where on this scale the media should be allowed to go. Developing consensus positions is especially difficult when views change as they affect individuals. This will be all the more so as marketing continues to become more focused, and as the need for personal information about the audience for a particular form of mass media becomes ever more important and the risk of exposing individual information in a way that is unexpected thus increases.

Information about the number of people who might be reached through a particular program or publication is no longer sufficient to attract advertisers. Instead, the advertisers want to see that the "right" kind of people for their product will be attracted by the content. Advertisers attracted to the Web site www.CollegeHumor.com are very different from those that advertise on network telecasts of a golf tournament. As the amount of information about a viewer becomes more sophisticated and more personalized, advertising can be more targeted. Internet sites that sell advertising, for example, can now determine which advertisement to show based on the viewing and browsing habits of the individual visiting the site.

Another dimension of personal privacy has emerged as the result of the digitization of entertainment content such as music, video, and movies over the past decade. Digitization has allowed new mechanisms for distribution of those forms of content, but has also allowed the possibility of perfect copying of a digital work. Such perfect copying, in which no information (and thus no quality) is lost, was not economical with analogue versions of these kinds of content. But with a standard computer, it is possible to make an unlimited number of copies of digital content without degrading the original in any physical manner, a capability that has led the owners of the intellectual content of such works to worry that they are losing (or have already lost) control of that property. The result has been an attempt to reassert the property rights of these owners, and such reassertion has privacy implications. In particular, content owners have sought to create new technologies for digital rights management (or DRM) that will allow the owners of the intellectual property to control copies of that property even when it has been sold to the consumer and is no longer physically under the direct control of the initial owner. These technologies may have a serious impact on the privacy of the consumers of the content.

DRM technologies would allow the original content owners (such as the producers of a movie or the distributor of a music CD) to control when and where that content could be used and, more importantly, how that content could be copied. The privacy concern, which is discussed more fully in Chapter 8, is that ensuring such control means that the content owner will be able to trace what content a person buys, what devices are used to view or listen to the content, how often the content is accessed, what parts the user finds most interesting, and perhaps even where the content is accessed, all in a manner that is entirely impossible with traditional media.

There is also the worry that information gathered in the name of protecting intellectual property will in fact be repurposed to other ends, since that information will be gathered and owned by the companies producing the content. Such information, not available in content without digital rights management, could lead to the establishment of even more invasive databases for marketing purposes.

6.8 STATISTICAL AND RESEARCH AGENCIES[21]

A large number of federal agencies have a role in collecting data from individuals, households, farms, businesses, and governmental bod-

---

[21]This section is based largely on National Research Council, *Expanding Access to Research Data: Reconciling Risks and Opportunities*, The National Academies Press, Washington, D.C., 2005; and National Research Council, *Private Lives and Public Policies: Confidentiality and Accessibility of Government Statistics*, National Academy Press, Washington, D.C., 1993. Another

ies and disseminating those data for a variety of statistical purposes, including the development and dissemination of large, general-purpose data sets based on censuses, surveys, and administrative records. They also include the collection and analysis of personal data in experimental research with human subjects. A few federal statistical agencies conduct general or multipurpose programs (e.g., the Bureau of the Census), but many others conduct specialized programs or activities (e.g., the Bureau of Labor Statistics and the National Center for Education Statistics). Some programmatic agencies conduct some statistical activities (e.g., the Federal Aviation Administration and the Internal Revenue Service). The data collected by these agencies help policy makers understand the state of the nation—from the national economy to household use of Medicare—and support both the evaluation of existing programs and the development of new ones.

Agencies work with both statistical and administrative data. To carry out their basic functions, government agencies collect enormous amounts of data, most of which are used directly for various administrative purposes and much of which is personally identifiable information. Those data collected exclusively for statistical and research purposes form a tiny fraction of the total. Data collected for administrative purposes (which include matters such as determination of benefit eligibility and amounts) are often useful and appropriate for statistical purposes, as when patterns of Food Stamp applications are used to trace the effects of program changes. In contrast, data collected for research and statistical purposes are inappropriate for administrative uses, and privacy concerns can arise if data subjects worry that their provision of data intended for statistical purposes might be used administratively. (For example, a Census survey respondent might be worried that his or her survey answers might be turned over to the Internal Revenue Service and make him or her more vulnerable to a tax audit.)

All of the statistical agencies work to protect individual respondents (data subjects) against the use of statistical data for administrative purposes. In some cases, these protections are provided through statutes. Government-wide legislation includes the Privacy Act of 1974, the Freedom of Information Act of 1966, and the Paperwork Reduction Act of 1980. Agency-specific legislation further specifies the confidentiality and data access policies that those specific agencies must follow (e.g., the Bureau of the Census and the National Center for Health Statistics). How-

---

useful reference is G.T. Duncan, "Exploring the Tension Between Privacy and the Social Benefits of Governmental Databases," in Peter M. Shane, John Podesta, and Richard C. Leone, eds., *A Little Knowledge: Privacy, Security, and Public Information after September 11*, The Century Foundation, New York, 2004.

ever, the confidentiality policies of some agencies are not backed by statutory provisions. Instead, these agencies rely on persuasion, common-law tradition, and other means to protect identifiable statistical records from mandatory disclosure for nonstatistical uses, and such means may not always be successful.

In part to ensure that statistical data are not used for administrative purposes, agencies give data subjects pledges of confidentiality, both explicit and implicit. But when those pledges are not backed by statutory assurances, the pledges may not necessarily be honored (and statutory assurances can themselves be changed retroactively).

These pledges of confidentiality also lead to another set of privacy concerns. For analytical purpose, it is sometimes valuable to release to the public microdata data sets, that is, data sets consisting of some of the individual survey responses that were collected for statistical purposes. But the confidentiality pledges require that these data sets be released in a form that does not allow individual identification in any form or in any way, and promoting access to microdata increases the risks of breaching the confidentiality of the data.

One approach to honoring the confidentiality pledge in this context is the use of statistical disclosure limitation techniques (discussed in Section 3.8.2.2) to transform data in ways that limit the risk of identity disclosure. Use of such a procedure is called masking the data, because it is intended to hide personal information associated with data subjects. Some statistical disclosure limitation techniques are designed for data accessed as tables, and some are designed for data accessed as records of individual data subjects (microdata). Statistical disclosure limitation techniques almost always degrade data to some extent, although the degradation involved may not matter for a given purpose.

6.9 CONCLUSION

Many types of organizations face privacy issues. Some of these, like financial institutions, have long been recognized as holding large amounts of sensitive information about individuals and have had some scrutiny in their handling and use of that information. Other organizations, such as retail businesses merchants, data aggregation services, and noncommercial groups, are not so clearly identified with privacy issues, either in the public eye or through regulation, but are beginning to be seen as gathering many of the same kinds of information and of having many of the same vulnerabilities that can lead to concerns about privacy.

This brief examination of a variety of privacy issues centering on institutions and organizations makes it clear that the interaction of information technology and privacy is not an issue in only some isolated areas of society. Large amounts of information are being gathered by agencies in many areas of U.S. society, whether it be government, the private commercial sector, or the noncommercial sector. This information is being aggregated, mined, and exchanged in ways about which most of us are unaware. Although some situations (such as the use of RFID tags) have attracted public attention, others (such as the aggregation of information in data services such as ChoicePoint) are not known about until a major breach is announced.

Another feature of privacy that this chapter illustrates is that often it is not the gathering of information itself that is a violation of privacy, but rather the use of that information. Schools, for example, need to gather large amounts of information about their students to be able to design classes for those students, among other purposes. But that same information can be used to provide marketing information, and that secondary use can lead to the perception of a violation of privacy.

BOX 6.3
Questions for Judgments and Policies About Privacy

1. Goals—Have the goals been clearly stated, justified, and prioritized? Are they consistent with the values of a democratic society?
2. Accountable, public, and participatory policy development—Has the decision to apply the technique been developed through an open process, and if appropriate, with the participation of those to be surveilled? This involves a transparency principle.
3. Law and ethics—Are the means and ends not only legal but also ethical?
4. Opening doors—Has adequate thought been given to precedent-creation and long-term consequences?
5. Golden rule—Would the watcher be comfortable in being the subject rather than the agent of surveillance if the situation were reversed? Is reciprocity or equivalence possible and appropriate?
6. Informed consent—Are participants apprised of the system's presence and the conditions under which it operates? What exceptions to informed consent are deemed legitimate? Is consent genuine (i.e., beyond a response to deception or unreasonable seduction) and can participation be refused without dire consequences for the person?
7. Truth in use—Where personal and private information is involved, does a principle of unitary usage apply, whereby information collected for one purpose is not used for another? Are the announced goals the real goals?
8. Means-ends relationships—Are the means clearly related to the end sought and proportional in costs and benefits to the goals?
9. Can science save us?—Can a strong empirical and logical case be made that a means will in fact have the broad positive consequences its advocates claim?
10. Competent application—Even if in theory it works, does the system (or operative) using it apply it as intended?

There can even be differences in the perceived threat to privacy for the same action seen from different viewpoints. For example, information on past purchases can be used by marketing organizations to send out more targeted catalogs; this is seen by the marketing organizations as a way of cutting down the number of catalogs that a consumer receives (and thus is a way of giving that customer better, more personalized service). But some customers see this use of information as a mechanism to build a dossier of the customer's likes and dislikes, and therefore as a violation of the privacy of the customer.

Abstracting across the domains outlined in Sections 6.2 to 6.8, a number of generic questions are suggested by the privacy issues these domains raise (Box 6.3). Asked about any proposed collection of personal information, these questions can help to indicate the complexity of these issues.

There are no simple answers in this complex of issues surrounding privacy. The principles implied in these issues are not necessarily of equal

11. Human review—Are automated results with significant implications for life chances subject to human review before action is taken?
12. Minimization—If risks and harm are associated with a tactic, is it applied to minimize risk and harm with only the degree of intrusiveness and invasiveness that is absolutely necessary?
13. Alternatives—Are alternative solutions available that would meet the same ends with lesser costs and greater benefits (using a variety of measures, not just financial measures)?
14. Inaction as action—Has consideration been given to the principle that sometimes it is better to do nothing?
15. Periodic review—Are there regular efforts to test the system's vulnerability, effectiveness, and fairness and to review policies?
16. Discovery and rectification of mistakes, errors, and abuses—Are there clear means for identifying and fixing these (and in the case of abuse, applying sanctions)?
17. Right of inspection—Can individuals see and challenge their own records?
18. Reversibility—If evidence suggests that the costs outweigh the benefits, how easily can the surveillance be stopped (e.g., extent of capital expenditures and available alternatives)?
19. Unintended consequences—Has adequate consideration been given to undesirable consequences, including possible harm to watchers, the watched, and third parties? Can harm be easily discovered and compensated for?
20. Data protection and security—Can data collectors protect the information they collect? Do they follow standard data protection and information rights as expressed in the Code of Fair Information Protection Practices and the expanded European Data Protection Directive?

SOURCE: G.T. Marx, "Seeing Hazily (But Not Darkly) Through the Lens: Some Recent Empirical Studies of Surveillance Technologies," *Law and Social Inquiry* 30(2):339-400, 2005.

weight and are sometimes even in tension. They touch on other issues involving innovation, property rights, the desire to provide customers better and more personalized services, and improvement of efficiency and profitability by gathering more information. Furthermore, their applicability will vary depending on perceptions of crisis and across contexts (e.g., public health, law enforcement, and national security may involve exemptions that would be inappropriate for the private sector or individuals). A snapshot view of these institutions selectively illustrates some of the problems that will have to be addressed in thinking about privacy in an age of information.

7

Health and Medical Privacy

Health and medical information (including medical records, prescription histories, patient data, surgical records, and so on) is one of the most obvious of those types of information that have long been considered to be personal and deserving of privacy protection. Not only are the intuitions of most people nearly universal regarding the need for privacy in the medical and health arena, but the need to keep private the information about a patient's health has also been recognized as a requirement since the time of the Hippocratic oath. Yet trends in the collection, storage, and use of health information collectively have made this area one of the most worried about by those who believe that privacy is being eroded.

7.1 INFORMATION AND THE PRACTICE OF HEALTH CARE

Information has traditionally been a central aspect of health care, touching the science, the practice, the equipment, and the business of medicine. Health and medical information is also basic to the interpersonal and institutional relationships of individuals (e.g., involving expectations about sharing intimate health information with close friends or undergoing health exams for employment). Moreover, advances in the science of medicine have led to more types of information being relevant to patient care.

Health care information also has particular relevance apart from an individual's health. Taken in the aggregate over many people, long-term large-scale population studies allow the discovery of statistical correlations between environmental factors and disease and are also used to help assess the efficacy of treatments, to determine the overall costs of particular kinds of treatment regimes, and to conduct epidemiological research that can generate insight into the genesis, development, and spread of disease.

In addition, advances in the integration of computing with sensing devices have led to new generations of instruments for the medical profession, from enhanced magnetic resonance imaging devices to improved equipment for testing blood chemistry. These devices now generate information about individuals which would, in a very real sense, not have been possible to obtain without the information revolution, and the information they provide is more revealing than what was available in the past. Such advances are the latest manifestation of an evolution of medical practice from a near-exclusive focus on the present-day symptoms of a patient to a search for root causes of those symptoms, and an increasing ability to determine predispositions and susceptibility, in advance, for preemptive medical action.

The greater availability of more types of patient information has changed how medicine is practiced. The model of 50 years ago, where each person had a single physician who dealt with all of the medical aspects of the patient, has been replaced with group practices and health maintenance organizations in which groups of specialists work together to deal with the needs of a patient. Even if an individual has a primary health care provider, that provider may be a nurse practitioner as well as a physician, and may well be the agent of referral to other specialists rather than the single source of medical care. In turn, the need for medical specialists is directly related to the growth in medical knowledge—much more is known now about disease and treatment than was understood in the not-so-distant past, and no single doctor can be asked to know all of the complexities and details associated with all of this information or to keep up with the ongoing rapid changes in knowledge.

The new information environment for medicine has been driven both by new instrumentation and new information technology. New instruments enable new kinds of information to be gathered about patients, and the increasing volume of information can be managed only with the use of information technology. Furthermore, the ability to store, retrieve, and transfer information from caregiver to caregiver supports the continuity of care that has to be maintained from one specialist to another, as patient records can be collected, collated, and interpreted by all of the members (perhaps geographically dispersed) of the medical team.

These changes in the practice of medicine have correlates in changes in the business of medicine that also have been enabled and encouraged by the use of information technology. The expanding number of people involved in providing medical care to an individual has been more than paralleled by the growing number of those involved in paying for that care. The payment trails from office and hospital practice through insurance company and employer all make extensive use of information technologies.

7.2 PRIVACY IN MEDICINE

Privacy has been a part of medical practice since the 4th century B.C. The classical version of the Hippocratic oath for physicians states, "What I may see or hear in the course of the treatment or even outside of the treatment in regard to the life of men, which on no account one must spread abroad, I will keep to myself, holding such things shameful to be spoken about."[1]

It is not surprising that medical practice requires privacy. The patient is the source of much of the information that relates to his or her health, and if the physician (or more generally, the caregiver) is to obtain the information needed to make good medical decisions about the patient, the patient must be persuaded to provide it. Put differently, patient candor is an essential element of health care and depends heavily on the patient's confidence that the information provided will indeed be kept private. Patient cooperation is also needed for laboratory testing and analysis and for treatment, particularly when treatment is ongoing.

From the patient's perspective, medical information is often the most privacy-sensitive personal information that they provide. For these reasons, protecting medical privacy has long been recognized as an essential element of any regulatory system in health care.

As a point of departure, consider the issue of privacy as it relates to certain medical issues. Using the anchoring vignette approach described in Section 2.4 (see Box 2.2), a possible survey question might be, *To what degree does [your/ "Name's"] doctor respect [your/his/her] privacy?* Here are a number of possible vignettes:

1. [Renée] is ill and goes to the hospital to consult with the doctor. After she steps into the consultation room, the doctor closes the door and tells her that everything she says is confidential.
2. [Alioune] is ill and goes to the hospital to consult with the doctor. While he is in the consultation room, a nurse opens the door several times

---

[1]The modern version reads as follows: "I will respect the privacy of my patients, for their problems are not disclosed to me that the world may know." For both versions, see http://www.medterms.com/script/main/art.asp?articlekey=20909.

to give messages to the doctor, allowing people in the waiting room to catch parts of his conversation with the doctor.

3. [Chandikha] is ill and goes to the hospital to consult with the doctor. The doctor forgets to close the door of the consultation room. As a result, individuals in the hallway or waiting room are able to hear their conversation.

4. [Ben] is ill and goes to the hospital to consult with the doctor. The doctor takes notes of their conversation and orders a number of tests to be done. The doctor misplaces this file, including the notes and orders for tests, among the magazines in the waiting room. Individuals in the waiting room are thereby able to see the file.

5. [Paul] is ill and goes to the hospital to consult with the doctor. The hospital maintains an electronic database of all diagnoses, tests, and treatments. The database is hacked and all the information, including that of [Paul's] visit, is posted online.

By design, this set of anchoring vignettes constitutes one specific domain of privacy, capturing some of the essential issues that face patients, doctors, hospitals, and public policy makers. Due to changes in information technology, for example, protecting medical privacy is more difficult today than just a few years ago for many reasons:

• More patient information is collected, both in volume and in types of information.

• More people have access to patient information, including medical caregivers, researchers, and administrators in the health care system and, in many cases, employers and government agencies outside it.

• Patient information is more easily accessible because it is increasingly stored in digital form (and so it can be transmitted more easily than in paper form).

• Patient information is held for very long periods of time, and the longer it remains in existence the greater the opportunities for abuse.

• More patient information is being collected by types and in volumes that are intended to aid medical practitioners in predicting future medical conditions with greater accuracy.

• Patient information (such as DNA information) is being (or soon will be) collected that has relevance to individuals related to the patient (parents, siblings, current and future offspring), thus raising the potential for significant violations of medical privacy and complicating both the technical and ethical issues involved in managing such information.

Such factors make individuals nervous about their medical privacy, since in a very real sense the individual is no longer in control of what persons, or even what organizations, have access to their medical records. Box 7.1 provides additional discussion.

These concerns are enhanced by the fact that the collected medical records provide a storehouse of information that can be used in a variety of ways other than those intended when the information was first collected. These records can also be used for the marketing of particular drugs, or for the denial of medical health insurance coverage. Such uses, often seen as invasions of privacy, are more than just hypothetical possibilities; actual cases in which medical information has been used and misused in such ways have been reported in the press, leading to fears about the overall privacy of medical information. In an industry that combines business, treatment, and research, it is often difficult to draw clear lines delineating where information gathered for one of these purposes slips into being used for another.

The issue of the repurposing of personal information in areas unexpected by the individual recurs as a theme throughout this report as it affects a variety of domains of privacy, and it is no less important here. As a point of departure, consider the issue of privacy as it relates to the repurposing of personal health information. Using the anchoring vignette approach, a possible survey question might be, *When obtaining a medical diagnosis from [your/"Name's"] doctor, how much privacy [do you/does he/she] have about that medical condition?* Here are a number of possible vignettes:

1. [Alexandra] is diagnosed with diabetes. Her doctor makes a note of the diagnosis in his own patient database.

2. [Margareta] is diagnosed with diabetes. Her doctor makes a note of the diagnosis to the insurance company, which uses the information to calculate reimbursements and then discards the diagnosis.

3. [Gerard] is diagnosed with diabetes. His doctor makes a note of the diagnosis to the insurance company, which uses the information to calculate reimbursements and then adds it to an internal database of all medical histories of its clients.

4. [Bobbie] is diagnosed with diabetes. His doctor makes a note of the diagnosis in the university hospital database. This information is available to university researchers, and [Bobbie] receives several solicitations for participation in a diabetes study being conducted by the university's public health school.

5. [Danny] is diagnosed with diabetes. His doctor makes a note of the diagnosis in the hospital database. The hospital then enters into a joint venture with a multinational drug company, and [Danny] receives numerous sample diabetes drugs via mail from that company.

6. [Joanna] is diagnosed with diabetes. Her doctor makes a note of

---

BOX 7.1
Personal Health Information, the Availability of
Health Insurance, and Privacy

The privacy of personal health information looms large in many policy debates, and most people believe that such information is entitled to a very high degree of privacy. The essential public policy argument is over whether personal health information should be available to companies that offer health insurance, for use either as a screening device or as a mechanism to set rates for the primary provider of information or even for relatives who are tied to that information. (For purposes of this discussion, the health care payers' needs for specific information related to payments for medical procedures already performed are not at issue; there is little controversy associated with the need for personal health information to prevent fraudulent billing.)

The argument against allowing insurance companies to have access to such information often asserts that nothing is more personal than personal health information, and holds that an individual should not be forced, either explicitly (as a requirement for coverage) or implicitly (by being given possible rate incentives) to reveal this information to outside parties such as health insurance companies.

Moreover, the argument goes, individuals—based on their genetic propensity toward a disease or on their personal medical history—might be denied health coverage and thus effectively health care, which without insurance would be prohibitively expensive. Since these are the people who are most likely to need access to that health care system, denial of coverage is inherently improper and should be contrary to public policy.

The health insurers argue that their economic well-being depends on their being able to use personal health information to assign each applicant to the appropriate risk pool, thereby enabling them to run their business in a more accurate and efficient manner. In this view, DNA information or HIV status or mental health history or family history should be treated no differently than any other kind of personal health information.

Further, health care insurers fear a world in which those seeking insurance have more information about their future health probabilities than is available to the insurance companies. In that case those unlikely to have health care problems could remove themselves from the shared risk pool, whereas those at a high risk for future disease would enroll. Insurance companies denied access to personal health information would be unable to do the actuarial assessments necessary to set their rate structures differentially so as to provide service to a broad population and to prosper as companies. Conversely, health care insurers believe it is to their advantage to be able to "cherry pick," by providing coverage preferentially or at lower cost to those unlikely to use a great deal of medical care, and the availability of personal health information helps them to identify such individuals.

Seen in this light, the fundamental underpinnings of the health care privacy/health

---

the diagnosis in the hospital database. The database is hacked and the information is posted online. A software company extracts the information and sells the database on CD to pharmaceutical companies.

A key issue here is the repurposing of information in unexpected areas. The importance of medical information to individuals, businesses, researchers, and doctors explains why this is such a sensitive issue. More-

insurance debate concern whether or not access to medical care is a basic right that should be guaranteed for all. Those arguing for the privacy of certain kinds of personal health information (at least with regards to denying access to health insurance companies) tend to believe that health insurance is a requirement for access to medical care, and that such access is a basic need that should not be denied to anyone. The insurers, on the other hand, see health insurance as a product being offered by profit-making companies, which can obtain an adequate return on their investments only if they are able to set rates based on the future risk calculated on the individual being insured. If this risk is too high, then the individual can be denied coverage, or given coverage only at very high prices.

From the standpoint of an individual wondering about providing personal health information, the relevant issue is a matter of privacy. That is, given the lack of national consensus on whether or not health care is a basic right, his or her only decision—as an individual—is whether or not to provide information that might ultimately result in the denial or excessive pricing of health care services. But at the policy level, there is in addition to the debate over privacy another debate about the right to and the mechanisms for access to the health care system in this country. The latter debate is important and is being discussed in many venues. However, these two debates should not be conflated.

The addition of DNA information to the personal health information of an individual creates complexities of a different order. Indeed, sensitivities have arisen in recent years due to the possibility—indeed the high likelihood—that medical records will soon contain increasing amounts of information about a person's DNA.

The expected benefits of DNA information are large, because it can be used to predict the probability of future disease in an individual or the success of any given treatment for that individual. But DNA information can be extraordinarily revealing about a person's medical predispositions. Perhaps more significantly, the DNA information of an individual reveals genetic truths (and secrets) not just about that individual, but also about his or her relatives—a dimension much less present for other kinds of personal health information. This is not to say that DNA information is necessarily more sensitive or more deserving of protection than information about an individual's HIV status, for example. But DNA information and to a much lesser extent familial history raise the question of the party or parties that should be identified as the providers or the owners of such information, and therefore whose interests are compromised when an individual chooses to release "his" or "her" DNA information.

As an illustration, consider that it is controversial today to base coverage decisions on conditions beyond an individual's control; such a case would surely involve DNA information as an instance. Consider also the implications that an individual's father or child might be denied medical coverage on the basis of the individual's provision of DNA information.

over, the trend toward increased collection of medical data, coupled with increased sharing of that information for a multitude of purposes, is accelerating. The vignettes given above, ordered from most to least protective of privacy, help to provide a context that is relevant for informed decision making about what level of privacy is acceptable or required in the medical domain.

The recent mapping of the human genome, which would have been impossible without the increased power of information-processing equipment, continues to open new areas for the collection of data about each of us that has the potential to aid in the prevention, diagnoses, and treatment of disease as well as to increase the knowledge of medical science concerning the genetic components of health and longevity. However, the possibilities for the abuse of such information are immense and of great concern to those who want to ensure the privacy of personal health information. Although the technology for obtaining this information is being developed rapidly, we have yet to answer the important questions of who should have access to that information and for what purposes—and the longer such questions go unanswered, the greater the long-term risk of irreversible consequences.

7.3 ADDRESSING ISSUES IN ACCESS TO AND USE OF HEALTH DATA

This section examines four approaches to addressing the challenges posed by questions regarding access to and use of individuals' health and medical information: industry self-regulation, legislation and regulation, consumer/patient awareness, and official advocacy. Of course, these are not necessarily mutually exclusive, but we provide examples from each to demonstrate the variety of strategies being explored in this space.

7.3.1 Industry Self-regulation

A direct attempt to deal with issues about the privacy of medical information is the Ethical Force program of the American Medical Association (AMA),[2] which lays out principles for the ethical treatment of patients and information about those patients. In addition, the program seeks to formulate performance measures to enable evaluation of whether or not those principles are being followed.

As would be expected from a program staffed by and directed toward professionals in the health care industries,[3] the Ethical Force program reflects a keen awareness of the tensions and requirements of

---

[2]Ethical Force Program, *Protecting Identifiable Health Care Informationl Privacy: A Consensus Report on Eight Content Areas for Performance Measure Development*, American Medical Association, December 2000, available at http://www.ama-assn.org/ama/pub/category/7726. html.

[3]The Ethical Force program is intended to apply to every individual or organization that has access to or uses identifiable health care information. However, the primary constituency of the AMA is physicians, thus leaving open the question of comparable efforts by professional organizations related to nurses, laboratory technicians, hospital administrators, and so on.

the business, treatment, and science aspects of medicine. As such, its principles for the privacy of individually identifiable information are both complex and nuanced. Based on the concepts of informed consent for the collection and use of information, limitations on the information collected, and limitations on the use to which the collected information is put, each of these principles is seen not as an absolute, but rather as a starting point from which exceptions can be identified.

The notion of informed consent is justified by an appeal to "well-accepted principles of autonomy and respect for persons."[4] Informed consent for the collection or use of personally identifiable information should be obtained "whenever feasible"; however, the AMA report on the Ethical Force program then goes on to note that there are circumstances in which such consent is either not feasible or not needed. Cases where the consent is not feasible should be reviewed by some "formal, authoritative, and publicly accountable process." Furthermore, in cases where the sharing of identifiable health information "confer[s] direct therapeutic or diagnostic benefit on the person whose information is at issue," no informed consent is needed at all. Interestingly, the sharing of information with an insurance company for the payment of medical claims is considered to confer a direct therapeutic effect on the individual, and hence does not require any form of informed consent.

A second principle of the Ethical Force guidelines is that of limiting the information collected to that which is "required for current needs, or reasonably projected future needs, which are made explicit at the time consent is obtained." This principle is reinforced in the notion of use-limitation; even when limits have been observed in the collection of information, the use of that information should also be limited to those purposes for which the information was originally obtained. (Of course, because modern information technology facilitates the long-term storage of information, the future will almost certainly see many possible uses of information that cannot be foreseen today.)

A third principle is that patients should have access to their records and be able to amend or append information to such files (although not necessarily to delete information, even if that information is found to be in error).[5]

The Ethical Force guidelines also recognize that there will be excep-

---

[4]Ethical Force Program, *Protecting Identifiable Health Care Informational Privacy*, December 2000.

[5]An important policy question arises regarding the deletion of erroneous information. On the one hand, the presence of information known to be erroneous may cause subsequent confusion or misunderstanding—a point that argues for deleting it. On the other hand, information that is found to be in error can be useful for monitoring the process of patient care—a point that argues for flagging it but not deleting it.

tions to the principles established. One such exception, having to do with the ability to release information when it is for the direct therapeutic benefit of the individual, is noted above. In addition, the guidelines recognize that legal requirements from law enforcement or public health agencies sometimes require the release of personally identifiable information without the consent of the individual. In addition, information can be released if it is released in a form that allows only statistical study and not the identification of the individuals whose data are released (Box 7.2 addresses this topic in more detail). Finally, the guidelines allow the release and use of such information that would otherwise be in violation of the guidelines if that use has been approved by an agency (such as an institutional review board) that has followed some well-defined, publicly accountable process of review.

The nuances in the Ethical Force principles echo the complexities of the balance between medicine as a business, as a service to individuals, and as a science. The need to share information freely with other medical professionals for the therapeutic good of the patient is a clear reflection of the overriding concern of treating the patient, along with the specialization in and collaborative nature of current medical practice. The inclusion of sharing information with insurers to allow payment for the treatment received reflects the business aspect of medicine. But the exceptions for access in accordance with the law reflects the history of public health in this country, where laws have been passed that recognize the need to violate the privacy of the individual in cases where the health of the general public is put at risk. Finally, the ability to override the privacy of the individual if allowed after review by a publicly accountable board ensures the possibility of using information in medical records for the purpose of scientific studies.

In most cases, the normative preferences of many individuals would allow some consideration of the balance between the privacy of the individual's medical information and the advances in scientific knowledge possible for society if that information is available to researchers. But this is not a trivial issue in the medical domain, and the issue can be put quite starkly: If it weren't for prohibitions on access to information due to privacy concerns, it might be possible to help many people live longer and more healthy lives. Determining what portions of individual information are acceptable to protect or distribute then becomes a critical issue.

To illustrate, consider the issue of privacy as it relates to researchers obtaining personal health information. Using the anchoring vignette approach, a possible survey question might be, *During [your/"Name's"] [most recent] hospital treatment, how much privacy did [you/she/he] have from medical researchers?* Here are a number of possible vignettes:

1. [George] is a cancer patient at the university hospital. The hospital maintains a policy of complete separation of research and treatment, and assures him that his file will never be accessed by anyone but his doctor.

2. [Elaine] is a cancer patient at the university hospital. As a condition of being a patient, she must let data on her recovery be used anonymously in a study of several thousand cancer patients nationwide. Her tests will only be reported as a small part of an average across all patients.

3. [Tinika] is a cancer patient at the university hospital. As a condition of being a patient, she must release her file to the hospital, to be used as an anonymous case study for the hospital training manual.

4. [Mark] is a cancer patient at the university hospital. The hospital requires that all patients allow their medical files to be used for research purposes. Any medical researcher may obtain [Mark's] file.

7.3.2 Legislation—HIPAA and Privacy

The most comprehensive legislative attempt to address the issues around the uses of individual health information is the Health Insurance Portability and Accountability Act (HIPAA) of 1996. This act, one of the outcomes of the Clinton administration's attempt to deal with the overall state of health care in the United States, had as its purpose the protection of health insurance coverage for workers and their families when workers changed or lost their job. However, as is often the case in such bills, the attempt to provide portability of coverage grew to encompass a number of other areas, as well.

Portability required that the insurance companies adopt a common way of representing the medical information about the insured. This common format was also seen as a way of introducing efficiencies in the transmission and payment of claims from health care providers to the insurance companies, and so the effort toward portability also included establishing standards for electronic health care transactions, as well as national identifiers for providers, health plans, and employers. The hope was that by enabling a common format, the industry could adopt electronic means of transmitting and settling claims, which would in turn allow a reduction in the administrative costs of the health system. This administrative cost has been estimated to be 25 percent of the overall cost of the health system in the United States, and so reductions of such costs could have a significant impact on the overall cost of health care.

Although using standardized format for medical information to enable electronic transfer of information was intended to lead to considerable savings and efficiencies, legislators also realized that such standardization and transmission opened the possibility of misuse and privacy invasion. Because of this, the HIPAA legislation addressed the concerns of privacy

---

BOX 7.2
The Anonymization and De-identification of Data

Both the American Medical Association's Ethical Force guidelines[1] and the privacy regulations related to the Health Insurance Portability and Accountability Act (HIPPA) make a distinction between the use of personally identifiable medical information and the use of that same information put into a form that cannot be traced back to the individuals associated with that information. If this is possible, questions of personal privacy having to do with access to that information become moot. However, it turns out that it is very difficult to draw a bright or even a stable line between these two kinds of information.

There is a class of information that is obviously identifying of individuals, such as their Social Security number, the combination of their name and address, or a listing of the names of the immediate family members. (Under HIPAA, personal identifiers include name, address including city and zip code, telephone number, fax number, e-mail address, Social Security number, date of birth, medical record number, health plan identification number, and dates of treatment.) The excising of such information from a listing of medical data is generally what is thought of by most when they think of de-identification of a medical record.

However, statistical techniques can be used to determine the identity of individuals given far less obvious markers. For example, given the location of residence at the level of granularity of a voting district, and the date of birth of a subject (both the day and the year), there is a high probability that a single individual will be identified. This is surprising to many, but is simply an outcome of the statistical distribution of birth dates and the size of voting districts.

---

[1]Ethical Force Program, *Protecting Identifiable Health Care Informational Privacy: A Consensus Report on Eight Content Areas for Performance Measure Development*, American Medical Association, December 2000, available at http://www.ama-assn.org/ama/pub/category/7726.html.

---

and security. While the bill itself did not include any provisions governing the privacy and security of personal health information, it did contain language committing Congress to pass legislation addressing those concerns. Further, if Congress was unable to pass such legislation within 3 years of the passage of the HIPAA bill itself, the legislation directed the Department of Health and Human Services to draw up a regulation covering those areas.

The HIPAA bill was passed and signed into law in 1996. By 1999 it was clear that Congress was not going to be able to draft and pass a bill that addressed the privacy and security concerns that had been outlined in the original bill. At that time, the Department of Health and Human Services began drafting regulations designed to improve the privacy of personal health information and the security of such information as it was

The ability to perform such statistical identification has a significant impact on medical research that mines historical data. Researchers in this area are generally unable to obtain informed consent from those whose records are being used because of the large sample sizes that are mined in such studies. Often many of the subjects are unavailable to provide such consent, either because they are deceased or because the contact information in the record is out of date. Without such consent, both the ethics of the profession and current federal privacy regulations mandate that the information be rendered anonymous.

There are technologies for anonymization that have been developed for statistical disclosure limitation. As noted in Chapter 3, the core concept behind such technology is to randomly scramble the information in complex records in such a way as to make it impractical to correlate an individual record and a particular person while maintaining the statistical relationships between those parts of the record being analyzed. However, such technologies can often mask just the kinds of relationships that medical research is trying to discover. When the information to be correlated is known before the anonymization occurs, such techniques are often valuable. However, often these studies are an attempt to discover correlations that are not known before examining the data. In such cases, de-identification can mask the very correlations that are the goal of the study.

Part of the problem with the notion of anonymization of records is that the regulations regarding the use of anonymized information treat the notion as a binary relation—either the record has been anonymized, or it is individually identifiable information. However, since much of the information is such that it lends itself to statistical correlation, the notion of anonymization is more accurately represented as a probability that the collection of information can be used to identify an individual out of a target population at an affordable cost. If the probability must be zero, much of the wealth of medical information that is available for long-term statistical study will be far more difficult to obtain or use in such research.

A further confusion is that guidelines and regulations often speak of "de-identified" information even though a close reading suggests that they mean anonymized (i.e., information for which re-identification is for practical purposes impossible).

stored and transmitted by those entities covered by the HIPAA law. These regulations became final in 2002, and their phased introduction began in April 2003.

Like the policy set forward by the AMA Ethical Force program, the privacy regulation that is part of HIPAA is based on the principle of informed consent. With certain statutory exceptions (such as use of information for the purposes of treatment, payment, or health care operations, or for law enforcement or research purposes), consent of the individual must be obtained for all uses and disclosures of personally identifiable health information. In addition, the HIPAA privacy regulations require that all covered entities (a category that includes all government health plans, private sector health plans and managed care organizations, health care providers who submit claims for reimbursement and payment clearinghouses—effectively, all members of the health care industry other than certain small self-administered health plans) must train every member of their workforce in privacy protection, must appoint a privacy officer, and must provide notice of their privacy policies to all of their members and patients. Individuals can request copies of health care information kept about them, and can request corrections and amendments of that information.

The privacy regulation acknowledges that the burden of receiving informed consent may be unreasonable for researchers attempting to do large-scale studies based on collections of personally identifiable medical information. Both the use of de-identified information and the use of personally identifiable information whose use has been approved by an institutional review board are allowed by the HIPAA privacy regulations, although the latter is the case only if the conditions for waiver specified under the so-called Common Rule are met,[6] or under a few other limited circumstances. However, the guidelines for when such use is allowed are not clear to practitioners in the field. Nor are they without cost; protecting patient privacy is an overhead expense that might not be incurred absent HIPAA regulations.

While the privacy regulation focuses on the rights of the individual, it does not give the individual the right of action against those that are claimed to have violated the regulation. Individuals who believe that their privacy rights under the regulation have not been met must first complain to the Health and Human Services Office of Civil Rights, which is the government agency charged with enforcing the regulation.

The HIPAA privacy regulation was met with considerable trepidation by members of the health care industry. The regulation was complex enough (at 31 pages) that it was difficult to know what was required for compliance; some of the requirements that were understood (such as those having to do with training of staff or mass notification of patients about their privacy rights under HIPAA) involved considerable cost.

The overall efficacy of informing patients of privacy policies seems minimal, much as has been the case in the financial industry with the similar requirements of Gramm-Leach-Bliley, and there has been some degree of confusion among care providers about the nature and extent of personal health information that may be provided, and to whom and

---

[6]The Common Rule directs research institutions to assure the federal government that it will provide and enforce protections for human subjects of research conducted under its auspices. These institutions are responsible for assessing research proposals in terms of their risks to subjects and their potential benefits, and they must see that the Common Rule's requirements for selecting subjects and obtaining informed consent are met. Common Rule requirements are set forth in Title 45 of the Code of Federal Regulations, Part 46, Subpart A.

under what circumstances.[7] Whether this confusion merely reflects a transitional effect between pre-HIPAA and post-HIPAA regimes remains to be seen.

The requirement for training has been seen by some as a way of changing the culture of the medical provider profession in a way that is positive albeit costly. The impact on researchers, especially those wishing to do large-scale and long-term investigations across sets of medical records, is currently unknown; however, the formulation of the privacy regulation has created a mechanism for dialog between researchers and regulators.

Finally, there remains the question of enforcement of HIPAA's privacy regulations. In June 2006, the *Washington Post* reported that in the 3 years since the HIPAA regulations went into force, thousands of complaints alleging violations have resulted in two criminal prosecutions, no civil fines, and many agreements to fix problems that may have occurred without any penalty.[8] These complaints have included allegations that personal medical details were wrongly revealed, information was poorly protected, more details were disclosed than necessary, proper authorization was not obtained, and that patients were frustrated in obtaining their own records. One administration official was quoted as saying that "our first approach to dealing with any complaint is to work for voluntary compliance." Critics have asserted, however, that a lack of aggressive enforcement has made providers and insurers complacent about complying.

In the long run, an enforcement regime of some sort is likely to be needed to ensure substantial compliance with the regulations. But as with the confusion about the circumstances under which what personal health information may be provided to which parties, the long-term results of the current approach to compliance remain to be seen.

7.3.3 Patient Perspectives on Privacy

7.3.3.1 Notifications of Privacy Policy

As noted above, HIPAA mandates a number of privacy protections for personal health information. The concept of informed consent is important to these protections, and thus health care providers are required to

---

[7]Rob Stein, "Patient Privacy Rules Bring Wide Confusion: New Directives Often Misunderstood," *Washington Post*, August 18, 2003, available at http://www.washingtonpost.com/ac2/wp-dyn/A7124-2003Aug17.

[8]Rob Stein, "Medical Privacy Law Nets No Fines: Lax Enforcement Puts Patients' Files at Risk, Critics Say," *Washington Post*, June 5, 2006, available at http://www.washingtonpost.com/wp-dyn/content/article/2006/06/04/AR2006060400672_pf.html.

provide privacy-relevant information to patients about how their personal health information will be used.

However, patients have been notified of privacy and information-handling policies in forms that are largely incomprehensible to the average patient. For example, a readability analysis of HIPAA privacy notices indicated that they were written at a level that requires college-level reading skills. The analysis concluded that the writing styles use too many words per sentence, too many complicated sentences, and too many complicated and uncommon words.[9] Going beyond this analysis, the concepts (or implications) of non-perishable data, quasi-unidentifiable data, semi-permeable security systems, and information-sharing principles that allow abrogation of privacy for business (insurance reimbursement) or research reasons, are likely to be beyond the experience or expertise of most people who will have to make decisions based on these concepts. Under such circumstances, it is not unreasonable to expect that many people will ignore such notices rather than seek assistance in understanding them.

7.3.3.2 Privacy Implications of Greater Patient Involvement in Health Care

Information technology is now beginning to be used as a market differentiator in health care by HMOs and private health care partnerships to allow patients to view some or all of their medical information over the Internet, e-mail their caregivers with questions, or send in their blood glucose readings by e-mail or fax so that the caregivers can evaluate the quality of the patient's disease management. This trend benefits patients by helping them to better understand their state of health, and by reinforcing their role as an active member of the health care team, which has been shown to correlate with better patient self-care.

One consequence of this active partnership with the patient is that personal health information will increasingly be made available to the patient outside the confines of the health care setting per se (e.g., at home). To the extent that this information is made available online, many concerns about the end user's ability to manage security on his or her own come to the fore. Considering the high vulnerability of many end users to Nigerian scam letters and "phishing" attacks, a substantial amount of health information could be compromised directly from end users.

A related point is that search engines are capable of storing individual search histories (identified by the IP address originating the search).

---

[9]Mark Hochhauser, "Why Patients Won't Understand Their HIPAA Privacy Notices," Privacy Rights Clearinghouse, April 10, 2003, available at http://www.privacyrights.org/ar/HIPAA-Readability.htm.

Given that the Internet gives individuals the ability to search the Web for information about specific medical conditions and treatments, an extensive search history can be quite revealing about the health conditions of the individual searching for those terms. Note that such information would not, in general, be protected by any health care privacy legislation, although it might enjoy some protection under more general statutes.

7.3.3.3 Improper Interpretation and Unintended Consequences of HIPAA Privacy Regulations

In the early days of HIPAA implementation, confusion was common over what was and was not allowed under HIPAA. HIPAA privacy regulations were designed to prevent the inappropriate transfer of personal health information. However, as health care establishments sought to implement these regulations, they often went overboard and withheld information even when they would have been authorized to provide it. For example, in one instance, and citing HIPAA regulations, a hospital refused to release the medical records of a heart donor on privacy grounds to the physicians treating the heart recipient.[10] In other instances, patients and their family members have been unable to access their own personal health information because health care providers were erring on the side of caution in providing such information. In some such instances, patients have been exposed to unnecessary medical risk.

As health care providers have developed more experience with HIPAA regulations, such incidents have become fewer in number. But they still do occur from time to time, and the early days of HIPAA implementation provide a cautionary tale of some of the things that can go wrong when privacy legislation or regulation is first implemented.

More recently, HIPAA privacy regulations have impeded the efforts of patients to untangle problems associated with their medical records or payments for medical services received.[11] In particular, some patients have been the victim of medical identity theft, in which another person assumes a patient's identity for the purpose of receiving medical services. Medical identity theft has both a medical and a financial impact on the victim, whose health care records come to contain health information that is not associated with the victim and whose finances are compromised by liability for medical services never received. However, victims of medical identity theft report many difficulties in obtaining their

---

[10]Rob Stein, "Patient Privacy Rules Bring Wide Confusion: New Directives Often Misunderstood," *Washington Post*, August 18, 2003, p. A01.

[11]Joseph Menn, "ID Theft Infects Medical Records," *Los Angeles Times*, September 25, 2006.

records so that they can investigate what might have happened. In some cases, the victim's investigations are stymied because a victim's medical record now has personal health information on another person (the thief), and some hospitals argue that HIPAA prevents them from turning over documents that contain information on other people even under these circumstances.

7.3.3.4 Spillover Privacy Implications of Receiving Health Care Services

In April 2005, the Target Corporation (operators of a large chain of department stores that often include pharmacies) began to require photo identification for the purchase of certain over-the-counter cold medicines. Identity information is recorded in a database along with the purchase so that Target can limit customers to two packages every 2 weeks and can see if they have purchased other cold medicine from Target. The stated reason for the policy is that these medicines contain pseudoephedrine, which can be converted to methamphetamine (also known as crystal meth)—an addictive and illegal drug.[12] Although Target states that it obeys all federal and state laws regarding the privacy of such information, this policy was promulgated by Target on its own initiative and not at the behest of any state or federal law.

For many years, medication has been provided by prescription or over the counter, and the privacy implications of such medications were clear. Prescription drugs required the presentation of identification under the rationale that such medications were specifically prescribed for the individual in question by a physician who had examined him or her and made a determination about the appropriateness and safety of the drug. Over-the-counter medications could be purchased by essentially anyone, without presenting identification.

Whether or not Target's purpose in adopting this policy is appropriate or socially beneficial, the policy changes this traditional paradigm by requiring presentation of identification and storage of such information for over-the-counter drugs in pursuit of non-medical goals. As a rule, consumers have many choices about where to purchase over-the-counter medications, but Target's policy regarding cold medicines does illustrate how privacy can be eroded in a service as vital as health care.

---

[12] C. Benjamin Ford, "Target Wants Photo ID for Cold Medicine," *The Gazette*, February 15, 2006, available at http://www.gazette.net/stories/022406/polia%20s195144_31962.shtml.

7.3.4 Institutional Advocacy

The notion of institutional advocacy most commonly arises when there is no natural constituency for a certain perspective. For example, there are many short-term incentives for exploiting the environment for economic reasons, but few similar incentives to refrain from exploiting the environment. Thus, the Environmental Protection Agency was established in large part to reduce this imbalance.

In the domain of health care, there are similarly many incentives to use patient information, and very few to refrain from using it. The issues involved with health care privacy are also complex and highly conditional and situational. Under these circumstances, some privacy analysts suggest that an institutional advocate is needed to help balance the scales. Indeed, there are today chief privacy officers in many corporations that deal with personal information on a large scale. The role of such officers is to ensure that adequate attention to privacy is paid in decision making that might have an effect on privacy, and HIPAA itself stipulates that organizations covered by the act must designate a "privacy official" responsible for the "development and implementation" of the policies and procedures necessary for compliance with the HIPAA privacy requirements.

Similar arguments could be made on a larger scale as well. On this view, issues related to medical privacy are too complex for the average consumer to understand, let alone take informed action about. Thus, an institutional advocate for medical privacy in the U.S. government, or in state governments, would help to ensure that adequate attention to privacy is paid in policy making that might have an effect on privacy.

7.4 OPEN ISSUES

Although the questions surrounding privacy have been discussed for years in the context of individual health information, it is not clear that any of the issues in this area are either less controversial or less murky as a result. The traditional approach, in which the privacy of the patient could be controlled by that patient's doctor and in which the information about that patient was kept in files owned and controlled by the doctor and not easily shared physically, is no longer a viable model. This model has been made impractical by changes in how the information itself is stored and how medical treatment is paid for and delivered. Adding in the growing realization that medical information traditionally regarded as private holds promise for changing the way the science of medicine can be conducted, it is clear that there are additional pressures on the traditional notions of medical privacy and that the rules of practice relevant to medical information will continue to evolve.

Because of the way medicine has evolved, it is helpful though sometimes difficult, to distinguish clearly the following aspects:

• The practice of medicine, which is concerned with the medical care of individuals and communities, both to maximize current and future health and to track and monitor current disease;
• The science of medicine, which is concerned with the advancement of medical knowledge and technique;
• The business of medicine, which determines how and where medical care is provided and how best to ensure that the costs of medical care are held to a reasonable level, as well as what is reasonable in highly competitive profit-driven sectors of the business; and
• The regulation of medicine, which is society's way of ensuring that medicine is practiced competently and in safe settings.

Even within this very particular domain, there are multiple contexts—business, practice, science, and law and regulation—in which privacy considerations as well as other concerns have to be evaluated, and each entails different tradeoffs. For example, it is easy to imagine a patient who is perfectly willing to share very sensitive information for the purpose of improving her medical care but is far less comfortable with providing that information for inclusion in a longitudinal research study. She might also be made uneasy by realizing that the same information might be entered into records that will make their way to an insurance company that will than make decisions about the extent and nature of her coverage (or that of her relatives), or might be made available to a public health laboratory for epidemiological purposes.

There are even subcontexts that are relevant. In the general context of medicine as business, one might identify the business of medicine per se and the business of the fields that surround medicine. The pharmaceutical industry is commonly seen as an adjunct to the health care industry, but pharmaceutical companies are often held to business and ethical standards very different from those that apply to such clearly health-related businesses as hospitals or medical clinics. Insurance companies, which are more and more the payer of the costs of medical treatment, provide yet another subcontext, given that it is the rare person in the United States who is able to obtain consistent medical care without the use of these insurance companies and abiding by their sometimes-onerous information requirements.

To illustrate, consider the issue of privacy as it relates to the availability of health insurance. Using the anchoring vignette approach, a possible survey question might be, *How much privacy [do you/does "Name"] have from [your/his/her] health insurance provider?* Here are a number of possible vignettes:

1. [Jordan] wants to sign up for health insurance. The application requests basic information such as his name, address, age, and prior medical insurance providers.

2. [Suzanne] wants to sign up for health insurance. The application asks her for basic personal information as well as an immunization record.

3. [Mandy] wants to sign up for health insurance. The application asks her for basic personal information, as well as a detailed description of all prior illnesses.

4. [Andrew] wants to sign up for health insurance. The application requires him to list all doctors who have treated him, to answer specific questions about his behaviors, and to give permission for a financial background check.

5. [David] wants to sign up for health insurance. The application consists of a copy of his full files from prior insurance providers and doctors, a detailed medical history, and an interview as well as a physical examination that includes blood and urine tests.

6. [Joanna] wants to sign up for health insurance. The application consists of a copy of her full files from prior insurance providers and doctors, a detailed medical history, and an interview as well as a physical examination that includes blood and urine tests. In addition, the health insurance company purchases customer information from local grocery store membership programs so that it can consider her dietary habits.

Given such a variegated landscape, the lines between proper and improper use of health information are unclear. The use of information for the treatment of an individual is generally accepted, but the scope of the set of people who might need to use the information for that purpose is becoming less and less clear. The right of a society to ensure the public health of all its members has long been seen as taking precedence over the privacy of the individual when it comes to the incidence of infectious disease, as illustrated by the tracing by public health authorities of an infected person's sexual contacts in the case of sexually transmitted disease. Some see the release of health information to insurance companies to allow payment for services to the individual as having direct benefit to the patient and therefore not subject to the informed consent required for other kinds of release of that information, but do not see direct benefit in the release of such information to pharmaceutical companies.

Determining the proper balance between access to information and protection of privacy in the business, practice, and science aspects of medicine under the new realities of medical treatment is not something that can or should be done casually or by some small group either inside or outside the industry. The decisions made in this area will have an impact on the lives of everyone, and will affect the cost, efficacy, and range of treatments. Greater clarity regarding what the tradeoffs are between individual privacy and the use of this information would allow more informed discussion of alternatives for decision making. There is a certain urgency for making these decisions, as every day the techniques of medical information gathering and sharing improve. Although we now have some handle on the notion of what constitutes personal health information, a time will come when current notions surrounding those ideas will not be adequate.

Perhaps the largest policy driver in the near term is the push for substantially greater use of electronic medical records. The privacy issues associated with such records are well understood in a theoretical sense,[13] although how these issues will play out in the ubiquitous national deployments of electronic medical records envisioned in current policy plans is quite uncertain. What can be said with confidence is that they *will* play out, and policy makers cannot assume that the existing policy regime will necessarily be adequate in an era of widespread deployments.

---

[13]See, for example, National Research Council, *For the Record: Protecting Electronic Health Information*, National Academy Press, Washington, D.C., 1997.

8

Libraries and Privacy

Libraries have played a central role in American life for over a century. And the issues raised today about privacy are very similar to those associated with library privacy: tensions between values and between reality and perception; the potential for use of technology to help ensure privacy as well as compromise it; issues that affect all age groups; and issues related to national security, law enforcement, and commercial use.

Libraries have been at the forefront of discussions about the uses of technology to expand access to and use of information. Libraries of all types (e.g., local public libraries, metropolitan libraries, university research libraries, corporate libraries) see their core mission as storing and organizing information so that it can be accessed by their patrons. What may be surprising to some is that for more than 50 years libraries and librarians have been at the forefront of discussions concerning privacy. In fact, the American Library Association's Code of Ethics for members (Box 8.1) explicitly recognizes a responsibility to protect the rights of library users to privacy and confidentiality regarding information that they have sought or received and resources that they have consulted, borrowed, acquired, or transmitted.

Unlike some who see privacy as a right or a good in and of itself, the library community sees privacy as a necessary condition for the accomplishment of its primary goal, which is to provide the atmosphere and the resources for patrons to educate themselves in whatever way they desire. For libraries, privacy is seen primarily as an instrumental good, but one that has been discussed and thought about to such an extent that

---

BOX 8.1
The American Library Association's Code of Ethics

The American Library Association's (ALA's) Code of Ethics for members was adopted by the ALA Council on June 28, 1995.

As members of the American Library Association, we recognize the importance of codifying and making known to the profession and to the general public the ethical principles that guide the work of librarians, other professionals providing information services, library trustees and library staffs.

Ethical dilemmas occur when values are in conflict. The American Library Association Code of Ethics states the values to which we are committed, and embodies the ethical responsibilities of the profession in this changing information environment.

We significantly influence or control the selection, organization, preservation, and dissemination of information. In a political system grounded in an informed citizenry, we are members of a profession explicitly committed to intellectual freedom and the freedom of access to information. We have a special obligation to ensure the free flow of information and ideas to present and future generations.

The principles of this Code are expressed in broad statements to guide ethical decision making. These statements provide a framework; they cannot and do not dictate conduct to cover particular situations.

---

the members of the American Library Association have become fierce advocates for the privacy of their patrons.

Libraries come in almost as many different varieties as the people they serve. Indeed, the American Library Association estimates that there are "117,418 libraries of all kinds in the United States today,"[1] a number that includes public libraries (large and small), school libraries, university libraries, research libraries, law libraries, institutional (or special) libraries, and medical libraries.

This chapter presents the library community as a case study in the pursuit and protection of privacy. First, it examines what the library community sees as its primary goal, tracing the evolution of that goal from

---

[1]See American Library Association, "Number of Libraries: ALA Fact Sheet 1," September 2005, available at http://tinyurl.com/if19.

I. We provide the highest level of service to all library users through appropriate and usefully organized resources; equitable service policies; equitable access; and accurate, unbiased, and courteous responses to all requests.

II. We uphold the principles of intellectual freedom and resist all efforts to censor library resources.

III. We protect each library user's right to privacy and confidentiality with respect to information sought or received and resources consulted, borrowed, acquired or transmitted.

IV. We recognize and respect intellectual property rights.

V. We treat co-workers and other colleagues with respect, fairness and good faith, and advocate conditions of employment that safeguard the rights and welfare of all employees of our institutions.

VI. We do not advance private interests at the expense of library users, colleagues, or our employing institutions.

VII. We distinguish between our personal convictions and professional duties and do not allow our personal beliefs to interfere with fair representation of the aims of our institutions or the provision of access to their information resources.

VIII. We strive for excellence in the profession by maintaining and enhancing our own knowledge and skills, by encouraging the professional development of co-workers, and by fostering the aspirations of potential members of the profession.

SOURCE: See the American Library Association Web site at http://www.ala.org/alaorg/oif/ethics.html.

the first establishment of public libraries in the United States to the ways in which those libraries fulfill that goal today. It then explores why this community has decided throughout its history that the preservation of privacy is required for it to accomplish that goal. Next, it looks at the ways in which libraries have responded to technological change, with respect to both their primary goal and efforts to secure the privacy of their patrons. Finally, it outlines some of the new technological developments that will affect the practices of librarians and describes actions that the library community is already taking to ensure that it will be able to guarantee the privacy of library patrons in the face of these developments.

8.1 THE MISSION OF LIBRARIES

Public libraries were established in the United States at a time when the average level of education was not much beyond elementary school, and at a time when large numbers of immigrants were coming to the country. The public library movement was based on the conviction that democracy in the United States could only be furthered if members of the public were able to educate themselves, and to have access to information that would allow them to make informed decisions. The public library was seen as a way of allowing individuals to find information that would enable them to form opinions on current issues and in general become more informed citizens.

This ideal, combining practical access to information with the notion that, given the chance, people would educate themselves, drove the development of public libraries and shaped the role of the librarian. Rather than seeing themselves as caretakers of information, librarians saw themselves as educators and enablers whose stock in trade was helping others to access information. Rather than hoarding information and protecting it from those outside the library, the librarian's job was to spread the information contained in the library to the community in which the library was located. The information to be distributed was not to be determined by the tastes of the librarian, but rather by the interests and desires of library patrons. It was the job of the librarian to help when needed, but it was up to the patron to decide what he or she wanted to read, study, or learn.

This historical background can still be seen in the mission statements of public libraries. For example, the Louisville, Kentucky, Public Library's mission statement begins, "The Louisville Public Library is committed to providing its citizens: The benefit and pleasure of learning and discovery through its collections, services, and staff";[2] the Greene County, Ohio, Public Library's mission statement begins, "The Greene County Public Library system is the community connection to reading, lifelong learning, and personal and professional enrichment for people of all ages."[3]

While the mission of public education was first articulated as part of the movement to establish public libraries, this mission now has been adopted by all kinds of libraries. For example, research libraries that are part of universities might be seen as having a mission more narrowly directed toward the needs of the university community, but the mission statements of such institutions look remarkably like those of the public libraries. In all of these cases, a primary mission of the library is to enable its users to gain access to materials that will allow them to learn.

---

[2]City of Louisville Public Library, "Mission Statement of the Louisville Public Library," November 17, 2004, available at http://www.ci.louisville.co.us/library/mission.asp.

[3]Greene County Public Library, "Mission," available at http://www.gcpl.lib.oh.us/mission.asp, accessed June 12, 2006.

8.2 LIBRARIES AND PRIVACY

To meet their primary mission, libraries have had to ensure that the atmosphere they provided did not discourage patrons from investigating any subject that they found of interest. In a statement that is strikingly relevant today, the American Library Association stated in 1953 that:

> . . . reading is among our greatest freedoms. The freedom to read and write is almost the only means for making generally available ideas or manners of expression that can initially command only a small audience. The written word is the natural medium for the new idea and the un-tried voice from which come the original contributions to social growth. It is essential to the extended discussion that serious thought requires, and to the accumulation of knowledge and ideas into organized collec-tions. . . .[4]
>
> In order to provide this right, librarians have affirmed as a part of their contract with their patrons that they will "protect each individual's pri-vacy and confidentiality in the use of library resources and services."[5]

The connection between privacy and the goal of enabling individual learning reflected several different considerations. Many patrons of the early public libraries were members of the waves of immigrants that came to the United States during the late 19th and early 20th centuries. The public libraries were seen as a way of helping those immigrants assimi-late into a new country and culture. Many of the newcomers came from countries whose governments took great care to monitor the interests of their citizens, often to the citizens' detriment. The library community felt that it was necessary to protect the privacy of these patrons so that they would feel free to use the libraries, and so that their self-education would not be, or appear to be, subject to government scrutiny. This consider-ation is still a major concern for librarians in areas with large immigrant populations.[6]

For librarians, similar considerations applied even when library

---

[4]American Library Association, "The Freedom to Read Statement," adopted June 25, 1953, by the ALA Council and the AAP Freedom to Read Committee, available at http://www.ala. org/ala/oif/statementspols/ftrstatement/freedomreadstatement.htm.

[5]American Library Association, "Libraries: An American Value," adopted February 3, 1999, available at http://www.ala.org/ala/oif/statementspols/americanvalue/librariesa-merican.htm.

[6]For example, the committee took testimony in April 2003 from the director of the Queens-borough Public Library in New York City, which serves a population that is predominantly immigrant. He indicated that as the result of such concerns, the library took several steps to protect the privacy of patron information, including the separation of the library's informa-tion retention policies into "paper" and "electronic," the delinking of electronic book/patron information when the book is returned, and the daily destruction of Internet usage sign-up sheets.

patrons were native to the United States. The goal of self-education was meant to allow patrons to explore controversial and unpopular ideas and ideologies. To engage in this sort of exploration, patrons of the library needed to feel that their choice of reading material would not be subject to the scrutiny of neighbors, friends, or employers, even though concerns about government scrutiny were perhaps less common among the non-immigrant U.S. population. For citizen and non-citizen alike, the interest in privacy extended even to scrutiny by the librarians themselves; it dictated that librarians should not try to guide their patrons' self-education activities, but instead should merely enable whatever study a patron wished to undertake.

This connection between self-education and privacy is made explicit in the official interpretation of the American Library Association's Library Bill of Rights (Box 8.2).[7] This interpretation conceptualizes privacy as follows: "In a library (physical or virtual), the right to privacy is the right to open inquiry without having the subject of one's interest examined or scrutinized by others."

This conception of a privacy interest in one's intellectual pursuits is arguably different from an interest in maintaining the confidentiality of one's medical records or in resisting broad law enforcement surveillance tactics for privacy reasons. While one might worry about embarrassment resulting from the disclosure of medical information, or about interference by government or law enforcement in the study of politically or socially unacceptable ideas, the concern for intellectual privacy also rests on a more general fear of the ostracism, ridicule, or loss of social status that could result if the subject matter of inquiry were generally known. The kind of privacy that libraries seek to guarantee also is different from the kind of privacy that might be needed by the patron of an abortion clinic, pawnshop, or drug rehabilitation center. In those other cases, the privacy interest extends to the actual use of the service being provided. In the case of the library, worries about privacy do not center on the fact that a person is a patron of a library, but rather about the content of that patron's use. Indeed, the interpretation states that "when users recognize or fear that their privacy or confidentiality is compromised, true freedom of inquiry no longer exists."

Well before the advent of modern information technology, the desire to ensure patron privacy led librarians to develop techniques for tracking books checked out of the library that minimized leakage of information

---

[7]American Library Association, "Privacy: An Interpretation of the Library Bill of Rights," adopted June 19, 2002, by the ALA Council, available at http://www.ala.org/Template.cfm?Section=interpretations&Template=/ContentManagement/ContentDisplay.cfm&ContentID=76546.

BOX 8.2
The American Library Association's
Library Users' Bill of Rights

The American Library Association's (ALA's) Library Users' Bill of Rights was adopted by the ALA Council on June 18, 1948. It was amended on February 2, 1961, and January 23, 1980, and inclusion of "age" was reaffirmed on January 23, 1996.

The American Library Association affirms that all libraries are forums for information and ideas, and that the following basic policies should guide their services.

I. Books and other library resources should be provided for the interest, information, and enlightenment of all people of the community the library serves. Materials should not be excluded because of the origin, background, or views of those contributing to their creation.

II. Libraries should provide materials and information presenting all points of view on current and historical issues. Materials should not be proscribed or removed because of partisan or doctrinal disapproval.

III. Libraries should challenge censorship in the fulfillment of their responsibility to provide information and enlightenment.

IV. Libraries should cooperate with all persons and groups concerned with resisting abridgment of free expression and free access to ideas.

V. A person's right to use a library should not be denied or abridged because of origin, age, background, or views.

VI. Libraries which make exhibit spaces and meeting rooms available to the public they serve should make such facilities available on an equitable basis, regardless of the beliefs or affiliations of individuals or groups requesting their use.

SOURCE: See the American Library Association Web site at http://www.ala.org/work/freedom/lbr.html.

---

about who was reading which books. Many libraries were early adopters of systems in which patrons were identified by the numbers on their library cards. Only the library could make the correlation between the numbers and the people to whom they were assigned. The records of who had checked out the books (often available on paper cards placed in the books when those books were on the shelves) contained only the numbers. Further, more complete records linking numbers to names were destroyed soon after the book had been returned.

Although there are no federal laws protecting the privacy of library patrons, 48 states and the District of Columbia have passed laws and the other two states have prevailing opinions from their attorneys general.

The language of these laws varies from state to state. The American Library Association recommends that librarians understand state confidentiality laws and that libraries have in place procedures for cooperating expeditiously with law enforcement officers when a subpoena or other legal order for records is made within the framework of state law.[8]

8.3 LIBRARIES AND TECHNOLOGY

Modern information technology has become central to all parts of a modern library. Libraries were early adopters of computerized systems and have used these systems to organize their holdings, to keep track of which patrons have checked out which items, and to expand the range of materials that they are able to offer to patrons. In all of these applications, the privacy of patrons has been a major concern. The library community also has taken a proactive approach to evaluating the potential and the privacy implications of new technologies, and has recognized that raising questions about privacy is much more difficult after a technology has been adopted.

One of the first uses of information technology in libraries was for tracking the books checked out by patrons. Many systems adopted by libraries needed to be altered so that records associating patrons with the books they had checked out would be purged from the system as soon as possible. Even though that information might be useful for tracking the popularity of some titles or the interests of the library's patrons, enabling secondary use of circulation information was considered improper because this capability might enable use of the information for other purposes in ways that could compromise patron privacy. Rather than risk compromising privacy, the library community generally has required that information systems purchased for library use be tailored to capture only the minimum amount of data necessary to track who has checked out a book, and to ensure that the information is purged as soon as possible after the book has been returned. In this way, the computer-based systems adopted by librarians would provide the same privacy guarantees as the non-computerized systems previously in use.

Indeed, librarians are constantly looking for ways to use technology to enhance the privacy protections they offer to their patrons. Michael Gorman has talked about an example of a technology that might help preserve patron privacy and intellectual freedom in libraries. He describes how self-service book checkout systems might make a "signal contribu-

---

[8]American Library Association, "State Privacy Laws Regarding Library Records," available at http://www.ala.org/alaorg/oif/stateprivacylaws.html, accessed June 12, 2006.

tion to the library right to privacy."[9] Patrons might be more willing to borrow sensitive or controversial material if they know that the transactions will be handled entirely by the checkout machine.

For similar reasons, libraries have developed computerized catalog systems that do not require identification of the patron using the catalog. This ensures that patrons' searches of the catalog will remain private. Libraries have made this decision even though records of past searches might be used to help patrons find other holdings of interest. There is also some interest in recommender systems that can suggest to a given user that he or she might be interested in certain references, based on the preferences and access behavior of other members of the user community, though these systems do not make reference to specific user identities.

Perhaps the most visible and dramatic change that information technology has brought about in libraries relates to the holdings of those libraries. Modern libraries are far more than book repositories. Over the years, libraries have expanded their holdings to include music, movies, and most recently access to the Internet (especially that part of the Internet known as the World Wide Web). All these developments further the goal of providing educational materials to the public. But as libraries have expanded their holdings beyond books to other forms of media and other methods of information access, the pressures on their commitment to protecting the privacy of their patrons have intensified. The provision of access to music and film can be seen as a simple extension of the traditional role of the library as a place to access books, but the provision of Internet access seems different.

Public access to the Internet is now nearly universal in modern libraries, both through computers connected to the Internet that are owned by the library and through access to networks owned and maintained by the library to which individuals can connect their own computers. Indeed, many libraries now offer unrestricted wireless network access, allowing patrons to connect to the Internet not only inside the library itself but also from an area around the library. In many ways, the Internet seems to be the ultimate mechanism for fulfilling the goal of public libraries, as it opens up to all library patrons a vast world of information that they can explore at their leisure. The Internet multiplies the holdings of any library by allowing access to information stored anywhere in the world, without expanding the physical space needed for the library.

But there are also aspects of the Internet that make it different from

---

[9]Michael Gorman, "Privacy in the Digital Environment—Issues for Libraries," 67th IFLA Council and General Conference, August 16-25, 2001, available at http://www.ifla.org/IV/ifla67/papers/145-083e.pdf. This paper is adapted from a chapter in the author's *Our Enduring Values*, American Library Association, Chicago, 2000.

the other means of information access that have traditionally been offered by libraries. The most obvious of these is that unlike the physical holdings of a library, which are chosen by the library staff after being vetted by publishers, the offerings on the Internet are not required to be selected by either a librarian or a publisher. Anyone can publish on the World Wide Web with little or no expense. This means that while there are great amounts of information on the Web, there is also a great amount of misinformation on the Web. Along with expanded access to information of great educational value, the Web offers access to sites that contain racist, sexist, and homophobic diatribes, as well as sexually explicit material.

Access to the Internet is also different from the traditional access to information offered by libraries, because the Internet is a two-way mechanism for communication. This means that not only can patrons of a library use the Internet to access information, but they also can use that access to send communications of their own. In providing patrons with Internet access, libraries are also providing patrons with a communication mechanism that is generally difficult to trace.

The American Library Association has developed a toolkit to help individual libraries develop policies designed to address both of these aspects of Internet use.[10] This toolkit acknowledges that there is content on the Internet that is both inappropriate and, in some cases, illegal, but also emphasizes the importance of ensuring patron privacy, allowing patrons free use of the tools that enable access to information, and ensuring that the dignity and autonomy of individual patrons is not compromised.

In general, the library community rejects the notion that librarians should act as guardians or gatekeepers of their patrons' access to the Internet. In the case of patrons who are children, the American Library Association's policy toolkit makes explicit that the primary responsibility for enforcing restrictions on Internet access for children rests with the parents of those children, not with the librarians.[11]

The Children's Internet Protection Act of 2002 (P.L. 1060-554) sought to change this approach by conditioning eligibility for certain federal funding on a library's willingness to block all patrons' access to sexually explicit material deemed harmful to minors. The American Library Association (ALA) challenged this law, and in 2002 a three-judge panel in the federal court for the Eastern District of Pennsylvania overturned the law, ruling that it violated the First Amendment rights of library patrons. However, the federal government appealed this decision, and in 2003 the

---

[10]See http://www.ala.org/ala/oif/iftoolkits/litoolkit/librariesInternet.htm.

[11]American Library Association, "Libraries and the Internet Toolkit: Key Messages," updated December 1, 2003, available at http://www.ala.org/Template.cfm?Section=litoolkit&Template=/ContentManagement/ContentDisplay.cfm&ContentID=50645.

Supreme Court ruled that the law was valid.[12] The ALA now suggests that if libraries install filtering software, such software be placed "at the least restrictive level."[13] Better yet, the ALA advises that libraries comply with the law by educating their patrons on the appropriate use of the Internet rather than restricting such use.

The use of the Internet and networked information services (such as some specialized databases) also brings third-party suppliers into the relationship between the library and its patrons. Many of the databases that libraries wish their patrons to be able to access require that users log on or otherwise identify themselves. While this can be done through the library's computer system, and the library can ensure that it does not keep information about which patron uses what database, the library has little or no control over whether the database provider gathers information on the subjects of interest to the library patrons.

Although libraries are the primary customers for computer systems used to track the circulation of library materials, they are simply patrons of the database service (and often patrons requesting discounted fees). As such, they often cannot dictate the privacy policies that will be enforced by the database service. In such cases, librarians are put in the delicate position of having to choose between being able to offer the service and being able to ensure adherence to the standards of privacy to which they have become accustomed. Some libraries, with better bargaining power, have addressed this issue through detailed policies and agreements with vendors. Columbia University, for instance, requires that "[s]ervices licensed by Columbia that gather user or marketing data . . . notify users in each session how and why this data is being collected and . . . provide users the option of not having such data collected about them."[14]

Patrons' use of the Internet as a communication medium raises other issues that are more complex. In some cases,[15] threatening e-mail has been sent from an Internet connection provided by a library, and the library subsequently has made the computer from which the threat was sent available to law enforcement officers seeking to identify the person who sent the threat. These libraries did not, however, keep records that enabled law enforcement personnel to discover this information, nor did

---

[12]*United States v. American Library Assn., Inc.* (02-361) 539 U.S. 194 (2003), 201 F. Supp. 2d 401, reversed.

[13]American Library Association, "Libraries and the Internet Toolkit: Libraries, the Internet and Filtering," updated December 1, 2003, available at http://www.ala.org/Template.cfm?Section=litoolkit&Template=/ContentManagement/ContentDisplay.cfm&ContentID=50667.

[14]See Columbia University's "Information Sheet for Database Vendors," updated December 6, 2005, available at https://www1.columbia.edu/sec/cu/libraries/staffweb/digital/ner/vendor_data.html.

[15]Carla Stoffle, University of Arizona, testimony to the committee, January 30, 2003.

the librarians believe that such record keeping would comport with the library's commitment to ensure privacy.[16]

There are other emerging technologies suggested for use within libraries that have caused additional privacy concerns. The two most commonly cited are radio-frequency identification (RFID) tags and digital rights management systems, discussed further in Section 8.5.

8.4 LIBRARIES AND PRIVACY SINCE 9/11

In the wake of the terrorist attacks of 2001 and the subsequent increased focus on national and homeland security, libraries have seen their commitment to privacy questioned in the name of the need for safety. As repositories of information, libraries have been seen by some as fertile grounds for the education of terrorists. With their policy of open access to the Internet, libraries also have been seen as venues from which terrorists can safely communicate with each other. Certainly a factor in the increasing scrutiny of libraries was the revelation that some of the September 11 terrorists, including Mohammed Atta himself, had used publicly available library computers to access e-mail[17] and possibly conduct terrorist business.

The traditional privacy policies of libraries have come into conflict with some of the provisions of laws passed in response to the 9/11 attacks and the continued worries about terrorism. Legislation passed in the post-9/11 period, including the USA PATRIOT Act, has expanded the authority of law enforcement to conduct surveillance and gather data on individu-

---

[16]Under the provisions of 18 U.S.C. 2709, an "electronic communication service provider" must comply with "a request for electronic communication transactional records in its custody or possession made by the Director of the Federal Bureau of Investigation." However, Section 5 of the USA PATRIOT Act Additional Reauthorizing Amendments Act of 2006, P.L. 109-178, exempts libraries from this requirement if they provide Internet access but are not themselves "providing" the users with "the ability to send or receive wire or electronic communications." According to the Congressional Research Service, a reasonable interpretation of this definition suggests that to be considered an electronic communication service provider under this law, a library must *independently* operate the means by which transmission, routing, and connection of digital communication occur. In contrast, a local county library usually has a service contract with an Internet service provider (ISP) to furnish the library with the electronic communication service, as many businesses and individuals do; the fact that the library has set up a computer with Internet access for the use of its patrons probably does not, by itself, turn the library into a communications service "provider." Under this characterization, the actual "provider" of Internet access is the ISP, not the library. See Brian Yeh and Charles Doyle, "USA PATRIOT Improvement and Reauthorization Act of 2005: A Legal Analysis," RL Order Code 33332, Congressional Research Service, Washington, D.C., March 24, 2006.

[17]"Privacy and Security: A Librarian's Dilemma," *The San Francisco Chronicle*, February 2, 2003, p. D4.

als even when there is not probable cause to believe that the individuals targeted for surveillance are engaged in any criminal activity. Although law enforcement officials have always had the ability to seek grand jury subpoenas (with no court order required) to compel the production of any information from any party, including libraries, that is (merely) relevant to a criminal investigation, Section 215 of the USA PATRIOT Act expanded the authority of the FISA Court to issue an order compelling the production of any tangible object from any source as part of an investigation to protect the United States from international terrorism or clandestine intelligence activities (Box 8.3).

The American Library Association has been very active in opposing some sections of the USA PATRIOT Act, passing a resolution on January 29, 2003, that states, in part, "The American Library Association (ALA) opposes any use of governmental power to suppress the free and open exchange of knowledge and information or to intimidate individuals exercising free inquiry. . . . ALA considers that sections of the USA PATRIOT

BOX 8.3
Section 215 of the USA PATRIOT Act

"The Foreign Intelligence Surveillance Act previously allowed senior officials of the Federal Bureau of Investigation to apply for a court order, in connection with a foreign intelligence investigation, for access to the records of common carriers, public accommodation providers, physical storage facility operators, and vehicle rental agencies (50 U.S.C. 1861-1863 [2000 ed.]).

"Section 215 rewrites those provisions. Assistant special agents in charge of the FBI field offices may now also apply. The court orders extend to any tangible object held by anyone. Items sought need not relate to an identified foreign agent or foreign power as was once the case, but they may be sought only as part of an investigation to protect the United States from international terrorism or clandestine intelligence activities. Nor may they be sought in conjunction with the investigation of an American or permanent resident alien predicated solely on the basis of activities protected by the First Amendment. There is a good faith defense for anyone who produces items in response to a court order under the section, and production does not constitute a waiver of applicable privilege. Under the USA PATRIOT Improvement and Reauthorization Act of 2005, Section 215 will expire on December 31, 2009, unless it is explicitly made permanent by an additional act of Congress."

SOURCE: Charles Doyle, "Terrorism: Section by Section Analysis of the USA PATRIOT Act," Order Code RL 31200, Congressional Research Service, Washington, D.C., 2001, available at http://fpc.state.gov/documents/organization/7952.pdf.

Act are a present danger to the constitutional rights and privacy rights of library users."[18]

An example of the library community's view of the dangers appears in the writing of a Washington state librarian who refused an FBI request for circulation records associated with a biography of Osama bin Laden and wrote about the USA PATRIOT Act's implications for her profession (Box 8.4). The ALA also has urged librarians to review the records that they currently keep to ensure that they maintain only those that are absolutely needed, and that all other information about patrons is purged as soon as possible.

It should be noted that the phenomenon of law enforcement personnel or agencies looking to libraries for information about particular people and their reading (or Web-surfing) habits is certainly not new.[19] Indeed, during the 1980s, there was widespread concern within the library community regarding the FBI's Library Awareness program (part of a foreign counterintelligence program that sought to discover what was interesting to people from Eastern Europe when they visited premier university research libraries). In the 1950s, the library community was sometimes approached in attempts to find evidence of communist sympathy. At those times, as now, the library community held to its commitment to privacy in the face of pressures in the name of security.

8.5 EMERGING TECHNOLOGIES, PRIVACY, AND LIBRARIES

As mentioned in the discussion of technology drivers (Chapter 3), advances in technology have often led to new concerns about the impact of those advances on privacy. Emerging technologies that affect library operations such as digital rights management technologies (DRMTs) and RFID tags are timely illustrations and are already topics of controversy.

Consider, for example, DRMTs, whose overall goal is to ensure that digital content is not copied and distributed without the knowledge and consent of the providers of that content. Some proposals for such technologies envision enabling content providers to trace every use of every copy, including not only who the purchaser might be but also who is actually viewing the content. If such technologies become widely used in connection with the digital content held by libraries, the difficulty of ensuring the privacy of patrons who view such content will increase. If every viewing is subject to the content provider's being able to learn the

---

[18]American Library Association, "USA PATRIOT Act and Intellectual Freedom," available at http://www.ala.org/ala/oif/ifissues/usapatriotact.htm, accessed June 14, 2006.

[19]Much of this story is told, from the perspective of the library community, at http://www.ala.org/ala/oif/ifissues/fbiyourlibrary.htm.

> ## BOX 8.4
> ## A Librarian's View of the USA PATRIOT Act
>
> On June 8, 2004, an FBI agent requested from the Deming branch of the Whatcom County Library System in northwest Washington state a list of people who had borrowed a biography of Osama bin Laden. The FBI said that a library patron had sent the FBI the book after discovering some words written in the margin: "If the things I'm doing is considered a crime, then let history be a witness that I am a criminal. Hostility toward America is a religious duty and we hope to be rewarded by God."
>
> The library system attorney told the FBI that it would have to go through legal channels before the board of trustees would consider releasing the names of the borrowers, and also that a Google search indicated that the words in the margin were almost identical to a statement by bin Laden in a 1998 interview.
>
> The FBI served a subpoena on the library a week later demanding a list of everyone who had borrowed the book since November 2001. After deliberation, the board of trustees voted unanimously to go to court to quash the FBI subpoena. Fifteen days later, the FBI withdrew its request.
>
> However, for the library, the circumstances had been fortuitous. The subpoena had not been issued pursuant to the USA PATRIOT Act of 2001, which would have allowed the FBI to demand library records. It also could have prevented the library from revealing that it had received an order to surrender patron information, and thus could have prevented appeal or independent review of the order.
>
> As the librarian writing about this situation noted, if the FBI had returned with an order from a secret court under Section 215 of the USA PATRIOT Act, the FBI might now know which residents in that part of Washington state had simply tried to learn more about bin Laden. Faced with a USA PATRIOT Act order, the library would have been forbidden to disclose even the fact that it had received the order, and the librarian would not have been able to write the op-ed article.
>
> SOURCE: Adapted from Joan Airoldi, "Librarian's Brush with FBI Shapes Her View of the USA PATRIOT Act," *USA Today*, May 18, 2005, available at http://www.usatoday.com/news/opinion/editorials/2005-05-17-librarian-edit_x.htm.

identity of the viewer, libraries will find it difficult to assure patrons that these records have been kept confidential, have been deleted as soon as possible, and have not been used for purposes other than that of ensuring that borrowed materials were returned.[20]

---

[20]The problems posed for privacy protection are not necessarily insurmountable. For example, it might be possible for a library to provide users with a smart card keyed to allow access to DRM-protected content. There is no particular need for the smart card to be associated with a specific library patron, and indeed a library could present the patron with a bin of smart cards with different electronic identifiers that he or she could pick at random and/or trade in at any time. The bin itself could be made available only on presentation of

---

BOX 8.5
Digital Millennium Copyright Act
and Digital Rights Management

The protection afforded to digital files by digital rights management technologies (DRMTs) is bolstered by federal law. The Digital Millennium Copyright Act (DMCA), enacted in 1998, instituted a variety of penalties related to circumvention of technical protection measures applied to copyrighted works. In addition, other recent changes to the copyright laws are designed to assist copyright owners in their attempts to limit the flow of unauthorized, unprotected copies. In particular, the Online Service Provider Liability Limitation Act, enacted in 1998 as Title II of the DMCA and codified at Section 512 of the Copyright Act, grants online service providers (OSPs) immunity from secondary copyright infringement liability in exchange for their cooperation in stemming the flow of unprotected content on the Internet.

Title I of the DMCA, codified at Sections 1201-1204 of the Copyright Act, establishes legal protection for DRMTs. This protection consists of two main prohibitions. First, the statute prohibits the circumvention of technologies that effectively control access to a copyrighted work. Second, it proscribes the manufacture and distribution of technologies or devices that can be used to circumvent either access-control technologies or technologies that protect a right of the copyright owner (e.g., copy-control technologies and the like).[1] Both prohibitions are subject to a variety of narrow exceptions for a variety of activities ranging from reverse engineering to nonprofit library acquisition decisions.

Section 512, meanwhile, establishes procedures for OSPs that provide Web hosting or information location services to remove infringing material upon receipt of notice

---

[1]A device falls within this prohibition if (1) it is primarily designed or produced for circumvention, (2) it has only limited commercially significant purpose or use other than to circumvent, or (3) it has been knowingly marketed for use in circumvention. See 17 U.S.C. 1201(a)(2), (b).

The Digital Millennium Copyright Act (DMCA) further complicates matters from a privacy perspective. As noted in Box 8.5, Title I of the DMCA prohibits technological attempts to circumvent DRMTs deployed to protect digital content, and thus eliminates (or at least reduces significantly) the availability of such circumvention technologies to the public— and in particular to members of the public who are interested in protect-

---

an ID (e.g., a library card), but the gap between the act of presenting the card and picking a smart card from the bin would ensure the patron's privacy. Nevertheless, the easiest, most straightforward, and least expensive way to enable access to DRM-protected materials is indeed to use the library card infrastructure (presumably electronic) to provide such access, in which case the potential privacy problems described above become far more real.

from the copyright owner. While OSPs are not required to comply with these provisions, those that do comply are granted immunity from contributory infringement liability. An OSP is ineligible to claim the shelter of the notice-and-takedown provisions, however, if it receives a direct financial benefit from the infringing activity and has the right and opportunity to control the activity, or if it knows or has reason to know of the infringing activity and takes no action to stop it.

Section 512 also includes a provision authorizing a copyright owner to apply to the clerk of any federal district court for a subpoena requiring an OSP to furnish personal identifying information about a subscriber who is an alleged infringer identified in a takedown notice. Copyright owners also have attempted to use this provision to discover information about individuals alleged to be using Internet access services to trade copies of copyrighted works via peer-to-peer networks. However, two federal courts of appeal have rejected the argument that the subpoena provision should be read to apply to any subscriber, including subscribers who simply use an Internet connection supplied by the OSP.[2] Copyright owners are now using a procedural device known as the "John Doe" lawsuit to discover information about these subscribers via judicially authorized subpoenas.[3]

Finally, at the behest of the motion picture industry, there is currently a movement underway at the state level to enact laws prohibiting the attachment of unauthorized devices to communications networks. Although these laws are described as simply targeting unauthorized and unpaid access to telecommunications and cable services, their breadth leaves them open to much broader interpretation, potentially encompassing any device that can be attached to a personal computer connected to the Internet. For this reason, they have been dubbed "mini DMCAs."

---

[2]See *RIAA v. Verizon Internet Services, Inc.*, 351 F.3d 1229 (D.C. Cir. 2003), *cert. denied*, 125 S. Ct. 309 (2004); *In re* Charter Communications, Inc., Subpoena Enforcement Matter, 393 F.3d 771 (8th Cir. 2005).

[3]See *Sony Music Entertainment, Inc. v. Does 1-40*, 326 F. Supp. 2d 556 (S.D.N.Y. 2004).

ing their anonymous access to such content. It also eliminates or reduces the availability of these technologies to libraries that might otherwise be inclined to take affirmative steps in protecting patron privacy.

DRMTs and the DMCA thus pose a potential threat to libraries' current practice of ensuring that the content viewed by patrons of the library is kept private. The potential privacy problems have much in common with the problems libraries have already encountered in connection with patron access to information in subscription digital databases, discussed briefly above. However, the database access privacy is a problem that can be dealt with contractually between the libraries and the database vendors. Approaching the problem of privacy in the context of DRMTs may require that libraries negotiate with content providers regarding terms that do not compromise the privacy of users—an approach that might significantly raise the cost of obtaining those terms. On the other hand, in much the same way that some online subscription databases simply require identification of the library as the entity responsible for access, content providers might be satisfied simply with measuring the number of accesses to protected content, the number of individual users per month, or the peak number of simultaneous users in a month.

Concerns have also been raised about the use of RFID tags in library books.[21] Some proposals envision placing RFID tags in all of the physical materials held by libraries. These tags could then be used to control loss and to speed checkout—another application of information and information technology to improve the efficiency of libraries and perhaps even enhance patron privacy, as the library staff would not have to conduct the checkout procedures. The privacy concern is that anyone with an RFID reader could then surreptitiously discover what any patron of the library was checking out by simply getting close enough to the patron to read the RFID tags of the books in the patron's possession when he or she left the library. This assumes, however, that the individual doing the surreptitious reading of the tag would also have access to the database that linked the tag identification to the book title or ISBN.

This worry is more evident in the community of privacy advocates than it is in the library community itself. Indeed, the attitude of the library community seems best summed up by David Dorman, who wrote,

> . . . Forgive me for being skeptical of all the hullabaloo, but I just can't get too worked up about a library book broadcasting its bar code for several feet to any and all who care to lug around portable RFID readers and eavesdrop on the reading habits of passersby carrying library books. However, if that thought bothers some folks, I recommend they campaign for encrypting the barcode number in the RFID tag rather than foment (or buy into) vague apprehensions about a very useful and rather benign library inventory control tool.[22]

8.6 CONCLUSION

Leadership for privacy within libraries has come from within that sector itself. Libraries have long been advocates of personal privacy, seeing privacy as a necessary condition for libraries' fulfillment of their primary

---

[21]Beth Givens, "RFID Implementation in Libraries: Some Recommendations for 'Best Practices'," Privacy Rights Clearinghouse, posted January 10, 2004, available at http://www.privacyrights.org/ar/RFID-ALA.htm.

[22]David Dorman, "RFID Poses No Problem for Patron Privacy," *American Libraries Online*, December 2003, available at http://www.ala.org/ala/alonline/techspeaking/2003columns2/december2003.htm.

function as facilitators of access to information. This function, in turn, serves libraries' ultimate goal of enabling the ongoing education and cultural advancement of their patrons. Such an orientation makes the library community fundamentally different from other communities, such as businesses (as discussed in Chapter 6) or the medical establishment (discussed in Chapter 7), that have been perceived as compromising privacy from within, and on which privacy requirements have been imposed by law. Library professionals have championed laws protecting the privacy of library patrons as mechanisms to shore up their own guarantees of privacy to their patrons.

Libraries have always had to keep significant amounts of personal information about their patrons. Because of this, and because of the close connection between library use and patrons' intellectual lives, libraries have long been aware of the privacy problems that are now besetting other industries. The library community has a long and rich tradition of debate and policy formation around privacy and has taken seriously the problem of ensuring privacy. Librarians also have experience confronting and evaluating the asserted need to make tradeoffs between privacy and such other values as efficiency, law enforcement, and security.

Electronic information technology has engendered a new cycle of debate about these tradeoffs. Whether it is the use of electronic systems to maintain checkout records or the new ways in which information can be accessed via the Internet, the library community has had to consider again whether and to what extent the privacy of its patrons should be compromised to enable full utilization of the new technologies. Without exception these decisions have come down on the side of privacy to the fullest extent permitted by law. Librarians have also become proactive in assessing the privacy implications of emerging technologies, such as digital rights management and RFID tags.

Not all of these decisions have been left to the library community. Given the kind of information that library records might reveal about individuals, the law enforcement and intelligence communities have shown great interest in gaining access to that information. They have hoped that the information could be used to discover patterns of inquiry that might indicate threats to the United States. The library community has strenuously resisted such attempts, and continues to challenge recent laws that it believes compromise the privacy of library patrons. If history is any indication, attempts to use library information for these other means will be short lived and ultimately unsuccessful. The tradeoff between the freedom to read (and the associated freedoms of thought and expression) and the enhancement to security that might be gained from breaching the privacy guarantees provided by libraries has been examined many times in the past, and the end result has always been in favor of privacy as a means of ensuring freedom.

However, it would be short-sighted to think that the only threat to the privacy of library patrons comes from governmental attempts to access library records in an attempt to discover what citizens are thinking or studying. As the format of the content that libraries offer their patrons becomes more and more digitally based, attempts by the providers of that content to ensure that they retain control of it may become as great a threat as that posed by the government, because of the financial implications of such control. While statutes like the USA PATRIOT Act may define the current battleground for the library community's attempt to ensure patron privacy, DRMTs may well define the next battleground.

9

Privacy, Law Enforcement, and National Security

The tension between individual privacy and law enforcement or national security interests has been an enduring force in American life, its origins long predating the advent of new media or current technologies. Nowhere else is the tension between "it's none of your business" and "what have you got to hide" so easily seen.[1]

Although these tensions predate the information revolution, new technologies, new societal contexts, and new circumstances have sharply intensified that conflict, and even changed its focus. Section 9.1 focuses on the uses of information technology in law enforcement and discusses the pressures that such uses place on individual privacy. Section 9.2 does the same for national security and intelligence.

---

[1]As an illustration of the latter, Houston police chief Harold Hurtt referred to a proposal to place surveillance cameras in apartment complexes, downtown streets, shopping malls, and even private homes to fight crime during a shortage of police officers and told reporters at a police briefing, "I know a lot of people are concerned about Big Brother, but my response to that is, if you are not doing anything wrong, why should you worry about it?" See Pam Easton, "Houston Eyes Cameras at Apartment Complexes," *Associated Press Newswire*, February 15, 2006.

9.1 INFORMATION TECHNOLOGY, PRIVACY, AND LAW ENFORCEMENT

9.1.1 Background

By its very nature, law enforcement is an information-rich activity. The information activities of law enforcement can be broken into three categories.

1. Gathering and analyzing information to determine that a law has been violated;
2. Gathering and analyzing information to determine the identity of the person or persons responsible for a violation of law; and
3. Gathering and analyzing information to enable a legal showing in court that the person or persons identified in fact were guilty of the violation.

All of these gathering and analysis activities have been altered in basic ways by functional advancements in the technologies that have become available for collecting, storing, and manipulating data.

In actual practice, these categories can overlap or the activities in each category can occur in several temporal sequences. When a police officer observes someone breaking a law, the officer is determining that a law has been violated, gathering information about who broke the law (presumably the person he or she is observing), and gaining evidence that may be introduced in court (the testimony of the officer).

The essential difference between these categories is the locus or subject about which the information is gathered. In the first category concerning the breaking of a law, the locus of information is the event or activity. In the second sort of activity, the locus is the determination of an individual or set of individuals involved in the activity. In the third category, information associated with categories one and two are combined in an attempt to link the two in a provable way.

Although activities in the first category usually precede those in the second, this is not always the case. Law enforcement authorities have been known to start with "suspicious people" and then seek to discover what laws they might have broken, might be breaking, or might be planning to break. This is one of the rationales for certain kinds of undercover activity and is frequently regarded as more controversial.

These distinctions are important because they help to differentiate cases that generate concern about invasions of privacy from those that involve less controversial uses of the state's investigatory power.

Concerns about privacy invasions often involve the possibility that law enforcement officials can cast an unduly broad net, or one that is seen as discriminatory, as they gather information about persons in the absence of specific reasons to suspect that these individuals have violated some particular law.

A case in which an individual is targeted to see if he or she has violated a law is conceptually (and legally and morally) different from a case in which information is gathered about an individual as part of an investigation into a known or suspected violation of law or in which there are other grounds for suspicion. In the former case, information may be gathered about individuals who in fact were not involved in a violation—which is different in kind from the task of assembling information about an individual in the hope of finding a violation of law.

The potential for data gathering targeted at a particular individual or set of individuals to aid in the discovery of previously unknown violations of the law, or the risk that data gathered by law enforcement may be used for political or harassment purposes, often underlies efforts to restrict the kinds of information that law enforcement agencies can gather and the ways in which it is gathered. Even if the information is never used, the very fact that considerable amounts of data have been collected about individuals who have not been accused or convicted of a crime ensures that substantial amounts of information about non-criminals will end up in the databases of law enforcement agencies. Moreover, with such data a permanent part of their files, citizens may be concerned that this information will eventually be misused or mistakenly released, even if they are not suspects in any crime. They may even engage in self-censorship, and refrain from expressing unpopular opinions. For individuals in this position, issues such as recourse for police misbehavior or carelessness are thus very important.

Nor are worries about the gathering of information by law enforcement agencies restricted to how that information could be used in legal proceedings. Such proceedings are governed by the laws and professional ethics that protect the privacy of the individual, and the inappropriate use (in a criminal context) of information gathered by law enforcement agencies can be balanced by judicial review. However, even the suspicion of wrongdoing or being a "person of interest" can have an effect on an individual's ability to fly in a commercial airliner, obtain certain kinds of permits, gain some kinds of employment, obtain financial services, or conduct business. For example, watch lists, such as those used by the Transportation Security Agency, are not subject to the same level of scrutiny as evidence in a court of law yet can still affect the lives of those whose names appear on such lists. These uses of information are often not balanced by judicial or any other kinds of review, leaving the individual at a severe disadvantage when information is inaccurate or incomplete.[2]

None of these concerns about balancing the need for law enforcement agencies to gather information and the need of the citizen for privacy are new. What is new are the modern information technologies that law enforcement agencies can now use to observe situations and identify individuals more quickly, more accurately, and at less expense than ever before. These technologies include surveillance cameras, large-scale databases, and analytical techniques that enable the extraction of useful information from large masses of otherwise irrelevant information.

The sections that follow describe a number of technologies that allow law enforcement agencies expanded capabilities to observe, to listen, and to gather information about the population. Just as the ability to tap phone lines offered law enforcement new tools to gather evidence in the past century, so also these new technologies expand opportunities to discover breaches in the law, identify those responsible, and collect the evidence needed to prosecute. And just like the ability to tap telephones, these new technologies raise concerns about the privacy of those who are—rightly or wrongly—the targets of the new technologies. Use of the technologies discussed requires careful consideration of the resulting tension posed between two legitimate and sometimes competing goals: information gathering for law enforcement purposes and privacy protection.

9.1.2 Technology and Physical Observation

As a point of departure, consider the issue of privacy as it relates to government authorities conducting surveillance of its citizens. Using the anchoring vignette approach described in Chapter 2 (see Box 2.2), a possible survey question might be, *How much does [your/"Name's"] local town or city government respect [your/"Name's"] privacy in [your/her/his] routine local activities?* Here are a number of possibilities:

1. [Anita] lives in a city that prohibits any form of video or photographic monitoring by government agencies.
2. [Bita] commutes to work every day into a city that automatically photographs each car to see whether it runs a particular stoplight.
3. [Jake] lives in a city that videotapes all cars on city-owned property.

---

[2]See, for example, Peter M. Shane, "The Bureaucratic Due Process of Government Watch Lists," Ohio State Public Law Working Paper No. 55, February 2006, available at http://ssrn.com/abstract=896740.

4. [Beth] lives in a city that videotapes all people inside the hallways of city-owned buildings.

5. [Mark] lives in a city that uses a device in police cars to detect whether individuals are at home.

6. [Juanita] lives in a city that uses an imaging device in police cars that can see through walls and clothes.

These vignettes, ordered from most to least privacy-protecting, illustrate only a single dimension of privacy (namely image-based personal information), but they are a starting point for knowing what must be analyzed and understood in this particular situation, and what decisions society will have to make with respect to the issues the vignettes raise.

Whether it is used to see that a law has been or is being broken, to determine who broke the law, or to find a suspect for arrest, physical observation has historically been the main mechanism by which law enforcement agencies do their job. Physical observation is performed by law enforcement officers themselves, and also by citizens called as witnesses in an investigation or a trial. The vignettes above suggest that physical observation has evolved far beyond the in-person human witness in sight of the event in question.

When individuals are watched, particularly by the state with its special powers, privacy questions are obviously relevant. The usual expectation is that, unless there is a reason to suspect an individual of some particular infraction of the law, individuals will not be under observation by law enforcement agencies. But because of advances in technology, the means by which law enforcement can conduct physical observation or surveillance have expanded dramatically. New technologies that provide automated surveillance capabilities are relatively inexpensive per unit of data acquired; vastly expand memory and analytical ability, as well as the range and power of the senses (particularly seeing and hearing); and are easily hidden and more difficult to discover than traditional methods. They can be used to observe violations of law as well as a particular individual over extended periods of time unbeknownst to him or her.

Today, for example, the use of video cameras is pervasive. Once only found in high-security environments, they are now deployed in most stores and in many parks and schools, along roads, and in public gathering places. A result is that many people, especially in larger cities, are under recorded surveillance for much of the time that they are outside their homes.

Law enforcement officials, and indeed much of the public, believe that video cameras support law enforcement investigations, offering the prospect of a video record of any crime committed in public areas where they are used. Such a record is believed to have both investigatory value (in identifying perpetrators) and deterrent value (in dissuading would-be perpetrators from committing crimes).[3] However, these cameras also give those who operate them ever more information, often in the form of a reusable and possibly permanent record regarding where many law-abiding individuals are, who they are with, and what they are doing.

Another example concerns automobiles equipped with tracking systems, such as General Motors' OnStar system, that permit the location tracking to a fairly fine resolution of anyone holding a cell phone. (Such systems may be based on the use of GPS or on cell phones that provide location information as part of E-911 services.) By tracking people's position over time, it is also possible to track their average speed,[4] where they have been, and (by merging the positional information for multiple people) with whom they might have met. If such tracking is recorded, correlations can be made at any time in the future. Indeed, given the right monitoring equipment and enough recording space, it is even possible that the locations of every person for much of a lifetime could be made available to law enforcement agencies or even family members or researchers.

Similar issues regarding data reuse arise with respect to the use of video cameras for the enforcement of traffic regulations. In many cities the traffic lights have been equipped with cameras that allow law enforcement agencies to determine violations of red-light stop zones simply by photographing the offending vehicles as they pass through the red light. Such images allow local police agencies to automatically send red-light-running tickets to the vehicle owners. Even such a seemingly straightforward use of surveillance technology, however, brings up a host of privacy

---

[3]It is unquestionable that video records have had forensic value in the investigations of crimes that have already been committed. The deterrent effect is less clear. A study done for the British Home Office on the crime prevention effects of closed-circuit television (CCTV) cameras systematically reviewed two dozen other empirical studies on this subject and concluded that, on balance, the evidence suggested a small effect on crime reduction (on the order of a few percent) and only in a limited set of venues (namely, car parks). The deployment of CCTV cameras had essentially no effect in public transportation or in city-center contexts. Welsh and Farrington also noted that poorly controlled studies systematically indicated larger effects than did well-controlled ones. See Brandon Welsh and David Farrington, *Crime Prevention Effects of Closed Circuit Television*, Home Office Research Study 252, August 2002, available at http://www.homeoffice.gov.uk/rds/pdfs2/hors252.pdf.

[4]A lower-tech version of this capability is inherent in toll systems on highways. For some highways, periodic toll plazas on turnpikes were replaced by a system in which the driver picked up a ticket at the point of entry that was then used to determine the toll at the location where the car exited. Given that these tickets included the time of entry into the turnpike, there were concerns that the tickets could also be used upon exit to determine if the car had exceeded the speed limit. Stories of such secondary use have the ring of urban myth, but they continue to surface on the Internet and are certainly consistent with what the technology enables.

issues. For example, consider that these cameras could also be used to trace and record the presumed locations of people based on the observed time and location of their cars. That is, they could take pictures even when no car was running a red light. Such a concern is based on the future possibilities for repurposing the information gathered by such cameras rather than on the purpose for which these cameras were originally deployed.

Note that nothing intrinsic in the use of a video system to catch those running traffic lights enables secondary use of the information. The system could be designed in such a way that only those images showing someone running a red light were kept, and all other images were discarded immediately. Such a system could not be used to track the location of any but a small number of vehicles. Designing such a system in this way is simple to do when the system is first being built but is far more difficult once the system has been installed. However, privacy concerns associated with possible secondary uses are usually not raised when a system is designed, if nothing else because those secondary uses are not yet known or anticipated.

It could be argued that a video camera at the stoplight is no different in principle from posting a live police officer at the same place. A police officer can issue a ticket for a car that runs a red light, and if a live police officer on traffic detail at the intersection is not a threat to privacy, then neither is the placement of a video camera there. Others, however, would argue that a live officer could not accurately record all vehicles passing lawfully through the intersection, and could not be used to trace the movements of every vehicle passing through a busy intersection—lawfully or not—in the way that a video camera can. The image-retention capacity of a video system vastly exceeds that of even the most astute human observer and thus allows the tracking of all vehicles, not just those that are of interest at the time they move through the intersection. The images stored by the video system can, in principle, be not just those of vehicles that have violated the law, but of all vehicles that have passed by the camera.

In addition, information gathered by a video camera ostensibly deployed to catch cars running a red light can be used for other purposes, such as tracking the location of particular cars at particular points in time, or finding speeders (this would require combining of information from multiple cameras at multiple locations)—purposes that are not possible with a human officer. Further, when the images are stored, law enforcement agencies gain the capability to track what individuals have done in the past, and not just what they are currently doing. The worry is that once the information has been gathered and stored, it will be used in a variety of ways other than that for which it was originally intended. Such "feature creep" is possible because what is stored is the raw information, in image form, which can be used in a variety of ways.

Finally, video surveillance is far less expensive than the use of many human officers. From an economic point of view, it is impossible in large jurisdictions to station officers at every intersection, but placing a video camera at many intersections is much less expensive and within the means of many police departments. An important check on executive power has always been based on the allocation of resources, and if technology can enable a greater amount of police activity—in particular, more surveillance—for the same cost, the introduction of that technology changes the balance of power. Perhaps most importantly, this change in the balance of power is often unnoticed or not discussed—and when it is, a dispute about the amount of police activity must be resolved explicitly on policy grounds rather than implicitly on economic grounds.

Beyond video technologies such as those discussed above, there is also the prospect that emerging technologies can extend the reach of observation from public spaces into what have traditionally been private spaces. There has been some use of infrared detectors to "look through" walls and see into a suspect's home;[5] although the Supreme Court recently suggested that such law enforcement surveillance tactics might violate the resident's "reasonable expectation of privacy" (Section 1.5.5), the courts have not categorically rejected the use of such sophisticated imaging devices. If environmental sensors become pervasive, it may in the near future become possible to infer the location of people from the information gathered for purposes such as energy conservation—and to infer identities by correlating that information with other recorded information (such as building access records).

The conditions under which law enforcement agencies will or should have access to such information raises difficult questions both of law and of policy. Concern over the potential use of such sensitive information lies at the heart of many privacy-based concerns about the deployment of such technologies. The deepest concern, from the privacy perspective, is the potential for combining constant and non-obvious data gathering and the ability to assemble the data gathered to give the effect of largely constant observation of any space, whether public or private. Such a prospect, combined with the temporally permanent nature of the data when they are stored, appears to give law enforcement agencies the ability to constantly monitor almost any place and to have access to a history of that

---

[5]A number of court cases have been brought addressing the question of whether the use of a thermal-imaging device aimed at a private home from a public street to detect relative amounts of heat within the home constitutes a "search" within the meaning of the Fourth Amendment. The definitive ruling on this point is the decision of the U.S. Supreme Court in *Kyllo v. United States*, No. 99-8508 and decided on June 11, 2001, which held that it *is* a search and thus must be governed by the apparatus designed to protect the public against unreasonable searches.

place. Together with the ability to aggregate and mine the data that have been gathered (discussed below), this prospect would appear to give law enforcement enormous amounts of information.

The most serious issues arise if and when such technologies enable monitoring of specific individuals. Many present-day technologies indicate bodies, but not the identities of the persons who own those bodies. Future technologies may enable the identification of individuals—that is, the high-accuracy association of specific names with the bodies within view—in which case the privacy concerns are accentuated many-fold. (Even today, modern cell phones with location identification capabilities yield information about the whereabouts of individuals, because of the generally unviolated presumption that individuals carry their cell phones with them.)

9.1.3 Communications and Data Storage

Both communication and data storage technologies have long been of interest and use to the law enforcement community. Being able to observe and overhear the discussions of those suspected of breaking the law and to obtain records of criminal activity has been an important means for gaining evidence—but has also created inevitable threats to principles of privacy.

The primary difference between records and communications is that by definition, records are intended to persist over time, whereas communications are more transient. Transient phenomena vanish, and they are generally more private than persistent entities that can be reviewed anew, copied, and circulated. For this reason, technologies that threaten the privacy of records are often seen as less problematic than those that threaten the privacy of communications.

For keeping records private, the most common technique used has been to hide the records in a location known only to their owner. One can "hide" records by placing the file in a secret location (e.g., in an "invisible" directory on one's disk, on a CD-ROM stored under the mattress or under a rock in the back yard or in a safe deposit box, or embedded secretly in another document). Today, there are few generally applicable technologies that enable law enforcement authorities to find records in a secret location without the (witting or unwitting) cooperation of their owner. Thus, debates over the appropriate balance between the privacy of records—even digital records—and the needs of law enforcement authorities for those records have been relatively straightforward, and based on the ability of law enforcement authorities to compel or trick the owner into revealing the records' location. (The use of encryption to hide records, discussed in more detail below, presents a wrinkle in this debate, but the same techniques are available to law enforcement authorities to compel or trick the owner or others into revealing the decryption keys that would allow law enforcement access.)

But history paints a much different picture when it comes to communications. For the interception of telephone conversations, e-mail, and Internet-based communication, the proper balance between the claimed needs of law enforcement for access to such communications, and the privacy interests of persons who are the participants in the targeted communication, has been elusive and more difficult to define.

When the Bill of Rights was enacted, communication consisted either of spoken language (which could only be heard directly) or written. Written communications are a type of record, and such records can be obtained by law enforcement personnel as the result of a search (under rules covered by the Fourth Amendment). But what of written communications being sent through the mails—were these communications more like utterances made in public, and therefore not subject to the same explicit protections of privacy, or were they more like records private and covered by the protections of the Fourth Amendment?

In the case of mail carried by the U.S. Postal Service, the decision was that the outside of the mail (such as the address and return address) was public information, and not covered by the need for a search warrant,[6] but that any communication inside the envelope was considered private and any viewing of that information by law enforcement required a search warrant obtained under the requirements of probable cause.[7]

As communication technologies advanced, the distinction between what was publicly available and what was private in those technologies became the crux of the debates about the privacy of those communica-

---

[6]*Ex Parte Jackson*, 96 U.S. (6 Otto) 727,733 (1877).

[7]The process by which national security investigators have obtained mail cover information has been governed by U.S. postal regulations for nearly 30 years. See 39 C.F.R. 233.3. The authority to use mail covers for law enforcement purposes first appeared in the 1879 postal regulations. Section 212 statutorily authorizes the continued use of mail covers in national security investigations. A "mail cover" is the process by which the U.S. Postal Service furnishes to the FBI the information appearing on the face of an envelope addressed to a particular address: i.e., addressee, postmark, name and address of sender (if it appears), and class of mail. The actual mail is delivered to the addressee, and only the letter carrier's notation reaches the FBI. A mail cover does not include the contents of any "sealed mail," as defined in existing U.S. postal regulations (see 39 C.F.R. 233.3(c)(3)) and incorporated in Section 212. Although the Supreme Court has not directly addressed the constitutionality of mail covers (the Court has denied certiorari in cases involving the issue), lower courts have uniformly upheld the use of mail covers as consistent with the requirements of the Fourth Amendment. See *Vreeken v. Davis*, 718 F.2d 343 (10th Cir. 1983); *United States v. DePoli*, 628 F.2d 779 (2d Cir. 1980); *United States v. Huie*, 593 F.2d 14 (5th Cir. 1979); and *United States v. Choate*, 576 F.2d 165 (9th Cir.), cert. denied, 439 U.S. 953 (1978).

tions and what access law enforcement agencies had to the communication. Perhaps the best example concerns communication by telephone. When telephones were first introduced, the circuits were connected by an operator who often needed to listen in on the call to monitor quality, and most of the telephone lines were shared or "party" lines, allowing conversations to be heard by anyone with whom the line was shared (although good manners suggested not listening when the call was not for you).

With this history, it was generally held that discussions over a telephone were like discussions in public, so that law enforcement agents could listen in on such conversations, and could use in criminal prosecutions the contents of what they heard, with no oversight and without the consent of those whose words were monitored. Indeed, in *Olmstead v. United States*, 277 U.S. 438 (1928), the U.S. Supreme Court held that "the reasonable view is that one who installs in his house a telephone instrument with connecting wires intends to project his voice to those quite outside, and that the wires beyond his house, and messages while passing over them, are not within the protection of the Fourth Amendment. Here those who intercepted the projected voices were not in the house of either party to the conversation." In so holding, it ruled that "the wire tapping here disclosed [in the case] did not amount to a search or seizure within the meaning of the Fourth Amendment," and thus that telephone conversations were not protected or privileged in any way over ordinary speech outside the home. There was, in this view, no (rational) expectation of privacy for such conversations (although the term "expectation of privacy" had not yet come into use).

This view of telephone conversations lasted until 1967,[8] when the Supreme Court ruled that there was, in fact, a constitutional expectation of privacy in the use of the telephone. By this time, operators were hardly ever used for the connection of circuits and were not expected to monitor the quality of phone conversations, nor were most phone lines shared. However, the decision that there was an expectation of privacy in such conversations lagged significantly behind the technological developments that created such an expectation. At this point, the court decided that telephone calls were like physical mail, in which each call had a public "outside" and a private "contents." The public envelope contained the information necessary to establish the circuit for the call (including the phone from which the call was being made and the phone to which the call was made) but did not include the contents of the call, which was considered private. Gaining legal access to that part of the call required a warrant issued by a judge after a showing of probable cause.

The last two decades have seen a novel set of communication technol-

---

[8] *Katz v. United States*, 389 U.S. 347.

ogies become generally available. The Internet, encompassing both electronic mail and the World Wide Web, has provided new mechanisms for communication. The Web allows one-to-many communication, enabling nearly everyone to be a publisher for very little cost. Electronic mail allows communication between parties in ways that are fast, efficient, and highly resilient to failure. The cell phone network has changed many of the old limitations on telephony, allowing conversations between people who are mobile. New emerging technologies such as voice-over-IP, in which telephone-like communication can be carried over the same Internet using protocols first designed for data transmission, merge the functionality of voice networks with the underlying technologies of data networks.

New communication technologies are of obvious interest to law enforcement agencies. Some law enforcement officials see the Web sites that a person visits, or the e-mail that a person sends or receives, as information that could be relevant to the prosecution of criminals. On that basis, they have argued that law enforcement agencies should have legal access to such information equivalent to that available for telephone conversations. Law enforcement officials currently have access to pen registers and trap-and-trace registers on telephone calls, which show what calls were made from a particular phone (pen registers) or to the phone (trap and trace). The installation or attachment of pen registers and trap-and-trace registers does require a court order, but obtaining such an order need not overcome a high standard of probable cause, requiring only a request by the law enforcement agency. Similarly, because agents can discover the source and destination of paper mail simply by observing an envelope, it has been argued by analogy that law enforcement agencies should have access to the destinations of Web browsing and e-mail messages. Those who are troubled by this analogy note (correctly) that on the Internet addressing information cannot easily be separated from the content of the message, a distinction that is central to the availability of routing information for telephone calls and paper mail (Box 9.1).

In a similar fashion, cell phone networks are quite different from those that connect landlines. Cell phone networks allow the users to move while a call is in progress. This new functionality requires that the "circuit" connecting the cell phone and the rest of the network go through a series of connections, depending on the cell that is handling the phone. As the phone moves from one cell to another, technical hand-off protocols allow the voice traffic to be moved from cell to cell without the interruption of service. While the voice service being offered is similar to that provided by landlines, the technology underlying the network is very different.

The claim that law enforcement should have access to Internet and cell phone communication rests on analogies drawn between these sorts of communication and more traditional communication mechanisms such as landline phones and physical mail. However, the technology needed to provide the same capabilities is very different, as the characteristics of the networks underlying the communication mechanisms are very different. The separation of information that made it possible to provide the "public" information without compromising the "private" information is a property of the underlying network. While it is possible to separate seeing the addressing information on a piece of sealed physical mail from seeing its content (although the letter could always be surreptitiously opened), there is no easy equivalent physical separation for electronic mail.

Debates over law enforcement access to Internet and cell phone communications also reveal another point of contention that is rarely acknowledged explicitly: whether the protection of privacy should be a property or a characteristic or a feature afforded by technology or by policy. Those taking the position that the protection of privacy should be technologically based argue that technologically based assurances of privacy cannot be easily circumvented by capricious changes in policy or by law enforcement personnel acting outside their authority. A more moderate version of this position is to build technology that enforces policy rigidly, so that, for example, a wiretap that requires legal authorization from a judge cannot physically be performed without a one-time-use key (physical or logical) that is available only from a judge. Thus, grounding privacy protection in technology eliminates or reduces the need to trust law enforcement authorities to respect privacy rights of law-abiding citizens, and advocates of this position often justify their position by references to past government violations of privacy.

By contrast, those who argue that policy considerations should be the source of privacy protections note that without special attention, changing technologies can also change the pre-existing balance between privacy protection and law enforcement access—a balance that has been obtained through the policy-making process, and thus should be changed only by that process (rather than by technological advancement). Further, they argue, procedural protections—such as excluding evidence obtained through improperly obtained techniques and strict enforcement of internal regulations against improper behavior—suffice to deter abuse of authority. Thus, proponents of this position argue that technological developments in communications should be guided or regulated in such a way that they do not compromise the communications access capabilities that prior policy decisions have endorsed and sanctioned. Policy decisions and law, rather than ever-changing technology, should determine functionality and use.

These differences in perspective have played out many times in recent years, notably in debates over the Communications Access for Law

---

BOX 9.1
Telephone Networks, Data Networks, and the Law

Much of the law having to do with access by law enforcement and national security agencies to data networks has been drawn from similar laws dealing with telephone networks. Indeed, notions of tapping a communication line and establishing pen registers, and decisions about when a warrant is needed for data communications, often make explicit reference to the decisions and laws governing the phone network. Intuitively, such an extension from the phone system to data networks like the Internet makes sense. Both are communication networks, and much of the traffic that is now carried over the Internet (such as e-mail and newsgroups) was originally carried over the phone lines. However, these analogies lead to confusing and contradictory results, since the technology underlying data networks such as the Internet and the technology that underlies phone networks are intrinsically different in ways that are relevant to the decisions that have been made.

Traditional phone networks are circuit based. When a phone call is initiated, information is supplied to the network that allows a bidirectional connection to be made between the caller and the phone being called. In early incarnations of the phone network, this was done by calling an operator, who would literally connect a cable that would complete the connection between the two phones. Automated switching and dialing have eliminated the operator, but the idea is the same; when you dial a call, the switching hardware is used to create a connection between the two phones that is unshared, is bidirectional, and carries the signal that is the conversation between one phone and the other.

Unlike the traditional phone network, the protocols that are the basis of the Internet are packet based. Rather than establishing a circuit between the sender of information and the receiver and then sending the information over that circuit, any message is broken into chunks, with each chunk being wrapped with information about its destination and each being sent over the network. These packets are sent from one machine to another, with each machine looking at the information having to do with where the packet is to be sent and forwarding that packet. Different packets may take very different routes to the same destination. At the final destination, the packets are reassembled into a single message, which is then delivered to the intended recipient.

One of the major differences between a packet-based network and a circuit-based network is that a packet-based network mixes the routing information with the information being sent over the network. In a circuit-based network, the routing information is used only to establish a circuit; once the circuit is established this information is not needed. Further, during the establishment of the circuit, no content is sent or revealed. Packet-based networks make no such separation between the routing information and the content—indeed, these two kinds of information are present in all of the packets.

Enforcement Act (CALEA) and over encryption. CALEA required that telecommunications providers build into their networks and switching systems the capability to provide the contents of voice communications to law enforcement authorities (subject to all of the existing restrictions on such wiretaps imposed by law) regardless of the technology used. Thus,

These differences may seem minor until we see how the law has been extended from one kind of network to the other. For example, the law concerning interception of communication on a traditional phone network distinguishes between a pen register, which allows the recording of the establishment of a call (essentially, a trace of all of the calls made from a particular phone, showing the numbers to which the calls were made) and tapping the phone, which allows listening in on the conversation. The burden of proof for a pen register is much lower than that for a phone tap. Such a distinction makes sense in the case of the traditional phone network, where the information gathered as part of the pen register is concerned with the setting up of the circuit, which happens in a fashion that is distinct from the carrying of information over the circuit.

Extending the distinction between a pen registry and a full tap is not so easy in the case of a packet-based network. As with phone networks, requests by law enforcement agencies for information about the recipients of messages from a computer require much less cause for granting than requests to intercept the content of such messages. However, since the routing information is mingled with the content, it is not clear how the observation of the routing information can be done in such a way that the content of the messages is not also revealed.

Circuit-based networks also dedicate a separate circuit to each connection, keeping the contents of each circuit separate. This allows the tapping of a particular telephone conversation to be done without the observation of the contents of other telephone conversations. In packet-based networks, there is no such isolation of contents. Packets from all communications are mixed together on the same network, and it is only by the observation of the packets that one can tell which packet is part of which communication. This also means that any attempt to view the contents of one communication on such a packet-based network can require the observation of many other communications over that network.

There have been attempts to interpose technology on packet-based networks in an attempt to allow pen registries and isolated tapping of communications in such networks. One such attempt was the Carnivore program,[1] which interposed a piece of specialized hardware between the network and the observers of network communications. The purpose of the hardware was to pass along to law enforcement officials only those packets that they had legal authorization to read, but to do so the hardware had to observe all packets passing by. However, critics noted that the hardware was under the control of the very agencies that were doing the observation, and that the process required trust in the law enforcement agency using the hardware to configure it properly (i.e., to pass along only the legally authorized information) without external oversight.

---

[1]For more information on Carnivore, see *Independent Technical Review of the Carnivore System Final Report*, IIT Research Institute, December 8, 2000, available at http://www.usdoj.gov/jmd/publications/carniv_final.pdf.

debates have arisen about the extent and nature of technological measures needed to comply with this regulation with technologies in use such as voice-over-IP and cellular technology.

In the case of encryption, the past 20 years have seen a revolution in easy access to encryption technology, and easy access to high-grade cryptography has the potential to change the balance between individuals and their government (Box 9.2). With encryption widely available today, it is now possible for agencies to have physical access to data but not be able to interpret the data without the cooperation of parties with access to the relevant decryption keys.

Law enforcement authorities have expressed concerns that the use of encryption by criminals would stymie access to communications and records important to prosecution. A problem arises because encryption is also a tool that can be used to prevent many crimes—theft of proprietary data, identity theft, non-authorized wiretapping, and so on.

To address this issue, the U.S. government proposed in the 1990s a concept of encryption known as key escrow, in which strong encryption systems would be allowed subject to the proviso that the decryption keys for such systems be placed in a database that could be accessed by the government under certain conditions.[9] While the initial plans for such a database required that access be protected by ensuring court review, privacy objections to the plan were based on the inability of the government to guarantee that such review would always be required and that the requirement for such a review would always be followed. Furthermore, implementing key escrow would potentially introduce additional security vulnerabilities that non-governmental entities could exploit. For these and other reasons unrelated to the protection of personal privacy, key escrow systems for communications have largely been abandoned.[10]

9.1.4 Technology and Identification

Observation of the physical presence of a person, or the ability to intercept the communications of a person, is most useful to law enforcement if the person who is being observed, or whose communications are intercepted, can be identified. Identification is essential to enable multiple observations or communications to be correlated. It is the identity of the individual that allows a coherent picture to be pieced together from the set of observations and communications that have been taken. Even when sure identification of the individual is impossible, the ability to limit the identity to a member of a small group might be enough to make

---

[9]For more discussion, see National Research Council, *Cryptography's Role in Securing the Information Society*, Kenneth W. Dam and Herbert S. Lin, eds., National Academy Press, Washington, D.C., 1996.

[10]However, key escrow systems for data storage have been deployed with some success, simply because there are good business reasons for such systems. In these systems, keys for emergency decryption are stored in a database controlled by the owner of the records being stored, and if that owner loses the decryption keys, the backup keys still remain available.

BOX 9.2
Encryption

For many years, strong encryption algorithms were the property and province of government, since the ability to generate good encryption algorithms and to build the machinery to employ those algorithms was prohibitively expensive for most corporations, let alone individuals. However, the combination of much faster computing machinery and the development of public-key cryptosystems (along with the expanded interest in other cryptographic systems) have brought within the abilities of an individual the capacity to encrypt all of his or her data in a way that makes it extremely difficult (or impossible) and costly for law enforcement agencies to read that data.

Such cryptographic techniques are no longer limited to computer-based communication systems. As more and more communication systems move to a digital base, it becomes progressively easier to apply the same cryptographic techniques used in computers to those other communication channels. Cell phones, which are now reaching the computational capacity found only on desktop computers as recently as 3 to 5 years ago, are now capable of performing reasonable-grade cryptography on voice communications.

One method to prevent criminal use of encryption would be to forbid private encryption, making the private possession of encryption devices an offense by itself. This is not feasible for two reasons. First, it would necessarily outlaw the legitimate applications of cryptography, such as those used to secure networks, enable safe electronic commerce, and protect intellectual property. Second, it would be largely impossible to enforce, since any general-purpose computer (including anyone's desktop machine) can be programmed to provide encryption capabilities. Consider, for example, software cryptographic systems such as Pretty Good Privacy (PGP) that are easily obtained in open-source form and can be built and run by users with little technical sophistication, or commercial operating systems such as Mac OS X and Windows that include features that allow all of the user's data to be encrypted (in the case of the Macintosh, using a U.S. government-approved encryption algorithm). Utilities such as the secure shell (SSH) allow easy encryption of data over the network.

Historically, the U.S. government's position on cryptography reflected the premises that drove the asserted need for national security access to data. By limiting the economic viability of developing strong cryptographic systems (by, for example, making it difficult for U.S. information technology vendors to export such systems), the spread of strong cryptography internationally was inhibited for many years, and this phenomenon had the collateral effect of inhibiting the domestic use of cryptography as well. Law enforcement considerations were much more prominent in the key escrow proposal, which the administration floated in the mid-1990s as an intermediate step between weak encryption and the widespread availability of strong encryption.

the information useful in an investigation. Further, the ability to identify an individual is essential to the capturing of that individual once it has been determined that there is reason to prosecute that individual for some violation of law.

The most common form of identification is that which occurs when some other person directly observes and identifies a suspect or target. However, such identification requires that the person to be identified must first be known to the person doing the identification. The most common form of identification not dependent on personal knowledge of the suspect or target involves the use of identification documents. Such documents are often government issued, although there is currently no single governing standard in the United States for whom and under what circumstances such a document is issued. Indeed, the chain of documents used to establish identity often leads through multiple governmental bodies; passports (which are issued by the federal government) are often issued based on identity established via a driver's license (issued by the state government) and a birth certificate (usually issued by the city or county). This documentation chain is long enough and the connections between the documents tenuous enough that it is often possible to obtain fraudulent identification.[11]

The task of identification in the law enforcement context is complicated by at least two factors. The first is that the person who is the subject or target may wish to remain anonymous, and will thus have done whatever is possible to preclude or at least hamper accurate identification. This process does not entail identification in the sense of authentication, where all that is at issue is whether or not the subject is who he or she claims to be with respect to some (often non-personal) standard of eligibility, but rather full-fledged identification, where the task is to determine, often in the face of falsified evidence or testimony, a person's true identity.[12] The second complicating factor is that law enforcement can seek to identify a subject at various times during an investigation, using different types of evidence. Such evidence might be the reports of an eyewitness or might involve more circumstantial evidence (such as the use of a computer or cell phone at a particular time).

Biometrics is a technology that has long been used to aid in the identification of persons. Perhaps the best known biometric identification system involves the use of fingerprints. The use of fingerprints for

---

[11]National Research Council, *IDs—Not That Easy: Questions About Nationwide Identity Systems*, Stephen T. Kent and Lynette I. Millett, eds., National Academy Press, Washington, D.C., 2002.

[12]Recall that Section 1.5.1 of this report comments on the issue of a person's "true" identity.

identification is possible because of two factors: the putative uniqueness of a person's fingerprints and their relatively unchanging nature over time. Because of these characteristics, fingerprints can be used to identify a subject as the same person over time (although not identify who that person is, unless there are prior records that associate a particular fingerprint with a particular individual on the basis of still other records or accounts).

The ability to identify a person consistently over time is all that is needed to knit together the information that might be gathered about an individual through observation (either direct or indirect) or through the interception of communications. Technology is beginning to provide a number of such biometric measures that are of interest to law enforcement agencies. Emerging as an identification mechanism on a par with fingerprints is DNA profiling, which has been used in court cases to establish that a subject is (or is not) the person who left some DNA at a crime scene. Other biometrics that can aid in uniquely identifying a person, such as palm prints or retinal scanning, are being investigated as mechanisms to ensure the identity of a person, both by law enforcement agencies and to aid in the control of access to secure areas. None of these forms of identification is foolproof, with some (like fingerprints and DNA profiling) offering a high degree of accuracy, and others (such as palm prints, retinal scanning, or voice prints) having a lower degree of accuracy today. Most must be measured either in the laboratory or in carefully controlled conditions.

The aforementioned biometric mechanisms share a third characteristic: most currently require that the person being identified be in close proximity to or in actual contact with the device that is doing the reading of the biometric identifier, and are therefore seldom if ever used without the knowledge (and, often, without the consent and active participation) of the person being identified. Of even greater interest to the law enforcement community and relevance to issues of privacy are a set of biometric identification techniques that can be used from a distance without the knowledge or consent of the person being identified. Such remote identification techniques offer the promise of being able not only to identify individuals as part of routine observation, but also to aid in the capture of fugitives by enabling covert identification in a broad set of contexts.

Perhaps the best known remote identification technique is automated facial recognition, which attempts to identify a person from the characteristics of his or her face. This technology is currently being used in a number of prototype systems. The technology allows automated matching from a database of pictures to images that can be taken from photographs or video streams. Especially in the case of video streams, facial recognition technology promises to allow the identification of individuals from a distance and without their knowledge (or consent). However, the results of the use of this technology have been mixed, at best, in all but the most controlled of conditions. In addition, there have been few real tests of the efficacy of facial recognition technology in the kinds of environments that are of most interest to law enforcement agencies that have not been conducted by self-interested parties (e.g., the vendors of such technology). Without independent analysis by uninvolved parties, it is difficult to assess the real promise of such technology.

In the same way that facial recognition technology might be combined with the visual observation technologies to enable the tracking of the activities of a person, the biometric of voice recognition can be used as an identification mechanism for vocal forms of communication. Voice recognition technologies are reasonably robust in controlled environments (making them excellent choices for some forms of access control) but are less so in noisy environments.

Other biometric identification mechanisms have also been proposed or are being actively studied. Among those listed by the International Biometric Group[13] as having "reduced commercial viability or in exploratory stages" are odor recognition, through which an individual can be identified by his or her smell, and gait recognition, in which a person can be recognized by the way in which he or she walks.

Today, the technology is relatively immature for remote biometric identification and/or identification without the consent or participation of the individual being identified, and in no meaningful sense can remote biometric identification technology be said to usefully work. Thus, there exists an opportunity for discussion of the privacy aspects of the technology to begin before the systems have been fully formed.[14] This fact allows, for example, discussions of such things as the repurposing of the identification information or the long-term storage of information coming from such systems before the systems are actually built. The premature deployment of these technologies has made everyone more aware of the problems that can arise because of false positive identifications. By understanding the limitations of these technologies, it is also possible to design

---

[13]International Biometric Group, "What Are the Leading Biometric Technologies?," available at http://www.biometricgroup.com/reports/public/reports/biometric_types.html, accessed June 14, 2006.

[14]Non-consensual and/or remote identification of individuals poses by far the most serious privacy issues, as compared to identification techniques that require consent. However, this is not to say that biometrics of all kinds do not pose other issues. A forthcoming CSTB report on biometrics will address these points in greater detail than is possible here, but as one example, consider the possibility that a biometric identifier might somehow be compromised. "Gummi bear" fingerprint duplicates have been used to fool fingerprint readers, thus raising the question of how a biometric identifier might somehow be revoked.

the systems using the technologies for those contexts in which they can be most valuable, rather than thinking that they can be extended to any environment.

Presented in such a way, the debate over the use of biometrics could be an example of how the development of such technology can be more effectively, more rationally, and less contentiously considered in relation to privacy and related values. The technology has great promise but also is open to significant abuse. By raising the issue before it is too late to shape the direction of the technology, the development of biometric identification might offer a model case study for future technologies that pose issues arising from conflicting societal needs.

Biometrics technology by itself is not inevitably privacy invasive. However, when combined with the various forms of surveillance technologies discussed in the previous section, such identification technologies (especially those that allow identification at a distance in a non-invasive fashion) permit the repeated collection of information about individuals and linking of information to that individual. This in turn can be used to populate a database that stores information on where a person has been and when he or she has been there.

9.1.5 Aggregation and Data Mining

Databases, generally in paper format, have long been created and maintained on the habits, histories, and identifying characteristics of those who have been arrested, convicted of breaking laws, or are otherwise considered by law enforcement agencies to be a "person of interest." For example, collections of fingerprints of individuals have been assembled and kept at both the local and national level since the early parts of the 20th century, when it was determined that identification by fingerprint could be used in linking individuals to violations and in locating them for arrest and trial.

Computers were adopted early by law enforcement agencies in order to improve their ability to collect, collate, manipulate, and share information. Moving information into computer databases, rather than keeping it in paper files, allowed the information to be searched, located, shared, and cross-referenced in ways that were previously impossible. By vastly increasing the amount of information that could be gathered and stored and by introducing new ways in which that information could be retrieved and correlated, the computer soon became an indispensable tool in law enforcement.

What has changed is the amount of digital information generated and stored about everyone. Almost every activity in modern life, from grocery shopping to surfing the Web to making a phone call, generates some record in a database somewhere. The sum total of these records, which might be described as our "digital shadow," provides a view into the activities of a person that can reveal activities, interests, tastes, and routines. For law enforcement agencies, these digital shadows can also provide a rich environment for investigation and evidence gathering.

How much of this digital shadow is available to law enforcement agencies, and under what circumstances that information should be available, are currently open questions. Some databases compiled by the federal government, such as those of the Census Bureau, are protected by statutorily enforced confidentiality guarantees, and law enforcement agencies do not have legal access to them. General federal databases are open to law enforcement examination but are governed by the Privacy Act of 1974, which requires that databases containing individually identifying information be identified to the public and that those whose information is stored in those databases be allowed to have access to the information and to correct or amend the information within the database. (This issue is addressed further in Section 9.3.)

Also of interest (and concern) from the privacy perspective are the data gathered and stored by non-governmental agencies. This information would include most of the digital shadow of any individual, including financial information, transaction histories, and the myriad other forms of data that are accumulated about each of us in our everyday lives. Some of this information (such as personal health information stored in one's medical record) is mostly private under existing law. But the vast majority of the information gathered and stored by third parties (such as banks or other financial institutions) has been determined by the courts and legislation not to be private records and is routinely available to law enforcement agencies. When that information is stored electronically, there are fears that the information can be shared and linked even more easily. The end result is that the amount of information that is available to a law enforcement agency about any particular individual is considerable, and the tools that can be used to comb through that information continue to grow in sophistication.

The valid concerns created by the vast amount of information available to law enforcement agencies should be tempered by the realization that the process of aggregating such information is not a simple undertaking. When talking about the information that is gathered by law enforcement agencies, people often speak as if there were a single database containing all of the information about a particular person, or even a single database containing all of the information about all persons. In fact, this is far from the case. Different law enforcement agencies at different levels of government (local, state, federal) do not share a single mega-database of information. Different agencies even at the same level of government maintain their own distinct data repositories. Even within a particular law enforcement agency, there are many different databases, in many different forms, containing the information gathered on individuals. These databases may not share formats, or even have compatible mechanisms for identifying an individual.

As discussed in Section 3.9, aggregation of the information in such databases is not a trivial undertaking. Generally these databases have been designed with different keys, different fields, and different ways of interpreting the fields.

The task of formulating queries that will be understood by multiple databases or in interpreting the results from any such queries requires that the person formulating the query know the details of each of the databases. This task can easily become more complex than current techniques can handle, although in any given instance and with sufficient work, the task is often doable. For example, consider the seemingly simple problem of identifying a person in multiple databases. The name of the person is generally not sufficient for unique identification. Some number can be assigned to the individual, but it is unlikely that the number will be the same from one database to the next unless that number has some other significance (such as being the person's Social Security number).

Nor is it the case that the information gathered by law enforcement, even when in digital form, can always be easily manipulated or aggregated with other information. For example, the video taken from observation cameras may be in digital form, but it is not captured in a form that can easily be manipulated by the computer or correlated with other digital information. To correlate the digital shadow of an individual with the movements of that person as shown by video cameras requires that the video camera images be identified as those of a particular individual. To convert from data that represents information about the light that entered the video lens to information about the location of some person requires the ability to recognize the pictures on the video as particular individuals. As noted above, remote identification technology that will aid in this conversion is currently being developed, but it is far from being in a state that allows even the most sophisticated of government agencies to routinely convert observation information into something that could be used in data-mining applications.

In fact, very little technology exists that allows the automatic conversion of the kinds of raw data collected by the sophisticated sensors discussed above into a format that permits the data to be mined or otherwise collated. If law enforcement agencies have the raw data (in the form of, say, video images from cameras in public places) that would allow them to trace the movements of a person, the technology today will allow that tracing only by the application of large amounts of human effort (a law enforcement agent watching all of the tape for all of the places that a person might have been). Nor is there any feature today that permits these raw data to be converted into information in a fully automated fashion. While there have been attempts to automate such a conversion in the fields of image processing, years of research have failed to move the techniques to a level beyond the most basic, in which images of people (rather than a particular person) can be distinguished from images of other environmental features such as houses or plants. The same also holds for thermal imaging devices, which yield only very crude representations of heat patterns and cannot provide much identification information by themselves. Today, it appears that the automated recognition of individuals will be a labor-intensive activity for the foreseeable future.

Even the much simpler task of identifying the drivers of vehicles that have been photographed running a stoplight cannot currently be automated. In this case, all that is required is identifying the license number on the car, a much simpler task than recognizing a person from a photo of his or her face. But even this seemingly simpler process cannot be executed with the level of fidelity needed for law enforcement purposes, which requires human mediation in the recognition of which car was pictured.

The ability of the police to reconstruct movements of a person of interest has been misconstrued by many as an indication that law enforcement agencies can follow the movements of anyone in an ongoing fashion. However, reconstructions (which often use as data positional information from cars, video images from various public and commercial locations, and the like) are time-consuming, human-intensive activities that can only be done by using the known location of the individual at a given time to reduce the search space of possible locations at a previous time. Connecting the dots, in such cases, is possible only because a human being is looking for a known person at each of the locations where the known "dot" might be present, and when finding such a location is using that information to cut down on the next places to search. It is not an activity that can be fully automated, nor is it one that could be easily and routinely performed for broad segments of the population.

Even if we restrict the supposed data mining to the information in an individual's digital shadow, there are problems inherent in data aggregation. The same information can be represented in very different ways in different databases. Correlating information between those databases is a non-trivial problem, generally requiring significant design and programming to ensure that the information can be interpreted in a consistent way across the databases.

Somewhat ironically, the very fact that the law enforcement agencies were early adopters of information technology now works against their ability to use the cutting edge of that technology. As early adopters, those agencies made significant investments in technology that is now obsolete. Further, those early technologies were developed in a fashion that makes them far more difficult to knit together into integrated systems, instead leaving "silos" of information in the various systems that cannot be correlated in the ways that reflect the worst privacy invasion nightmares. For example, the Federal Bureau of Investigation has struggled for many years to integrate and upgrade its systems,[15] with the end result at this writing that the FBI is still using an antiquated system with capabilities far below those envisioned by people concerned about the use of the system to violate personal privacy.

Law enforcement authorities can also obtain significant amounts of personal information from data aggregation companies, as described in Section 6.5. As noted in that section, there is particular concern over the use by law enforcement agencies of the aggregated information assembled by these companies. The laws and regulations that govern the gathering of information by the law enforcement establishment do not necessarily apply (or do not apply with clarity) to these data aggregators, and there is some concern that by contracting with these companies law enforcement will be able to avoid the restraints that have been placed on it to ensure the privacy of the individual citizen.

9.1.6 Privacy Concerns and Law Enforcement

Any modern society requires an effective and rational law enforcement system. Gathering, storing, and analyzing extensive information are vital to the law enforcement process, even though some information will also be gathered about persons who are manifestly beyond suspicion.

Privacy concerns arise most clearly when law enforcement agencies gather information about those who have broken no law and are not suspects, or when such information is used for purposes other than the discovery or prosecution of criminals, or when the very process of gathering the information or the knowledge that such information is being gathered changes the behavior of those who are clearly innocent and above reproach.

One of the basic safeguards against potential abuse by law enforcement agencies of information gathering is the long-standing constitutional

---

[15]See, for example, National Research Council, *A Review of the FBI's Trilogy Information Technology Modernization*, James McGroddy and Herbert S. Lin, eds., The National Academies Press, Washington, D.C., 2004; and Dan Eggen and Griff Witte, "The FBI's Upgrade That Wasn't: $170 Million Bought an Unusable Computer System," *Washington Post*, August 18, 2006, available at http://www.washingtonpost.com/wp-dyn/content/article/2006/08/17/AR2006081701485_pf.html.

barrier to the use in court of evidence that has been obtained unlawfully—for example, through a warrantless search or other means that violate a suspect's or defendant's rights. While prosecutors are sometimes—or often, depending on the authorities queried on the matter—able to introduce evidence that came to light as a consequence of illegality in law enforcement, the barrier against official exploitation of a suspect's privacy is an important protection against excesses and abuses in information gathering. (The primary loophole in the exclusionary rule is that if law enforcement authorities are not themselves guilty of unlawful warrantless searches, it does not matter very much how evidence was brought to the attention of those authorities.)

Moreover, prosecutors are usually obligated to reveal the content and sources of evidence they wish to use at trial against a defendant, thus adding further to the safeguards and protections. In a manner consistent with the principles of fair information practices (Chapter 1), courts generally insist that the accused should have access to relevant information that has been gathered about him or her, and the ability to challenge and correct that information should it be introduced in court.

One extreme in the spectrum of views is that the collection of information by various branches of government about those governed is part of the price that must be paid for the continued security of the whole. In this view, the ability of government to collect data should not be limited, as the individual cannot be harmed by the information gathered unless the individual was in fact doing something wrong. Such a view holds that these government agencies are well intentioned and therefore will not use the information gathered for illicit or mischievous purposes. The laws that exist ensure that abuses cannot be used against the citizen even if they do occur.

This view adopts a narrow construction of what "harm" might be possible. That is, it requires a belief that a law-abiding individual is not "harmed" if personal information (e.g., buying habits, reading history, mental health status) is viewed by people who have no reason to have access to that information but who as a consequence of their jobs do have such access. In this view, a large-breasted woman whose clothed body is viewed close-up through the zoom telephoto lens on a remotely controlled surveillance camera by security guards during daylight hours suffers no harm.[16] Nor is a farmer harmed who misses a flight because his

---

[16]Jeffrey Rosen, "Being Watched: A Cautionary Tale for a New Age of Surveillance," *New York Times Magazine*, October 7, 2001. Rosen noted that a group of "bored, unsupervised men in front of live video screens" with the ability to "zoom in on whatever happens to catch their eyes" tends to spend "a fair amount of time leering at women." He reported on one control room in which there were close-up shots of women with large breasts taped onto the walls.

or her name is put onto a do-not-fly list because of recent large purchases of ammonium nitrate and fuel oil and a truck rental.

There is a different view that arises from the sheer imbalance between the power of the state and that of the individual. This imbalance makes some citizens understandably anxious about the information-gathering abilities of the state. Consequently, the disparity in resources that can be brought to bear by the state versus those that are available to most individuals also justifies the imposition of certain limits on government's information gathering—even if such limits complicate or impede the task of law enforcement agencies.

9.2 INFORMATION TECHNOLOGY, PRIVACY, AND NATIONAL SECURITY

Nowhere is the disparity of power and resources greater than that between the individual citizen and the federal government. At the same time, it is primarily the federal government that needs to gather information not only for law enforcement purposes but also to ensure the national security of the country. Such data-gathering activity differs in several respects from similar activities performed for law enforcement, notably in the procedures that must be followed, the oversight that constrains the intelligence agencies, and the ability of those about whom data is gathered to view and amend or correct that data.

9.2.1 Background

The general category of national security comprises many functions of government, including those performed by the armed forces and federal law enforcement agencies. However, the term "national security" has recently become associated with the agencies of the federal government that are most directly involved in the gathering and analysis of intelligence information relating to threats against the United States, and those agencies of other governments that play a similar role for other countries. The tension between individual privacy and national security arises, for the most part, with regard to these intelligence-gathering and analysis functions for national security.

While the information-gathering role of the government in law enforcement serves mainly to aid detection and conviction of a suspect after a law has been violated, the role of government agencies charged with protecting national security often entails gathering information about possible future threats, and identifying possible ways to change or control that future. Indeed, the role of an intelligence agency can be characterized as ensuring that its government knows all the secrets of its adversaries or potential adversaries while at the same time ensuring that these adversaries know none of the government secrets. Given this role, the technologies developed for intelligence may define both the boundary for technology that can be privacy invasive, and the boundary for those technologies that help to ensure privacy. Furthermore, in order to maintain advantages over foreign adversaries, the nature and the extent of intelligence-related technological capabilities are often kept secret.

Because the mission of national security agencies is quite open-ended, limiting the scope of inquiry by such agencies becomes far more difficult and complex than imposing comparable limits on law enforcement. While law enforcement data gathering may be reviewed by other agencies and confined to active investigations, intelligence agencies are not required to demonstrate in advance the potential relevance of the information they gather. Instead, such agencies often try to compile as much information as possible that might be potentially relevant to their tasks, and then analyze all of that data in an attempt to define and describe potential adversaries. As *Information Technology for Counterterrorism* put it:[17]

> Because terrorists are not clearly identified with any entity (such as a nation-state) whose behavior can be easily studied or analyzed, their individual profiles of behavior and communication are necessarily the focus of an intelligence investigation. Most importantly, it is often not known in advance what specific information must be sought in order to recognize a suspicious pattern, especially as circumstances change. From the perspective of intelligence analysis, the collection rule must be "collect everything in case something might be useful." Such a stance generates obvious conflicts with the strongest pro-privacy rule "Don't collect anything unless you know you need it."

The notion of intelligence agencies being compelled to respect the privacy of the individual seems almost as quaint as Henry Stimson's justification for shutting down the original cryptography section in the State Department, stating in 1930 that "gentlemen do not read other gentlemen's mail." Since the time of World War II, it has been the role of the intelligence agencies to read nearly everyone's mail (or cables, or radio transmissions) to protect national security. The role of the intelligence agency is, in effect, to violate the privacy of those individuals and countries that might jeopardize national security.

The second aspect of intelligence gathering for national security that makes this activity different from the gathering of information for law enforcement is the inherent need for secrecy in the very process itself.

---

[17]National Research Council, *Information Technology for Counterterrorism: Immediate Actions and Future Possibilities*, John L. Hennessy, David A. Patterson, and Herbert S. Lin, eds., The National Academies Press, Washington, D.C., 2003.

Any information gathered by law enforcement agencies and subsequently used as evidence in the prosecution of an individual eventually becomes public and is open to challenge by the person being prosecuted. Much of the information gathered by intelligence agencies for national security, however, must be kept secret. Secrecy is required not only to keep an adversary from learning what is known about him, but also to ensure that the sources of information cannot be identified and compromised. The need for secrecy in this realm means that those who might be the subjects of interest for information gathering cannot know what information is gathered about them (or even if information is being gathered about them), much less check or challenge the accuracy of that information.

The balance between individual privacy and national security is often seen as a balance between the types of information necessary to ensure national security, and the constraints imposed on those that gather the information. There is a common belief that the more the ability to gather information is constrained, the more likely it is that information of potential relevance to national security will be lost or overlooked.[18] This tension, like its counterpart in the realm of law enforcement, is as old as the republic. What has changed is the technology of information gathering and analysis that can be used by the intelligence agencies.

Along with the changes in the technology, there has been a major change in the nature of the national security endeavor itself. The traditional intelligence endeavor, shaped by World War II and the ensuing Cold War, was focused on the preservation of the state from the threats posed by other states. These threats were long term, comparatively overt, and carried out on a stage on which all of the players were known to each other. The decrease in this sort of threat, occasioned largely by the ending of the Cold War, has been replaced by a far more amorphous threat coming from non-governmental bodies using non-traditional tactics. While perhaps best illustrated by the terrorist attacks on the World Trade Center and the Pentagon on September 11, 2001, these groups perform acts of terrorism meant to destabilize governments by undermining the sense of security of the citizens of those governments. While U.S. citizens tend to focus on the threat to the United States and its allies, the threat from terrorists is not confined to any particular country or region. These combatants, who are hard to identify and willing to sacrifice their own lives in the course of their attacks, now form a threat whose proactive neutralization is one of the main objects of national security.

---

[18]This view is not necessarily true. Indeed, there is an opposing view that the more information gathered, the more likely it is that relevant information will be lost in the flood of irrelevant data. In this view, quantity of information is not the only thing that should be sought; the quality and the relevance of the information are of greater importance.

9.2.2 National Security and Technology Development

While law enforcement agencies were among the early adopters of information technology, the agencies involved in intelligence gathering and analysis have often been the generators of technological innovation. Since the efforts during World War II to break the codes of other countries and to ensure that U.S. codes could not be broken, the intelligence community has directly developed, collaborated in the development, or funded the development of much of the current information infrastructure.

Many of the technologies that are used to gather, sift, and collate data were developed initially by the intelligence agencies either for the purposes of cryptography or to allow them to sift through the vast amounts of information that they gather to find patterns for interpretation. At the same time, the cryptographic techniques that can be used both to ensure the privacy of stored information and to secure channels of communication trace their roots back to the same intelligence services, in their role as securers of the nation's secrets. Moreover, many of the concepts of computer security, used to ensure that only those with the appropriate rights can access sensitive information, have been leveraged from developments that trace back to the intelligence or defense communities.

There is considerable uncertainty outside the intelligence community about the true nature and extent of national capabilities in these areas. Many of those concerned about protecting privacy rights assume that the technology being used for intelligence purposes has capabilities far above technology available to the public. Rightly or wrongly, it is often assumed that the intelligence community can defeat any privacy-enhancing technology that is available to the general public, and has a capability of gathering and collating information that is far beyond any that is commercially available. Given the secret nature of the national security endeavor, this assumption is understandably neither confirmed nor denied by either those intelligence-gathering groups themselves or the governmental bodies that are supposed to oversee those groups.

9.2.3 Legal Limitations on National Security Data Gathering

Analysis of the limitations on national security-based data gathering is complicated by the distinction between U.S. citizens and non-citizens, especially lawfully resident aliens. Some constitutional rights extend to all persons; thus, the Supreme Court ruled as early as 1896 (and has repeatedly reaffirmed as recently as 1982) that aliens could invoke the equal protection clause against invidious discrimination as readily as could U.S. citizens.[19] But some protections (such as privileges and immunities)

---

[19]The 1982 reaffirmation is found in *Plyler v. Doe*, 457 U.S. 202, 102 S. Ct. 2382 (1982), which also provides a plethora of historical Court citations supporting the notion that even aliens

apply only to citizens; indeed the Supreme Court has held that states may, if they wish, make U.S. citizenship an essential qualification for certain occupations (notably teaching in the public schools[20] and being police officers[21]) if the qualification has a rational basis.

The problem arises with respect to rights and liberties that are neither expressly confined to citizens nor available alike to citizens and aliens. In fact, most of the safeguards of the Bill of Rights fall into this third category, leading to intense debate over such issues as whether a lawfully resident alien may be deported for advocacy or political activity for which a citizen could not be punished under the First Amendment. Limited precedent may be cited on both sides of that debate, and the issue is one that the Supreme Court seems consciously to have avoided.

When it comes to information gathering, even citizens have few rights to object to the placement of their sensitive personal information into a government database, regardless of whether the information is obtained legally or illegally.[22] However, even in cases where such an objection is raised, it is not clear that the citizens have any recourse on the gathering of that information. If that is true for citizens, it is at least equally true for non-citizens, even those who have long and lawfully resided in the United States. Moreover, a non-citizen who is not physically present in this country—even though formerly a lawful resident—has severely attenuated legal claims (as, for example, would have been the fate of the Guantanamo detainees absent the agreement between the United States and Cuba that gave the naval base quasi-domestic status). Thus, the grounds on which a non-citizen might object to information gathering and data storage in the interests of national security seem remote. The issues of focus for this report are those that might be raised by U.S. citizens. And as a practical matter, the committee is concerned only about information gathering within the United States (i.e., information gathering on subjects located on U.S. soil), though noting that citizens do retain certain rights even when they are out of country.

The distinction between the rights of citizens and those of others matches the perception (and, perhaps, the historical reality) that the gravest national security threats originate beyond our borders. Until rela-

---

whose presence in this country is unlawful are "persons" guaranteed due process of law by the Fifth and Fourteenth Amendments.

[20]*Ambach v. Norwick*, 441 U.S. 68, 99 S. Ct. 1589, 60 L. Ed. 2d 49 (1979).

[21]*Foley v. Connelie*, 435 U.S. 291, 98 S. Ct. 1067, 55 L. Ed. 2d 287 (1978).

[22]In *Bartnicki et al. v. Vopper*, 121 S. Ct. 1753, 149 L. Ed. 2d 787, 29 Media L. Rep. 1737 (2001), the Supreme Court held that a radio station could not be held liable for broadcasting the contents of an audio recording that had been obtained in an illegal wiretap. Since it would be hard to argue that any information broadcast on the radio waves to the public is somehow private, it would seem that the contents of the audio recording could in fact be placed into a government database—even if the contents had been obtained illegally. How far the precedent of *Bartnicki et al. v. Vopper* extends remains to be seen.

tively recently, neither the military nor the U.S. foreign intelligence agencies were allowed to gather information about purely domestic activity, even if that activity seemed to pose a national security threat. Under this premise, if actions of U.S. citizens and resident aliens within the United States evoke suspicion on security grounds, any investigation would be conducted by the FBI and other domestic law enforcement agencies. That precept was recently reinforced when the Department of the Army formally apologized for having interrogated participants at a University of Texas conference on women and Islam, making clear in the apology that any such inquiry should have been handled by the FBI and not by the military (or for that matter the Central Intelligence Agency). This division of labor partly reflects the difficulty of distinguishing legitimate and protected dissent from genuine security threats, and an abiding fear that government power of inquiry could be abused if the more secretive U.S. foreign intelligence agencies possessed such domestic authority.

In this regard, as with the limits placed on the law enforcement agencies, the United States is somewhat different from other countries. Outside the United States, it is common for a country to have a domestic intelligence service whose job it is to accumulate information on citizens and those within the borders of the country for the purposes of national security. There have been times that some parts of the U.S. federal government have performed this function within the United States, but such activities have been rare and either were discontinued after a period of national emergency or became the cause of major scandal when they were generally discovered. Further, when such activities were undertaken, they were often undertaken as an adjunct activity for a law enforcement agency (such as the FBI) rather than as part of the activity of an organization whose primary charter was the gathering of domestic intelligence for the purpose of national security.

An important part of the current legal framework for national security intelligence gathering in the United States was established by the Foreign Intelligence Surveillance Act (FISA). As noted in Section 4.3.1, FISA was passed in order to regulate executive branch authority to conduct wiretaps in intelligence matters and thus could be fairly regarded as a privacy protection measure. FISA, and a series of executive orders based on it, cover the surveillance (both electronic and non-electronic) of "a foreign power or an agent of a foreign power," including U.S. persons who fall under the definition of an agent of a foreign power. FISA establishes a special court of 11 federal district court judges who review requests for warrants. These warrants can cover electronic surveillance (including wiretapping and electronic eavesdropping) and covert physical searches.

To obtain a warrant, law enforcement authorities must demonstrate to the FISA Court that there is probable cause to believe that the target of the warrant is an agent of a foreign power. Unlike standard search warrants obtained for criminal cases, applications for FISA warrants do not require a statement of what information is being sought through the warrant, nor is there a requirement that the party granted the warrant return to the court a listing of what information was obtained through the warrant. While FISA warrants cannot be granted for the purpose of criminal prosecution, information obtained secondarily via a FISA warrant has been allowed in criminal trials.

Since the intelligence process depends on gathering information, one premise of the current system is that the entities whose information is being obtained do not know the extent of what is known about them or the sources of that information. Thus the FISA law forbids any person upon whom a FISA Court subpoena is served from disclosing that fact to anyone other than a colleague or subordinate whose involvement is vital to obtain the subpoenaed information.[23] Moreover, the FISA procedure for information gathering differs sharply from what is allowed under standard law enforcement search and seizure rules. While judicial approval of the FISA Court is required for national security searches, the proceedings of that court (and even the identity of its members) are secret. The substantive standard required for issuance of such a secret warrant is also said to be far lower than for a regular warrant, requiring no specific evidence of actual complicity in or even specific contribution to any terrorist activity.

---

[23]Non-disclosure orders are not unique to FISA. Indeed, five other federal statutes authorize the government to issue a non-disclosure order pursuant to a "national security letter" that requests communications providers, financial institutions, and credit bureaus to provide to appropriate intelligence agencies certain types of customer business records, including subscriber and transactional information related to Internet and telephone usage, credit reports, and financial records. These laws include 12 U.S.C. 3414 (access to financial records); 15 U.S.C. 1681u (access to credit reports for the FBI), 15 U.S.C. 1681v (access to credit reports for U.S. government intelligence agencies), 18 U.S.C. 2709 (access to stored wire and electronic communications and transactional records for the FBI), and 50 U.S.C. 436 (access to financial information for purposes of law enforcement, counterintelligence, or security determination). Section 115 of the USA PATRIOT Improvement and Reauthorization Act of 2005 created a mechanism for judicial review of a national security letter as well as any associated nondisclosure order. See Brian Yeh and Charles Doyle, "USA PATRIOT Improvement and Reauthorization Act of 2005: A Legal Analysis," Order Code RL 33332, Congressional Research Service, Washington, D.C., March 24, 2006. According to the Associated Press, the FBI sought information on 3,501 U.S. citizens and legal residents in 2005 from their banks and their credit card, telephone, and Internet companies using the national security letter mechanism. It also received FISA Court approval under Section 215 for the examination of business records.

9.2.4 Recent Trends

Traditionally, as noted in the previous section, the separation between intelligence gathering for national security purposes and law enforcement surveillance has served to protect the privacy at least of U.S. citizens and to some degree that of permanent resident aliens while they are in the United States. Gathering information on such persons had been generally forbidden except in aid of law enforcement or if a person was determined to be an agent of a foreign power. This meant that the gathering of information could happen only in an attempt to investigate the breaking of a particular law, and the obtaining of information was subject to the kinds of restrictions and third-party judicial reviews that have characterized law enforcement information gathering.

The events of September 11, 2001, and the subsequent efforts to identify, find, and eliminate the threat from both the terrorists directly responsible and others who support groups that have been identified with similar tactics have caused many to call into question the traditional separation of law enforcement and national security intelligence gathering. National security was traditionally seen as served by gathering information about threats from other countries; suddenly the highest level of threat seemed to be from non-governmental entities. National security intelligence was gathered from outside the borders of the United States; suddenly the threat seemed to be within those borders as well as without. The domestic collection of information was bound to the prosecution of crimes; suddenly there was a perceived need for the domestic collection of information for intelligence purposes. The traditional notion of limiting intelligence gathering to outside the borders of the United States and to other than U.S. persons appeared to be dangerously out of date.

One indication of this trend is the adoption, in October 2001, of the Uniting and Strengthening America by Providing Appropriate Tools Required to Intercept and Obstruct Terrorism (USA PATRIOT) Act. This act is seen by its supporters as an overdue response to restrictions on intelligence gathering that had impeded cooperation and collaboration among agencies, and that needed to be relaxed or removed if the nation was to protect itself from the new threats to national security, identified not as other governments but as smaller, non-governmental organizations willing to launch suicide attacks. Opponents of the act, however, charge that many of its provisions seriously threaten or erode basic rights and liberties enshrined in the Constitution, as well as jeopardizing privacy to an unprecedented degree.

One of the difficulties of judging between these two viewpoints is the complexity of the act itself, which is a collection of amendments and additions to other laws rather than a stand-alone act. In some cases, the act defines limitations on technologies that had not been addressed in law before; in other cases the act expands or clarifies the scope of previously existing law.

In general, the USA PATRIOT Act eased a number of restrictions on foreign intelligence gathering within the United States and granted the U.S. intelligence community somewhat greater access to information unearthed during a criminal investigation.[24] For example, the USA PATRIOT Act authorizes the release to federal intelligence and immigration officials of information obtained during the course of a grand jury investigation, whereas such information was previously protected under very strict disclosure rules. The act codified the use of trap-and-trace devices and pen registers, already established under long-standing FISA Court practices, for treating electronic communications such as e-mail in a similar way to telephone communications. Section 215 of the USA PATRIOT Act also allowed the FISA Court to issue orders granting access to any records and tangible items from any entity (e.g., bookstores, libraries, department stores, schools), not just common carriers, public accommodation facilities, physical storage facilities, and car rental facilities, as under previous law; this provision substantially enlarged the range of items subject to FISA jurisdiction. Finally, the act also allowed "roving" surveillance of a subject, where previously FISA had required the identification of a particular scope (e.g., a specific telephone number or physical location) where the surveillance would occur.

To guard against official abuse, the USA PATRIOT Act established a claim against the United States for certain communications privacy violations by government personnel and expanded the prohibition against FISA orders based solely on the exercise of an individual's First Amendment rights. In addition, the USA PATRIOT Improvement and Reauthorization Act of 2005 provided greater congressional oversight, enhanced procedural protections, more elaborate application requirements, and a judicial review process for the exercise of Section 215 authorities. Finally, the USA PATRIOT Act Additional Reauthorizing Amendments Act of 2006 establishes a judicial review procedure for Section 215 nondisclosure orders that allows recipients of a Section 215 production order to challenge the nondisclosure requirement 1 year after the issuance of the production order. In response to such a challenge, the FISA Court judge has the discretion to modify or set aside a nondisclosure order, unless the attorney general, deputy attorney general, an assistant attorney general, or the director of the FBI certifies that disclosure may endanger the national

---

[24]This discussion of the USA PATRIOT Act's impact on FISA is based on Charles Doyle, "The USA PATRIOT Act: A Sketch," Order Code RS 21203, Congressional Research Service, Washington, D.C., April 18, 2002.

security of the United States or interfere with diplomatic relations (unless the judge finds that the certification was made in bad faith).[25]

From a FISA perspective, more important than any of the particular sections of the USA PATRIOT Act is the fact that the law encourages the sharing of information from law enforcement with intelligence agencies. The success of the September 11, 2001, attacks has been seen by many as a result of the distinction drawn between law enforcement and intelligence gathering; in this view if all of the relevant information held by both the law enforcement agencies (such as the FBI) and the intelligence community had been put together and seen correctly, the attacks could have been predicted and stopped. Not sharing such information was faulted as a reflection of the distinction between law enforcement and intelligence gathering for national security, a distinction that had historically been drawn in part to ensure the privacy of U.S. citizens.

It is in this context that the sharing with law enforcement officials of information derived from intelligence operations has proven controversial. Under the USA PATRIOT Act, FISA Court orders need no longer serve the primary purpose of gathering foreign intelligence information, but may now be authorized by the FISA Court under a less stringent standard of serving a "significant purpose" of obtaining such information. Generally, the concern about such sharing has been that the privacy (and other) protections embedded in the processes of domestic law enforcement may be circumvented or mooted by the use of intelligence processes that are less subject to such protections.

For example, an airline (JetBlue) acknowledged a September 2003 incident in which it violated its stated privacy policy by sharing personal information on 1.1 million customers with a Pentagon contractor investigating issues in connection with the CAPPS II airline security program.[26] A few months later, Northwest Airlines acknowledged that it had also provided months of reservation data to NASA's Ames Research Center, after asserting in September 2003 that it "did not provide that type of information to anyone." In its acknowledgment, Northwest Airlines said it participated in the NASA program to assist the government's search for technology to improve aviation security, and denied that its actions violated its privacy policy, which it said was aimed at preventing the

---

[25]See Yeh and Doyle, "USA PATRIOT Improvement and Reauthorization Act of 2005," 2006.

[26]Michelle Maynard, "JetBlue Moves to Repair Its Image After Sharing Files," *New York Times*, September 23, 2003, available at http://www.nytimes.com/2003/09/23/business/23AIR.html?ex=1379649600&en=1e13d100496b900d&ei=5007&partner=USERLAND.

sale of passenger information to third parties for marketing purposes.[27] Another example is the recently revealed (late 2005) wiretaps of communications involving certain U.S. persons in pursuit of intelligence related to al-Qaeda without the approval of the FISA Court (Box 9.3). As this writing, the program is still controversial amidst many calls for further investigation.

The quest for more and better technologies for analyzing information for national security purposes also raises privacy concerns. In particular, one common view of the failure to foresee and stop the events of September 11, 2001, is that the failure was not one of a lack of information, but rather a lack of putting together the information that was already available. In this view, better analysis tools are needed more than (or in addition to) the ability to gather more information.

One attempt at creating such tools taken by the DOD's Defense Advanced Research Projects Agency (DARPA) was the Total (later Terrorist) Information Awareness (TIA) program (Box 9.4). The exact goals of this program are difficult to determine, as they shifted significantly over the time the program was active. However, the goals were always centered on developing and providing technology that would allow the detection and tracking of terrorist or suspected terrorist activities by aggregating data that are collected by both government and non-government agencies and then mining that data to find patterns of behavior that are highly correlated with future terrorist actions.

A full analysis of the privacy implications of the TIA program has appeared elsewhere and is not repeated here.[28] The point that is important to make is that one of the legacies of the September 11 attacks is the willingness of the intelligence agencies charged with the national defense to gather information about U.S. persons in their attempt to track and find terrorists. In addition, the TIA program shows the willingness of these agencies to use or invent technologies that will help them in that undertaking, even when those technologies may be privacy invasive.

---

[27]Sara Kehaulani Goo, "Confidential Passenger Data Used for Air Security Project," *Washington Post*, January 17, 2004, available at http://www.washingtonpost.com/ac2/wp-dyn/A26037-2004Jan17.

[28]Technology and Privacy Committee (TAPAC), *Safeguarding Privacy in the Fight Against Terrorism*, Department of Defense, Washington, D.C., March 1, 2004. This report (1) concluded that TIA was a flawed effort to achieve worthwhile ends; (2) argued that although data mining is a vital tool in the fight against terrorism, it could present significant privacy issues if used in connection with personal data concerning U.S. persons; (3) stressed the importance of government actions to protect privacy in developing and using data-mining tools; and (4) noted that existing legal requirements applicable to the government's data-mining programs were numerous, disjointed, and often outdated, with the possible effect of compromising privacy protection, public confidence, and the nation's ability to craft effective and lawful responses to terrorism.

BOX 9.3
National Security Agency Domestic Surveillance and Data Mining of Calling Records

In 2002, the president authorized the National Security Agency (NSA) to begin conducting surveillance of electronic communications in the United States without a court-approved warrant. Since the public became aware of this program late in 2005,[1] many questions have been raised about both its legality and its constitutionality.

According to what has been revealed publicly in news reports, the classified NSA program has focused on intercepting, without a warrant, phone calls and e-mails of U.S. persons that are believed to be linked, directly or indirectly, to the al-Qaeda terrorist organization. It is further said to be limited to only domestic-to-international communication; warrants are obtained when both parties in the communication are within U.S. borders. Although official sources have not provided an authoritative description of the activities and scope of this program, the administration has defended it—and its ability to monitor possible terrorist group activity—as both legal and within the authority granted to the president under the Authorization for Use of Military Force (AUMF) against al-Qaeda,[2] passed by Congress on September 14, 2001. The AUMF authorized the president to "use all necessary and appropriate force against those nations, organizations, or persons he determines planned, authorized, committed, or aided the terrorist attacks that occurred on September 11, 2001, or harbored such organizations or persons, in order to prevent any future acts of international terrorism against the United States by such nations, organizations or persons." Additionally, the administration contends that the president's inherent constitutional authority as commander in chief authorizes the president to take whatever action is necessary to combat terrorism.[3]

Critics, however, debate the legality and constitutionality of the program that was authorized outside the Foreign Intelligence Surveillance Act (FISA) of 1978, which provides explicit legal guidance on how domestic surveillance can be conducted.[4] Recently amended in 2001 by the USA PATRIOT Act, FISA was passed to balance the need

---

[1]James Risen and Eric Lichtblau, "Bush Lets U.S. Spy on Callers Without Courts," *New York Times*, December 16, 2005, available at http://www.nytimes.com/2005/12/16/politics/16program. html?ex=1292389200&en=e32072d786623ac1&ei=5090&partner=rssuserland&emc=rss. Additionally, the *New York Times* did not release the story for over a year at the request of the administration for national security concerns.

[2]P.L. 107-40, 115 Stat. 224 (2001); for the legislative history, see Congressional Research Service, "Authorization for Use of Military Force in Response to the 9/11 Attacks (P.L. 107-40): Legislative History," January 4, 2006, available at http://www.fas.org/sgp/crs/natsec/RS22357.pdf.

[3]The Department of Justice response to the House and Senate Intelligence Committees defending the program is available at http://www.fas.org/irp/agency/doj/fisa/doj122205.pdf. See also a white paper released by the Department of Justice, "Legal Authorities Supporting the Activities of the National Security Agency Described by the President," January 19, 2006, available at http://files.findlaw.com/news.findlaw.com/hdocs/docs/nsa/dojnsa11906wp.pdf.

[4]Among the sources of criticism of the program are American Bar Association, "Task Force on Domestic Surveillance in the Fight Against Terrorism," February 15, 2006, available at http://www.abanews.org/docs/domsurvrecommendationfinal.pdf. Also see "A Response to the Department of Justice on Warrantless Surveillance," by a group of 14 constitutional scholars and former government officials, January 9, 2006, available at http://www.fas.org/irp/agency/doj/fisa/doj-response.pdf.

for foreign intelligence surveillance for national security purposes with an individual's constitutional rights. It established procedures for the oversight of domestic surveillance activities conducted by U.S. intelligence agencies, including the creation of the Foreign Intelligence Surveillance Act Court, an independent body designed to grant surveillance authority rather than its being determined by the intelligence agency itself. Additionally, the legislation addressed circumstances in which surveillance could be conducted without a warrant, including after a declaration of war for a period of 15 days and in times of emergency when warrants could be obtained ex post facto within 72 hours. Critics argue that changes to domestic surveillance procedures should be authorized by Congress and should take place through amendments to FISA. Furthermore, critics underscore that FISA legislation was drafted on the basis that the president's constitutional power is "inherent" but should not be exclusive, and that Congress, rather than the executive branch, has the power to regulate the exercise of that authority.

A number of analysts have also raised a variety of concerns about the implications of this program and the legal basis used to authorize it. Among the concerns is the reliance on AUMF as a legal basis for electronic domestic surveillance activities, which could also be used to authorize warrantless physical search and seizures. Related questions have been raised in terms of the admissibility in a court of law of information obtained without a warrant.[5] The inclusion in the program of phone and Internet traffic from U.S. telecommunications companies has also raised concerns that the scope of the program was not limited to domestic-to-international communication as initially described by the administration.[6] Broader constitutional questions also have been raised by the authorization of this program that has taken place outside a system of checks and balances designed to protect individuals' rights from possible abuses by government authorities.[7]

Similar concerns have arisen as the result of an NSA program to use the calling records of the customers of AT&T, Verizon, and BellSouth. Reported in *USA Today* on May 11, 2006,[8] the program supposedly uses these data to analyze calling patterns in an effort to detect terrorist activity. Calling records do not involve the content of the calls themselves, but do include, at a minimum, the originating number, the called number, the duration of the call, and the time of day of the call. Such records are usually protected less stringently than the content of phone calls, but their disclosure to government authorities has historically entailed an explicit legal authorization, albeit with lower standards of cause, to produce such records. As in the case of content surveillance, controversy arises because the carriers in question may have provided the records without such authorization in hand.

---

[5]Chitra Ragavan, "The Letter of the Law," *U.S. News and World Report*, March 27, 2006, available at http://www.usnews.com/usnews/news/articles/060327/27fbi.htm.

[6]James Risen and Eric Lichtblau, "Spy Agency Mined Vast Data Trove," *New York Times*, December 24, 2005, available at http://www.nytimes.com/2005/12/24/politics/24spy. html?ex=1293080400&en=016edb46b79bde83&ei=5090.

[7]See American Bar Association, "Report of the Task Force on Domestic Surveillance in the Fight Against Terrorism," February 15, 2006, available at http://www.abanet.org/op/greco/memos/ aba_house302-0206.pdf.

[8]Leslie Cauley, "NSA Has Massive Database of Americans' Phone Calls," *USA Today*, May 11, 2006.

BOX 9.4
The Total Information Awareness Program

The Total Information Awareness (TIA) program caused considerable worry among many Americans across the political spectrum, much of it provoked by bad public relations and the political concerns raised over those in charge of the program. Notably absent from the debate over the TIA program was any discussion of exactly what technology was being sought by the program, and whether or not the technology being sought was actually possible. This was in part due to a constant changing of the goals articulated for the program; it was hard to determine exactly what the technology being developed was supposed to do. But even the various alternatives that were proposed at different times were not examined in the light of their technological possibilities or the repercussions of that technology if it were possible. This is especially odd given that the agency sponsoring the TIA program, DARPA, is a research agency charged with just this kind of technical evaluation.

A number of the proposed components of the TIA program were never the focus of controversy; these had to do with automated translation aids and tools for standardizing the format of information being gathered by intelligence agencies. More controversial were the proposed tools that would allow discovery of patterns of activity. These tools would mine a consolidated database built from the information gathered by governmental and non-governmental entities, which would include data on commercial transactions. In one version of the TIA statement of goals, the analysis tools would scan this database for events or sets of events of interest (such as the purchase of one-way rental trucks coupled with the purchase of large amounts of fertilizer) and identify persons who had participated in such transactions, allowing those persons to come to the attention of the national security agencies. The result would be an automated mechanism for "connecting the dots." Such a system would solve the problem of not seeing the patterns in the information that had been acquired, which some thought was the main failure that made the attacks of September 11, 2001, possible.

Such a system is not technically feasible, however. To aggregate the information from the various sources into a single database would require a solution to the problem of data integration (Section 3.9). Different databases store data in different forms, meaning that the information held in one database cannot be read or manipulated by programs that understand the second database. To allow a program to use both databases requires some form of data integration, which in turn requires converting one

---

While the USA PATRIOT Act, the warrantless National Security Agency surveillance of certain U.S. persons, and the Total Information Awareness program are perhaps the most obvious examples of changes in law and attitude on the balance between privacy and national security after the events of September 11, they are hardly the only examples. The establishment of "do not board" watch lists by the Department of Homeland Security, in which information from unknown sources can be used

(or both) of the database formats into some common format that can be manipulated and understood by a single program. This problem has existed in industry for the past 40 years; all attempts to solve the problem even on a small scale have succeeded only for very simple aggregations and have proven to be exceptionally expensive. To hypothesize a single aggregation, whether virtual or physical, of all of the databases, both public and private, as is done in this version of the TIA program, is to hypothesize a general solution to the still-unsolved data integration problem.

Even if the data integration problem could be solved, the solution sought by the TIA program would require the ability to evaluate arbitrary sets of events in that database to find patterns. However, the set of possible events grows at a pace that makes the general evaluation of all of those sets computationally infeasible. The number of sets of events that can be formed from a group of individual events is equal to 2 to the power of the number of events; that is, for 20 different events the number of distinct sets of those events is 2^{20}, or more than 1,000,000 different sets of events. If we were to look at each commercial transaction in the United States as a separate event, the set of possible sets made up of those events is far larger than the number of atoms in the universe.

A second version of the TIA goal avoided this problem of computational complexity by stating that the tools would allow analysts to identify a person of interest, and then use the tools to track all of the activities of that person that were traced in all of the databases that had been aggregated. This approach eliminated the problem of the prior goal by concentrating on a particular subject or set of subjects and picking out the events associated with that subject. By starting with a subject of interest, the events in the database could be examined individually to see if they involved that individual, thus keeping the complexity of the search proportional to the size of the database (rather than growing exponentially with the size of the database). This goal still assumed that the aggregation of databases into a single search set would be possible, but even if only a small number of databases were aggregated, this goal could provide a more complete picture of an individual than could be found in any of the single databases.

The problem with this narrower goal is that, even if it can be achieved, it is unlikely that it will help disrupt terrorist attacks before they are carried out. The ability to find out more information about known persons does not help in the identification of potential terrorists with no previous records of such involvement or other reason to fall under suspicion—and there is no shortage of such individuals in the world.

to place even U.S. citizens on lists that make it difficult or impossible to board commercial airline flights, has come to light because of recent cases of people being placed on such a list erroneously. One problem with such watch lists, as they now appear to be implemented, is that it is difficult to find out if a particular person has been placed on such a list and, if placed on the list, to find out the information that caused that placement. There is no formal mechanism for challenging either the placement on the list or the information that was used to make the determination. Even Edward Kennedy, senior senator from Massachusetts, has had problems getting his name off the watch list.[29]

Even if corrective mechanisms were in place, lists such as these suffer from a cluster of problems having to do with establishing the identity of those who are being compared to the list. If a list is kept in terms of names, its usefulness is limited by the fact that a single name can be shared by many different people. A combination of name and address may be better, but falls prey to the ease with which people move from place to place, and the time lag between such a move and the time at which all relevant records have been updated to reflect the new address. Indeed, such lists seem to presume, contrary to fact, that there is a way (or set of ways) to uniquely identify each person who might appear on such a list. There is no such mechanism available today, and establishing such a mechanism is far from simple.[30]

9.2.5 Tensions Between Privacy and National Security

In many ways, the tension between privacy and national security parallels the tension between privacy and law enforcement. Both law enforcement and national security require government to amass large amounts of information about people, including much information that the subject or target might want to keep private and information that will ultimately not prove useful for any mission-related function. Both law enforcement and national security require that that information be analyzed to try to infer even more about a person. Both are heavy users of technology, and both use technology to gather information, identify individuals, and analyze that information.

National security differs from law enforcement, however, in two significant ways. First, law enforcement authorities are usually (though not always) called in when a criminal act has been committed, and the criminal act itself serves to focus investigative resources—that is, they tend to be reactive. National security authorities are most interested in preventing hostile acts from taking place—they tend to be proactive. Second, most of the information gathered by law enforcement and used to prosecute a person for the violation of a law will eventually be made public, along with the mechanisms used to gather that information. Intelligence gathering

---

[29]Rachel L. Swarns, "Senator? Terrorist? A Watch List Stops Kennedy at Airport," *New York Times*, August 20, 2004.

[30]See National Research Council, *Who Goes There? Authentication Through the Lens of Privacy*, Stephen T. Kent and Lynette I. Millett, eds., The National Academies Press, Washington, D.C., 2003.

for the purposes of national security, on the other hand, is an intrinsically non-public activity. The mechanisms used to gather information, along with the information itself, are not made public, even when the information is used in a way that has an impact on the life of the subject of that information.

This greater need for secrecy makes it unlikely that citizens will be able to discover if the agencies charged with national security are violating their privacy. The mechanisms for gathering information are often unknown, so those wishing to ensure privacy may not know the techniques against which they must guard. The information gathered must remain secret, and so there is no easy way to know what information is gathered, if that information is accurate, whether it might be subject to different interpretations, or how to correct the information if it is inaccurate or incomplete. The only thing known with certainty is that there is an entity that is capable of gathering information about foreign governments, and it is reasonable to presume that such an entity can easily gather information about private citizens in the United States.

Because of the secret nature of the information gathered by national security agencies, it can be difficult to establish a trust relationship if one does not already exist between the citizens about whom the information is gathered and the agencies doing the gathering. There are few in the United States who would worry about the gathering of information even within the borders of the United States and about U.S. citizens if they could be assured that such information was only being used for genuine national security purposes, and that any information that had been gathered about them was accurate and appropriately interpreted and treated. How to obtain that assurance is a public policy issue of the utmost importance. This is why oversight is so important, all the more so in times of crisis. Accountability need not mean indiscriminate transparency; rather, trusted agents such as members of Congress or special commissions should be entrusted with offering, and hopefully can be trusted to offer, needed assurances.

9.3 LAW ENFORCEMENT, NATIONAL SECURITY, AND INDIVIDUAL PRIVACY

Even before the formation of our nation, government was seen as posing the principal threats to individual privacy. Many of the grievances against the English crown that were detailed in the Declaration of Independence reflected an erosion of the right to be left alone, and many provisions of the Bill of Rights sought to codify limitations on government power which the framers saw as vital to the new nation. While the Constitution nowhere expressly recognizes a "right to privacy," several provisions (especially, but not only, the Fourth Amendment) unmistakably limit the power of government to invade the lives of citizens.

When law enforcement and national security are concerned, the sources of concern about privacy rights are readily apparent. On the one hand, law enforcement must be able to gather information about individuals in order to identify and apprehend suspects and to enforce criminal law and regulatory standards. National security agencies gather and analyze information about individuals and organizations in order to protect and enhance national security. On the other hand, the very process of gathering and using such information may pose serious risks to individual privacy.

A somewhat similar set of tensions apply to data that have already been collected for some purpose other than law enforcement or national security. As noted in earlier chapters, a wide variety of personal information on individuals is collected for a wide variety of purposes by both government agencies (e.g., the Internal Revenue Service, the Census Bureau) and private sector organizations such as banks, schools, phone companies, and providers of medical care. In some instances (such as survey data collected by the Census Bureau), such information has been collected under a promise, legal or otherwise, that it would be used for a certain purpose and only for that purpose, and would otherwise be kept confidential.[31] If and when external circumstances change (e.g., the nation comes under attack), some would argue strongly that it is criminal to refrain from using all resources available to the government to pursue its law enforcement and national security responsibilities. Others would argue just as strongly that the legal restrictions in effect at the time of data collection effectively render such data unavailable to the government, legally if not physically.

According to scholars William Seltzer and Margo Anderson,[32] an example of such government use of privileged data occurred during World War II, when the Bureau of the Census assisted U.S. law enforcement authorities in carrying out the presidentially ordered internment

---

[31]One exception is that the USA PATRIOT Act of 2001 allows the attorney general to obtain a court order directing the Department of Education to provide to the Department of Justice data collected by the National Center for Education Statistics (NCES) if such data are relevant to an authorized investigation or prosecution of an offense concerning national or international terrorism. However, the law also requires the attorney general to protect the confidentiality of the data, although the standards used for such protection are formulated by the attorney general "in consultation with" the Department of Education. Prior to the passage of the USA PATRIOT Act, NCES data were to be used only for statistical purposes.

[32]William Seltzer and Margo Anderson, "After Pearl Harbor: The Proper Role of Population Data Systems in Time of War," paper presented at the annual meeting of the Population Association of America, Los Angeles, California, March 2000, available at the American Statistical Association's Statisticians in History Web site.

of Japanese-Americans. In a meeting of the Census Advisory Committee held in January 1942, J.C. Capt, director of the census, was reported to say, "We're by law required to keep confidential information by [sic] individuals. But in the end, [i]f the defense authorities found 200 Japs missing and they wanted the names of the Japs in that area, I would give them further means of checking individuals."

It is not known if the Census Bureau actually provided information on individual Japanese-Americans, but Seltzer and Anderson cite documents indicating that the Census Bureau clearly did provide mesodata (i.e., census results tabulated for very small geographic units, some as small as a city block) that did facilitate the internment process. Indeed, on the Monday after the December 7 attack on Pearl Harbor (which occurred on a Sunday), the Census Bureau initiated the production of reports on the distribution of Japanese-Americans across the United States based on macrodata (data from the 1940 census aggregated in terms of large geographic units).

Seltzer and Anderson note also that the Census Bureau has recognized possible threats to privacy arising from certain kinds of mesodata, and in response has progressively introduced stricter disclosure standards. Indeed, the bureau has indicated that under the standards now in place the release of mesodata from the 1940 census on Japanese-Americans would have been severely restricted.

A number of points are worth noting about this example. First, whether or not the Census Bureau provided information on individuals, the use of census data violated the spirit of the confidentiality law in the sense that respondents provided information under promises of confidentiality[33]—information that was subsequently used against them. Second, Capt's remarks suggest a willingness to exploit legal loopholes in order to cooperate with the internment order. Third, even if the actual wording of the confidentiality promise made a "fine print" provision for "other legally authorized uses," it would still have left survey respondents with the impression that their responses were confidential.

---

[33]For example, President Herbert Hoover's proclamation in 1929 for the 15th census said that "the sole purpose of the census is to secure general statistical information regarding the population and resources of the country. . . . No person can be harmed in any way by providing the information required. The census has nothing to do with . . . the enforcement of any national, state, or local law or ordinance. There need be no fear that any disclosure will be made regarding any individual person or his affairs. . . ." In addition, the 1940 census enumeration form itself said that "only sworn census employees will see your statements. Data collected will be used solely for preparing statistical information concerning the Nation's population, resources, and business activities. Your Census Reports Cannot Be Used for Purposes of Taxation, Regulation, or Investigation" [capitalization in the original]. See Thomas F. Corcoran, "On the Confidential Status of Census Reports," *The American Statistician* 17(3):33-40, 1963.

Issues related to privacy in a law enforcement or national security context are hard for citizens to assess. Citizens are not told what information these agencies are capable of gathering or what they do gather, because that knowledge being made public can limit the very information that agencies will be able to gather. In addition, the stakes are higher because these agencies can use information they gathered to imprison citizens. Citizens are asked to trust that abuses are not occurring and to trust in the oversight mechanisms that often require one part of the government to ensure that another is not generally overstepping appropriate bounds.

Similarly, law enforcement and national security agencies are put into a difficult position regarding the gathering and analysis of information. If these agencies fail to gather enough information to accomplish their missions, they are faulted for not using the latest techniques and technologies. However, if these agencies are perceived as gathering too much information about ordinary citizens, they are faulted for invasion of privacy.

Unfortunately, it is often impossible to determine, before the fact, who is going to be a law breaker or terrorist in the future. There is no way for law enforcement and national security agencies to determine about whom they should gather information without requiring that these agencies also know the future. The conundrum is further accentuated by a declaratory national policy that emphasizes prevention of terrorist attacks rather than prosecution or retaliation after they occur. That is, law enforcement activities must take place—successfully—in the absence of the primary event that usually focuses such activities. With few definitively related clues to guide an investigation, a much more uniform spread of attention must be cast over those who might have some contact or connection, however tenuous, to a possible terrorist event in the future.

The best that can be expected is that these agencies put into place the appropriate safeguards, checks, and balances to minimize the possibility that they gather information in an inappropriate way about citizens. But the more such safeguards are in place, so the argument goes, the more likely it is that mistakes are made in the opposite direction, and that these agencies will miss some piece of information that is vital for the performance of their function.

Yet areas of overlap between privacy and law enforcement and national security also exist. For example, citizens who have faith in their government and who believe that it generally follows democratic rules (one reflection of which is respect for privacy) will be more likely to cooperate with law enforcement in providing information and other forms of support. In that sense, just as it is sometimes said that privacy is a good business practice, it might also be said that a law enforcement agency's respect for a citizen's privacy, rather than necessarily being in opposition to, can be supportive of law enforcement goals.

An important influence on the process of balancing governmental and societal needs for safety and security and individual privacy is the fact that public safety is—almost by definition—a collective benefit, while government infringements of privacy in the name of public safety tend to affect individuals or relatively small or politically marginal groups of people, at least in the short term. Under such circumstances, it is easier for public safety officials to dismiss or minimize privacy concerns that their actions might raise. As an illustration of the sentiment, Harvard Law School Professor William Stuntz has asserted that "reasonable people can differ about the balance, but one could plausibly conclude that the efficiency gains from profiling outweigh the harm from the ethnic tax that post-September 11 policing is imposing on young men of Middle Eastern origin."[34]

The flip side of this sentiment, of course, is that community involvement and good will may well be an essential element, perhaps the most important element, of a strategy that seeks to counter terrorists concealing themselves in the nation's communities. That is, tips about unusual and suspicious behavior are most likely to emerge when the communities in which terrorists are embedded are allied with, or at least not suspicious of, law enforcement authorities—and singling out young men of Middle Eastern origin for special scrutiny is not an approach that will create a large amount of good will in the affected communities.

These tensions have been magnified since the terrorist attacks of September 11. There are many who feel that if the right information had been available, along with the right tools to analyze that information and the right governmental structures that would allow the sharing of the information between law enforcement and national security agencies, those attacks could have been avoided. Part of the reaction to those attacks was the passing of laws and the creation of policies that made it easier for agencies to collect and share information and the weakening of some traditional checks and balances in the hope of enhancing national security.

At the same time, there is worry that the increasingly sophisticated technology available for surveillance, data sharing and analysis, and data warehousing, when joined with the weakening of rules protecting individual information, will allow law enforcement and national security agencies a vastly expanded and largely unseen ability to monitor all citizens. The potential for abuse given such an ability is easy to imagine—for example, a law enforcement agency might be able to monitor the group gatherings of citizens objecting to a certain government policy, identifying who they meet with and perhaps what they talk about. Most citizens do not know what is technically possible, either now or in the near future. Because of this, there is often a tendency to believe that the technology

---

[34]See William Stuntz, "Local Policing After the Terror," *Yale Law Journal* 111:2137, 2002.

is capable of far more than it can actually do, either currently or in the foreseeable future. The problem may not be in what these government agencies are capable of doing with technology, but rather with what the citizens believe those agencies can do.

These comments should not be taken to suggest that policy makers in government agencies are unaware of privacy interests. For example, under the E-Government Act of 2002, any federal agency contemplating a substantially revised or new information technology system is required to develop a privacy impact assessment (PIA; Box 9.5) for such a system before work on that system begins in earnest. In the case of the Department of Homeland Security (DHS), DHS officials indicate that findings of PIAs are, to some extent, folded into the requirements development process in an attempt to ensure that the program or system, when deployed, is at least sensitive to privacy considerations. (It should also be noted that DHS officials reject the paradigm that privacy trades off against security; they assert that the challenge is enhancing security while protecting privacy.) Nevertheless, the concern from the privacy advocates remains regarding the extent to which privacy considerations are taken into account, and the specific nature of the privacy-driven system or program adaptations.

BOX 9.5
The Department of Homeland Security
Privacy Impact Assessment

A privacy impact assessment (PIA) is an analysis of how personally identifiable information is collected, stored, protected, shared, and managed. "Personally identifiable information" is defined as information in a system or online collection that directly or indirectly identifies an individual whether the individual is a U.S. citizen, legal permanent resident, or a visitor to the United States.

The purpose of a PIA is to demonstrate that system owners and developers have consciously incorporated privacy protections throughout the entire life cycle of a system. This involves making certain that privacy protections are built into the system from the start, not after the fact when they can be far more costly or could affect the viability of the project.

Personally identifiable information is information in a system, online collection, or technology (1) that directly identifies an individual (e.g., name, date of birth, mailing address, telephone number, Social Security number, e-mail address, zip code, address, account numbers, certificate and license numbers, vehicle identifiers including license plates, uniform resource locators, Internet Protocol addresses, biometric identifiers, photographic facial images, or any other unique identifying number or characteristic), or (2) by which an agency intends to identify specific individuals in conjunction with other data elements, that is, indirect identification. These data elements may include

Finally, the discussion in this chapter raises the question of what must be done when law enforcement authorities or intelligence agencies invade the privacy of Americans who are law-abiding or who pose no threat to national security. It is unrealistic to expect that the number of false positives (i.e., the number of people improperly implicated) can be reduced to zero, and thus public policy must necessarily anticipate that some such cases will arise. One option is to minimize the number of false positives, and in the event of a false positive, the person improperly implicated simply absorbs the cost and consequences of the false positive (e.g., loss of privacy and any consequential costs, such as personal embarrassment, financial loss, and so on) on behalf of the rest of society. But these costs and consequences can be dire indeed, and at least in principle our society has generally adopted the principle that individuals suffering the consequences of improper or mistaken government behavior are entitled to some kind of compensation. Providing recourse for citizens improperly treated by government authorities is generally thought to make government authorities more careful and more respectful of rights than they might otherwise be.

---

a combination of gender, race, birth date, geographic indicator, and any information that reasonably can be foreseen as being linked with other information to identify an individual.

In some cases the technology might only collect personal information for a moment. For example, a body-screening device might capture the full scan of an individual, and even if the information was not retained for later use, the initial scan might raise privacy concerns, and thus the development and deployment of the technology would require a PIA.

Questions asked by the PIA include the following:

Section 1.0 Information collected and maintained

1.1 What information is to be collected?
1.2 From whom is information collected?
1.3 Why is the information being collected?
1.4 What specific legal authorities, arrangements, or agreements define the collection of information?
1.5 Privacy Impact Analysis: Given the amount and type of data being collected, discuss what privacy risks were identified and how they were mitigated.

Section 2.0 Uses of the system and the information

2.1 Describe all the uses of information.
2.2 Does the system analyze data to assist users in identifying previously un-

continued

BOX 9.5
Continued

known areas of note, concern, or pattern (sometimes referred to as "data mining")?

2.3 How will the information collected from individuals or derived from the system be checked for accuracy?

2.4 Privacy Impact Analysis: Given the amount and type of information collected, describe any types of controls that may be in place to ensure that information is used in accordance with the above described uses.

Section 3.0 Retention

3.1 What is the retention period for the data in the system?

3.2 Has the retention schedule been approved by the National Archives and Records Administration (NARA)?

3.3 Privacy Impact Analysis: Given the purpose of retaining the information, explain why the information is needed for the indicated period.

Section 4.0 Internal sharing and disclosure

4.1 With which internal organizations is the information shared?

4.2 For each organization, what information is shared and for what purpose?

4.3 How is the information transmitted or disclosed?

4.4 Privacy Impact Analysis: Given the internal sharing, discuss what privacy risks were identified and how they were mitigated.

Section 5.0 External sharing and disclosure

5.1 With which external organizations is the information shared?

5.2 What information is shared and for what purpose?

5.3 How is the information transmitted or disclosed?

5.4 Is a memorandum of understanding (MOU), contract, or any agreement in place with any external organizations with whom information is shared, and does the agreement reflect the scope of the information currently shared?

5.5 How is the shared information secured by the recipient?

5.6 What type of training is required for users from agencies outside DHS prior to receiving access to the information?

5.7 Privacy Impact Analysis: Given the external sharing, describe what privacy risks were identified and how they were mitigated.

Section 6.0 Notice

6.1 Was notice provided to the individual prior to collection of information? If yes, please provide a copy of the notice as an appendix. (A notice may include a posted privacy policy, a Privacy Act notice on forms, or a system-of-records notice published in the Federal Register Notice.) If notice was not provided, why not?

6.2 Do individuals have an opportunity and/or right to decline to provide information?

6.3 Do individuals have the right to consent to particular uses of the information, and if so, how does the individual exercise the right?

6.4 Privacy Impact Analysis: Given the notice provided to individuals above, describe what privacy risks were identified and how they were mitigated.

Section 7.0 Individual access, redress and correction

7.1 What are the procedures that allow individuals to gain access to their own information?

7.2 What are the procedures for correcting erroneous information?

7.3 How are individuals notified of the procedures for correcting their information?

7.4 If no redress is provided, are alternatives available?

7.5 Privacy Impact Analysis: Given the access and other procedural rights provided for in the Privacy Act of 1974, explain the procedural rights that are provided and, if access, correction, and redress rights are not provided, explain why not.

Section 8.0 Technical access and security

8.1 Which user group(s) will have access to the system?

8.2 Will contractors to DHS have access to the system? If so, please submit to the Privacy Office with this PIA a copy of the contract describing their role.

8.3 Does the system use "roles" to assign privileges to users of the system?

8.4 What procedures are in place to determine which users may access the system, and are they documented?

8.5 How are the actual assignments of roles and rules verified according to established security and auditing procedures?

8.6 What auditing measures and technical safeguards are in place to prevent misuse of data?

8.7 Describe what privacy training is provided to users either generally or that is specifically relevant to the functionality of the program or system.

8.8 Are the data secured in accordance with FISMA requirements? If yes, when were certification and accreditation last completed?

8.9 Privacy Impact Analysis: Given access and security controls, describe what privacy risks were identified and how they were mitigated.

Section 9.0 Technology

9.1 Was the system built from the ground up or purchased and installed?

9.2 Describe how data integrity, privacy, and security were analyzed as part of the decisions made for your system.

9.3 What design choices were made to enhance privacy?

SOURCE: Department of Homeland Security, Privacy Impact Assessments: Official Guidance, DHS Privacy Office, available at http://www.dhs.gov/interWeb/assetlibrary/privacy_pia _guidance_march_v5.pdf.

Part IV

Findings and Recommendations

10

Findings and Recommendations

10.1 COMING TO TERMS

Finding 1. The meaning of privacy is highly contextual, and it can vary depending on the specific circumstances at hand, such as the situation and relationships at issue, the intentions of the parties involved, and the historical context, technology, and political environment.

Chapters 1 and 2 of this report take note of the fact that in both everyday discourse and in the scholarly literature, a commonly agreed-upon abstract definition of privacy is elusive (Section 1.2). For example, "privacy" under discussion may involve protecting the confidentiality of information; enabling a sense of autonomy, independence, and freedom to foster creativity; wanting to be left alone; or establishing enough trust that individuals within a given community are willing to disclose data under the assumption that it will not be misused.

Nevertheless, it is often possible to find agreement on the meaning of privacy in specific contexts (Section 2.4). In other words, the meaning of privacy depends on many specifics about the situation at hand, e.g., the situation and relationships at issue, the intentions of the parties involved, and the historical context, technology, and the political environment. For example, informational privacy involving political and religious beliefs raises different issues than does health information with respect to a contagious disease. A conversation with one's attorney is different from a speech in a public park or a posting on an Internet bulletin board. Agreement on the meaning of "privacy" outside the specified context is

305

not necessary, but for making progress in a specific context, a common understanding is essential. In many cases, simply clarifying the terms constitutes progress in itself, and indeed may on occasion be sufficient to reduce the need for further argument.

Because the committee found that common to almost all notions of privacy is a privileged status for personal information (privileged in the sense of information that is not immediately known or accessible to others), this report has focused on the meaning and implications of privacy as it relates to the gathering, aggregation, analysis, distribution, and use of personal information. A successful discussion about privacy policies requires the clear identification of both the nature of the personal information in question and the relevant contextual factors.

Regarding the nature of the personal information, it is important to probe in several areas discussed in Section 2.1.3:

- Data capture, which includes the type(s) of personal information in question (e.g., Social Security number, medical information, publicly available information) and the circumstance and means of its capture;
- Data storage, which includes the time period for which data will be retained and available for use and the circumstances and means of storage (e.g., media used), and the protections for personal information while it is available for a specific use;
- Data analysis and integration, which includes the nature of the process through which the information is analyzed and the links that might be made to other data; and
- Data dissemination, which includes the parties who will have access to the information, the form(s) in which the information is presented, the type of harm that might result from unwelcome disclosure or dissemination, and the extent to which this information has privacy implications for other individuals.

Regarding the relevant contextual factors, it might be useful to probe about the following:

- What is the relevant and applicable social and institutional context? For example, are rewards or benefits offered for sharing personal information? Is coercion used in the form of withholding benefits when personal information is not shared? Does the individual retain control over the initial and potential future uses of her information? Does she have the opportunity to review and correct personal information?
- Who are the actors and institutions involved? These might include the subject of the information, the provider of the information (which may not be the subject), the original recipients of the information, subsequent

recipients, and other individuals who might be affected without their active involvement—and the relationships among them.

• What are the stated and unstated motivations, goals, or purposes of the actors? Why do the recipients of the information want it? How might the information be repurposed—used for a purpose other than that for which it was originally collected—in the future?

• How are decisions made when there are competing interests regarding personal information, for example, public health needs versus individual privacy or national security versus civil rights interests?

• What are the informational norms in question? As noted in Chapter 2, informational norms specify how different kinds of information about various actors in the given context can flow. These norms can be illuminated in many instances through the technique of applying anchoring vignettes as described in Chapter 2. Relevant issues concerning these norms might include:

—The extent to which information is provided voluntarily (e.g., is the providing of information required by law, is the information acquired covertly or deceptively);

—The extent to which information can be passed along to third parties and the circumstances of such passing (e.g., is it part of a financial transaction);

—The extent to which reciprocity exists (is the subject entitled to receive information or other benefits from the recipient);

—The extent to which the gathering of information is apparent and obvious to those to whom the information pertains;

—Limitations on the use of the information that are implied or explicitly noted;

—Whether or not the act of subsequently providing information is known to the subject; and

—The extent to which collected information can/might be used for or against others (e.g., relatives, other members of a class).

One important corollary of Finding 1 is that policy debates are likely to be sterile and disconnected if they are couched simply in abstract terms. It should thus be expected that policy debates involving privacy will be couched in the language of the specific context involved—and such context-dependent formulations are desirable. The reason is that even if the issues themselves seem to carry over from one context to another, the weighting of each issue and hence the relationships of issues to each other are likely to depend on the specific context.

A second corollary is that because privacy has meaning only in context, the incidence of privacy problems (e.g., violations of privacy) is poorly defined outside specific contexts, and overall quantitative measures of privacy are not particularly meaningful. What may be more meaningful is careful delimitation of claims that are made based on domain-specific data. An example from the identity theft domain might involve hypothesizing the number of individuals per year whose names and Social Security numbers were potentially compromised by a security breach, rather than asserting these numbers as indicating identity theft.

A third corollary is that privacy is not primarily a technological issue—technology cannot violate or guarantee privacy. Technology can enhance or detract from the secrecy of information or the anonymity of an actor, but these are not the same as privacy. The nature and extent of privacy in any given context are tied to many factors, including the way in which information is accessed, the intentions of those accessing the information, and the trust relationships between the user of the information and the subject of the information.

10.2 THE VALUE OF PRIVACY

Finding 2. *Privacy is an important value to be maintained and protected, although it is not an absolute good in itself.*

As noted in Chapter 2, privacy is an important value to be maintained and protected. Certain types of privacy (e.g., those involving religious beliefs and political ideas or certain aspects of the body) approach the status of fundamental human rights. They are related to our most cherished ideals of the dignity of the person, the family, liberty, and democracy.

At the same time, the committee does not view privacy as an intrinsic and absolute good independently of particular situations. There are times when crossing the informational borders of the person is appropriate and to fail to do so would be irresponsible. That is, the committee recognizes situations and contexts in which society negotiates appropriate tradeoffs between privacy and other values (as discussed below) such as public health and safety. To note this is not to deny the centrality of privacy to human dignity, candor, and intimacy as well as to a democratic society. Privacy is thus also a means as well as an end, and the committee recognizes considerable instrumental value in privacy—privacy in the service of other important goals. Beyond instrumentality, privacy has important symbolic value in demonstrating societal respect for the individual.

Finding 3. *Loss of privacy often results in significant tangible and intangible harm to individuals and to groups.*

In one obvious example, protecting the privacy of one's personal information helps to make one safer from crimes such as fraud, identity theft, and stalking. (When undertaken on a large scale, identity theft can also have important and negative effects on society, as suggested by the use of identity theft as an element in the financing of terrorist groups and their operations (see Box 4.1).) But such tangible harms, striking though they are, affect far fewer people compared with those who suffer less tangible harms (as suggested in Section 1.3). These intangible harms could be regarded as the consequential damages to individuals and to society that result from the loss or compromise of privacy, and they are no less real or significant for being intangible rather than tangible. Consider:

- A person whose personal information (name, address, Social Security number, and so on) may have fallen into the hands of identity thieves may not in fact suffer from an actual fraudulent purchase made in her name. But if the breach is identified and the subject learns of it, she will likely worry about being victimized and thus must look over her shoulder for a very long period of time. She may have to scrutinize her credit card statements more carefully; she may have to subscribe to a credit-monitoring service; she may have to put a freeze on her credit report and thereby deny herself the convenience of obtaining instant credit at a store. She may live in fear of assault, public embarrassment, or defamation, not knowing who has the information or how it might be used. Thus, absent the protection of her information, she stands to lose real benefits and the intangible peace of mind that she would otherwise enjoy, even if no actual direct harm occurs, not to mention the many dozens of hours needed to repair her records and relationships. Furthermore, it takes only a few such well-publicized incidents (i.e., a small number compared with the number of possible instances where it could happen) to cause a very large number of people to lose trust in electronic commerce and related matters—and thus to refrain from engaging in such commerce. Such broader impacts have larger consequences for the economy as a whole than simply the impact on the individuals directly affected by identity theft.
- Under public surveillance, many people change their behavior so that they are not seen as acting anomalously in any way, even if their behavior absent surveillance would be perfectly legal and ethical. For example, an interracial couple may walk down the road holding hands and even sneak a kiss. With surveillance cameras visibly trained on the road, they may not kiss, they may not hold hands, and they may even change their route so that they are not under video surveillance. Public surveillance may reduce the likelihood that someone would attend a public demonstration in which he might otherwise participate. In short, surveillance often has the effect of influencing the behavior of people in the direction of greater conformity and homogeneity. Greater conformity is sometimes defensible, as might be the case when safe driving can be linked to automatic traffic camera surveillance. But surveillance in some

instances has negative consequences, and in a culture and society that celebrate diversity and embrace tolerance, such chilling effects are not at all positive. In short, privacy supports many democratic societal values, such as the right to freely associate, the embrace of social diversity, and even the use of secret ballots in support of free elections, and consequently the loss of privacy can affect the entire society.

• Through the analysis of a variety of personal information, the U.S. government has placed many individuals on "watch lists" as suspected terrorists who should be denied airplane boarding privileges or entry into the United States. Individuals on these watch lists cannot know of their status until they are denied boarding or entry—and if they are in fact not terrorists, they suffer the consequences of mistaken identity. Further, they have no recourse—no way to be made whole—for the consequences they suffer.

• Workplace surveillance changes the workplace environment, almost by definition. But unlike most unfocused public surveillance, the very purpose of workplace surveillance is to change the behavior of everyone within its purview. From the standpoint of employees under poorly explained surveillance (which is often simply offered as a fait accompli), surveillance can result in a deadened work environment perceived as hostile and restrictive in which workers are not trusted and "are treated like children." Ironically, work monitoring seen to be unreasonable is likely to be responded to in ways that undermine the goals of the organization, and such surveillance may raise the level of stress among workers in ways that limit their productivity.

• A voter without privacy is subject to coercion in casting his or her vote. Indeed, it was for just this reason that the secret ballot was gradually introduced in the United States in the late 19th century. With a secret ballot, there is no way to prove how an individual voted, and thus a voter can cast his or her vote freely without fear of later retribution. Secret ballots also impede vote buying, since a voter can vote one way and tell his or her paymaster that he voted the way he or she was paid to vote.

• The availability of personal information about an individual enables various organizations to provide him or her with information or product and service offerings customized to the interests and patterns reflected in such information. While such information and offerings do have benefit for many people who receive them, they can have negative effects as well. For example, personal medical information made available to drug manufacturers may result in drug advertisements being targeted to individuals with certain diseases. Receipt of such advertisements at one's family home can compromise the privacy of the individual's medical information if the diseases associated with such drugs are socially stigmatizing.

• People who lose control of their personal information can be subject to discrimination of various kinds (Section 2.3). As a society, we have made a choice that discrimination based on race and religion (among other things) should be illegal as a matter of public policy. But there are many other distinctions that can be made when detailed personal information is available that facilitates the classification and assignment of people to groups—groups defined not by race or religion but by some nameless statistical sorting on multiple dimensions. Members of groups so defined can be denied services, information, opportunities, or employment to which they would otherwise be entitled if that personal information had been kept private. For example, political campaigns can use collections of personal information to tailor different messages to members of different groups that are designed to appeal to their particular views and attitudes. Such practices work against full disclosure and a community-wide consideration of the issues.

These examples underscore the committee's categorical rejection of the notion that if you have done nothing wrong, you have nothing to fear from a loss of privacy.

It should also be noted that the *ability* to put individuals under surveillance is often as significant in changing behavior as the reality of such surveillance. From dummy surveillance cameras intended to deter crime to fellow diners in a cafeteria who *might* be listening to a private conversation, there are many ways in which potential surveillance can affect behavior.

Finding 4. *Privacy is particularly important to people when they believe that the entity receiving their personal information is not trustworthy and that they may be harmed by sharing that information.*

Trust is an important issue in framing concerns regarding privacy. In the context of an individual providing personal information to another, the sensitivities involved will depend on the degree to which the individual trusts that party to refrain from acting in a manner that is contrary to his or her interests (e.g., to pass it along to someone else, to use it as the basis for a decision with inappropriately adverse consequences). As an extreme case, consider the act of providing a complete dossier of personal information on a stack of paper—to a person who will destroy it. If the destruction is verifiable to the person providing the dossier (and if there is no way for the destroyer to read the dossier), it would be hard to assert the existence of any privacy concern at all.

But for most situations in which one provides personal information, the basis for trust is less clear. Children routinely assert privacy rights to their personal information against their parents when they do not trust that parents will not criticize them or punish them or think ill of them as a result of accessing that information. (They also assert privacy rights in many other situations.) Adults who purchase health insurance often assert privacy rights in their medical information because they are concerned that insurers might not insure them or might charge high prices on the basis of some information in their medical record. Many citizens assert privacy rights against government, although few would object to the gathering of personal information within the borders of the United States and about U.S. citizens if they could be assured that such information was being used only for genuine national security purposes and that any information that had been gathered about them was accurate and appropriately interpreted and treated (as discussed in Section 9.2.5). Perversely, many people hold contradictory views about their own privacy and other people's privacy—that is, they support curtailing the privacy of some demographic groups at the same time that they believe that their own should not be similarly curtailed. This dichotomy almost certainly reflects their views about the trustworthiness of certain groups versus their own.

In short, the act of providing personal information is almost always accompanied to varying degrees by a perceived risk of negative consequences flowing from an abuse of trust. The perception may or may not be justified by the objective facts of the situation, but trust has an important subjective element. If the entity receiving the information is not seen as trustworthy, it is likely that the individuals involved will be much more hesitant to provide that information (or to provide it accurately) than they would be under other circumstances involving a greater degree of trust.

10.3 PRESSURES ON PRIVACY

The discussion in earlier chapters suggests that there are many pressures that are increasingly limiting privacy. Among them are advancing information technologies; increasing mechanisms for obtaining information; the value of personal information to business and government; and changing social norms and needs.

Finding 5. *Although some developments in information technology (IT) and other technologies do have considerable potential to enhance privacy, the overall impact of advancing technology including IT has been to compromise privacy.*

One obvious pressure on privacy is the evolution of information technology writ large, an evolution that has resulted in greater capability to invade and compromise privacy more deeply and more easily than ever before. One might ask whether this result was inevitable—whether under a different set of societal structures and different notions of power and privilege the evolution of IT might have done more to enhance privacy. But even though some developments in IT do indeed have the potential to enhance privacy, there is little doubt that the overall impact of advancing IT has been to compromise privacy in important ways.

For example, the rapidly decreasing cost of storing information has meant that personal information on an individual, once collected, may generally be available for potential use forever unless special measures are taken to destroy it (Chapter 3). Even when there is no particular need to keep information for a long time, it is often kept by default, because it is more expensive to decide on what to destroy or delete than to maintain it in storage. Such information is easily if not routinely added to existing databases on the individual, which means that the volume of information about an individual only grows over time.[1]

A second example is the proliferation of smaller, less expensive, and more easily deployed sensors that can readily obtain information in their ambient environment, information that is sometimes personal information about individuals.

Technology has also facilitated greater access to information (Section 3.4). Nominally public records stored on paper are vastly more inaccessible than if their contents are posted on a Web site or are available online, and in that sense are more private apart from any rules regulating access to them. For example, property tax records have been available to the public in most municipalities for decades. The inconvenience of access has prevented widespread knowledge of neighbors' property values, but when such information is available via the Internet, it is disseminated much more broadly.

More generally, information technology is a rapidly changing field. New information technologies—and new sensor, biometric, and life science technologies, too—often offer capabilities poorly understood and considered in public debates or in individuals' expectations of privacy. Traditional expectations about information are in a sense under continuous bombardment from such changes, and prior beliefs, understandings, and practices are not necessarily an adequate guide or control with respect to the torrent of new developments. The net result is that the appearance

---

[1]An example is a person's medical history, much of which is irrelevant to an individual's current medical status. (Information regarding major medical events (surgeries, major diseases) and associated significant data such as reports on operations, X rays, and pathology reports continue to be useful, but much of the medical record over time becomes filled with data that may be maintained for medical legal purposes but has little value to the treating physician long after the fact. Such data might, for example, include lab work taken during a critical event or during routine care many years in the past.)

of new technologies rekindles debates and arguments that might otherwise have been regarded as settled.

Finding 6. *Businesses, researchers, and government agencies increasingly find value in the exploitation of personal information, which leads to many pressures for repurposing of collected data.*

A second pressure is the fact that the IT-enabled exploitation of personal information has many benefits for modern business in enhancing the economic bottom line (Chapters 6 through 8). Activities such as increasing consumer choice, reducing economic risks, directing customized product offerings to consumers, and hiring and placing employees in the most cost-effective fashion become feasible as business strategies only when there is personal information available to support them. Researchers rely on collections of personal information to derive statistical trends of importance to public policy makers. Government authorities increasingly seek better and more ways of using personal information to provide services (Section 6.8), administer benefits, and enhance security (Chapter 9).

Furthermore, the ways in which personal information can be exploited to benefit the bottom line of businesses or the mission capabilities of government agencies seem to be limited only by the creativity of the human mind (Section 6.1). This is significant because data, once collected for a given purpose, can easily be used for a different purpose in the future—this is especially true because the data can be retained indefinitely at little cost. Today's databases for the most part have not been designed to restrict the use of the data they contain to any specific purpose. Many of the privacy concerns discussed in this report center on cases in which information gathered for one purpose is reused for a different purpose with neither notice nor consent. Whether it is the use of medical information for the marketing of pharmaceuticals, the conversion of timestamps on toll-road tickets for the calculation of average speed (and the subsequent issuing of speeding tickets), or the reuse of information collected from patients in a long-term epidemiological research study, repurposing of previously collected data creates myriad privacy concerns.

A particularly interesting kind of personal information is information that today is not easily personally identifiable but may be more identifiable in the future. For example, surveillance cameras in public places take many pictures of people. Today, the automated recognition of facial images taken by such cameras is difficult and unreliable—but the technology of facial recognition will almost certainly improve in the future. As the technology improves, and databases of facial images are populated, it is entirely possible that businesses and government will develop new ways of exploiting personal information that is not identifiable today.

Finding 7. *Privacy considerations are relevant throughout the life cycle of personal information that is collected, and not just at the beginning of the collection process.*

The collection and use of personal information is typically not a single event, but a process with considerable duration and organizational support. Finding new ways to exploit already-collected information extends the life cycle even further. Thus, privacy considerations need to be taken into account on a continuing basis.

Finding 8. *Businesses and government agencies have developed many mechanisms—both voluntary and intrusive—for obtaining personal information.*

Because institutions both public and private find high value in the IT-enabled large-scale availability of personal information, they continually find ways to maintain and expand the availability of such information from individuals. Though there are many variants, such ways can be grouped in a few categories:

• *Mandated disclosure* is, by definition, coercive. For example, taxpayers must provide detailed financial information on income tax returns. Convicted felons in a number of states must provide DNA information for entry into a database to which law enforcement officials have access. Convicted sex offenders must register with law enforcement authorities, and communities must be notified about the presence of such individuals living therein. Most importantly, failure to provide such information is punishable by law.

• *Incentivized disclosure* is arguably voluntary. Individuals are persuaded to provide personal information by the offer of some incentive—an offer that may be difficult to refuse. For example, merchants often offer customers "loyalty" cards, the presentation of which at the cash register entitles the customer to a discount on the merchandise being bought. In exchange, the merchant obtains a record of all purchases (and patterns over time) made using this loyalty card. The use of this data may enable the merchant to better tailor product offerings to its customers' revealed preferences. Customers who prefer that no record be made of their purchases need not present a loyalty card, and in some cases they may request that a generic loyalty card be used to provide the discount.

• *Conditioned disclosure* lies between incentivized disclosure and mandatory disclosure. Obtaining a certain good or service is conditioned on the recipient providing personal information. Furthermore, the good or service in question is arguably very important—perhaps nearly essential—to the activities of one's daily life or the obligations of citizenship.

Driving a car, traveling on an airplane, voting, and being employed are voluntary activities in some sense, but one must provide personal information in order to engage in them. Walking in a public plaza watched by surveillance cameras is voluntary, but even if notices of surveillance are posted (which may not be the case), avoiding the plaza may not be particularly convenient—and thus surveillance photos of the walker may be taken. Taking a drug test may be a requirement of keeping one's job— and the results of a urine test may be stored in an employee's personnel file. Thus, the disclosure of personal information is not quite mandated, because one may indeed make a choice to not obtain the good or service. But it is not quite voluntary either, because doing without the good or service in question would constitute a hardship or a substantial inconvenience for the individual.

• *Entirely voluntary disclosure.* People engaged in social interactions with others often exchange information about themselves, but they themselves decide what they will share. A person may have a sense of the other person involved, or of the cultural norms that suggest the nature of the exchange, but for the most part they still decide if and how much information to provide. In other situations, people sometimes voluntarily provide information about themselves as a gesture of affiliation or as evidence of competence, understanding, or empathy ("Yes, that happened to me too; I understand just how you feel"). To the extent that these interactions do not reflect differential power relationships, these can be regarded as entirely voluntary disclosures, and they need not be governed by the expectation of tangible or direct personal benefit or exchange.

• *Unannounced acquisition of information.* In such situations, information is not even "disclosed," since disclosure implies that the individual realizes that he or she is revealing information. But there are many situations in which people disclose personal information without realizing it. Most individuals who make toll-free calls do not realize that the numbers from which they are calling are provided to the called party, and caller-ID services operate without notice to callers. Web bugs and cookies covertly provide information about the Web surfing behavior of individuals. Building entry is often recorded as individuals swipe their electronic ID cards into an access control system. Surveillance photos are often taken at a distance. In some of these cases, individuals subject to these acquisitions of information are in some sense given notice of that fact, but these notices are often provided in such a way that they are easy to ignore or forget.

Finding 9. Changing social trends and sentinel events put strong pressures on privacy.

Some forms of privacy invasion that are technically possible may in practice not take place in certain social contexts. Beyond formal law, for example, various professional codes of ethics require practitioners to preserve certain kinds of privacy, and in many cases these codes are sufficient to reassure individuals that personal information revealed to these practitioners will remain private and confidential. Social and cultural norms regarding propriety and civility have also tended to keep certain kinds of personal information that were nominally public from being widely circulated (e.g., information about a public figure's divorce or extramarital affairs). Manners and common sense can also be important in limiting disclosure and notice.

Nevertheless, a number of social trends have significantly eroded much of the privacy protection that may have resulted from such norms (Section 1.4.3). Once information becomes public, it is virtually impossible to fully expunge it, no matter how privacy invasive, offensive, or incorrect it may be. Personal information that is available is likely to be exploited by those who see economic, political, or other strategic value to its use, independent of societal approval or disapproval. DNA evidence has led to the freeing of imprisoned individuals and convicted others, putting pressure on obtaining it. Sexual offender notices have led to the harassment and murder of convicted offenders who have served their sentences.[2]

Sentinel events (i.e., dramatic changes in circumstance such as terrorist events and public health crises) often change the privacy environment (Section 1.4.4). Furthermore, the resulting media coverage and political rhetoric often lead to a political environment in which privacy can be reduced or curtailed in ways not previously accepted by the public. This was dramatically illustrated by the speed with which the USA PATRIOT Act was passed in the wake of the September 11, 2001, terrorist attacks.

Finding 10. *The power of the state and large private organizations to gather personal information and to act on that information is much greater than the power of the individual to withhold personal information from the state or those organizations or to prevent improper or unjustified actions from being taken.*

As noted in Section 9.1.6, there is almost always a substantial imbalance between the power of the state and that of the individual regarding the gathering of information about individuals. Some regard this imbalance as dangerous and improper, and infer that external limits are thus necessary to constrain the ability of government officials to act improperly, even if such constraints complicate or impede the task of law enforcement agencies. Others trust that government officials will use such power only

---

[2]Emily Bazar, "Suspected Shooter Found Sex Offenders' Homes on Website," *USA Today*, April 18, 2006, available at http://www.usatoday.com/news/nation/2006-04-16-maine-shootings _x.htm.

in the interest of the citizenry and thus do not believe that such constraints are necessary, especially if these constraints complicate or impede the task of law enforcement agencies. Whatever one's views on this matter, it is a reality that must be factored strongly into the debate over privacy.

Similar comments apply to the balance between large private organizations and individuals, although the texture of that balance is different. It is difficult to withhold information from both government and many large private organizations with which individuals choose to do business. Government and private organizations are subject to some degree of oversight, by the independent branches of government in the former case and by boards and ombudsmen in the latter case. But individuals have no choice in the government laws and regulations under which they live short of moving away,[3] and they often have only some choices in the private organizations with which they interact. Moreover, private organizations do not directly hold coercive powers such as imprisonment, which are reserved for the state. Concerns regarding private organizations parallel those regarding government. That is, some people are highly concerned about the imbalance between individuals and private organizations, and thus infer that regulation is thus necessary to constrain their ability to act in ways that harm individuals, even if such constraints complicate or impede their business and operational missions. Others believe that the power of the marketplace is sufficient to constrain their behavior, and reject external constraints because they would complicate or impede their business and operational missions.

10.4 MAKING TRADEOFFS

Finding 11. *Privacy is a value that must often be traded off against some other desirable societal value or good.*

At the same time that the committee strongly believes privacy is central to notions of the dignity of the person and is a requisite for a decent and democratic society, it also recognizes the complexity of society and the existence of competing values (Section 1.2). For example, the protection of privacy is sometimes detrimental to economic efficiency—in the absence of certain kinds of information, two otherwise equal parties may not make the most economically efficient decision. Privacy claims can be

---

[3]Of course, citizens in a democracy can vote to support candidates who support changes in laws and regulations that they regard as objectionable. However, this does not change the fact that citizens are obligated to obey all applicable laws and regulations on the books at any given moment, and their only choices at that moment are to accept such responsibility or to move to a location where they are not subject to the reach of those laws or regulations.

used to shield criminal acts, and they can also be used to limit scrutiny of acts and behavior that—though not technically illegal—are arguably antisocial or otherwise disapproved.

Depending on one's weighting of the values at stake, such tradeoffs may mean more privacy and less of X (X being the other value or values at stake) or vice versa. Deciding the right mix of privacy and X in any given situation sometimes entails a tradeoff with respect to other values, and understanding the nature of those tradeoffs is necessary before one can think systematically about decisions involving tradeoffs.

A central feature of many policy tradeoffs involving privacy is the fact that privacy—in the terms usually most relevant to the policy debate—relates to the privacy of individuals, whereas the other X at stake relates to a collective value or good. That is, some individual members of society are asked to accept reductions in privacy in order to benefit the entire society. If these individual members are politically marginalized (e.g., because they are few in number or have no vocal advocates), the political process will similarly marginalize their privacy concerns. (In the past, such groups have included Japanese-Americans in World War II and the U.S. citizens and organizations subjected to National Security Agency communications surveillance in the decade beginning in the early 1960s, many of whom among the latter were active in the antiwar and civil rights movements.[4]) Whether the actions taken are viewed as desirable or undesirable, or as necessary or unnecessary, will vary depending on the conditions, but they should be recognized for what they are.

A similar tradeoff occurs when researchers seek to obtain statistical information from large aggregations of personal information from many individuals. For example, epidemiologists often use personal health information of many individuals to understand patterns of disease propagation. Although personal health information is generally collected for the benefit of individual patients, epidemiological research generally does not require the identities of these patients. Society as a whole benefits from epidemiological research, but the potential costs of using putatively anonymized personal health information are borne by the individuals whose identities might be compromised inadvertently. It is for this reason that the nature and the scope of privacy assurance regarding personal health information are so important from a policy perspective.

The fact that tradeoffs are made is not new in public policy. But one implication of the information age—in which information is collected and

---

[4]*Warrantless FBI Electronic Surveillance,* Book III of the Final Report of the Select Committee to Study Governmental Operations with Respect to Intelligence Activities, United States Senate, April 23, 1976.

disseminated with increasing ease and individuals are more and more interconnected—is that routine administrative and bureaucratic processes (one might even call these processes autonomic) for making many such decisions are no longer sufficient, and that engaged, reflective decision making, perhaps at higher levels than before, will become increasingly necessary.

The reason is that in the absence of countervailing forces, privacy will tend to be eroded when considered in relation to some more tangible and immediate objective that is also desirable. Indeed, privacy is something that is noticed mostly when it is gone or missing or compromised. People are much more likely to notice that their privacy is being violated than they are to notice that their privacy is being respected. Thus, it is easy for autonomic decision making to sacrifice a good—privacy—that is noticeable mostly in its absence in favor of the more tangible and visible benefit promised by those seeking another legitimate end. We must become aware of this tendency and be sure that decision makers give adequate weight to values having different characteristics.

Finding 12. *In the public debate about balancing privacy and other societal interests, there is often a lack of clarity about the privacy interests involved and too often a tendency to downplay and to be dismissive of the privacy issues at stake.*

Because policy makers recognize the political risks involved in appearing to compromise citizen privacy, they often offer assurances that legitimate citizen privacy will in fact be protected. That is, they assert that they have in fact guarded against sacrificing privacy needlessly or inappropriately—whether or not they have in fact done so.

The committee believes that for public policy purposes, a vital element of making tradeoffs is the enhancement of transparency in the process. This strategy consists of two components. The first is the provision of a clear statement of what meaning of "privacy" is being used and why. The goal is to ensure that everyone in the discussion means the same thing by "privacy" and/or by "X" (whatever privacy is being traded against). (By clarifying the meaning of privacy rather than obfuscating it, the public debate could also serve an educational role for the public that often does not appreciate the issues attendant to privacy.) From an analytical perspective, Sections 10.1 and 2.4 (see Box 2.2) describe one process—the use of anchoring vignettes—for coming to terms about meaning, and there are of course other ways of doing so as well.

Note that debates seeming to be about privacy can in fact involve very different matters. For example, the debate about access to DNA information by insurance companies is actually a debate about access to health care, employment, or mobility and whether or not insurance companies should be allowed to deny coverage on the basis of one's genetic profile. Those making policy should take care to make sure that debates that seem to center on privacy do not, in fact, use privacy as a screen to cover other fundamental disagreements. This does not mean that privacy is irrelevant to such a discussion—for example, individuals asserting a right to privacy may be using the only weapon that they have to protect their self-interest in such a situation. But privacy may not be the only or even the primary issue at stake.

Indeed, the point about identifying the source of disagreement is worth expanding. Although privacy considerations are generally important in policy discussions (both public and private), there are a number of logically prior antecedents. The most important of these antecedents is the desirability of any particular policy goal in the first place. Some particular contemplated action may have many and deep privacy implications, but if the goal to be served by that action is an inappropriate one—however that may be decided—it may not be necessary to address the privacy implications at all. If health insurance were a right to be enjoyed by all citizens, the debate over access to DNA information by insurance companies would have a much different character. A program that collects the personal information of Elbonian-Americans has definite privacy implications. But if the goal of the program is to enable the identification of Elbonian-Americans for possible deportation, it may make sense for the nation to assess whether or not the deportation of Elbonian-Americans is a good or a bad policy goal.

The second component of a transparency strategy is discussed below.

Finding 13. *When privacy is at issue, bland assurances that privacy will not be harmed offered by policy makers can do more to raise skepticism than would honest assessments of tradeoffs.*

Transparency also requires that tension be recognized when it is present. Recognizing that there is often tension in a "privacy versus X" relationship (e.g., personal privacy versus video surveillance for transportation safety), it is important to make clear how the various stakeholders view the situation and the factors that decision makers consider. Public debate and discourse are undermined when policy makers simply deny the existence of tradeoffs between privacy and other values and assert without evidence that it is possible to "have it all." Policy makers of good conscience and good will can legitimately come to different conclusions about the right balance in any given situation, but it is unreasonable to assert without evidence that there will be no diminution or narrowing of privacy if and when these other values are given a new and higher priority.[5]

It is true that in making a tradeoff, it is sometimes possible to develop privacy-respecting solutions that reduce the conflict between privacy and other values. For example, policy makers may decide to make greater use of a system that collects certain kinds of personal information on individuals in order to enhance energy efficiency in a building. But the potential infringement on privacy may well come from the long-term retention of such information—and so restructuring the system to erase that information after it is no longer necessary (e.g., after an hour, when it is no longer needed to manage the building heating and air conditioning system) might mitigate the privacy concerns substantially without damaging the goal of conserving energy. Drivers on toll roads need to be charged, but the time at which they enter or leave a toll road is irrelevant to whether or not they have paid. Thus, a toll system that does not record entry and exit times cannot be used to calculate the driver's speed between those two points and thus cannot be used as a basis for issuing speeding tickets.[6] In general, explicit attention to privacy considerations (e.g., collecting only information that is directly relevant, or showing only the degree of intrusiveness and invasiveness necessary for the stated goal) can reduce the privacy downside for some proposed action.

If a solution is available or developed that does mitigate privacy concerns, it should be discussed explicitly, so that there is clear evidence for what would otherwise be an empty assertion made simply for public relations purposes. And even in the cases in which no mitigating solution is available, an explicit discussion of costs to privacy and benefits regarding the other values would be much more credible than stock assertions.

If the public is to give up some measure of privacy, there should be a reasonable expectation of public information about the benefits in other dimensions that will result from that loss. Because a loss is certain (by definition), it is not sufficient to offer speculative benefits as justification. The benefits themselves may be uncertain because they are probabilistic,

---

[5]Perhaps a prior issue is whether or not some proposed action should be taken at all, irrespective of privacy considerations. For example, if a proposed action is demonstrably not cost-effective in achieving some goal, privacy considerations may not be relevant at all, since decision makers in both the private and the public sectors should not be taking cost-ineffective actions in the first place.

[6]Of course, one might argue that the use of a toll system to catch speeders (but only certain types of speeders) is an appropriate and efficient use of technology designed for other purposes, and that such "dual use" should be encouraged rather than discouraged. From a public policy perspective, this may well be true—but the committee believes that in such cases, both purposes ought to be openly discussed, and if the outcome of the public policy process is that both uses are determined to be desirable, then so be it.

but at the very least the analytical basis that led to the decision must be publicly articulated.

Put differently, it is necessary to make explicit the evidentiary or other basis for concluding that the action in question will serve a stated policy goal. While there is a reasonable debate to undertake about an action that compromises privacy to some extent and that demonstrably advances a stated policy goal, it makes little sense to take an action that does the former but not the latter. If some action does not demonstrably advance a stated policy goal, it may not be necessary to consider the privacy implications of that action at all, as the action may not make sense for reasons entirely unrelated to privacy. Yet in the rush to "do something" in response to a shocking event, privacy-compromising actions are often taken that have little real relationship to advancing a stated goal.

Finding 14. Privacy-invasive solutions to public policy problems may be warranted, but when they are implemented as measures of first rather than last resort, they generate resistance that might otherwise be avoided if other alternatives were tried first.

Privacy-respecting solutions that reduce the cost of making a trade-off are often difficult to find. But there is one type of solution that is worth special notice—the approach in which privacy-reducing actions are employed as a last rather than a first resort. Before demanding solutions that require that citizens provide more personal information, policy makers crafting solutions to problems would do well to fix problems by making more effective use of the personal information to which they already have access. For example, if the bottleneck in processing intercepted phone calls is the lack of linguists that understand the language in which those calls are made, it may not make much sense to intercept even more calls until more linguists are available.

10.5 APPROACHES TO PRIVACY IN THE INFORMATION AGE

As noted above, the pressures on privacy are many and the inherent protections for privacy few. It is thus worth considering explicit approaches that can be used to support privacy.

10.5.1 Principles

The committee identified a number of principles that it believes should guide efforts to achieve an appropriate balance between privacy and other issues. These include the following:

- *Avoid demonization.* Most threats to privacy do not come from fundamentally bad people with bad intentions. Rather, they are consequences of trying to address real needs (such as national security, law enforcement, open government, business efficiency, fraud prevention, and so on) either without giving adequate thought to the privacy consequences, or because they assign to the other needs a higher priority than they assign to privacy. Although demonization of an opponent is a staple of today's political rhetoric, it tends to make compromise and thoughtful deliberation difficult.

• *Account for context and nuance.* As noted in Section 10.1 and elsewhere in this report, privacy is a complicated subject with many nuances. Whose privacy is at issue? Against what parties? What information is in question? What are the circumstances? What precedents may be created? In the policy-making process (whether for public policy or organizational policy), taking these nuances into account will often be necessary if common ground is to be found. Without context and nuance, the debate quickly polarizes into "pro-privacy" and "anti-privacy"/"pro-X" camps.[7] (For X, substitute any issue of public importance—security, law enforcement, the economy, for example.)

• *Respect complexity.* Privacy is a moving target, as the numerous social and technical factors with which it is intertwined change over time. Many choices made today to settle some privacy issue will almost certainly lead to surprising results and require further adjustment, either by modifying the original choices, or by adding further mechanisms to compensate for newly discovered problems. Thus, solutions to privacy problems are more likely to be successful if they can begin with modest and simple steps, guided by well-formulated principles that produce operational real-world experience and understanding that can then be used to shape further actions, always with an eye to the dynamic nature of the topic.

• *Be aware of long-term costs and risks.* As noted in Section 3.10, privacy protections are—in practice—based on a mix of culture, technology, and policy. But all systems are deployed in a cost-sensitive environment, and it is important to consider how economic cost might have an impact on this mix. On the one hand, retrofitting privacy protections to information systems or business practices is often more expensive than design-

---

[7]An analogy from the world of computer security may be helpful. Operating systems often have facilities for protecting the privacy of files. If the privacy question is formulated simply as, Should other people be able to have access to a given user's files?, most people would say no. But if the question is decomposed into finer questions such as, Who can know about the existence of this particular file?, Who has permission to read its contents?, Who can change its contents?, and, Who can change these permissions?, it becomes possible to have a more useful discussion about privacy requirements and the necessary system capabilities to support those requirements.

ing these systems or practices from the start to be privacy-protective or respecting. Indeed, there is substantial empirical experience that indicates that this is the case. On the other hand, it is clearly simpler and less expensive to design systems or business practices without attention to privacy at all. Because the policy process often seems easier to manipulate than technological development (particularly after the technology is in place), the temptation is great to rely heavily on policy to protect privacy. The committee believes that in the long run, policy-based privacy protections introduced without providing for adequate technology enforcement are likely to result in unintended violations of privacy. (It is also axiomatic that absent an adequate policy framework for protecting privacy, the best technology is unlikely to succeed.) This scenario is likely to result in costly retrofits and may also result in unfavorable publicity and perhaps significant economic liability. Thus, organizations that handle personal information are well advised to invest up front in adequate technological privacy protection from the very beginning.

10.5.2 Individual Actions

Finding 15. Individuals can take steps to enhance the privacy of their personal information. They can also become better informed about the extent to which their privacy has been compromised, although the effectiveness of these measures is bound to be limited.

Individuals have some ability to take steps to enhance the privacy of their personal information, and to be better informed about the extent to which their privacy may be compromised (Section 3.8.1).[8] Most of these steps involve tradeoffs involving convenience, access, and cost. Individuals can tailor their privacy protection practices to their specific situation. As in the physical world, people whose privacy has been compromised with harmful, costly, or inconvenient results will almost certainly increase the degree of inconvenience and cost they are willing to accept for greater protection in the future.

To reduce the amount of personal information that may be compromised, individuals can:

• Improve the security of their local computing environments using tools such as firewalls and encryption;
• Make use of re-mailers, proxies, and other anonymization techniques if anonymity is desired;

---

[8]A fuller discussion of measures that individuals may take to thwart surveillance can be found in Gary Marx, "A Tack in the Shoe: Neutralizing and Resisting the New Surveillance," *Journal of Social Issues* 59(2):369, 2003.

- Use secure and encrypted e-mail;
- Take anti-phishing measures to reduce the likelihood of identity theft;
- Install software from reliable sources to block third-party cookies, Web bugs, and other devices that enable the tracking of activity across various Web sites; and
- Install software that reliably deletes all relevant information from one's computer when one deletes a file.

To reduce the amount of unwanted information that they receive, individuals can:

- Block spam e-mail;
- Employ pop-up blockers and ad blockers;
- Use special e-mail addresses for important correspondents and faked or infrequently checked e-mail addresses for others;
- Take advantage of all opt-out opportunities, such as do-not-call lists (for both home and mobile numbers) and options for not receiving postal or electronic mail;
- Put credit freezes or fraud alerts on their credit reports; and
- Avoid using toll-free numbers and block caller-ID when making calls.

To monitor one's online privacy, individuals can:

- Search the Internet periodically for sensitive personal information, such as one's Social Security number or an unlisted phone number from an anonymized account or a computer that cannot be traced to the individual. (So-called vanity searches, in which one searches the Internet for references to one's name, can also be revealing to many people.) One may (or may not) be able to do anything about the online existence of such information, but at least one would know that it was available in such a fashion;
- Periodically monitor their credit ratings; and
- Use personal e-mail addresses that are specifically created to monitor the implementation of policies of a Web site operator. For example, a site such as merchant.com might post a privacy policy that said, "Your e-mail address will never be given to anyone else." Given the volume of spam e-mail that one receives, it would ordinarily be difficult to trace to a specific merchant the unauthorized release of one's e-mail address. However, if one used an e-mail address that was tailored for the site in question, receipt of a marketing e-mail from anyone else to that address would be convincing proof that the site did not adhere to its posted policy.

Additional steps for individuals can be found on the Web sites of the Electronic Frontier Foundation,[9] the Center for Democracy and Technology,[10] and the Electronic Privacy Information Center.[11]

In general, the actions described above are technically oriented—that is, they protect the individual only against technologically based intrusions of privacy (though they would do a better job of doing so if they were less cumbersome in actual use), and whether they are worth the trouble depends on the individual's cost-benefit calculus about the value of privacy. But they cannot defend against intrusions of privacy that occur as a matter of policy or routine bureaucratic practice (e.g., routine sharing of information that is allowable under the law or policy). And they do not in general enable the user to know if these actions are effective in protecting one's privacy.

In such instances, the only privacy-enhancing measure that one can take as an individual is to provide false or incomplete information when personal information is requested. Of course, providing false information has other consequences. In some cases, it is illegal to provide false information (as on a tax return). In other cases, providing the false information may result in being denied certain benefits that providing true information would enable. In addition, providing false information may not be an entirely reliable technique for protecting one's identity, because some data-correcting techniques—intended to catch errors made when the data are recorded—may also be able to correct false information under some circumstances. More to the point, an individual is unlikely to know if his or her attempt to provide false information is in fact succeeding in protecting his or her identity.

It is important to note that in identifying actions that individuals can take to enhance their privacy, the committee is not "blaming the victim" or arguing that individuals who fail to take such actions are solely or even primarily responsible for invasions of their privacy. The fact that individuals can take steps to protect their personal information does not imply that other societal actors, such as government and private organizations, have no responsibility for privacy. Indeed, private and personal actions are not equally available to all members of society, especially in contexts of inequality where the resources for self-protection are not equally distributed, and so personal actions may need to be supported by the kinds of organizational and public policy actions considered below.

---

[9]See http://www.eff.org/Privacy/eff_privacy_top_12.html.
[10]See http://www.cdt.org/privacy/guide/basic/topten.html.
[11]See http://www.epic.org/privacy/2004tips.html.

Recommendation 1. **If policy choices require that individuals shoulder the burden of protecting their own privacy, law and regulation should support the individual in doing so.**

If a policy choice is made that places the onus on individuals to fend for themselves, the individual's ability to do so should be facilitated by law and regulation. That is, all reasonable efforts must be made to inform the individual about the options available and the consequences of selecting any of those options. (Reasonableness necessarily takes into account an assessment of the relative costs and benefits of providing such information.) Such a precedent exists in the legislative mandate for credit-monitoring agencies to provide free credit reports to consumers periodically and for consumers to demand corrections for erroneous entries in their credit reports. In the future (and simply for illustrative purposes), law and regulation could mandate requirements that published privacy policies be easily readable (e.g., at a 7th-grade reading level), that statements related to repurposing illustrate possible secondary purposes, and that information is well publicized about technical options for individuals to protect their privacy.

10.5.3 Organization-based Actions

Finding 16. *Self-regulation is limited as a method for ensuring privacy, although it nevertheless offers protections that would not otherwise be available to the public.*

Organizations that use technology to manage large volumes of personal information (both in the private sector and in government) can establish privacy policies (e.g., on Web sites) that specify self-imposed restrictions on their use of information that they collect—or could collect—about those with whom they interact. The desire to maintain public trust and good will is a powerful motivator for many organizations to protect privacy on a voluntary basis.

To strengthen the force of privacy assurances, as well as to make it easier for organizations to establish appropriate privacy protections, organizations that are committed to particular standards and to mutual policing have banded together in associations such as TRUSTe,[12] BBBOnline,[13] and the Direct Marketing Association[14] in an attempt to improve their members' public images by forming larger "regions of trust." In general,

---

[12]See http://www.truste.org/.
[13]See http://www.bbbonline.org/.
[14]See http://www.dmaconsumers.org/.

members of these organizations agree to adhere to established privacy principles and agree to comply with a variety of oversight and consumer resolution procedures.

Some argue that self-regulating associations have at least the appearance and perhaps embody the fact of "the fox guarding the henhouse," and even self-regulation advocates recognize that such associations cannot provide a complete solution. For example, the existence of a privacy policy per se does not indicate whether that policy actually protects privacy. Membership is voluntary, and so organizations whose regular practices are very different from the voluntary guidelines may not even apply for membership or may have been kicked out because of violations. Moreover, resources available for policing depend in part on dues paid by the members, and to encourage a large membership, there is a temptation to keep dues low and policing light. Nevertheless, a declared policy is often an organization's first step toward a meaningful privacy protection regime.

Recommendation 2. **Organizations with self-regulatory privacy policies should take both technical and administrative measures to ensure their enforcement.**

An important next step is the enforcement of a declared privacy protection policy. This is a non-trivial task, and even the most stringent privacy policies cannot provide protection if they are subverted by those with access to the personal information, either legitimate access (the insider threat) or illegitimate access (the hacker threat). Thus, data custodians almost always use some form of technical protection to limit access to, and use of, personal information (e.g., passwords and other access control devices to prevent unauthorized people from accessing protected data).

Sometimes this is as simple as using file or database system access controls, or encrypting the data and limiting access to the decryption keys, or even using physical measures such as guards and locks for a facility that houses personal information. But more sophisticated measures may be needed. Section 3.8 describes several technologies relevant to maintaining the privacy of personal information in an organizational setting: auditing queries to databases containing personal information, designing systems whose data requirements and data retention features are narrowly tailored to actual needs, restricting access to information from which individual identities can be inferred, and implementing machine-readable privacy policies as a way of better informing users about the nature of those policies.

Administrative measures are also necessary to support enforcement. For example, administrative actions are needed to promulgate codes of behavior and procedures that govern access to stored personal information. Penalties for violating such codes or procedures are also needed, as technological enforcement measures sometimes fail or do not cover certain eventualities.

Recommendation 3. **Organizations should routinely test whether their stated privacy policies are being fully implemented.**

Because automated privacy audits are rarely comprehensive (except at great expense), red-teaming of an organization's privacy policy and its implementation is often in order. In the security domain, red-teaming refers to the practice of testing an organization's operational security posture through the use of an independent adversary team whose job it is to penetrate the defenses of the organization. Red-teaming in a privacy context refers to efforts undertaken to compare an organization's stated privacy policy to its practices. In general, red-teaming for privacy will require considerable "insider" access—the ability to trace data flows containing personal information. As in the case of security red-teaming, results of a privacy red-teaming exercise need to be reported to senior management, with a high-level executive in place with responsibility for ensuring and acting as an advocate for privacy as an individual and a collective good.

Recommendation 4. **Organizations should produce privacy impact assessments when they are appropriate.**

It is often the case that information practices—adopted entirely for non-privacy-related reasons—have unforeseen or surprising impacts on privacy that may not even have been considered in the adoption of those practices. Inadvertent effects on privacy could be reduced if privacy were systematically considered before adopting new information practices or changing existing practices. Privacy impact assessments—analogous to environmental impact assessments—can be established as a regular part of project planning for electronic information systems. Explicit attention to privacy issues can be valuable even if these assessments remain internal to the organization. However, public review can encourage consideration from other perspectives and perhaps reduce unintended consequences that could generate additional rounds of feedback, costly retrofitting, and/or unnecessary erosion of privacy.

Federal agencies are already required to produce privacy impact assessments (PIAs) under the E-Government Act of 2002. Illustrative PIAs produced by two agencies can be found at the Department of Homeland Security and National Science Foundation Web sites.[15] But the advantages of producing PIAs are not limited to government agencies, and the committee believes that they may have considerable utility in the context of private organizations as well.

Recommendation 5. **Organizations should strengthen their privacy policies by establishing a mechanism for recourse if an individual or a group believes that they have been treated in a manner inconsistent with an organization's stated policy.**

Finally, the limits on self-regulation must be acknowledged. As noted in Section 9.2.4, organizations are sometimes willing to violate their stated policies without advance notice under some circumstances, especially when those circumstances are both particularly exigent and also unanticipated. For these reasons, it is important to consider mechanisms other than self-regulation to protect privacy. Public policy is one source of such mechanisms. But an organization that establishes a mechanism for recourse should its policy be violated does much to enhance the credibility of its stated policy.

Recommendation 6. **Organizations that deal with personal information should establish an institutional advocate for privacy.**

Organizations that deal with personal information would benefit from some kind of institutional advocacy for privacy, as many health-care-providing organizations have done in response to the Health Insurance Portability and Accountability Act of 1996 (Section 7.3.4). By analogy to an organizational ombudsman who provides high-level oversight of everyday activities conducted in the name of the organization that might not be entirely consistent with the organization's stated policies or goals, an organizational privacy advocate could have several roles. For example, it might serve as an internal check for the organization, ensuring that the organization has and makes public some stated privacy policy. It might also help to ensure that the privacy policy is actually followed by the organization. Internally, it might serve a red-team role, pushing on the

---

[15]The NSF Web site includes a PIA for its Personnel Security System and Photo Identification Card System (http://www.nsf.gov/publications/pub_summ.jsp?ods_key=pia0503); the DHS Web site includes a PIA for the US-VISIT program (for the automatic identification of non-immigrants exiting the United States at certain land points of entry; see http://www.dhs.gov/interweb/assetlibrary/privacy_pia_usvisitupd1.pdf).

privacy mechanisms instituted by the organization and testing them for their adequacy. Finally, it could be responsible for the generation and periodic review of privacy impact statements, which would be reviews of the privacy implications of new programs or policies being instituted by an organization. It could also help anticipate emerging privacy issues.

Some precedents for institutional advocates do exist, although their function and purpose vary. Under the Bankruptcy Abuse Prevention and Consumer Protection Act of 2005, a consumer privacy ombudsman must be appointed by the bankruptcy court before certain kinds of consumer information are sold or leased. Verified Identity Pass, Inc., a private firm that offers a voluntary, biometric "fast pass" system to support the Transportation Security Administration's registered traveler program for expedited security screening at airports, has an independent, outside privacy ombudsman whose responsibility is "to investigate all privacy complaints, gather the facts, and respond to members, as well as to post responses publicly and prominently on [the firm's] website."[16] Bell Canada has designated a privacy ombudsman to oversee compliance with the Bell Code of Privacy.[17]

A number of companies have created the position of chief privacy officer. In those companies where this title does not primarily designate a public relations position that puts the best face on company privacy practices or a legal position that merely ensures compliance with existing privacy laws, the chief privacy officer can serve as an effective organizational advocate who ensures high-level management attention to privacy issues, serves as a liaison to other privacy expert stakeholders, and anticipates future needs. This role is symbolic as well as instrumental.

10.5.4 Public Policy Actions

Finding 17. *Governmental bodies have important roles to play in protecting the privacy of individuals and groups and in supporting and ensuring informed decision making about privacy issues.*

Historically, privacy concerns in the United States have most often been tied to government infringement of privacy at various levels. Many have also noted that government is at least willing, under many circumstances, to trade off privacy and other rights in pursuit of some other goal or objective. This has meant that in some cases government agencies have undertaken actions and activities that have violated citizen privacy and then subsequently noted the impropriety of such actions (e.g., the forced

---

[16]See http://flyclear.com/privacy_ombudsman.html.
[17]See http://www.bell.ca/support/PrsCSrvGnl_Privacy.page.

relocation of Japanese-Americans during World War II and the use of census data to identify such individuals (Section 9.3); the domestic surveillance in 1960s of participants in the civil rights movement). Against this historical perspective, a certain skepticism about the role of government as a guarantor of privacy is not surprising and may be helpful.

Nevertheless, the committee believes that various governmental bodies have important roles to play in protecting the privacy of individuals and groups, and in ensuring that decisions concerning privacy are made in a more transparent and well-informed fashion. As citizens become more concerned with privacy issues, it will become increasingly important for governmental agencies at all levels to address these concerns. Perhaps more importantly, actions and decisions of governmental entities on a variety of issues are likely to have significant privacy impacts. Whether it is something as obvious as decisions or policies concerning national security or as seemingly minor as making public-record information available on the World Wide Web, a great many actions taken by governments have privacy implications. Consequently, it is appropriate that privacy be at least a consideration if not a priority at all levels of government decision making.

10.5.4.1 Managing the Privacy Patchwork

Finding 18. The U.S. legal and regulatory framework surrounding privacy is a patchwork that lacks consistent principles or unifying themes. A less decentralized and more integrated approach to privacy policy in the United States could bring a greater degree of coherence to the subject of privacy.

The U.S. legal and regulatory framework surrounding privacy is a patchwork that lacks commitment to or guidance from a set of consistent principles or unifying themes. Because of the ad hoc way in which privacy has been approached by most policy makers, the current sets of privacy-related laws, rules, and regulations—at all levels of government—are confusing at best and inconsistent at worst.

Given the decentralized manner in which the United States has dealt with privacy issues (Section 4.4), this state of affairs is hardly surprising—and yet it has major costs. This patchwork is more than just a source of frustration and confusion—it is also inefficient and expensive. The current regulatory patchwork, in which laws governing privacy differ across the jurisdictions in which firms engage in business transactions, increases the economic costs of attending to privacy that these firms must bear.

The committee believes that a less decentralized approach to privacy policy in the United States could bring substantial benefits for the understanding and protection of privacy. Only with such an approach can different priorities and tensions be reconciled. At the same time, the committee cautions that less decentralization can also lead to a lowest-common-denominator approach to privacy, which might well weaken privacy protections enjoyed by some states. Further, the committee notes that in an increasingly global marketplace, some degree of harmonization of U.S. privacy law with the privacy laws and regulations of other nations is likely to be necessary when business-related data flows between the United States and these other nations involve personal information.

10.5.4.2 Reviewing Existing Privacy Law and Regulations

Recommendation 7. **The U.S. government should undertake a broad, systematic review of national privacy laws and regulations.**

As a first step in the direction of a less decentralized approach to privacy policy, the U.S. government should undertake a systematic review of the laws and regulations that affect the level and quality of privacy that Americans enjoy. This review should address:

- Areas of overlap and conflict in current national privacy law and regulation—special attention should be paid to the relationship of national law to state and local law extensively enough to generate a representative picture of those relationships;
- Assessment of the nature and extent of gaps between stated policies and implementation, and the causes of such gaps;
- Areas of privacy concern that the current legal and regulatory framework leaves unaddressed, such as the gathering, aggregation, and use of personal information by companies and other organizations that are currently not covered to any significant degree by any form of privacy regulation;
- A clear articulation of the value tradeoffs that are embedded in the current framework of laws and regulation, especially where those tradeoffs were not made explicit at the time of adoption;
- The economic and social impact, both positive and negative, of current privacy law and regulation;
- The extent to which the personal information of Americans held by various parties is covered by the principles of fair information practices;
- The interplay between state and federal privacy laws, taking into consideration matters such as the scope and nature of state laws as compared to federal laws; and
- The interplay between domestic and foreign privacy laws, taking into consideration matters such as the scope and nature of flows of personal information to and from the United States and instances in

which differences between foreign laws and domestic law might call for harmonization.

If undertaken in an authoritative manner, such a review would simplify the task of knowing how to comply with privacy regulations and might also make such compliance less expensive. Further, it would help individuals to understand their privacy rights, and it could facilitate such enforcement of those rights as is necessary for their enjoyment. By making the protection of privacy more efficient, more transparent, and more consistent, all members of the community should benefit. By anticipating future developments, future problems might also be avoided or minimized.

As to which part of the U.S. government should undertake this review, the privacy commissioner's office (the subject of Recommendation 14) is an obvious locus of such activity. But the recommendation for undertaking a review is independent of Recommendation 14, and what part of the U.S. government undertakes this review is less important than that it be undertaken.

10.5.4.3 Respecting the Spirit of the Law

Recommendation 8. **Government policy makers should respect the spirit of privacy-related law.**

The United States is a nation governed by law. It is thus axiomatic that the rule of law must be the supreme authority of the land. Common discourse recognizes the distinction between the spirit and the letter of the law, and the committee believes that both the spirit and the letter of the law play important roles in the protection of privacy. Conformance to the latter is what is needed "to not break the law." The spirit of the law is necessarily more imprecise than the letter of the law, but if fully respected, the spirit of the law has operational implications as well. For example, a number of laws provide for the confidentiality of data collected by certain federal agencies (e.g., the Census Bureau, the Internal Revenue Service, and so on). To the extent that government policy makers wish to merge protected data with commercial and other non-protected data in order to identify individuals, the committee believes that such actions are not consistent with the spirit of data confidentiality guarantees. Respecting the spirit of the law would result in decision-making processes that give legal limitations and constraints a wide berth rather than "pushing the envelope" and "looking for loopholes." This approach supports policy makers who engage in open and public debate and discussion when circumstances change rather than use such circumstantial changes to advance long-standing agendas that were previously blocked by public opposition.

Note, too, that these comments apply irrespective of any particular policy outcome or preference. They are a call for deliberation and moderation rather than hasty overreaction—whether the issue is revelation of a government abuse (that might lead to excessive curtailment of law enforcement or national security authorities) or a terrorist incident (that might lead to excessive intrusions on privacy). And they also imply a need to build into policy some mechanisms, such as "sunset requirements," that facilitate the periodic revisiting of these issues.

10.5.4.4 The Relevance of Fair Information Practices Today

Finding 19. The principles of fair information practice enunciated in 1973 for the protection of personal information are as relevant and important today as they were when they were first formulated.

Principles of fair information practice were first enunciated in 1973 (Section 1.5.4). At the time, they were intended to apply to all automated personal data systems by establishing minimum standards of fair information practice, violation of which would constitute "unfair information practice" subject to criminal penalties and civil remedies. Pending legislative enactment of such a code, the report also recommended that the principles be implemented through federal administrative action.

In 1974, the Privacy Act (Section 4.3.1) was passed, applying these principles to personal information in the custody of federal agencies. In addition, the Fair Credit Reporting Act (first passed in 1970 and amended thereafter several times) applies these principles to the accuracy, fairness, and the privacy of personal information assembled by private sector credit-reporting agencies. Many other private sector organizations have also adopted privacy policies that trace their lineage to some or all of the principles of fair information practice.

Since 1973, the environment surrounding the gathering and use of personal information has changed radically. Information technology is increasingly networked. Private sector gathering and use of personal information have expanded greatly since the early 1970s, and many private sector organizations that manage personal information, such as data aggregators (Section 6.5), are not covered by fair information practices, either under the law or under a voluntary privacy policy based on these principles. National security considerations loom large as well, and the risks of compromising certain kinds of personal information are arguably greater in an environment in which terrorism and identity theft go hand in hand (see Box 4.1 in Chapter 4).

For these reasons, the committee believes that the principles of fair information practice are as relevant today—perhaps more so—for the protection of personal information as they were when they were first formulated.

Recommendation 9. **Principles of fair information practice should be extended as far as reasonably feasible to apply to private sector organizations that collect and use personal information.**

Although some of the restrictions on government regarding the collection and use of personal information are not necessarily applicable to the private sector, the values expressed by the principles of fair information practice should also inform private sector policies regarding privacy.

Reasonableness involves a variety of factors, including an assessment of the relative costs and benefits of applying these principles. This recommendation is thus consistent with the original intent behind the 1973 Department of Health, Education, and Welfare report covering all organizations handling personal information (not just government agencies),[18] although the committee is explicitly silent on whether the legislative enactment of a code of fair information practices is the most appropriate way to accomplish this goal.

For the sake of illustration, another approach to encourage the broad adoption of fair information practices might be based on the "safe harbor" approach described in Section 4.7. That is, a private sector organization that collected or used personal information would self-certify that it is in compliance with safe harbor requirements, which would be based on the principles of fair information practice. Periodic assessment of the extent to which mechanisms for ensuring enforcement of these requirements have been developed and applied would be provided to the public. Adherence to these requirements would similarly take the form of government enforcement of the federal and state statutes relevant to unfair and deceptive business practices. In return, complying organizations could be granted immunity from civil or criminal action stemming from alleged mishandling of personal information.

Within the domain of fair information practices, the committee calls attention to two particularly important topics: the repurposing of data and the notion of choice and consent.

---

[18]U.S. Department of Health, Education, and Welfare, *Records, Computers and the Rights of Citizens,* Report of the Secretary's Advisory Committee on Automated Personal Data Systems, MIT Press, Cambridge, Mass., 1973.

Recommendation 10. **To support greater transparency into the decision-making process regarding repurposing, guidelines should be established for informing individuals that repurposing of their personal information might occur, and also what the nature of such repurposing would be, and what factors would be taken into account in making any such decision.**

While repurposing is not necessarily privacy invasive (e.g., medical information gathered for clinical decision making can be used to conduct epidemiological research in ways that are privacy preserving), there is an unavoidable tension between a principle that one should know how personal information collected from him or her will be used before it is collected and the possibility that information collectors might want to use that information in the future for a purpose that cannot be anticipated today. While this tension cannot necessarily be resolved in any given instance, it should be possible to provide greater transparency into the resolution process. Accordingly, guidelines should be established for informing individuals that repurposing might occur, and also about the nature of such repurposing and what factors would be taken into account in making any such decision. Educating the public about the nature of this tension is also important, and might be undertaken as part of the effort described in Recommendation 14.

Recommendation 11. **The principle of choice and consent should be implemented so that individual choices and consent are genuinely informed and so that its implementation accounts fairly for demonstrated human tendencies to accept without change choices made by default.**

Even with mandated disclosure, individuals have choices about whether or not they provide information. But only *informed choice*—choice made when the deciding individual has an adequate amount of the important information that could reasonably affect the outcome of the choice—is morally and ethically meaningful. Individuals are entitled to be informed about answers to the questions articulated in Section 10.1—and parties acquiring personal information are morally and ethically obligated to provide such information to subjects. Vague notices that obfuscate and presume high educational levels of their readers do not satisfy these obligations, even if they do technically comply with legal requirements. Moreover, as the issues of data collection become more complex, the task of providing usable and comprehensible information increases in difficulty.

The importance of default choices has been empirically demonstrated.

As noted in Section 2.2.5, the endless debate between the desirability of opt-in and opt-out regimes is a debate over which of these should be the information subject's default choice. In fact, it is easy to circumvent this Hobson's choice by requiring the individual to make an explicit choice to opt-in or to opt-out. Recall that opting in means that the individual must affirmatively allow the primary data recipient to share his or her information, while opting out means that the individual must affirmatively disallow such sharing of information. But consent requirements could be formulated so that the individual had to choose one of these options explicitly—either "I choose to share information" or "I choose to not share information"—and so that the selection of one of these options would be as essential to processing the form as the individual's Social Security number would be for a financial institution. Absent a choice, the form would be regarded as null and void, and returned to the individual for resubmission.

Recommendation 12. **The U.S. Congress should pay special attention to and provide special oversight regarding the government use of private sector organizations to obtain personal information about individuals.**

As noted in Chapter 6, government use of private sector organizations to obtain personal information about individuals is increasing. Fair information practices applied to data aggregation companies would go a long way toward providing meaningful oversight of such use. However, even if data aggregation companies are not covered by fair information practices in the future (either directly or indirectly—that is, through the extended application of fair information practices to *government* agencies that use such companies), the committee recommends that such use receive special attention and oversight from the U.S. Congress and other appropriate bodies so that privacy issues do not fall in between the cracks established by contracts and service agreements.

To illustrate what might be included under attention and oversight, the committee notes that two oversight mechanisms include periodic hearings (in this case, into government use of these organizations) and reporting requirements for U.S. government agencies that would publicly disclose the extent and nature of such use.

10.5.4.5 Public Advocates for Privacy

Finding 20. Because the benefits of privacy often are less tangible and immediate than the perceived benefits of other interests such as public security and economic efficiency, privacy is at an inherent disadvantage when decision makers weigh privacy against these other interests.

As noted in Section 10.4, privacy offers benefits that are often less tangible, visible, or immediate than those benefits offered by public safety, economic efficiency, and so on. The consequence is that privacy is at an inherent disadvantage in the decision-making competition for priority and resources.

For other issues in which short-term pressures tend to crowd out longer-term perspectives, the mechanism of institutionalized advocacy has found some success. For example, the Environmental Protection Agency was established to provide a bureaucratic counterweight to the forces of unrestricted economic development inside and outside government.

Today, a number of privately funded organizations, such as the Electronic Privacy Information Center and the Electronic Frontier Foundation, act as generalized advocates for privacy in the public policy sphere. Such groups, while an important ingredient in the debate concerning privacy, are generally focused at the national level, and resource limitations mean that they focus primarily on the most egregious threats to privacy if and when they come to notice. Perhaps most importantly, they do not have institutionally established roles in the public policy process, and they achieve success primarily based on the extent to which they can mobilize public attention to some privacy issue. In contrast, an organizational privacy advocate would have better access to relevant information from government agencies and possibly private organizations under some circumstances, legal standing, and greater internal legitimacy, thus enabling it to play a complementary but no less important role.

Recommendation 13. **Governments at various levels should establish formal mechanisms for the institutional advocacy of privacy within government.**

Institutionalized advocacy can take place at a variety of different levels—at the level of individual organizations, local government, federal agencies, and so on. An example of institutionalized advocacy is the Privacy Office of the U.S. Department of Homeland Security (DHS), whose mission is to minimize the impact of departmental activities on the individual's privacy, particularly the individual's personal information and dignity, while achieving the mission of the DHS.[19] The DHS Privacy Office is the focal point of departmental activities that protect the collection, use, and disclosure of personal and departmental information. In addition, the Privacy Office supports the DHS Data Privacy and Integrity Advisory Committee, which provides advice on programmatic, policy,

---

[19]This description is based on the DHS description of its Privacy Office, available at http://www.dhs.gov/dhspublic/interapp/editorial/editorial_0338.xml.

operational, administrative, and technological issues within DHS that affect individual privacy, as well as data integrity and data interoperability and other privacy-related issues. The Privacy Office also holds public workshops to explore the policy, legal, and technology issues surrounding government's, private sector's, and individuals' information and the intersection of privacy and homeland security.

A common complaint about standards issued at a national level—regardless of subject—is that they do not take into account local contexts and perspectives, and a "one-size-fits-all" mentality can easily lead to absurdities that undercut both public support and the spirit of the original standard. But local communities can have their own institutional advocates, and it may make sense to consider the idea of local enforcement of national standards as a way to obtain some of the efficiencies afforded by national standards and the benefits of local awareness of how those standards might sensibly be implemented in practice.

Recommendation 14. **A national privacy commissioner or standing privacy commission should be established to provide ongoing and periodic assessments of privacy developments.**

As discussed in earlier chapters (especially Chapters 1 and 3), rapid changes in technology or in circumstances can and often do lead to changes in societal definitions of privacy and in societal expectations for privacy. Solutions developed and compromises reached today may be solidly grounded a year from now, but 3 years is enough for a new "killer app" technology to emerge into widespread use (thus changing what is easily possible in the sharing of information), and a decade is enough for today's minority political party to become the majority in both the legislature and the executive branch. Any of these eventualities coming true is bound to require a new and comprehensive examination of privacy issues. Thus, it is unrealistic to expect that privacy bargains will become settled "once and for all" or that expectations will be static. Dynamic environments require continuous attention to privacy issues and readiness to examine taken-for-granted beliefs that may no longer be appropriate under rapidly changing conditions.

Of significance is the likelihood that the effects of changes in the environment will go unnoticed by the public in the absence of some well-publicized incident that generates alarm. Even for those generally knowledgeable about privacy, the total impact of these developments is difficult to assess because rapid changes occur in so many different sectors of the community and there are few vantage points from which to assess their cumulative effects.

For these reasons, it makes sense to establish mechanisms to ensure continuing high-level attention to matters related to privacy as society and technology change and to educate the public about privacy issues. Although a number of standing boards and committees advise individual agencies on privacy-related matters (e.g., the Information Security and Privacy Advisory Board of the Department of Commerce, the Data Privacy and Integrity Advisory Committee of the Department of Homeland Security), their inputs are—by design—limited to the concerns of the agencies with which they are associated. The committee believes that at the federal level, a "privacy commissioner" type of office or a standing privacy commission would serve this role very well. A permanent governmental body with the charter of keeping discussions about privacy in the foreground of public debate and discussion could do much to reduce the number and intensity of unwanted privacy-related surprises that occur in the future.

Areas of focus and inquiry for such an office could include the following:

• *A comprehensive review of the legal and regulatory landscape*, as described in Section 10.5.4.2. Such a review might be undertaken periodically so that changes in this landscape could be documented and discussed.

• *Trends in privacy-related incidents and an examination of new types of privacy-related incidents.* Prior to the widespread use of the Internet, certain privacy issues, such as those associated with online "phishing," never occurred. Because the deployment of new technologies is often accompanied by new privacy issues, warning of such issues could help the public to better prepare for them. Documented trends in privacy-related incidents would also provide some empirical basis for understanding public concerns about privacy. Note also that "incidents" should be defined broadly, and in particular should not be restricted to illegal acts. For example, "incidents" might include testing of specific privacy policies for readability, and with an appropriate sampling methodology information could be provided to the public about whether the average readability level of privacy policies was going up or down.

• *Celebration and acknowledgment of privacy successes.* Much as the Department of Commerce celebrates the quality of private companies through its Baldrige awards program, a privacy commissioner could acknowledge companies whose privacy protection programs were worthy of public note and emulation.

• *Normative issues in data collection and analysis.* Grounded in the information technology environment of the early 1970s, the principles of fair information practice generally presume that the primary source of personal information about an individual is that person's active and consensual engagement in providing such information to another party. This source is still quite important, but new sources of personal information have emerged in the past 30 years—video and infrared cameras, Internet usage monitors, biometric identification technology, electronic location devices, radio-frequency identification chips, and a variety of environmental sensors. In addition, new techniques enable the discovery of previously hidden patterns in large data sets—patterns that might well be regarded as new information in and of themselves.

These types of data acquisition devices and techniques have rarely been the subject of focused normative discussion. Currently, there are no principles or standards of judgment that would help public policy makers and corporate decision makers determine the appropriateness of using any given device or technique. (For example, the use of a given device or technique for gathering data may not be illegal, perhaps because it is so new that regulation has yet to appear, but the lack of legal sanctions against it does not mean that using it is the right thing to do.) Systematic attention to such principles by a privacy commissioner's office might provide valuable assistance to these decision and policy makers.

• *Collective and group privacy.* Historically, privacy regulation in the United States has focused on personal information—information about and collected from individuals. Issues related to groups have generally been addressed from the important but nevertheless narrow perspective of outlawing explicit discrimination against certain categories of individuals (e.g., categories defined by attributes such as race, religion, gender, sexual orientation, and so on). But new statistical profiling techniques, coupled with the increasingly ubiquitous availability of personal information about individuals, provide many new opportunities for sorting and classifying people in ways that are much less obvious or straightforward.

Originally undertaken to improve marketing, risk management, and strategic communications, statistical profiling has served as the basis for decisions in these areas—and thus may have served to inappropriately exclude people from opportunities that might otherwise improve their ability to grow and develop as productive members of society (even as others may be inappropriately included). However, the nature and scope of such exclusions are not known today, nor is the impact of these exclusions on the cumulative disadvantage faced by members of population segments likely to be victims of categorical discrimination. At the same time, others argue that equitable, efficient, and effective public policy requires the development of data resources that might require such sorting. A future review of privacy might examine these issues, as well as the potential constraining effects on options available to individuals and their ability to make truly informed and autonomous choices in their roles as citizens and consumers in the face of unseen statistical sorting.

• *Privacy, intimacy, and affiliation.* Although matters such as personal intimacy and affiliation are typically beyond the direct and formal purview of most public policy analysis, they are central to the good life. Indeed, one might well argue that a life without intimacy or without the freedom to affiliate with other people is a life largely shorn of meaning and fulfillment. It is at least plausible that the sense of privacy enjoyed by individuals affects the range of activity and behavior that might be associated with expressions of intimacy and affiliation. To the best of the committee's knowledge, no review of privacy has ever considered these issues, and since almost all of the attention to privacy questions focuses on the behavior of governments and organizations, a future review might examine them.[20]

• *Informing and educating the public about privacy.* The issues surrounding privacy are sufficiently complex that it may be unrealistic to expect the average person to fully grasp their meaning. A privacy commissioner's office could help to educate the public about privacy issues (in the management of health care data and in other areas). Because this educational role would be institutionalized, it is reasonable to expect that the information such an office provided would be more comprehensible than the information offered by sources and parties with an interest in minimizing public concern about threats to privacy (e.g., difficult-to-read privacy notices sent by companies with economic interests in using personal information to the maximum extent possible).

This educational role could have a number of components. For illustration only, it might include:

—Review of and recommendations for how schools teach about privacy and how understanding of it could be improved in the face of recent rapid changes. For example, social networking, as might be found on Facebook.com and MySpace.com, continue to present challenges to the privacy and safety of many of the young people who use such sites and services. As relatively recent developments indicate, education about how these people should approach such services has been lacking.

—Promotion among the manufacturers of surveillance equipment (whether tools for adults or toys for children) to include warning messages similar to those on other products such as cigarettes (e.g., use of the tools unless certain conditions are met is illegal). Instruction

---

[20]Among some recent work relevant to the issue, see J. Smith, *Private Matters*, Addison Wesley, Reading, Mass., 1997; R. Gurstein, *The Repeal of Reticence*, Hill and Wang, New York, 1996; C. Calvert, *Voyeur Nation*, Westview Press, Boulder, Colo., 2000; Gary T. Marx, "Forget Big Brother and Big Corporation: What About the Personal Uses of Surveillance Technology as Seen in Cases Such as Tom I. Voire?," *Rutgers Journal of Law and Urban Policy* 3(4):219-286, 2006, available at http://garymarx.net.

booklets for such equipment might also briefly mention the value issues involved and, in the case of toys with a double-edged potential, encourage parents to discuss the issues raised by covertly invading the privacy of others, even if such actions appear to be benign and are undertaken only in fun.

—Development of model discussions of privacy that could be used for instructional purposes.

The committee acknowledges that the notion of a privacy commissioner is controversial in a number of ways, emanating from many points along the privacy policy spectrum. Some believe that the establishment of such offices is in reality a mechanism to avoid coming to grips with the real policy issues of privacy. Others believe that the presence of such an office can be used to lend legitimacy to efforts that would otherwise be seen clearly as compromising privacy. Still others believe that the success of such a commissioner would be contingent on the power given to the commissioner and the policy decisions concerning what kinds of privacy are important to protect, and that such commissioners are rarely given enough explicit authority to make substantive policy decisions regarding privacy.

Another camp believes that such offices stultify real progress and are likely to be mismanaged. And there is no denying that such an office would mark a significant movement in the direction of giving government an important role in protecting privacy. Nonetheless, the committee believes that the value of having a national and institutionalized focal point for promoting public discourse about privacy outweighs these possible objections.

10.5.4.6 Establishing the Means for Recourse

Finding 21. *The availability of individual recourse for recognized violations of privacy is an essential element of public policy regarding privacy.*

Even the best laws, regulations, and policies governing privacy will be useless unless adequate recourse is available if and when they are violated. In the absence of recourse, those whose privacy has been improperly violated (whether by accident or deliberately) must bear alone the costs and consequences of the violation. This is one possible approach to public policy, but the committee believes this approach would run contrary to basic principles of fairness that public policy should embody. The committee also believes that when recourse is available (i.e., when individuals can identify and be compensated for violations), those in a position to act inappropriately tend to be more careful and more respectful of privacy policies that they might inadvertently violate.

Recommendation 15. **Governments at all levels should take action to establish the availability of appropriate individual recourse for recognized violations of privacy.**

These comments apply whether the source of the violation is in government or in the private sector, although the nature of appropriate recourse varies depending on the source. In the case of government wrongdoing, the doctrine of sovereign immunity generally protects government actors from civil liability or criminal prosecution unless the government waives this protection or is statutorily stripped of immunity in the particular kinds of cases at hand. That is, against government wrongdoers, a statute must explicitly allow civil suits or criminal prosecution for recourse to exist.

Against private sector violators of privacy, a number of recourse mechanisms are possible.[21] One approach is for legislatures (federal or state) to create causes for action if private organizations engage in certain privacy-violating practices, as these legislatures have done in the case of unfair and deceptive trade practices. Such laws can be structured to allow government enforcement actions to stop the practice and/or individual actions for damages brought by individuals harmed by the practices.

There are other possibilities as well. When local privacy commissioners or advocates have been legislatively chartered, their charge could include standing to take action on behalf of individuals who have been harmed, either tangibly or intangibly, by some privacy-violating action. Mediators or privacy arbitration boards might be established that could resolve privacy disputes; while this would still require those who thought their privacy had been violated to bring action against the violator, it might reduce the overhead of such actions in a way that would be acceptable to all.

---

[21]In pursuing remedies against private sector invasions of privacy by the news media, publishers, writers, photographers, and others, caution is in order respecting freedoms of speech and press, as noted in Section 4.2.

Appendixes

A

A Short History of Surveillance and Privacy in the United States

A.1 INTRODUCTION

Routine surveillance is an inescapable feature of daily life in the United States at the start of the 21st century. We all leave a trail of electronic traces that are picked up for processing by a variety of organizations and agencies. Constant exchanges thus occur in which personal information is involved. Sometimes people are able to negotiate the amount of data they are willing to disclose—for instance when filling out a product registration form for a new computer. At other times, an individual's leverage over the organization is minimal, as when people apply for business or government services such as loans or insurance. The interaction becomes even more unidirectional when personal data are collected from a distance, without the direct participation of the citizen or consumer.

"Surveillance" may be thought of as systematic attention to personal details for the purposes of influence, management, or control. Some surveillance is personal, face-to-face supervision, but the main concern in what follows is situations in which data are routinely collected. Such systematic collection of personal information is not a new phenomenon in American society. As far back as the colonial era, organizations were actively interested in the details of people's daily lives. While the inten-

NOTE: This appendix is based largely on work performed on contract to the committee by David Lyon, Queen's University, Canada (with extensive research assistance from Bart Bonikowski, Sociology, Duke University).

sity and scope of surveillance have varied since the 17th century, the same factors shape them: the interests of those in positions of power, the technology available to them, and the legal frameworks within which they operate.

The history of surveillance in the United States can be divided into five time periods, each characterized by particular political, legal, and technological developments. While these divisions are arbitrary, they highlight some of the main trends that have characterized the institutional collection of information and the corresponding moral and legal responses:

• The first phase, which spans the decades from the mid-17th century to the American Revolution, is dominated by the Puritan ethic of colonial New England, with its emphasis on the enforcement of a strict moral code by means of neighborly "watchfulness."

• The second covers the early American Republic, from its confederation to the Civil War—a time of rapid social and political change and of a marked shift in surveillance from being an informal practice based in religious dogma to becoming an embryonic political tool of the government.

• The third era stretches from the Civil War to the mid-20th century and is characterized by rapid technological growth, an increased reliance of government and business on surveillance, and the initial formulations of privacy as a legal right.

• The fourth stage is that of post–World War II America from 1950 to 1980, which gave rise to computerized and centralized surveillance but also to a first concerted social effort at developing a legal right to privacy as an effective countermeasure.

• The fifth period encompasses the main technological and political developments in surveillance and privacy from 1980 to the present, including the growth of computer interconnectivity, wireless technology, and the emergence of antiterrorism as the primary justification for intensified surveillance.

A.2 COLONIAL NEW ENGLAND (CA. 1650-1776)

Tensions between privacy and information gathering were present during the earliest colonial times. In New England, for example, the physical conditions of frontier life played an important role in shaping surveillance and privacy in the late 17th and early 18th centuries. The population of the Colonies in the 17th century was scattered among small settlements. Large families lived in small, crowded homes, many of which faced the town square or the main road, and frequently opened their doors to servants and lodgers, further reducing the amount of personal space available. It is not difficult to imagine how little personal information the inhabitants of New England were able to keep secret. In small, isolated communities where every face was familiar and information from the outside world was largely unavailable, people were involved primarily with one another's lives.

Surveillance and privacy were also affected by the strict adherence to the form of religious morality that lay at the heart of colonial New England's Puritan ethic. Members of the community were expected to divide their time between their occupation (usually farming), family obligations, and religious duties. Tobacco use, card playing, cursing, idleness, premarital and extramarital sex, breaking the Sabbath, and excessive drinking were seen as sinful and met with religious and criminal sanctions. The moral stigma also extended to solitary activities such as "night-walking" and living alone. Puritan congregations expected their followers not only to eschew those vices themselves, but also to keep watch on others to prevent them from wrongdoing. This mutual watchfulness was central to the colonial system of law enforcement and church discipline. Ironically, given the Puritans' aversion to the involvement of the state in religious matters, stemming from their persecution by English authorities in the 17th century, church and government law were closely intertwined in colonial New England.

It would seem reasonable, based on the description thus far, to conclude that the lives of New England settlers were under constant and intense surveillance. However, surveillance was partly restricted by the legal system of colonial New England. As early as 1647, Rhode Island adopted the principle that "a man's house is his castle," originally formulated by English jurist Sir Edward Coke. The colony outlawed "forcible Entry and Detainer" into a private dwelling, except by law enforcement officers acting under exceptional circumstances.[1] Massachusetts followed suit in 1659.

Meanwhile, a slow shift away from forced and self-incriminating testimony in the courtroom and the church, which laid the groundwork for the eventual construction of the Fifth Amendment of the Bill of Rights, was symptomatic of deeper changes in colonial society. America was gradually abandoning the strict ethic of the Puritan movement, a slow transition that continued well into the 19th century. During the 18th century, the Colonies also experienced rapid population growth, which increased the size of most towns, thereby altering the physical conditions that once facilitated mutual surveillance.

---

[1]David H. Flaherty, *Privacy in Colonial New England*, University Press of Virginia, Charlottesville, Va., 1972, p. 86.

It is also important to note that the type of surveillance widely conducted within the Puritan society differed significantly from surveillance in the 19th and 20th centuries. The political and religious institutions of colonial America were largely informal and unstructured. As a result, surveillance was less an institutional practice than a communal one. No organized police force was charged with investigating individuals, and no widespread enumeration of the populace took place. In fact, official records were nearly nonexistent, with the exception of court files, internal administrative records, and vital records (such as birth and death certificates). Instead, surveillance was an unsystematic activity carried out by particularly zealous members of the community, with varying repercussions for those under its gaze. Unlike its more concentrated bureaucratic form, which emerged in the following centuries, the power of colonial surveillance was widely dispersed among the population.[2]

A.3 THE EARLY REPUBLIC (1776-1861)

The influence of Puritan values on surveillance and privacy in America diminished throughout the 18th and early 19th centuries. The increasing mobility of individuals and the growth of urban centers made keeping tabs on one's neighbors increasingly difficult. Furthermore, improvements in literacy and education, combined with the ready availability of the press, meant that the interest of some also went beyond neighborhoods to include the national or international political forum. Although these privileges were principally limited to white males,[3] they contributed to changes in the social priorities of society as a whole. After all, these white males set social norms and government policies. The turning point in this phase of surveillance and privacy history was the American Revolution and the subsequent formation of an independent republic of the United States of America.

The origins of institutional surveillance in Western society can be generally traced back to the establishment of the modern bureaucracy, which had its beginnings in the military organization, the bureaucratic state, and

---

[2]This is not to say that some members of the community were not more disadvantaged than others—women, children, and ethnic minorities certainly had less power than white males, as was the case in all eras of American history. However, institutions had less surveillance power vis-à-vis individuals than they did in the later Republic.

[3]When the Constitution was voted on in 1787, the vast majority of people in America were still illiterate. Among 4,250,000 inhabitants of the Republic, 600,000 were slaves and 2,000,000 were women—both groups were denied the privileges of education. Of the remainder, about 250,000 were estimated to be literate—a number roughly equal to the total voter turnout for the vote on the Constitution. See Morris L. Ernst and Alan U. Schwartz, *Privacy: The Right to Be Let Alone*, Macmillan, New York, 1962.

the capitalist enterprise.[4] All three of these modern institutions came into existence in the United States at the end of the 18th century. The escalating tensions between the Colonies and the British government over the arbitrary levying of taxes and the stationing of British troops in New England led to the outbreak of the first skirmishes of the Revolutionary War at Lexington, Concord, and Bunker Hill. In response, the first modern American army was born, under the command of George Washington and by direction of the Continental Congress, the newly established system of revolutionary self-government. The new army replaced the scattered militia and came complete with army drill, regular roll call, and punishment for disobedience.[5]

A year earlier, in 1774, the early bureaucratic structure of American government had emerged with the First Continental Congress, which organized local committees in most towns, cities, and counties of the Colonies.[6] During the Constitutional Convention of 1787, which followed the War of Independence, this temporary structure was replaced by the present-form U.S. government, with three branches of power and a hierarchical organizational structure. The U.S. government soon became the primary site of institutional surveillance, as it gradually developed record-keeping practices to monitor its citizens.

While U.S. industry did not take shape until the latter half of the 19th century, the roots of capitalist enterprise in the United States can be found in early-19th-century shipping trade, the Southern plantations, the emergence of banking, and the westward search for gold. As U.S. businesses continued to grow, they developed bureaucratic record-keeping practices to keep track of contracts, loans, assets, and taxable revenues. These records of course included some information that referred to identifiable individuals.

The revolutionary era also marked the first instance of political-loyalty surveillance in the interest of national security. In the past, American colonists had felt endangered almost exclusively by "outside" forces, such as Native American tribes or the French and the Spanish. This sense of endangerment shifted during the Revolution, as the perceived threat began emanating from within the ranks of colonial society. As the tensions between the colonists and the British mounted in the 1770s, resentment against domestic supporters of British rule (Tories or Loyalists) became widespread. With the commencement of the Revolution, this antipathy

---

[4]Christopher Dandeker, *Surveillance Power and Modernity*, Polity Press, Cambridge, Mass., 1990.

[5]Richard W. Stewart, ed., *American Military History, Volume I: The United States Army and the Forging of a Nation, 1775-1917*, Army Historical Series, Center for Military History, Publication 30-21, Government Printing Office, Washington, D.C., 2005, pp. 48-50.

[6]Stewart, *American Military History*, Volume I, 2005, p. 50.

transformed into overt discrimination and abuse, as most Tories were ostracized and many fell victim to mob violence. The revolutionaries also persecuted Quakers, many of whom were pacifists opposed to the Revolution on moral and religious principle.

The surveillance capabilities of the new state were also used for other purposes. Since the Constitution of the United States called for the establishment of democratic popular elections and mandated a decennial census, the government needed to create organizational procedures that would regulate the proper fulfillment of these responsibilities. While electoral registration was an erratic practice whose application varied from state to state, the popular census of 1790 was the first attempt by the U.S. government to conduct systematic and universal gathering of information about its citizens. The census collected basic data on the gender, color, and identity of free males above the age of 16 years.[7] With time, this crude enumeration tool evolved into a sophisticated source of demographic information employed by social scientists, policy makers, and government officials throughout the country.

While the post-Revolution era gave rise to early surveillance practices by the government and the military, its primary contribution to the history of surveillance in the United States was the codification in the Constitution and the Bill of Rights of rules restricting invasive information gathering. Although the ideological bases for the American Republic are complex, some of the basic values contained in the Constitution require mention, since they bear directly on surveillance in the new Republic. Drawing largely on the philosophy of John Locke and the heritage of Puritanism, the U.S. Constitution sought to protect the rights of the individual, to ensure the limited role of government in American society, and to reinforce the central importance of private property for the exercise of individual liberty.[8] The Bill of Rights that emerged from these values was intended to shield citizens from unrestricted surveillance by those in positions of power and thus to avoid the development of authoritarian society, such as that of feudal Europe. The judicial interpretation of the Bill of Rights throughout the 19th and early 20th centuries rarely found solid grounds (especially based on the vague right to privacy) for curtailing government and corporate surveillance. Nonetheless, the sentiment of the founders against institutional intrusion in the life of citizens is unmistakable.

It must be stressed that the laws described above pertained to those

---

[7]Joseph Steinberg, "Government Records: The Census Bureau and the Social Security Administration," pp. 225-254 in S. Wheeler, ed., *On Record: Files and Dossiers in American Life*, Sage Foundation, New York, 1969.

[8]Alan F. Westin, *Privacy and Freedom*, Atheneum, New York, 1967, p. 330.

members of society who were viewed by the state as free citizens, which generally meant white male adults. The plight of those deprived of citizenship rights, such as African American slaves and Native Americans, was drastically different. Their individual rights were not protected by U.S. laws, since the former were seen as private property belonging to slaveholders, while the latter were treated as savages not worthy of legal protection. Consequently, slaves continued living in a state of almost total surveillance in which their every action was subject to scrutiny by overseers. Undesirable behavior was punished severely, with no legal recourse. Native Americans were banished to reservations and faced persecution and death if they resisted. Thus, when constitutional protections and restricted practices of state surveillance after the Revolution are spoken of, it must be remembered that such conditions were the norm only for a limited fraction of the U.S. population.

A.4 THE MODERN REPUBLIC (1861-1950)

Between the Revolution and the Civil War, surveillance and individual rights coexisted in a fragile balance. The growing desire of U.S. bureaucracies to keep track of citizens was offset by limited technological means of information gathering and by the constitutional, statutory, and common-law regulations developed in the new Republic. This is not to say that surveillance did not exist in those decades; however, its scope and intensity were relatively limited. The average free male's interaction with surveillance systems rarely went beyond reporting basic information in census surveys and furnishing land deeds during elections. This changed drastically in the years that followed the Civil War. The balance of surveillance and individual rights was upset by unprecedented technological development, the rapid growth of bureaucratic institutions (both governmental and commercial), and the failure of lawmakers to formulate adequate legal protections against surveillance practices.

Many contemporary surveillance technologies owe their existence to late-19th-century American enterprise. The steam engine enabled unprecedented rates of travel, and mechanization shifted work from the farm to the factory, a harbinger of greater mobility to come. Yet no technological developments had as much impact on the practice of surveillance in the 19th century as the inventions of the telegraph, the Dictograph recorder, the instantaneous photographic camera, and the punch-card-tabulating machine.

The telegraph, invented in the 1850s, created a completely new means of communication. For the first time, communication was separate from transport. However, as would be the case through much of U.S. history, the new medium also facilitated the interception of information sent through its channels. As early as the Civil War, during which the telegraph was first used on a wide scale, Confederate and Union forces tapped each other's telegraph lines to remain informed of their adversary's strategic decisions.[9]

Photographic and sound-recording technology made it possible to record people's actions and words from a distance and, on occasion, without their consent.[10] Photographic images also replaced the easily forged signature as a common identifier for bureaucracies eager to keep track of growing urban populations. With time, however, an efficient source of bodily identification—the fingerprint—further revolutionized the identification of citizens.

By 1902, fingerprints were systematically used by U.S. authorities, beginning with the New York Civil Service Commission. The practice quickly spread to prisons, the U.S. military, and police departments throughout the country. In 1924, the Federal Bureau of Investigation (FBI) received a legislative mandate to manage a national fingerprint card database, which contained 100 million records by 1946. Since that time, fingerprinting has been the predominant method of identification used by U.S. law enforcement agencies.

The final technological development of this era that had a marked impact on surveillance practices was the punch-card-tabulating machine. Invented by Herman Hollerith in 1889, the machine was designed to streamline the processing of the census. Hollerith's invention, which aggregated information from patterns of holes punched into cardboard cards, was first tested in the 1890 census, shortening its tabulation and analysis from 18 to 6 weeks. The device was an instant success, as it revolutionized record keeping, enabling quick information input and retrieval and decreasing the amount of space necessary for storing records.

The new surveillance technology was both a driving force in the growth of institutional surveillance and a product of increasing bureaucratic needs for information gathering. Both the bureaucratic institutional model and the technologies that it employed were the products of the pervasive pursuit of efficiency that dominated modern American society. The social fabric of the country changed dramatically in the late 19th century owing to immigration and industry, and a continent-wide railroad system allowed increasing mobility. Workers seeking employment were looking beyond their neighborhoods and towns, and the proportion of

---

[9]Alan F. Westin, *Privacy and Freedom*, 1967, p. 172.

[10]With older photographic technology, the subject had to stay still for some time in order for the camera to produce a sharp image, which limited the use of cameras for capturing candid moments.

those who could provide for themselves and their families by living off their land decreased rapidly.

U.S. bureaucracies began relying more heavily on records to keep track of the growing, increasingly mobile population. They collected vital records, school records, employment records, land and housing records, bank and credit records, professional licensing records, military records, church records, law enforcement records, and many others. Some of these information practices were not new—birth and death data and church records had been collected as far back as during the colonial era. However, the compilation of records became significantly more sophisticated at the end of the 19th century. Record keeping became more universal, more systematic, and more thoroughgoing than ever before in American history. Yet the records of this era differed from those of the mid-20th century in an important way: They were maintained predominantly at the local level. The lack of centralized management of record keeping limited its social control function, since a person could move to a different area to escape bad credit or a criminal investigation, although to do so would require the necessary resources.

Despite the predominance of uncoordinated local records in 19th-century America, it would be a mistake to conclude that no national surveillance practices existed before the 20th century. The decennial census had been the site of widespread information collection since 1790. By 1880, it was a sophisticated demographic tool under the jurisdiction of a newly established Census Office within the Department of the Interior.[11,12] While the early surveys collected only the most rudimentary information regarding the classes of people inhabiting a household, the 1880 census featured questions about the age, gender, marital status, place of birth, education, occupation, and literacy status of all household members.

Loyalty surveillance also played a role during the Civil War, and it re-emerged during World War I, although this time the lens of surveillance was focused on German Americans and antiwar activists.[13] Concerns about the war caused the government to pass the Espionage Act in June 1917. Peace protests were put down by police and the military; newspapers publishing antiwar articles were refused circulation by the Post Office Department; films with ostensible antiwar content were banned; and many professors critical of their universities' pro-war stance were

---

[11]In 1902 the Census Office, a permanent agency, was established in its place.

[12]Joseph Steinberg, "Government Records: The Census Bureau and the Social Security Administration," pp. 225-254 in S. Wheeler, ed., *On Record: Files and Dossiers in American Life*, Sage Foundation, New York, 1969.

[13]Morris Janowitz, "The Evolution of Civilian Surveillance by the Armed Forces," pp. 69-73 in M.B. Schnapper, ed., *Uncle Sam Is Watching You: Highlights from the Hearings of the Senate Subcommittee on Constitutional Rights*, Public Affairs Press, Washington, D.C., 1971.

fired. Interestingly, the Espionage Act remains coded in U.S. law to this day, though enforcement of its provisions has been reserved for times of war.[14]

After World War I, similar loyalty-surveillance tactics were used against Socialists and labor unions, and such tactics later re-emerged in full force during World War II against Japanese-Americans. According to scholars William Seltzer and Margo Anderson,[15] the Bureau of the Census assisted U.S. law enforcement authorities in carrying out the presidentially ordered internment of Japanese-Americans. Thus, a surveillance practice established for ostensibly benign statistical purposes was used for the implementation of the most oppressive domestic government action in U.S. history, aside from the negative treatment meted out against African American slaves and Native Americans. Although loyalty surveillance would never reach such overt extremes again, its presence would continue to dominate American political life from the 1950s to the late 1970s.

Another government agency highly dependent on gathering information from most U.S. citizens was the Bureau of Internal Revenue (which became the Internal Revenue Service in 1952). Initially set up as the office of the Commissioner of Internal Revenue, the agency was responsible for the collection of the first income tax in the United States between 1862 and 1872. However, the authority of the U.S. Congress to levy an income tax was not established until 1913, with the passage of the Sixteenth Amendment. Income tax in that year was graduated, and so the commissioner needed to keep track of the income of all taxpayers, giving rise to one of the first centralized document databases of the U.S. government.

By the 1930s, personal identification documents, whose proliferation was initially prompted by the outbreak of World War I, were important means for distinguishing those who were eligible for state programs from those who were not. Franklin D. Roosevelt's New Deal offered Americans new benefits, including Social Security and labor standards, in order to pull the country out of the Great Depression. Yet, at the same time, the New Deal substantially increased the government's administrative burden, requiring new surveillance procedures to keep track of the millions of new benefit recipients and minimize fraudulent claims. This uneasy combination of social benefits and regulatory mechanisms would come

---

[14]It was used again during the civil rights conflicts of the 1960s, since the United States was officially in a state of perpetual emergency from the time of the Korean War. See Howard Zinn, *A People's History of the United States*, HarperCollins, New York, 2003, pp. 542-544.

[15]William Seltzer and Margo Anderson, "After Pearl Harbor: The Proper Role of Population Data Systems in Time of War," paper presented at the Annual Meeting of the Population Association of America, Los Angeles, Calif., March 2000; also available at the American Statistical Association's Statisticians in History Web site.

to define the nature of bureaucratic surveillance in the 20th century, as it continually oscillated between the provision of care and the exercise of control. The Social Security Board (later to become the Social Security Administration), established in 1936 under the New Deal, embodied both of these contradictory values.

The development of surveillance was not limited to the political arena. In fact, some of the most overt uses of workplace behavior monitoring and record keeping took place in the burgeoning private sector. As would be the case for the remainder of the 20th century, early business surveillance focused on two distinct objectives: the monitoring of the worker and, increasingly, the investigation of consumer behavior. One could add a third objective, credit reporting, although this task was quickly taken over from individual businesses by a dedicated industry. Whatever the objective, private businesses were quick to recognize the potential profits to be made from consumer information.

Public policy and jurisprudence posed few constraints on the intensification of surveillance in bureaucratic record keeping, immigration, law enforcement, and the workplace. Whatever resistance to surveillance was mounted by private property rights before the Civil War largely failed to slow the spread of surveillance in industrial America. New surveillance technologies often did not breach private property. Microphones could be installed in adjacent apartments, telephone taps could be installed outside the home, and photographs could be taken from afar, thus upholding property rights. In the meantime, the less-intrusive forms of surveillance, such as bureaucratic record keeping, were simply seen by the law as necessary elements of a developing nation-state and were afforded few protective regulations.

The period from the late 19th to the early 20th centuries was a formative period for considering privacy rights. A key moment was Samuel Warren and Louis Brandeis's definition of privacy as the "right to be left alone."[16] The article described the progression of common law from the protecting of property and persons to the defending of spiritual and emotional states, as well as making the innovative observation that technology would soon make such discussions a more urgent concern.[17] It is not clear that their warning was heeded until the 1960s, 70 years after they offered it.

Another important development was the passage of the Telecommunications Act of 1934, specifically Section 605, which provided that "no

---

[16]Samuel D. Warren and Louis D. Brandeis, *Harvard Law Review* IV (December 15, No. 5):195, 205, 1890, available at http://www.lawrence.edu/fac/boardmaw/Privacy_brand_warr2.html.

[17]Alan F. Westin, *Privacy and Freedom*, 1967, p. 246.

person not being authorized by the sender shall intercept any communication and divulge or publish the existence, contents, substance, purport, effect, or meaning of such intercepted communication to any person." In two subsequent decisions, the U.S. Supreme Court held that the plain language of this section applied to federal agents,[18] that evidence obtained from the interception of wire and radio communications was inadmissible in court,[19] and that evidence indirectly derived from such interceptions was inadmissible as well.[20] Note, however, that the federal government subsequently continued to use wiretapping for purposes other than the collection of evidence to be introduced in court.[21]

A.5 COLD WAR AMERICA (1950-1980)

The three decades that followed World War II brought issues of surveillance and privacy into the light of serious public debate for the first time in U.S. history. Stories of excesses of government surveillance were featured prominently in the mass media, congressional hearings resulted in the passage of privacy laws, and new regulations emerged to govern the information practices within some private industries. Movies featured surveillance, and social scientists started to analyze it.[22]

Amidst all the attention given to privacy, surveillance was becoming ever more ubiquitous. Fueled by unprecedented rates of consumption, a new relationship developed between the individual and the retail sector, one governed by credit lending and surveillance-based marketing practices. Despite the advances of organized labor in the 1930s, the vast new middle class was under pressure in the workplace from hiring practices that demanded personal information and strict performance monitoring after the point of hiring. The political loyalty of citizens was questioned on a scale never before witnessed in American society as the anti-Communist mood swept the United States. And all these surveillance practices were facilitated by rapid technological development.

Beginning in the late 1950s, the computer became a central tool of organizational surveillance. It addressed problems of space and time in the management of records and data analysis and fueled the trend of cen-

---

[18]*Nardone v. United States*, 302 U.S. 397 (1937).
[19]*Nardone v. United States*, 302 U.S. 397 (1937).
[20]*Nardone v. United States*, 308 U.S. 338 (1939).
[21]*Warrantless FBI Electronic Surveillance*, Book III of the Final Report of the Select Committee to Study Governmental Operations with Respect to Intelligence Activities, United States Senate, U.S. Government Printing Office, Washington, D.C., April 23, 1976. (The Select Committee is popularly known as the Church Committee, after its chair, Frank Church, senator from Idaho.)
[22]Vance Packard, *The Naked Society*, David McKay, New York, 1964.

tralization of records. The power of databases to aggregate information previously scattered across diverse locations gave institutions the ability to create comprehensive personal profiles of individuals, frequently without their knowledge or cooperation. The possibility of the use of such power for authoritarian purposes awakened images of Orwellian dystopia in the minds of countless journalists, scholars, writers, and politicians during the 1960s, drawing wide-scale public attention to surveillance and lending urgency to the emerging legal debate over privacy rights.

One of the sectors that immediately benefited from the introduction of computer database technology was the credit-reporting industry. As was the case with most bureaucratic record systems, credit reporting began as a decentralized practice. In 1965, the newly established Credit Data Corporation (CDC)—a for-profit, computerized central agency—became the first national credit-reporting firm in the United States. It was soon followed by other firms, such as the Retail Credit Company, Hooper-Holmes, and the Medical Information Bureau (MIB), which served the insurance industry.

But the credit and insurance industries were not alone. Banks, utility companies, telephone companies, medical institutions, marketing firms, and many other businesses were compiling national and regional dossiers about their clients and competitors in quantities never before seen in the United States. The public sector was equally enthusiastic about the new capabilities of computers. Most federal, state, and local government agencies collected growing volumes of data and invested vast resources in the computerization of their systems. The U.S. military, the Internal Revenue Service, the Social Security Administration, and the Bureau of the Census were among the largest consumers of information and were thus some of the first to become computerized.

While record keeping was growing in all segments of society, the federal government continued its long-standing practice of loyalty surveillance—now increasingly computer-assisted. In the 1950s, the enemies were Communists; in the 1960s, black rights activists; and in the late 1960s and early 1970s, antiwar protesters. The existence of these groups was believed to justify the federal government's development of security records to monitor anyone deemed a threat. It used these security records for two purposes: to monitor the suitability of federal employees and to monitor subversive activity outside the government.

During the 1950s and 1960s, negative reactions to the growing centralization and computerization of records and the continued abuse of surveillance power by law enforcement authorities began to mount. Critics emerged from all sectors of society, including the academy, the mass media, churches, the arts community, and even the corporate world. Some politicians, who received increasing numbers of complaints from their constituents, began raising the issue in Congress. As a result, over the course of the 1960s and early 1970s a number of groundbreaking congressional committees began investigating the use of surveillance practices by the federal government and the private sector, most notably in connection with the Watergate scandal. Under the leadership of political leaders such as Senator Sam J. Ervin, Representative Cornelius Gallagher, and Senator Edward Long, the committees interviewed hundreds of public- and private-sector officials and analyzed thousands of internal documents, revealing the immense scope of surveillance in American society.

Aside from direct impacts on practices, the work of the congressional committees helped create public awareness and support for resisting surveillance. As a result of the hearings, the legislation of surveillance became one of the priorities of the U.S. government. With continued lobbying by individuals like Senator Ervin and Alan Westin, a leading expert on information privacy, the first concrete federal antisurveillance statutes were passed. Beginning in 1966, Congress began responding to the widespread calls for the regulation of surveillance. The Freedom of Information Act (FOIA), passed in 1966 and amended in 1974 and 1976; the Omnibus Crime Control and Safe Streets Act of 1968; and the Fair Credit Reporting Act of 1970 were important steps, respectively, in giving people control over their information, placing limits on police surveillance, and legislating accuracy and confidentiality for credit bureaus.[23]

In 1974, the Privacy Act was passed. For the first time, legislation explicitly identified and protected the right to privacy as a fundamental right. Although the original draft called for the regulation of information practices in federal, state, and local government as well as in the private sector, the final bill extended only to the federal government and the private companies with which it does business.[24] This continues to be the case, since private corporations generally only have to answer to self-government or sector-specific laws. The Privacy Act governed the collection of personal information and outlawed its disclosure without the consent of the individual in question. The exceptions to the antidisclosure clause included standard intraagency use, disclosure under FOIA, routine use for original purposes, and use for the purposes of the census, statistical research, the National Archives, law enforcement, health and safety administration, Congress, the Comptroller General, and court orders.[25]

A major challenge faced by the new privacy legislation was its proper enforcement. Even Senator Ervin, whose work led directly to the passing

---

[23]Richard F. Hixson, *Privacy in a Public Society: Human Rights in Conflict*, Oxford University Press, New York, 1987, pp. 186, 197, 219.
[24]Hixson, *Privacy in a Public Society*, 1987, p. 223.
[25]Hixson, *Privacy in a Public Society*, 1987, p. 224.

of the Privacy Act, was less than enthusiastic about its impact: "The Privacy Act, if enforced, would be a pretty good thing. But the government doesn't like it. The government has an insatiable appetite for power, and it will not stop usurping power unless it is restrained by laws they cannot repeal or nullify."[26] Indeed, failures to comply with surveillance regulations penetrated even the top tiers of the federal government. During the presidential campaign of 1972, five burglars with links to the Nixon administration were caught breaking into the Democratic National Committee offices in order to install surveillance equipment. The resulting Watergate affair revealed a wide array of secret government surveillance practices aimed at political opponents, journalists, and antiwar activists.[27] All this took place 4 years after the enactment of the Omnibus Crime Control and Safe Streets Act.

Court cases continued to bring privacy and freedom of information issues to the fore. In the 1965 Supreme Court case of *Griswold v. Connecticut*, the court rejected a statute forbidding the distribution of birth control information. Using this case as a basis, the *Roe v. Wade* ruling of 1973 eased the way to legal abortion, arguing that it was a privacy issue. Regardless of whether it was directly or indirectly related, privacy would continue dominating the surveillance discourse. Over the next two decades its role would become ever more crucial, as government and business surveillance continued to increase in intensity and scope, despite the modest legal victories of the 1960s and 1970s.

A.6 GLOBALIZED AMERICA (1980-PRESENT)

The end of the 20th century was a time of increasing globalization of America's economy. Computer interconnectivity allowed the leading corporations to expand their manufacturing and marketing bases to countries around the world, forming immense, multinational business networks, coordinated in real time.[28] This process was bolstered by the consolidation of many industries, as countless mergers and takeovers created business conglomerates in many sectors. With the convergence of corporate management came the convergence of company records and technologies. In the meantime, the rise of the personal computer in the 1980s, and networking along with wireless communication in the 1990s, were contributing to change in the daily lives of Americans. People's

---

[26]Hixson, *Privacy in a Public Society*, 1987, p. 207.
[27]Howard Zinn, *A People's History of the United States*, HarperCollins, New York, 2003, pp. 542-544.
[28]Manuel Castells, *The Rise of the Network Society*, Blackwell Publishing, Malden, Mass., 1996.

interactions with technology became routine, allowing them to accomplish many tasks from a distance. The growth of the electronics industry added momentum to continually growing consumerism, which too was facilitated by computer networking, popularizing credit and debit purchases. Since virtually all financial transactions became electronic, they were automatically tracked and recorded by computer databases.

Advances in science and technology redefined the human body as a site of information, making it a prime tool for surveillance practices. Closed-circuit cameras emerged in many retail locations to monitor customer and employee behavior. With time, they also became commonplace in public areas for the purpose of crime control. In the 1990s, the development of biometrics, the automatic identification technique based on bodily characteristics, suggested the possibility of identifying people without the need for documents. The emergence of DNA analysis and the subsequent mapping of the human genome promised revolutionary possibilities for identification and medical testing.

The marketing industry was transformed by information gathering. The development of demographic profiling based on consumer-behavior records led to the development of targeted marketing, which allowed companies to focus their promotional dollars on consumers they deemed desirable. Detailed information about the preferences and habits of consumers that facilitated such targeted marketing practices became a valuable commodity. So-called customer relationship marketing, which relies on sophisticated profiles based on purchasing and preference data,was developed as a major software tool for matching consumers to products and services.

In all its applications, surveillance was becoming increasingly rhizomic.[29] No longer were national data centers necessary, since information from decentralized databases could be aggregated and analyzed through the use of computer networks. And the rhizomes of surveillance systems were permeating every facet of American society. Highway toll systems, automatic teller machines, grocery store checkouts, airport check-ins, and countless other points of interaction with surveillance systems automatically fed information into computer systems, although not in ways that are interoperable or that allow easy data correlation among systems.

Against the backdrop of intensifying practices, Congress passed a number of laws to regulate surveillance within specific sectors, as described in Section 4.3.1. These bills have restricted the disclosure and misuse of personal information within particular industries, but such

---

[29]Kevin Haggerty and Richard Ericson, "The Surveillant Assemblage," *British Journal of Sociology* 51:605-22, 2001.

legislation has generally been narrowly drawn, and so problems outside of the specific purview of these bills have gone unaddressed.

Despite these limited attempts at bolstering the surveillance power of the government, many commentators believed that the role of the state in surveillance was weakening in the 1990s. Some went as far as to dismiss the very concept of a nation-state as an anachronism that would not survive the age of globalization. However, both arguments became moot after September 11, 2001. After the terrorist attacks on New York and Washington, D.C., the Bush administration forcefully reasserted the power of the state, launching the United States on a "war against terrorism."[30] One of the major components of this war was state-sponsored surveillance.

In the days immediately after September 11, the power of rhizomic surveillance was demonstrated to the public as the actions of the terrorists before the attack were reconstructed from bank records, closed-circuit television cameras, and airport systems. In order to enhance the existing surveillance infrastructure, the President and the Congress enacted the USA Patriot Act of 2001. The act gave the government greater surveillance power over citizens of the United States in order to increase security.

---

[30]David Lyon, *Surveillance After September 11*, Polity Press, Cambridge, Mass.; Blackwell Publishing, Malden, Mass., 2003.

B

International Perspectives on Privacy

This appendix presents a global overview of how various countries, regions, and cultures address privacy-related concerns about the processing of personal information. It outlines the principal similarities and differences among various national and regional regulatory measures for addressing these concerns. Comparison is made not only of regulatory strategies but also of various national, regional, and cultural conceptualizations of the ideals and rationale of privacy protection.[1]

B.1 CONCEPTUALIZATIONS OF PRIVACY AND RELATED INTERESTS

As noted in Chapters 2, 4, and 5 of this report, there has long been interest in the United States in privacy, and "privacy" is a frequently used concept in public, academic, and judicial discourse.[2] The concept has been especially prominent in discussion in the United States about the implications of the computerized processing of personal data. When this discussion took off in the 1960s, privacy was invoked as a key term for summing

---

[1]Much of the information on international conceptions of the rationale for privacy protection presented in this appendix is based on the work of Lee Bygrave. See, for example, L.A. Bygrave, *Data Protection Law: Approaching Its Rationale, Logic and Limits*, Kluwer Law International, The Hague/London/New York, 2002 (hereinafter cited as Bygrave, *Data Protection Law*, 2002). A full bibliography is available at http://folk.uio.no/lee/cv.

[2]See, generally, Priscilla Regan, *Legislating Privacy*, University of North Carolina Press, 1995 (hereinafter cited as Regan, *Legislating Privacy*, 1995).

up the congeries of fears raised by the (mis)use of computers.[3] However, privacy has not been the only term invoked in this context. A variety of other, partly overlapping concepts have also been invoked—particularly those of "freedom," "liberty," and "autonomy."[4]

The U.S. debate, particularly in the 1960s and early 1970s, about the privacy-related threats posed by computers exercised considerable influence on debates in other countries. As Hondius writes, "[a]lmost every issue that arose in Europe was also an issue in the United States, but at an earlier time and on a more dramatic scale."[5] Naturally, the salience of the privacy concept in U.S. discourse helped to ensure its prominence in the debate elsewhere. This is most evident in discourse in other English-speaking countries[6] and in international forums where English is a working language.[7] Yet also in countries in which English is

---

[3]See, for example, Alan F. Westin, *Privacy and Freedom*, Atheneum, New York, 1967. In this pioneering work that prompted global privacy movements in many democratic nations in the 1970s, Dr. Alan Westin, Professor of Public Law at Columbia University, defined privacy as the claim of individuals, groups, and institutions to determine for themselves when, how, and to what extent information about them is communicated to others. See also Arthur R. Miller, *The Assault on Privacy: Computers, Data Banks, and Dossiers*, University of Michigan Press, Ann Arbor, 1971 (hereinafter cited as Miller, *The Assault on Privacy*, 1971).

[4]The title of Westin's seminal work *Privacy and Freedom* (1967) is a case in point. Indeed, as pointed out further below, "privacy" in this context has tended to be conceived essentially as a form of autonomy—that is, as one's ability to control the flow of information about oneself.

[5]Frits W. Hondius, *Emerging Data Protection in Europe*, North Holland Publishing, Amsterdam, 1975, p. 6 (hereinafter cited as Hondius, *Emerging Data Protection in Europe*, 1975). Even in more recent times, discourse in the United States often takes up such issues before they are discussed elsewhere. For example, systematic discussion about the impact of digital rights management systems (earlier termed "electronic copyright management systems") on privacy interests occurred first in the United States: see particularly, Julie Cohen, "A Right to Read Anonymously: A Closer Look at 'Copyright Management' in Cyberspace," *Conn. L. Rev.* 28:981, 1996, available at http://www.law.georgetown.edu/faculty/jec/read_anonymously.pdf. Similar discussion did not occur in Europe until a couple of years later—the first instance being L.A. Bygrave and K.J. Koelman, "Privacy, Data Protection and Copyright: Their Interaction in the Context of Electronic Copyright Management Systems," Institute for Information Law, Amsterdam, 1998; later published in P.B. Hugenholtz, ed., *Copyright and Electronic Commerce*, Kluwer Law International, The Hague/London/Boston, 2000, pp. 59-124.

[6]See, for example, United Kingdom, Committee on Privacy (Younger Committee), *Report of the Committee on Privacy*, Cm. 5012, Her Majesty's Stationery Office, London, 1972; Canada, Department of Communications and Department of Justice, *Privacy and Computers: A Report of a Task Force*, Information Canada, Ottawa, 1972; Australian Law Reform Commission, *Privacy*, Report No. 22, Australian Government Publishing Service (AGPS), Canberra, 1983; and W.L. Morison, *Report on the Law of Privacy to the Standing Committee of Commonwealth and State Attorneys-General*, Report No. 170/1973, AGPS, Canberra, 1973.

[7]As is evident, for example, in the titles of the early Council of Europe resolutions dealing with information technology threats. See Council of Europe Resolution (73)22 on the

not the main language, much of the same discourse has been framed, at least initially, around concepts roughly equating with or embracing the notion of privacy—for instance, "la vie privée" (French),[8] "die Privatsphäre" (German),[9] and "privatlivets fred" (Danish/Norwegian).[10]

Nevertheless, the field of law and policy that emerged from the early discussions in Europe on the privacy-related threats posed by information technology (IT) has increasingly been described using a nomenclature that avoids explicit reference to privacy or closely related terms. This nomenclature is "data protection," deriving from the German term "Datenschutz."[11] While the nomenclature is problematic in several respects—not least because it fails to indicate the central interests served by the norms to which it is meant to apply[12]—it has gained broad popularity in Europe[13] and to a lesser extent elsewhere.[14] Its use, though, is being increasingly supplemented by the term "data privacy."[15] Arguably, the latter nomenclature is more appropriate, as it better communicates the central interest(s) at stake and provides a bridge for synthesizing North American and European policy discussions.

At the same time, various countries and regions display terminological idiosyncrasies that partly reflect differing jurisprudential backgrounds for the discussions concerned. In Western Europe, the discussion has often drawn on jurisprudence developed there on legal protection of personal-

---

Protection of the Privacy of Individuals vis-à-vis Electronic Data Banks in the Private Sector, adopted Sept. 26, 1973; and Council of Europe Resolution (74)29 on the Protection of the Privacy of Individuals vis-à-vis Electronic Data Banks in the Public Sector, adopted Sept. 24, 1974.

[8]See, for example, G. Messadié, *La fin de la vie privée*, Calmann-Lévy, Paris, 1974.

[9]See, for example, the 1970 proposal by the (West) German Interparliamentary Working Committee for a "Law for the protection of privacy against misuse of database information," described in H.P. Bull, *Data Protection or the Fear of the Computer*, Piper, Munich, 1984, p. 85.

[10]See, for example, Denmark, Registerudvalget [Register Committee], *Delbetænkning om private registre* [Report on Private Data Registers], No. 687, Statens Trykningskontor, Copenhagen, 1973.

[11]For more on the origins of "Datenschutz," see Simitis, *Kommentar zum Bundesdatenschutzgesetz*, 2003, pp. 3-4.

[12]Moreover, it tends to misleadingly connote, in U.S. circles, concern for the security of data and information or maintenance of intellectual property rights; see P.M. Schwartz and J.R. Reidenberg, *Data Privacy Law: A Study of United States Data Protection*, Michie Law Publishers, Charlottesville, Va., 1996, p. 5 (hereinafter cited as Schwartz and Reidenberg, *Data Privacy Law*, 1996).

[13]See generally, Hondius, *Emerging Data Protection in Europe*, 1975; and Bygrave, *Data Protection Law*, 2002.

[14]See, for example, G.L. Hughes and M. Jackson, *Hughes on Data Protection in Australia*, 2nd Ed., Law Book Co. Ltd., Sydney, 2001.

[15]See, for example, Schwartz and Reidenberg, *Data Privacy Law*, 1996; and C. Kuner, *European Data Privacy Law and Online Business*, Oxford University Press, Oxford, 2003 (hereinafter cited as Kuner, *European Data Privacy Law and Online Business*, 2003).

ity. Thus, the concepts of "Persönlichkeitsrecht" (personality right) and "Persönlichkeitschutz" (personality protection) figure centrally in German and Swiss discourse.[16] Norwegian discourse revolves around the concept of "personvern" (protection of person[ality]),[17] while Swedish discourse focuses on "integritetsskydd" (protection of [personal] integrity).[18] By contrast, Latin American discourse in the field tends to revolve around the concept of "habeas data" (roughly meaning "you should have the data"). This concept derives from due process doctrine based on the writ of habeas corpus.[19]

Many of the above-mentioned concepts are prone to definitional instability. The most famous case in point relates to definitions of "privacy." Debates in the United States over the most appropriate definitions of privacy[20] have counterparts in other countries centering on similar concepts.[21] Some of the non-U.S. debate concerns whether privacy as such is best characterized as a state/condition, or a claim, or a right. That issue aside, the debate reveals four principal ways of defining privacy.[22] One set of definitions is in terms of noninterference,[23] another in terms of limited accessibility.[24] A third set of definitions conceives of privacy as informa-

---

[16]See, for example, Germany's Federal Data Protection Act of 1990 (*Bundesdatenschutzgesetz—Gesetz zum Fortentwicklung der Datenverarbeitung und des Datenschutzes vom 20. Dezember 1990* (as amended in 2001) §1(1)), stipulating the purpose of the act as protection of the individual from interference with his/her "personality right" (Persönlichkeitsrecht); and Switzerland's Federal Law on Data Protection of 1992 (*Loi fédérale du 19. Juin 1992 sur la protection des données/Bundesgesetz vom 19. Juni 1992 über den Datenschutz*), Article 1, stating the object of the act as, inter alia, "protection of personality" (Schutz der Persönlichkeit).

[17]See Bygrave, *Data Protection Law*, 2002, pp. 138-143 and references cited therein.

[18]See Bygrave, *Data Protection Law*, 2002, pp. 126-129 and references cited therein.

[19]See further, A. Guadamuz, "Habeas Data vs. the European Data Protection Directive," *Journal of Information, Law and Technology*, 2001; and Fried, rapporteur, Organization of American States (OAS), Inter-American Juridical Committee, 2000, p. 107 et seq.

[20]For overviews, see Chapter 2 of Julie C. Inness, *Privacy, Intimacy, and Isolation*, Oxford University Press, New York, 1992; and Chapters 2 and 3 of J. DeCew, *In Pursuit of Privacy: Law, Ethics, and the Rise of Technology*, Cornell University Press, Ithaca, N.Y., 1997.

[21]See, e.g., *En ny datalag* [A New Data Law], Statens Offentlige Utredningar [State Official Reports], No. 10, pp. 150-161, 1993 (documenting difficulties experienced in Swedish data privacy discourse with respect to arriving at a precise definition of "personlig integritet").

[22]See generally Bygrave, *Data Protection Law*, 2002, pp. 128-129.

[23]See especially Samuel D. Warren and Louis D. Brandeis, "The Right to Privacy," *Harvard Law Review* IV (December 15, No. 5):195, 205, 1890 (arguing that the right to privacy in Anglo-American law is part and parcel of a right "to be let alone").

[24]See, for example, R. Gavison, "Privacy and the Limits of Law," *Yale Law Journal* 89:428-436, 1980, claiming that privacy is a condition of "limited accessibility" consisting of three elements: "secrecy" ("the extent to which we are known to others"), "solitude" ("the extent to which others have physical access to us"), and "anonymity" ("the extent to which we are the subject of others' attention").

tion control.[25] A fourth set of definitions incorporates various elements of the other three sets but links privacy exclusively to intimate or sensitive aspects of persons' lives.[26]

Definitions of privacy in terms of information control tend to be most popular in discourse dealing directly with law and policy on data privacy,[27] both in the United States and elsewhere. In Europe, though, the notion is not always linked directly to the privacy concept; it is either linked to related concepts, such as "personal integrity" (in the case of, e.g., Swedish discourse),[28] or it stands alone. The most significant instance of the latter is the German notion of "information self-determination" (informationelle Selbstbestimmung), which in itself forms the content of a constitutional right deriving from a landmark decision in 1983 by the German Federal Constitutional Court (Bundesverfassungsgericht).[29] The notion and the right to which it attaches have had considerable impact on development of data privacy law and policy in Germany[30] and, to a lesser extent, other European countries.

Despite the general popularity of notions of information control and information self-determination, these have usually not been viewed in terms of a person "owning" information about him-/herself, such that he/she should be entitled to, for example, royalties for the use of that information by others. Concomitantly, property rights doctrines have rarely been championed as providing a desirable basis for data privacy rules.[31] The relatively few proponents of a property rights approach have

---

[25]See, for example, Westin, *Privacy and Freedom*, 1967, p. 7 ("Privacy is the claim of individuals, groups, or institutions to determine for themselves when, how, and to what extent information about them is communicated to others").

[26]See, for example, Inness, *Privacy, Intimacy, and Isolation*, 1992, p. 140 (defining privacy as "the state of possessing control over a realm of intimate decisions, which includes decisions about intimate access, intimate information, and intimate actions").

[27]See generally Bygrave, *Data Protection Law*, 2002, p. 130, and references cited therein.

[28]See, for example, *En ny datalag* [A New Data Law], Statens Offentlige Utredningar [State Official Reports], No. 10, p. 159, 1993 (noting that the concept of "personlig integritet" embraces information control).

[29]Decision of December 15, 1983, BverfGE (*Entscheidungen des Bundesverfassungsgerichts*), Vol. 65, p. 1 et seq. For an English translation, see *Human Rights Law Journal* 5:94 et seq., 1984.

[30]Cf. S. Simitis, "Auf dem Weg zu einem neuen Datenschutzkonzept," pp. 714 ff. in *Datenschutz und Datensicherheit*, 2000 (detailing the slow and incomplete implementation of the principles inherent in the right).

[31]Opposition to a property rights approach is expressed in, inter alia, Miller, *The Assault on Privacy*, 1971, p. 211 ff.; Hondius, *Emerging Data Protection in Europe*, 1975, pp. 103-105; S. Simitis, "Reviewing Privacy in an Information Society," *University of Pennsylvania Law Review* 135:707, 718, 735-736, 1987 (hereinafter cited as Simitis, "Reviewing Privacy in an Information Society," 1987); K. Wilson, *Technologies of Control: The New Interactive Media for the Home*, University of Wisconsin Press, Madison, 1988, pp. 91-94; R. Wacks, *Personal Information:*

tended to come from the United States,[32] although sporadic advocacy of such an approach also occurs elsewhere.[33]

B.2 CONCEPTUALIZATIONS OF THE VALUES SERVED BY PRIVACY

In the United States, the discourse on privacy and privacy rights tends to focus only on the benefits that these have for individuals qua individuals. These benefits are typically cast in terms of securing (or helping to secure) individuality, autonomy, dignity, emotional release, self-evaluation, and interpersonal relationships of love, friendship, and trust.[34] They are, in the words of Westin, largely about "achieving individual goals of self-realization."[35] The converse of this focus is that privacy and privacy rights are often seen as essentially in tension with the needs of wider "society."[36] This view carries sometimes over into claims that privacy rights can be detrimental to societal needs.[37]

Casting the value of privacy in strictly individualistic terms appears to be a common trait in the equivalent discourse in many other countries.[38] However, the grip of this paradigm varies from country to country

---

Privacy and the Law, Clarendon Press, Oxford, 1989, p. 49; Y. Poullet, "Data Protection Between Property and Liberties—A Civil Law Approach," pp. 161-181 in H.W.K. Kaspersen and A. Oskamp, eds., *Amongst Friends in Computers and Law: A Collection of Essays in Remembrance of Guy Vandenberghe*, Kluwer Law and Taxation Publishers, Deventer/Boston, 1990; J. Litman, "Information Privacy/Information Property," *Stanford Law Review* 52:1283-1313, 2000; and Bygrave, *Data Protection Law*, 2002, p. 121.

[32]See, most notably, Westin, *Privacy and Freedom*, 1967, pp. 324-325; K.C. Laudon, "Markets and Privacy," *Communications of the Association for Computing Machinery* 39:92-104, 1996; J. Rule and L. Hunter, "Towards Property Rights in Personal Data," pp. 168-181 in C.J. Bennett and R. Grant, eds., *Visions of Privacy: Policy Choices for the Digital Age*, University of Toronto Press, Toronto, 1999; and L. Lessig, *Code and Other Laws of Cyberspace*, Basic Books, New York, 1999, pp. 159-163.

[33]See, for example, P. Blume, "New Technologies and Human Rights: Data Protection, Privacy and the Information Society," Paper No. 67, Institute of Legal Science, Section B, University of Copenhagen, 1998.

[34]See generally, Bygrave, *Data Protection Law*, 2002, pp. 133-134 and references cited therein.

[35]Westin, *Privacy and Freedom*, 1967, p. 39.

[36]See generally, Regan, *Legislating Privacy*, 1995, Chapters 2 and 8 and references cited therein.

[37]As exemplified in R.A. Posner, "The Right to Privacy," *Georgia Law Review* 12:393-422, 1978 (criticizing privacy rights from an economic perspective); and A. Etzioni, *The Limits of Privacy*, Basic Books, New York, 1999 (criticizing privacy rights from a communitarian perspective).

[38]See generally, C.J. Bennett and C.D. Raab, *The Governance of Privacy: Policy Instruments in Global Perspective*, Ashgate, Aldershot, 2003, Chapter 1 (hereinafter cited as Bennett and Raab, *The Governance of Privacy*, 2003).

and culture to culture. The variation is well exemplified when comparing the jurisprudence of the German Federal Constitutional Court with that of U.S. courts. The former emphasizes that the value of data privacy norms lies to a large degree in their ability to secure the necessary conditions for active citizen participation in public life; in other words, to secure a flourishing democracy.[39] This perspective is underdeveloped in U.S. jurisprudence.[40]

One also finds increasing recognition in academic discourse on both sides of the Atlantic that data privacy norms are valuable not simply for individual persons but for the maintenance of societal civility, pluralism, and democracy.[41]

A related development is increasing academic recognition that data privacy laws serve a multiplicity of interests, which in some cases extend well beyond traditional conceptualizations of privacy.[42] This insight is perhaps furthest developed in Norwegian discourse, which has elaborated relatively sophisticated models of the various interests promoted

---

[39] See, especially, the decision of December 15, 1983, BverfGE (*Entscheidungen des Bundesverfassungsgerichts*), Vol. 65, p. 1 et seq. For an English translation, see *Human Rights Law Journal* 5:94 et seq., 1984.

[40] See further, the comparative analyses in P.M. Schwartz, "The Computer in German and American Constitutional Law: Towards an American Right of Informational Self-Determination," *American Journal of Comparative Law* 37:675-701, 1989; P.M. Schwartz, "Privacy and Participation: Personal Information and Public Sector Regulation in the United States," *Iowa Law Review* 80:553-618, 1995; and B.R. Ruiz, *Privacy in Telecommunications: A European and an American Approach*, Kluwer Law International, The Hague/London/Boston, 1997.

[41] See, for example, S. Simitis, "Auf dem Weg zu einem neuen Datenschutzrecht" [On the Road to a New Data Protection Law], *Informatica e diritto* 3:97-116, 1984; Simitis, "Reviewing Privacy in an Information Society," 1987; R.C. Post, "The Social Foundations of Privacy: Community and Self in the Common Law," *California Law Review* 77:957-1010, 1989; R. Gavison, "Too Early for a Requiem: Warren and Brandeis Were Right on Privacy vs. Free Speech," *South Carolina Law Review* 43:437-471, 1992; Regan, *Legislating Privacy*, 1995; B.R. Ruiz, *Privacy in Telecommunications: A European and an American Law Approach*, Kluwer Law International, The Hague/London/New York, 1997); P.M. Schwartz, "Privacy and Democracy in Cyberspace," *Vanderbilt Law Review* 52:1609-1702, 1999; Bygrave, *Data Protection Law*, 2002; and Bennett and Raab, *The Governance of Privacy*, 2003.

[42] See, for example, O. Mallmann, *Zielfunktionen des Datenschutzes: Schutz der Privatsphäre, korrekte Information; mit einer Studie zum Datenschutz im Bereich von Kreditinformationssystemen* [Goal Functions of Data Protection: Protection of Privacy, Correct Information; with a Study of Data Protection in the Area of Credit Information Systems], Alfred Metzner Verlag, Frankfurt am Main, 1977; H. Burkert, "Data-Protection Legislation and the Modernization of Public Administration," *International Review of Administrative Sciences* 62:557-567, 1996; L.A. Bygrave, "Where Have All the Judges Gone? Reflections on Judicial Involvement in Developing Data Protection Law," pp. 113-125 in P. Wahlgren, ed., *IT och juristutbildning, Nordisk årsbok i rättsinformatik, 2000*, Jure AB Stockholm, 2001; also published in *Privacy Law and Policy Reporter* 7:11-14, 33-36, 2000; and Bygrave, *Data Protection Law*, 2002, Chapter 7.

by data privacy laws.[43] These interests include ensuring adequate quality of personal information, "citizen-friendly" administration, proportionality of control, and rule of law. In Norway, the insight that data-privacy laws are concerned with more than safeguarding privacy extends beyond the academic community and into regulatory bodies. Indeed, Norway's principal legislation on data privacy contains an objects clause specifically referring to the need for "adequate quality of personal information" (tilstrekkelig kvalitet på personopplysninger) in addition to the needs for privacy and personal integrity.[44]

The equivalent laws of some other European countries also contain objects clauses embracing more than privacy. The broadest—if not boldest—expression of aims is found in the French legislation: "Data processing shall be at the service of every citizen. It shall develop in the context of international co-operation. It shall infringe neither human identity, nor the rights of man, nor privacy, nor individual or public liberties."[45]

Also noteworthy is the express concern in the data privacy legislation of several German Länder for maintaining state order based on the principle of separation of powers, and, concomitantly, for ensuring so-called information equilibrium (Informationsgleichgewicht) between the legislature and other state organs. This "equilibrium" refers principally to a situation in which the legislature is able to get access to information (personal and/or nonpersonal) that is available to the executive.[46]

At the same time, however, considerable uncertainty still seems to reign in many countries about exactly which interests and values are promoted by data privacy laws. This is reflected partly in academic discourse,[47] partly in the absence in some laws of objects clauses formally

---

[43]See generally, Bygrave, *Data Protection Law*, 2002, p. 137 et seq. and references cited therein.

[44]See Norway's Personal Data Act of 2000 (*Lov om behandling av personopplysninger av 14. april 2000 nr. 31*), §1(2).

[45]See France's Act Regarding Data Processing, Files and Individual Liberties of 1978 (*Loi no. 78-17 du 6. janvier 1978 relative à l'informatique, aux fichiers et aux libertés*), §1.

[46]See further, Bygrave, *Data Protection Law*, 2002, p. 39; S. Simitis, ed., *Kommentar zum Bundesdatenschutzgesetz* [Commentary on the Federal Data Protection Act] 5th ed., Nomos Verlagsgesellschaft, Baden-Baden, 2003, p. 11.

[47]See, for example, D. Korff, "Study on the Protection of the Rights and Interests of Legal Persons with Regard to the Processing of Personal Data Relating to Such Persons," final report to E.C. Commission, October 1998, available at http://europa.eu.int/comm/internal_market/en/dataprot/studies/legalen.htm (accessed Oct. 10, 2003), p. 42 ("[t]here is a lack of clarity, of focus, over the very nature, aims and objects of data protection in the [European Union] Member States which is, not surprisingly, reflected in the international data protection instruments"); and B.W. Napier, "International Data Protection Standards and British Experience," *Informatica e diritto*, Nos. 1-2, pp. 83-100, 1992, p. 85, hereinafter cited as Napier, "International Data Protection Standards and British Experience," 1992) (claiming that, in Britain, "the conceptual basis for data protection laws remains unclear").

specifying particular interests or values that the legislation is intended to serve,[48] and partly in the vague way in which existing objects clauses are often formulated.[49]

B.3 SOCIETAL AND CULTURAL SUPPORT FOR PRIVACY: A COMPARISON

This section addresses the issue of whether some nations and cultures are more supportive of privacy than others are. It also addresses the factors that might contribute to such differences.

Making accurate comparisons of the degree to which given countries or cultures respect privacy is fraught with difficulty,[50] which is partly due to the paucity of systematically collected empirical data[51] and partly to the fact that concern for privacy within each country or culture is often uneven. In the United Kingdom (U.K.), for example, proposals to introduce multipurpose personal identification number (PIN) schemes similar to those in Scandinavia[52] have generally been treated with a great deal of antipathy, yet video surveillance of public places in the United Kingdom[53] seems to be considerably more extensive than that in Scandinavian countries.

---

[48]See, for example, the U.K. Data Protection Act of 1998 and Denmark's Personal Data Act of 2000 (*Lov nr. 429 af 31. maj 2000 om behandling af personoplysninger*).

[49]See, for example, Council of Europe Convention for the Protection of Individuals with Regard to Automatic Processing of Personal Data (European Treaty Series No. 108; adopted January 28, 1981), Article 1 (specifying goals as protection of "rights and fundamental freedoms, and in particular . . . right to privacy").

[50]This difficulty obviously carries over into comparative assessment of various countries' legal regimes for privacy protection. See, for example, C.D. Raab and C.J. Bennett, "Taking the Measure of Privacy: Can Data Protection Be Evaluated?" *International Review of Administrative Sciences* 62:535-556, 1996. Equally problematic is the accurate comparison of privacy levels across historical periods. Yet another issue, over which relatively little has been written, concerns discrepancies between various classes of persons within a given society in terms of the respective levels of privacy that they typically enjoy. For further discussion, see generally, Bennett and Raab, *The Governance of Privacy*, 2003, Chapter 2.

[51]As Bennett and Raab (*The Governance of Privacy*, 2003, p. 15) remark, "[U]nfortunately, we have little systematic cross-national survey evidence about attitudes to privacy with which to investigate the nature and influence of wider cultural attributes. Much of th[e] argumentation tends, therefore, to invoke anecdotes or cultural stereotypes: 'the Englishman's home is his castle,' and so on."

[52]Further on the Scandinavian PIN schemes, see, for example, A.S. Lunde, J. Huebner, S. Lettenstrom, S. Lundeborg, and L. Thygesen, *The Person-Number Systems of Sweden, Norway, Denmark and Israel*, U.S. Department of Health and Human Services, Vital and Health Statistics, Series 2, No. 84, DHHS Publication No. (PHS) 80-1358, 1980; also available at http://www.cdc.gov/nchs/data/series/sr_02/sr02_084.pdf (accessed Oct. 4, 2003).

[53]For more on this surveillance, see, for example, S. Davies, "Surveillance on the Streets," *Privacy Law and Policy Reporter* 2:24-26, 1995; *Der Spiegel*, July 5, 1999, pp. 122-124; and A.

It is clear that levels of privacy across nations and cultures and across broad historical periods are in constant flux. Moreover, the ways in which human beings create, safeguard, and enhance their respective states of privacy and the extent to which they exhibit a desire for privacy vary from culture to culture according to a complex array of factors.[54] At the same time, the desire for some level of privacy appears to be a panhuman trait. Even in societies in which apparently little opportunity exists for physical or spatial solitude, human beings seem to adopt various strategies for cultivating other forms of social distance.[55]

To the extent that a panhuman *need* for privacy exists, it appears to be rooted not so much in physiological or biological as in social factors. According to Moore, the need for privacy is, in essence, socially created. Moore's seminal study indicates that an extensive, highly developed concern for privacy is only possible in a relatively complex society with a strongly felt division between a domestic private realm and public sphere—"privacy is minimal where technology and social organization are minimal."[56]

However, technological and organizational factors are not the sole determinants of privacy levels. Also determinative are ideological factors. Central among these are attitudes to the value of private life,[57] attitudes

---

Webb, "Spy Cameras vs. Villains in Britain," United Press International, March 8, 2002, available at http://www.upi.com/view.cfm?StoryID=08032002-020813-4448r (accessed Nov. 6, 2003).

[54]See further, B. Moore, *Privacy: Studies in Social and Cultural History*, M.E. Sharpe, Publishers, Armonk, N.Y., 1984 (hereinafter cited as Moore, *Privacy*, 1984); J.M. Roberts and T. Gregor, "Privacy: A Cultural View," pp. 199-225 in J.R. Pennock and J.W. Chapman, eds., *Privacy: Nomos XIII*, Atherton Press, New York, 1971; I. Altman, "Privacy Regulation: Culturally Universal or Culturally Specific?," *Journal of Social Issues* 33:66-84, 1977; Westin, *Privacy and Freedom*, 1967; and Flaherty, *Privacy in Colonial New England*, University Press of Virginia, Charlottesville, 1972 (hereinafter cited as Flaherty, *Privacy in Colonial New England*, 1972).

[55]See, for example, Moore's study (*Privacy*, 1984) of the Siriono Indians in Bolivia; Flaherty's study (*Privacy in Colonial New England*, 1972) of colonial society in New England; and R. Lunheim and G. Sindre, "Privacy and Computing: A Cultural Perspective," pp. 25-40 in R. Sizer, L. Yngström, H. Kaspersen, and S. Fischer-Hübner, eds., *Security and Control of Information Technology in Society*, North-Holland, Amsterdam, 1993, a study of a village society in Rajasthan, North-West India (hereinafter cited as Lunheim and Sindre, "Privacy and Computing," 1993).

[56]Moore, *Privacy*, 1984, p. 276. Cf., inter alia, Lunheim and Sindre, "Privacy and Computing," 1993, p. 28 ("privacy is a cultural construct encountered in virtually every society of some economic complexity"); Raes, 1989, p. 78 (noting that privacy today "is as much a result of modern technology as technology is a threat to the private lives of citizens"). For a particularly incisive sociological analysis of historical changes in levels and types of privacy, see Shils, 1975, Chapter 18.

[57]See, for example, H. Arendt, *The Human Condition*, University of Chicago Press, 1958, p. 38 (noting that, in ancient Athenian culture, the private sphere was often regarded as a domain of "privation"). See also Moore, *Privacy*, 1984, p. 120 et seq. Moore, however, dis-

to the worth of persons as individuals,[58] and sensitivity to human beings' non-economic and emotional needs.[59] Concern for privacy tends to be high in societies espousing liberal ideals, particularly those of Mill, Locke, Constant, and Madison. As Lukes notes, privacy in the sense of a "sphere of thought and action that should be free from 'public' interference" constitutes "perhaps the central idea of liberalism."[60]

The liberal affection for privacy is amply demonstrated in the development of legal regimes for privacy protection. These regimes are most comprehensive in Western liberal democracies. By contrast, such regimes are underdeveloped in most African and Asian nations. It is tempting to view this situation as symptomatic of a propensity in African and Asian cultures to place primary value on securing the interests and loyalties of the group at the expense of the individual. However, care must be taken not to pigeonhole countries and cultures in static categories, and provision for privacy rights is increasingly on the legislative agenda of some African and Asian countries.

It is also important to note that the United States—often portrayed as the citadel of liberal ideals—has not seen fit to protect privacy as extensively as some other nations have, notably Canada and the member states of the European Union (E.U.). Consider, for example, the absence of comprehensive legislation on data privacy regulating the U.S. private sector and the lack of an independent agency (a data protection authority or a privacy commissioner) to specifically oversee the regulation of data privacy matters.[61] Thus, within the Western liberal democratic "camp,"

---

cerns growing enthusiasm and respect for private life among Athenians over the course of the 4th century B.C.; see Moore, *Privacy*, pp. 128-133.

[58]See, for example, M. Ethan Katsh, *The Electronic Media and the Transformation of the Law*, Oxford University Press, New York, 1989, p. 192 ("Part of the reason there was less privacy and less concern with privacy in earlier times is that the individual, the principal beneficiary of a right to privacy, did not have the same status in the ancient world as in the modern era"). See further, F.D. Schoeman, *Privacy and Social Freedom*, Cambridge University Press, Cambridge, 1992, Chapters 6 and 7 (describing factors behind the emergence of individualism and a concomitant concern for privacy in Western societies).

[59]See, for example, S. Strömholm, *Right of Privacy and Rights of the Personality: A Comparative Survey*, P.A. Norstedt and Söners Förlag, Stockholm, 1967, pp. 19-20 (viewing the development of legal rights to privacy as part and parcel of a "humanization" of Western law; i.e., a trend toward greater legal sensitivity to the nonpecuniary interests of human beings).

[60]Lukes, 1973, p. 62. Cf. Bennett and Raab, *The Governance of Privacy*, 2003, pp. 22-23 ("the political theory of privacy, in both the US and Europe, has largely operated within a liberal paradigm").

[61]See also Section B.4.2. For more on the differences between U.S. and European regulatory approaches in the data privacy field, see, for example, A. Charlesworth, "Clash of the Data Titans? US and EU Data Privacy Regulation," *European Public Law* 6(2):253-274, 2000; J.R. Reidenberg, "Resolving Conflicting International Data Privacy Rules in Cyberspace," *Stanford Law Review* 52:1315-1371, 2000; J.B. Ritter, B.S. Hayes, and H.L. Judy, "Emerging

considerable variation exists in legal regimes and readiness for safeguarding privacy.[62]

A variation in legal regimes need not reflect differences in the support for privacy in various nations. For example, the variation might be due, at least in part, to differences in the extent to which persons in respective countries can take for granted that others will respect their privacy (independently of legal norms).[63] In other words, it can be attributable to differences in perceptions of the degree to which privacy is or will be threatened. For instance, the comprehensive, bureaucratic nature of data privacy regulation in Europe[64] undoubtedly reflects traumas from relatively recent, firsthand experience there of totalitarian oppression.[65] This heritage imparts both gravity and anxiety to European regulatory policy. Conversely, in North America and Australia, for example, the paucity of firsthand domestic experience of totalitarian oppression tends to make these countries' regulatory policy in the field relatively lax.

Variation between the privacy regimes of Western states can also be symptomatic of differences in perceptions of the degree to which interests that compete with privacy, such as public safety and national security, warrant protection at the expense of privacy interests. In other words, the variation can be symptomatic of differing perceptions of the need for

---

Trends in International Privacy Law," *Emory International Law Review* 15:87-155, 2001; and D.H. Flaherty, *Protecting Privacy in Surveillance Societies*, University of North Carolina Press, Chapel Hill/London, 1989 (hereinafter cited as Flaherty, *Protecting Privacy in Surveillance Societies*, 1989).

[62]See, generally, Section B.4.

[63]It is claimed, for instance, that this difference accounts for the lack of judicial support in the United Kingdom for a tort of breach of privacy, in contrast to the willingness of U.S. courts to develop such a tort: see, e.g., J. Martin and A.R.D. Norman, *The Computerized Society*, Englewood Cliffs, N.J., 1970, p. 468. However, other explanations have also been advanced for the nondevelopment of a right to privacy in English common law: see, e.g., Napier, "International Data Protection Standards and British Experience," 1992, p. 85 (emphasizing the "narrow-mindedness" of English judges). For further detail on the divergent paths taken by English and American courts in developing a specific right of privacy under common law, see, inter alia, L. Brittan, "The Right of Privacy in England and the United States," *Tulane Law Review* 37:235-268, 1963; G. Dworkin, "Privacy and the Law," p. 113 et seq. in J.B. Young, ed., *Privacy*, Wiley, Chichester, 1978. In a decision of October 16, 2003, the House of Lords unanimously held that a tort of invasion of privacy is not part of English law, thus dealing a serious if not fatal blow to the development of a separate privacy tort under U.K. common law: see *Wainwright v. Home Office* [2003] U.K.H.L. 53, especially paragraphs 30-35, available at http://www.bailii.org/uk/cases/UKHL/2003/53.html (accessed Nov. 5, 2003). For an overview of other recent U.K. case law on privacy, see R. Jay and A. Hamilton, *Data Protection: Law and Practice*, Sweet and Maxwell, London: 2003, pp. 56-69.

[64]See further, Section B.4.2.

[65]See also K.S. Selmer, "Elektronisk databehandling og rettssamfunnet" [Electronic Data Processing and Legal Society], pp. 41-53 in *Forhandlingene ved Det 30. nordiske juristmøtet, Oslo 15.-17. august 1984*, Part II, Oslo, 1984.

surveillance and control measures. This is seen most clearly in the impact on U.S. regulatory policy of the terrorist attacks of September 11, 2001. In the wake of those attacks, the United States has been more willing to place limitations on privacy rights.[66]

Yet other factors can play a role too. For instance, U.S. and, to a lesser extent, Australian eschewal of omnibus data privacy legislation for the private sector is due partly to a distrust of a strong state role in influencing the economy, combined with skepticism toward legally regulating the private sector except where flagrant imbalances of power are proven to exist between private parties—imbalances that cannot be corrected except by legislative intervention.[67]

The above differences aside, concern and support for privacy on the part of the general public seem to be broadly similar across the Western world.[68] There is abundant evidence from public opinion surveys that these levels of concern and support are relatively high,[69] at least in the

---

[66]See generally, Electronic Privacy Information Center and Privacy International, *Privacy and Human Rights 2003: An International Survey of Privacy Laws and Developments*, EPIC/PI, Washington, D.C., 2003.

[67]With respect to U.S. attitudes, see, e.g., Schwartz and Reidenberg, *Data Privacy Law*, 1996, p. 6 et seq.; and J.H. Yurow, "National Perspectives on Data Protection," *Transnational Data Report* 6(6):337-339, 1983. For further analysis of the causes of divergence between Western countries' respective regimes for data privacy, see generally, C.J. Bennett, *Regulating Privacy: Data Protection and Public Policy in Europe and the United States*, Cornell University Press, Ithaca, N.Y., 1992, Chapter 6 (hereinafter cited as Bennett, *Regulating Privacy*, 1992).

[68]As Bennett notes, "In nature and extent, the public concern for privacy is more striking for its cross-national similarities rather than for its differences" (Bennett, *Regulating Privacy*, 1992, p. 43). It is, nevertheless, noteworthy that Germans seem often to take data privacy issues a great deal more seriously than other nationalities do. A remarkable case in point is the high response rate of German-based organizations and individuals to a pan-European Union questionnaire issued by the Commission of the European Communities in 2002 regarding certain data privacy issues. Respondents registering Germany as their place of residence accounted for approximately 40 percent of the total number of respondents for each questionnaire. See http://europa.eu.int/comm/internal_market/en/dataprot/ lawreport/docs/consultation-controllers_en.pdf (accessed Nov. 4, 2003); and http://europa. eu.int/comm/internal_market/en/ dataprot/lawreport/docs/consultation-citizens_en.pdf (accessed Nov. 4, 2003).

[69]See generally Bygrave, *Data Protection Law*, 2002, p. 110 and references cited therein; and Bennett and Raab, *The Governance of Privacy*, 2003, pp. 56-65 and references cited therein. The survey material referenced there derives mainly from the United States, Canada, Australia, Norway, Denmark, and the United Kingdom. Survey material from Hungary seems largely to fit with the findings from the other countries: see I. Székely, "New Rights and Old Concerns: Information Privacy in Public Opinion and in the Press in Hungary," *Informatization and the Public Sector* 2:99-113, 1994 . Note, though, that surveys of public attitudes to privacy can suffer from methodological weaknesses that make it unwise to rely on their results as wholly accurate indications of public thinking: see further, for example, William H. Dutton and Robert G. Meadow, "A Tolerance for Surveillance: American Public Opinion Concerning

abstract.[70] The concern for privacy is often accompanied by considerable pessimism over existing levels of privacy, along with a lack of trust that organizations will not misuse personal information.[71] Privacy concern tends to cut across a broad range of political leanings (within liberal democratic ideology),[72] although there are occasional indications of statistically significant variation in attitudes to privacy issues based on party or political attachments.[73] In terms of the roles played by other demographic variables, such as age, sex, and income level, results appear to vary a great deal from country to country and survey to survey.[74]

The survey evidence points toward increasing public sensitivity to the potential misuse of personal information. Certainly, one finds, for example, concrete instances in which items of information that previously were routinely publicized are now subject to relatively stringent requirements of confidentiality.[75] Perhaps more interesting, however, is whether indications exist of an opposite development—that is, an increasing acclimatization of people to situations in which they are required to divulge personal information and a concomitant adjustment of what they

---

Privacy and Civil Liberties," pp. 147-170 in Karen B. Levitan, ed., *Government Infostructures*, Greenwood Press, Westport, Conn., 1987.

[70]Privacy concerns tend often to be of second-order significance for the public, with problems such as public safety, unemployment, and financial security being ranked as more important: see Bygrave, *Data Protection Law*, 2002, p. 110 and references cited therein.

[71]Bygrave, *Data Protection Law*, 2002, p. 111 and references cited therein.

[72]See further, Bennett, *Regulating Privacy*, 1992, especially p. 147.

[73]See, for example, H. Becker,"Bürger in der modernen Informationsgesellschaft" [Citizens in the Modern Information Society], pp. 343-490 in *Informationsgesellschaft oder Überwachungsstaat*, Hessendienst der Staatskanzlei, Wiesbaden, 1984; pp. 415-416 cite survey results from (West) Germany showing that supporters of the Green Party (Die Grünen) were more likely to view data privacy as important than were supporters of the more conservative political parties.

[74]Compare, for example, I. Székely, "New Rights and Old Concerns: Information Privacy in Public Opinion and in the Press in Hungary," *Informatization and the Public Sector* 2:99-113, 1994 (Hungarian survey results appear to show that demographic variables play little role in determining public attitudes to privacy issues), with Australian Federal Privacy Commissioner, *Community Attitudes to Privacy*, Information Paper 3, Australian Government Publishing Service, Canberra, 1995 (demographic variables play a significant role in Australian survey results). Compare also, e.g., the latter study (privacy of personal information found to be more important to high-income than low-income earners) with L. Harris and Associates in association with A.F. Westin, *Harris-Equifax Health Information Privacy Survey 1993*, Equifax, Atlanta, Ga., 1994, p. 15 (low-income earners express higher concern about privacy than high-income groups, except in relation to medical privacy issues).

[75]See, for example, H. Torgersen, "Forskning og personvern" [Research and Privacy], pp. 223-239 in R.D. Blekeli and K.S. Selmer, eds., *Data og personvern*, Universitetsforlaget, Oslo, 1977; p. 237 notes that, in Norway, the quantity and detail of information publicly disclosed in connection with student matriculation were far greater in the 1960s than in the mid-1970s and onward.

perceive as problematic for their privacy. Unfortunately, there seems to be little survey evidence addressing this point.

Nevertheless, it is pertinent to note that public concern for privacy has rarely resulted in mass political movements with privacy protection per se high on their agenda.[76] In most Western countries and even more so on the international plane, the actual formulation of law and policy on data privacy has typically been the project of a small elite.[77]

It is tempting to draw a parallel between this state of affairs and the way in which privacy concerns were articulated and politically pushed in the 19th century, at least in the United States and Germany. The movement for the legal recognition of privacy rights in those countries and at that time had largely genteel, elitist traits. It was, as Westin observes, "essentially a protest by spokesmen for patrician values against the rise of the political and cultural values of 'mass society.'"[78] This would be, however, an inaccurate (and unfair) characterization of the modern "data privacy elite." The agenda of the latter is strongly democratic and egalitarian; it is much more concerned about the welfare of the citoyen (citizen) than simply about that of the bourgeois. And it self-consciously draws much of its power from the privacy concerns of the general public.[79]

B.4 REGULATORY POLICY ON PROTECTION OF PRIVACY AND PERSONAL INFORMATION (DATA PRIVACY)

A number of legal instruments exist at both international and national levels that deal directly with data privacy.[80] In addition, some instruments

---

[76]See generally, Bennett, *Regulating Privacy*, 1992, pp. 146, 243.

[77]Bennett, *Regulating Privacy*, 1992, p. 127 et seq.

[78]Westin, *Privacy and Freedom*, 1967, pp. 348-349. See further, James Barron, "Warren and Brandeis, The Right to Privacy (1890): Demystifying a Landmark Citation," *Suffolk U.L. Rev.* 13:875, 1979; and D.W. Howe, "Victorian Culture in America," pp. 3-28 in D.W. Howe, ed., *Victorian America*, University of Pennsylvania Press, Philadelphia, 1976. For a similar critique with respect to the ideological and class roots of German "Persönlichkeitsrecht," see P. Schwerdtner, *Das Persönlichkeitsrecht in der deutschen Zivilordnung*, J. Schweitzer Verlag, Berlin, 1977, especially pp. 7, 85, and 92.

[79]See also Bennett, *Regulating Privacy*, 1992, p. 129.

[80]At the risk of stating the obvious: to describe these instruments as dealing directly with "data privacy" is to indicate that they specifically regulate all or most stages in the processing of personal data—i.e., data that relate to, and facilitate identification of, an individual, physical/natural person (or, sometimes, collective entity)—with a principal formal aim of safeguarding the privacy and/or related interests of that person. The main rules applied to the processing of such data embody a set of largely procedural, "fair information" principles stipulating, e.g., the manner and purposes of data processing, measures to ensure adequate quality of the data, and measures to ensure transparency of the processing in relation to the person to whom the data relate ("data subject"). For more detail, see generally, Bygrave, *Data Protection Law*, 2002, particularly Chapters 1, 3, 5, 18, and 19.

are not legally binding in a formal sense but are nevertheless highly influential in the development of regulatory policy with respect to privacy.

The legal systems of many, if not most, countries contain a variety of rules that embody elements of the basic principles typically found in data privacy instruments or that can otherwise promote these principles' realization, albeit in incidental, ad hoc ways.[81] However, what is primarily of interest in the following overview is the degree to which countries have adopted rule sets that are directly concerned with promoting data privacy. Also of primary interest is the degree to which countries provide for the establishment of independent agencies (hereinafter termed "data privacy agencies") specifically charged with overseeing the implementation and/or further development of these rule sets.

B.4.1 International Instruments

The formal normative basis for data privacy laws derives mainly from catalogues of fundamental human rights set out in certain multilateral instruments, notably the Universal Declaration of Human Rights (UDHR)[82] and the International Covenant on Civil and Political Rights (ICCPR),[83] along with the main regional human rights treaties, such as the European Convention on Human Rights and Fundamental Freedoms (ECHR)[84] and the American Convention on Human Rights (ACHR).[85] All of these instruments—with the exception of the African Charter on Human and People's Rights[86]—expressly recognize privacy as a fundamental human right.[87] Not all human rights catalogues from outside the Western, liberal-democratic sphere repeat the African Charter's omission of privacy. For example, the Cairo Declaration on Human Rights in Islam[88] expressly recognizes a right to privacy for individuals (see the Declaration's Article 18[b]-[c]).

The right to privacy in these instruments is closely linked to the ideals and principles of data privacy laws, although other human rights, such as

---

[81]Rules concerning computer security, breach of confidence, defamation, and intellectual property are examples.

[82]United Nations (UN) General Assembly Resolution 217 A (III) of Dec. 10, 1948.

[83]UN General Assembly Resolution 2200A (XXI) of Dec. 16, 1966; in force March 23, 1976.

[84]European Treaty Series No. 5; opened for signature Nov. 4, 1950; in force Sept. 3, 1953.

[85]OAS Treaty Series No. 36; adopted Nov. 22, 1969; in force July 18, 1978.

[86]OAU Doc. CAB/LEG/67/3 rev. 5; adopted June 27, 1981; in force Oct. 21, 1986.

[87]See Universal Declaration of Human Rights (UDHR), Article 12; International Covenant on Civil and Political Rights (ICCPR), Article 17; European Court of Human Rights (ECHR), Article 8; American Convention on Human Rights (ACHR), Article 11. See also Article V of the American Declaration of the Rights and Duties of Man (OAS Resolution XXX; adopted 1948).

[88]Adopted Aug. 5, 1990 (UN Doc. A/45/421/5/21797, p. 199).

freedom from discrimination and freedom of expression, are relevant, too. The special importance of the right to privacy in this context is reflected in the fact that data privacy laws frequently single out protection of that right as central to their formal rationale.[89] It is also reflected in case law developed pursuant to ICCPR Article 17 and ECHR Article 8: both provisions have been authoritatively construed as requiring national implementation of the basic principles of data privacy laws.[90] Indeed, these provisions function, in effect, as data privacy instruments in themselves. However, case law has yet to apply them in ways that add significantly to the principles already found in other data privacy laws, and in some respects the protection that they are currently held to offer falls short of the protection afforded by many of the latter instruments.[91]

In terms of other international legal instruments, there does not exist a truly global convention or treaty dealing specifically with data privacy. Calls for such an instrument are occasionally made, although there are no concrete plans underway to draft one. The closest to such an instrument is the Council of Europe Convention for the Protection of Individuals with Regard to Automatic Processing of Personal Data (hereinafter termed the "CoE Convention").[92] While this is a European instrument, it is envisaged to be potentially more than an agreement between European states, as it

---

[89]See, for example, Article 1 of the Council of Europe Convention on data privacy (note 49 above), Article 2 of Belgium's 1992 Act Concerning the Protection of Personal Privacy in Relation to the Processing of Personal Data (Wet van 8. December 1992 tot bescherming van de persoonlijke levenssfeer ten opzichte van de verwerking van persoonsgegevens/Loi du 8. décembre 1992 relative à la protection de la vie privée à l'égard des traitements de données à caractère personnel); and the preamble to (and title of) Australia's federal Privacy Act of 1988.

[90]In relation to Article 17 of the ICCPR, see General Comment 16 issued by the Human Rights Committee on March 23, 1988 (UN Doc. A/43/40, pp. 180-183), paragraphs 7 and 10. In relation to Article 8 of the ECHR, see the judgments of the European Court of Human Rights in, e.g., *Klass v. Germany* (1978), Series A of the Publications of the European Court of Human Rights ("A"), 28; *Malone v. United Kingdom* (1984), A 82; *Leander v. Sweden* (1987), A 116; *Gaskin v. United Kingdom* (1989), A 160; *Kruslin v. France* (1990), A 176-A; *Niemitz v. Germany* (1992), A 251-B; *Amann v. Switzerland* (2000), Reports of Judgments and Decisions of the European Court of Human Rights 2000-I. See further, L.A. Bygrave, "Data Protection Pursuant to the Right to Privacy in Human Rights Treaties," *International Journal of Law and Information Technology* 6:247-284, 1998.

[91]For instance, the right of persons to gain access to information kept about them by others is more limited under Article 8 of the ECHR than it usually is under ordinary data privacy laws. Further, uncertainty surrounds the degree to which Article 8 may be applied in cases involving data-processing practices of the *private* sector. See further, L.A. Bygrave, "Data Protection Pursuant to the Right to Privacy in Human Rights Treaties," 1998.

[92]European Treaty Series No. 108; adopted Jan. 28, 1981; in force Oct. 1, 1985. Further on the CoE Convention, see, for example, F. Henke, *Die Datenschutzkonvention des Europarates* [The Data Protection Convention of the Council of Europe], Peter Lang, Frankfurt am Main/ Bern/New York, 1986; and Bygrave, *Data Protection Law*, 2002, especially p. 32.

is open to ratification by states not belonging to the Council of Europe (see Article 23 of the CoE Convention). However, it has yet to be ratified by a nonmember state.[93]

Within the European Union, several directives on data privacy have been adopted, the first and most important of which is Directive 95/46/EC on the Protection of Individuals with Regard to the Processing of Personal Data and on the Free Movement of Such Data (hereinafter termed the "E.U. Directive").[94] This instrument is binding on E.U. member states. It is also binding on nonmember states (Norway, Iceland, and Liechtenstein) that are party to the 1992 Agreement on the European Economic Area (EEA). It is further binding on the 10, largely East European states (Slovak Republic, Czech Republic, Malta, Poland, Hungary, Lithuania, Latvia, Estonia, Slovenia, and Cyprus) that became full-fledged members of the Union on May 1, 2004. In other words, the directive is primarily a European instrument for European states. Nevertheless, it exercises considerable influence over other countries, not least because it prohibits (with some qualifications) the transfer of personal data to those countries unless they provide "adequate" levels of data privacy (see Articles 25-26 of the E.U. Directive).[95] As shown below, many non-European countries are passing legislation in order to meet this adequacy criterion at least partly.[96]

---

[93]Note, though, that the European Union, or, more accurately, European Communities, has signaled a wish to accede to the CoE Convention. Amendments to the convention were adopted on June 15, 1999, in order to permit accession by the European Communities, but they are not yet in force. See further, Bygrave, *Data Protection Law*, 2002, p. 32.

[94]Adopted Oct. 24, 1995, Official Journal of the European Communities (O.J.), L 281, Nov. 23, 1995, p. 31 et seq. Two sectoral directives on data privacy have also been adopted. The first of these was Directive 97/66/EC of Dec. 15, 1997, concerning the Processing of Personal Data and the Protection of Privacy in the Telecommunications Sector (O.J. L 24, Jan. 30, 1998, p. 1 et seq.). This has now been replaced by Directive 2002/58/EC of July 12, 2002, concerning the Processing of Personal Data and the Protection of Privacy in the Electronic Communications Sector (O.J. L 201, July 31, 2002, p. 37 et seq.). Further on the general directive, see, for instance, D.I. Bainbridge, *EC Data Protection Directive*, Butterworths, London/Dublin/Edinburgh, 1996; S. Simitis, "From the Market to the Polis: The EU Directive on the Protection of Personal Data," *Iowa Law Review* 80:445-469, 1995; U. Damman and S. Simitis, *EG-Datenschutzrichtlinie: Kommentar* [E.C. Directive on Data Protection: Commentary] Nomos Verlagsgesellschaft, Baden-Baden, 1997; and Bygrave, *Data Protection Law*, 2002.

[95]See further, e.g., P.M. Schwartz, "European Data Protection Law and Restrictions on International Data Flows," *Iowa Law Review* 80:471-496, 1995, especially p. 483 et seq.; European Union, Data Protection Working Party, "Transfers of Personal Data to Third Countries: Applying Articles 25 and 26 of the EU Data Protection Directive," working document adopted July 24, 1998, available at http://europa.eu.int/comm/internal_market/privacy/docs/wpdocs/1998/wp12_en.pdf (accessed Oct. 11, 2003); C. Kuner, *European Data Privacy Law and Online Business*, Oxford University Press, Oxford, 2003, Chapter 4; and Bennett and Raab, *The Governance of Privacy*, 2003, pp. 81-85.

[96]Further on this influence: P.P. Swire and R.E. Litan, *None of Your Business: World Data Flows, Electronic Commerce, and the European Privacy Directive*, Brookings Institution Press,

Furthermore, the E.U. Directive stipulates that the data privacy law of an E.U. state may apply outside the European Union in certain circumstances, most notably if a data controller,[97] based outside the European Union, utilizes "equipment" located in the state to process personal data for purposes other than merely transmitting the data through that state (see E.U. Directive Article 4[1][c]).[98] All of these provisions give an impression that the European Union, in effect, is legislating for the world.[99]

Apart from the above legal instruments, there exist numerous international and regional instruments on data privacy that take the form of guidelines, recommendations, or codes of practice. Although "soft law" only, some of them carry a great deal of political and/or commercial weight; accordingly, they exercise considerable influence on the development of data privacy law. For advanced industrial states generally, the most significant of these instruments are the 1980 Guidelines Governing the Protection of Privacy and Transborder Flows of Personal Data (hereinafter termed "OECD Guidelines"), adopted by the Organisation for Economic Co-operation and Development (OECD).[100] The OECD Guidelines contain a set of data privacy principles similar to those stipulated in the CoE Convention. These guidelines have been very influential in the drafting of data privacy laws and standards in non-European jurisdictions

---

Washington, D.C., 1998; G. Shaffer, "Globalization and Social Protection: The Impact of E.U. and International Rules in Ratcheting Up of U.S. Privacy Standards," *Yale Journal of International Law* 25:1-88, 2000; and N. Waters, "The European Influence on Privacy Law and Practice," *Privacy Law and Policy Reporter* 9:150-155, 2003.

[97]A "data controller" is a person or organization that determines the purposes and means of processing personal data: see E.U. Directive, Article 2(d).

[98]See further, L.A. Bygrave, "Determining Applicable Law Pursuant to European Data Protection Legislation," *Computer Law and Security Report* 16:252-257, 2000; Kuner, *European Data Privacy Law and Online Business*, 2003, Chapter 3; and A. Charlesworth, "Information Privacy Law in the European Union: E Pluribus Unum or Ex Uno Plures?," *Hastings Law Journal* 54:931-969, 2003.

[99]Equally, they nourish accusations of "regulatory overreaching." See particularly the criticism of Article 4(1)(c) in Bygrave, "Determining Applicable Law Pursuant to European Data Protection Legislation," 2000. See also the more general criticism (from U.S. and Australian quarters) in A. Lukas, "Safe Harbor or Stormy Waters? Living with the EU Data Protection Directive," Trade Policy Analysis Paper No. 16, Cato Institute, Washington, D.C., Oct. 30, 2001; P. Ford, "Implementing the EC Directive on Data Protection—An Outside Perspective," *Privacy Law and Policy Reporter* 9:141-149, 2003.

[100]Adopted by OECD Council on Sept. 23, 1980 (OECD Doc. C(80)58/FINAL). For further discussion of the Guidelines, see P. Seipel, "Transborder Flows of Personal Data: Reflections on the OECD Guidelines," *Transnational Data Report* 4:32-44, 1981. The OECD has issued other guidelines also relating, albeit more indirectly, to data privacy: see *Guidelines for the Security of Information Systems* (adopted Nov. 26, 1992)—now replaced by *Guidelines for the Security of Information Systems and Networks: Towards a Culture of Security* (adopted July 25, 2002); *Guidelines for Cryptography Policy* (adopted March 27, 1997); and *Guidelines for Consumer Protection in the Context of Electronic Commerce* (adopted Dec. 9, 1999).

such as Australia, New Zealand, and Canada.[101] They have also been formally endorsed—but not necessarily implemented—by numerous companies and trade associations in the United States.[102] Furthermore, they constitute an important point of departure for the ongoing efforts by the Asia-Pacific Economic Cooperation (APEC) to draft a set of common data privacy principles for jurisdictions in the Asia-Pacific region.[103]

Of potentially broader reach are the United Nations (UN) Guidelines Concerning Computerized Personal Data Files (hereinafter termed "UN Guidelines"), adopted in 1990.[104] The UN Guidelines are intended to encourage the enactment of data privacy laws in UN member states lacking such legislation. These guidelines are also aimed at encouraging international organizations—both governmental and nongovernmental—to process personal data in a responsible, fair, and "privacy-friendly" manner. However, the UN Guidelines seem to have had little practical effect relative to the OECD Guidelines and the other instruments canvassed above.[105] Nevertheless, their adoption underlines the reality that data privacy is not simply a "First World," Western concern. Moreover, in several respects, the principles in the UN Guidelines go farther than some of the other international instruments.[106]

Note should also be taken of the numerous recommendations and codes that are of sectoral application only. The CoE Convention, for

---

[101]Reference to the OECD Guidelines is made in the preambles to both Australia's federal Privacy Act of 1988 and New Zealand's Privacy Act of 1993. Further on the OECD Guidelines' importance for Australian policy, see Ford, "Implementing the EC Directive on Data Protection—An Outside Perspective," 2003. In Canada, the OECD Guidelines formed the basis for the Canadian Standards Association's Model Code for the Protection of Personal Information (CAN/CSA-Q830-96), adopted in March 1996. The Model Code has been incorporated into Canadian legislation as Schedule 1 to the Personal Information Protection and Electronic Documents Act of 2000.

[102]See, for example, R.M. Gellman, "Fragmented, Incomplete, and Discontinuous: The Failure of Federal Privacy Regulatory Proposals and Institutions," *Software Law Journal* 6:199-238, 1993.

[103]See generally, the documentation collated at http://www.apecsec.org.sg/apec/documents _reports/electronic_commerce_steering_group/2003.html (accessed Nov. 8, 2003). See also G. Greenleaf, "Australia's APEC Privacy Initiative: The Pros and Cons of 'OECD Lite,'" *Privacy Law and Policy Reporter* 10:1-6, 2003; G. Greenleaf, "APEC Privacy Principles Version 2: Not Quite So Lite, and NZ Wants OECD Full Strength," *Privacy Law and Policy Reporter* 10:45-48, 2003. Further on APEC generally, see http://www.apecsec.org.sg (accessed Nov. 2, 2003).

[104]On the background to the OECD Guidelines, see, for instance, J. Michael, *Privacy and Human Rights: An International and Comparative Study, with Special Reference to Developments in Information Technology*, UNESCO/Dartmouth Publishing Company, Paris/Aldershot, 1994, pp. 21-26.

[105]This is partly reflected in the fact that they are frequently overlooked in data privacy discourse, at least in Scandinavia; see Bygrave, *Data Protection Law*, 2002, p. 33 and references cited therein.

[106]For details, see Bygrave, *Data Protection Law*, 2002, pp. 73, 350.

instance, has issued a large range of sector-specific recommendations to supplement and extend the rules in its convention on data privacy. These recommendations cover, inter alia, the police sector,[107] employment,[108] research and statistics,[109] and telecommunications.[110] Another noteworthy instance is the code of practice issued by the International Labor Organization (ILO) on data privacy in the workplace.[111]

The principal international instruments dealing specifically with data privacy tend to be aimed at encouraging not just the enactment of national rules but also the harmonization of these rules. In turn, the harmonization objective has several rationales, some of which are concerned not so much with enhancing data privacy as with facilitating the flow of personal data across national borders in order to maintain international commerce, freedom of expression, and intergovernment cooperation.[112] The latter concerns arise because many national data privacy laws—mainly European—have long operated with rules providing for restrictions of data flow to countries not offering levels of data privacy similar to those of the "exporting" jurisdiction.[113]

While the practical effect of such rules on actual transborder data flow tends to have been negligible for the most part,[114] the potential impact of these rules has caused much consternation, particularly for business interests. Concern to minimize this impact in order to safeguard trade is most prominent in the OECD Guidelines and E.U. Directive.[115] The

---

[107]Recommendation No. R (87) 15 Regulating the Use of Personal Data in the Police Sector, adopted Sept. 17, 1987.

[108]Recommendation No. R (89) 2 on the Protection of Personal Data Used for Employment Purposes, adopted Jan. 18, 1989.

[109]Recommendation No. R (83) 10 on the Protection of Personal Data Used for Scientific Research and Statistics, adopted Sept. 23, 1983, and Recommendation No. R (97) 18 on the Protection of Personal Data Collected and Processed for Statistical Purposes, adopted Sept. 30, 1997.

[110]Recommendation No. R (95) 4 on the Protection of Personal Data in the Area of Telecommunications Services, with Particular Reference to Telephone Services, adopted Feb. 7, 1995.

[111]*Protection of Workers' Personal Data*, I.L.O., Geneva, 1997.

[112]See generally, Bygrave, *Data Protection Law*, 2002, p. 40, and references cited therein.

[113]See further, inter alia, A.C.M. Nugter, *Transborder Flow of Personal Data Within the EC*, Kluwer Law and Taxation Publishers, Deventer/Boston, 1990; R. Ellger, *Der Datenschutz im grenzüberschreitende Datenverkehr: Eine rechtsvergleichende und kollisionsrechtliche Untersuchung* [Data Protection with Respect to Cross-Border Data Traffic: A Comparative Law and Conflict-of-Laws Study], Nomos Verlagsgesellschaft, Baden-Baden, 1990 (hereinafter cited as Ellger, *Der Datenschutz im grenzüberschreitende Datenverkehr*, 1990); and Schwartz, "European Data Protection Law and Restrictions on International Data Flows," 1995.

[114]See, for example, the extensive survey in Ellger, *Der Datenschutz im grenzüberschreitende Datenverkehr*, 1990.

[115]See Bygrave, *Data Protection Law*, 2002, p. 40 and references cited therein.

latter goes the farthest in securing transborder data flow by prohibiting E.U. member states from instituting privacy-related restrictions on data transfer to other member states (see E.U. Directive, Article 1[2]). This prohibition is primarily grounded in the need to facilitate realization of the European Union's internal market.[116] At the same time, however, the E.U. Directive goes the farthest of the international instruments in restricting transborder data flow, through its qualified prohibition of data transfer to non-E.U. states that fail to provide "adequate" levels of data privacy (E.U. Directive Article 25).

The adequacy criterion could be regarded as evidence that economic protectionism forms part of the E.U. Directive's agenda—that is, it reflects a desire to protect European industry from foreign competition. Allegations of economic protectionism have been directed at earlier European data privacy regimes,[117] but little solid evidence exists to support them.[118] While there is perhaps more evidence linking the origins of the E.U. Directive to protectionist concerns, the linkage is still tenuous.[119] Considerably more-solid grounds exist for viewing the adequacy criterion as prima facie indication that the directive is seriously concerned with safeguarding privacy interests and rights. This concern is also manifest in the preamble to the directive,[120] in recent case law from the European Court of Justice,[121] and increasingly in the E.U. legal system generally. Particularly noteworthy is the growing recognition in the European Union that the protection of data privacy is in itself (i.e., separate from the broader right to privacy) a basic human right.[122]

Despite their harmonizing objectives, the international instruments tend to leave countries a significant degree of leeway in the development

---

[116]See particularly Recitals 3, 5, and 7 in the preamble to the E.U. Directive.

[117]See, e.g., K.R. Pinegar, "Privacy Protection Acts: Privacy Protectionism or Economic Protectionism?" *International Business Lawyer* 12:183-188, 1984; R.P. McGuire, "The Information Age: An Introduction to Transborder Data Flow," *Jurimetrics Journal* 20:1-7, 1979-1980; J.M. Eger, "Emerging Restrictions on Transborder Data Flow: Privacy Protection or Non-Tariff Trade Barriers," *Law and Policy in International Business* 10:1055-1103, 1978.

[118]See the discussion in Bygrave, *Data Protection Law*, 2002, pp. 114-115 and references cited therein.

[119]See the discussion in Bygrave, *Data Protection Law*, 2002, pp. 114-115 and references cited therein.

[120]See particularly, Recitals 2, 3, 10, and 11.

[121]See judgment of May 20, 2003, in Joined Cases C-465/00, C-138/01, and C-139/01, *Österreichischer Rundfunk and Others* [2003] ECR I-0000, particularly paragraph 71 et seq.

[122]See Charter of Fundamental Rights of the European Union, adopted Dec. 7, 2000 (O.J. C 364, Dec. 18, 2000, p. 1 et seq.), Article 8 (providing for a right to protection of personal data) and Article 7 (providing for the right to respect for private and family life). See also the right to protection of personal data in Article 50 of the draft treaty establishing a constitution for Europe (Conv. 850/03, Brussels, July 18, 2003; available at http://european-convention.eu.int/docs/Treaty/cv00850.en03.pdf, accessed Oct. 25, 2003).

of their respective data privacy regimes. This is especially the case with the "soft law" instruments, but the legally binding instruments also allow for considerable national flexibility. The CoE Convention is not intended to be self-executing, and it permits derogations on significant points.[123] The E.U. Directive has more prescriptive bite than its counterparts, but it is still aimed only at facilitating an "approximation" as opposed to the complete uniformity of national laws (see particularly Recital 9 in its preamble). Accordingly, it leaves E.U. member states considerable margin for maneuver.[124]

Of all of the instruments canvassed above, the E.U. Directive has become the leading trendsetter and benchmark for data privacy around the world. Not only is it shaping national data protection regimes, it is also shaping international instruments. For example, the CoE Convention has recently been supplemented by a protocol containing rules that essentially duplicate the rules in the E.U. Directive dealing respectively with the flow of personal data to nonmember states and with the competence of national data privacy authorities.[125] Outside Europe, clear traces of the E.U. Directive are to be found in the draft Guidelines on the Protection of Personal Information and Privacy drawn up by the Asia Pacific Telecommunity (APT)[126] and in the draft Asia-Pacific Privacy Charter drawn up by the Asia-Pacific Privacy Charter Council (APPCC).[127]

Nevertheless, the leadership status of the E.U. Directive could face a serious challenge in the Asia-Pacific region if APEC is able to agree on a common set of data privacy principles for its 21 member states. There are indications that the principles are likely to be inspired more by the OECD Guidelines than by the E.U. Directive, and at the same time they are likely to be less privacy-protective than the directive and possibly than the guidelines.[128] Work on the principles signals a readiness among

---

[123]See P. Henke, *Die Datenschutzkonvention des Europarates*, 1986, especially pp. 57-60; and Bygrave, *Data Protection Law*, 2002, p. 34.

[124]See further, Bygrave, *Data Protection Law*, 2002, p. 34 and references cited therein. See also Section 4.6.

[125]Additional Protocol to the Convention for the Protection of Individuals with regard to Automatic Processing of Personal Data (ETS No. 108) regarding supervisory authorities and transborder data flows (adopted May 23, 2001; not yet in force).

[126]Draft of September 2003; on file with author but not publicly available. Further on the APT, see http://www.aptsec.org (accessed Oct. 26, 2003).

[127]See Version 1.0 of the charter, dated Sept. 3, 2003; on file with author but not publicly available. For more on the APPCC and its work, see G. Greenleaf, "The Asia-Pacific Privacy Charter Council: A Regional 'Civil Society' Initiative," *Privacy Law and Policy Reporter* 10:49-50, 2003; and the APPCC home page at http://www.austlii.edu.au/au/special/cyberlpc/appcc (accessed Oct. 25, 2003).

[128]See G. Greenleaf, "Australia's APEC Privacy Initiative: The Pros and Cons of 'OECD Lite'," *Privacy Law and Policy Reporter* 10:1-6, 2003. Cf. G. Greenleaf, "APEC Privacy Prin-

many of the APEC states to forge their own approach to data privacy without necessarily conforming to European norms. This approach would appear to foster data privacy regimes less because of concern to protect basic human rights than over concern to engender consumer confidence in business.[129]

B.4.2 National Instruments

Well over 30 countries have enacted data privacy laws, and their number is growing steadily.[130] Most of these countries are European. Indeed, Europe is home to the oldest, most comprehensive, and most bureaucratically cumbersome data privacy laws at both national and provincial levels. Moreover, as shown above, Europe—through its supranational institutions—is also a springboard for the most ambitious and extensive international initiatives in the field.

Common points of departure for national data privacy regimes in Europe are as follows:

- Coverage of both public and private sectors;
- Coverage of both automated and manual systems for processing personal data, largely irrespective of how the data are structured;
- Application of broad definitions of "personal data";
- Application of extensive sets of procedural principles, some of which are rarely found in data privacy regimes elsewhere;[131]
- More stringent regulation of certain categories of sensitive data (e.g., data relating to philosophical beliefs, sexual preferences, ethnic origins);

---

ciples Version 2: Not Quite So Lite, and NZ Wants OECD Full Strength," *Privacy Law and Policy Reporter* 10:45-48, 2003 (noting that more recent drafts of the principles have been strengthened, though certainly not to the level of the E.U. Directive).

[129]See R. Tang, "Personal Data Privacy: The Asian Agenda," speech given at 25th International Conference of Data Protection and Privacy Commissioners, Sydney, Sept. 10, 2003; available at http://www.privacyconference2003.org/program.asp#psa (accessed Oct. 10, 2003).

[130]See generally, Electronic Privacy Information Center and Privacy International, *Privacy and Human Rights 2003*, Electronic Privacy Information Center and Privacy International, Washington, D.C., 2003, which gives a fairly up-to-date overview of the state of data privacy regimes in more than 50 countries. A complementary, though less comprehensive, overview is given in M. Henry, ed., *International Privacy, Publicity and Personality Laws*, Butterworths, London, 2001.

[131]An example of a principle that is unique to European laws concerns fully automated profiling. The principle is that fully automated assessments of a person's character should not form the sole basis of decisions that impinge on the person's interests. The principle is embodied in Article 15 of the E.U. Directive: see further, Bygrave, *Data Protection Law*, 2002, pp. 319-328.

• Restrictions on the transborder flow of personal data;
• Establishment of independent data privacy agencies with broad discretionary powers to oversee the implementation and development of data privacy rules;
• Channeling of privacy complaints to these agencies rather than to the courts;
• Extensive subjection of data processing to the notification and/or licensing requirements administered by the data privacy agencies;
• Extensive use of "opt-in" requirements for valid consent by data subjects; and
• Little use of industry-developed codes of practice.[132]

The majority of these characteristics were originally typical for data privacy laws in West European countries. Owing largely to the E.U. Directive, they are now also typical for the laws of most East European countries. Nevertheless, it is important to note that each country has its own unique mix of rules;[133] concomitantly, a good deal of variation exists in the degree to which each country shares the above-listed traits.[134] For example, the Netherlands has always made relatively extensive use of

---

[132]See further, for example, Bygrave, *Data Protection Law*, 2002, especially Chapters 2 through 4, and Kuner, *European Data Privacy Law and Online Business*, 2003. For older accounts, see, for example, Hondius, *Emerging Data Protection in Europe*, 1975; and H. Burkert, "Institutions of Data Protection—An Attempt at a Functional Explanation of European National Data Protection Laws," *Computer/Law Journal* 3:167-188, 1981-1982.

[133]For in-depth treatment of, e.g., U.K. law, see R. Jay and A. Hamilton, *Data Protection: Law and Practice*, Sweet and Maxwell, London, 2003; of German law, see S. Simitis, *Kommentar zum Bundesdatenschutzgesetz* [Commentary on the Alliance Data Protection Law], 2003; of Italian law, see G. Buttarelli, *Banche dati e tutela della riservatezza: La privacy nella Società dell'Informazione* [Data Banks and the Protection of Confidentiality: The Privacy of Information in Society], Giuffrè Editore, Milan, 1997; of Swiss law, see U. Maurer and N.P. Vogt, eds., *Kommentar zum Schweizerischen Datenschutzgesetz* [Commentary on the Swiss Data Protection Act], Helbing and Lichtenhahn, Basel/Frankfurt am Main, 1995. For overviews of the data privacy laws of Denmark, Finland, Norway, and Sweden, see P. Blume, ed., *Nordic Data Protection*, DJØF Publishing, Copenhagen, 2001. Otherwise, see the more detailed analyses of Danish law in P. Blume, *Personoplysningsloven* [The Personal Data Act], Greens§Jura, Denmark, 2000; and K.K. Nielsen and H. Waaben, *Lov om behandling af personoplysninger—med kommentarer* [Act on Processing of Personal Data—with Commentary], Jurist-g Økonomforbundets Forlag, Copenhagen, 2001; of Norwegian law in M. Wiik Johansen, K.-B. Kaspersen, and Å.M. Bergseng Skullerud, *Personopplysningsloven. Kommentarutgave* [Personal Data Act. Commentary Edition], Universitetsforlaget, Oslo, 2001; of Swedish law in S. Öman and H.-O. Lindblom, *Personuppgiftslagen: En kommentar* [Personal Data Act: A Commentary], Norstedts Juridik, Stockholm, 2001. English translations of the principal data privacy laws of all current E.U. member states are collated in S. Simitis, U. Dammann, and M. Körner, eds., *Data Protection in the European Community: The Statutory Provisions*, Nomos Verlagsgesellschaft, Baden-Baden, 1992 (looseleaf, continually updated).

[134]See further, Korff, 2002.

industry-based codes of practice, and the E.U. Directive itself encourages greater use of such codes (see E.U. Directive, Article 27). Moreover, data privacy regimes in each country are far from static. For example, Swedish legislation originally operated with relatively extensive licensing and notification requirements; now it has dispensed entirely with a licensing scheme and cut back notification requirements to a minimum. There is movement too at a broader European level. For instance, while West European data privacy regimes have traditionally relied heavily on paternalistic control mechanisms,[135] they now show greater readiness to rely more on citizen action, supplemented by greater readiness to embrace market mechanisms for the regulation of data processing. This notwithstanding, European jurisdictions (in contrast to, say, the United States) generally still maintain a relatively non-negotiable legislative baseline for the private sector.

Across the Atlantic, Canada comes closest of the North American countries to embracing the European approach. There is now federal legislation in place in Canada to ensure the comprehensive protection of data privacy in relation to both the public and private sectors.[136] Some Canadian provinces have already enacted data privacy legislation in relation to provincial and local government agencies and/or the private sector.[137] Data privacy agencies exist at both federal and provincial levels. The Commission of the European Communities (hereinafter termed "European Commission") has formally ruled that, in general, Canada offers "adequate" protection for data privacy pursuant to Article 25 of the E.U. Directive.[138]

By contrast, the U.S. legal regime for data privacy is much more atomized. While there is fairly comprehensive legislation dealing with federal government agencies,[139] omnibus legislative solutions are eschewed with respect to the private sector. Legal protection of data privacy in relation

---

[135]That is, control exercised by government bodies (primarily data privacy agencies) on behalf and supposedly in the best interests of citizens (data subjects).

[136]See Privacy Act of 1982; Personal Information Protection and Electronic Documents Act of 2000.

[137]See, for example, Quebec's Act on Protection of Personal Information in the Private Sector of 1993.

[138]Decision 2002/2/EC of 20.12.2001 pursuant to Directive 95/46/EC of the European Parliament and of the Council on the adequate protection of personal data provided by the Canadian Personal Information Protection and Electronic Documents Act (O.J. L 2, Jan. 4, 2002, p. 13 et seq.).

[139]Most notably the Privacy Act of 1974 (P.L. 93-579) and the Computer Matching and Privacy Protection Act of 1988 (P.L. 100-503). Note also the limited protection of data privacy afforded under the Constitution as construed by the Supreme Court: see especially *Whalen v. Roe*, 429 U.S. 589 (1977). See further, for instance, Schwartz and Reidenberg, *Data Privacy Law*, 1996, Chapter 4.

to the latter takes the form of ad hoc, narrowly circumscribed, sector-specific legislation, combined with recourse to litigation based on the tort of invasion-of-privacy and/or breach-of-trade-practices legislation.[140] European-style data privacy agencies do not exist in the United States. At the same time, however, a "safe harbor" agreement has been concluded between the United States and the European Union allowing for the flow of personal data from the European Union to U.S.-based companies that voluntarily agree to abide by a set of "fair information" principles based loosely on the E.U. Directive. The scheme, which so far has attracted approximately 400 companies,[141] has been held by the European Commission to satisfy the E.U. Directive's adequacy test in Article 25.[142]

In South America, Argentina has come the farthest in developing a comprehensive legal regime for data privacy. It enacted legislation in 2000[143] modeled on the E.U. Directive and equivalent Spanish legislation and formally based on the right of habeas data provided in its Constitution (Article 43).[144] The European Commission has formally ruled that Argentina satisfies the adequacy criterion of the E.U. Directive.[145] Other South American countries, such as Brazil and Chile, also provide constitutional protections for privacy rights and habeas data, but otherwise their legislation on data privacy is relatively scant. They lack also data privacy agencies.[146]

In the Asia-Pacific region, there exist a handful of relatively comprehensive legislative regimes on data privacy—most notably those in

---

[140]See generally, the overview in Schwartz and Reidenberg, *Data Privacy Law*, 1996, especially Chapters 9 through 14.

[141]See http://web.ita.doc.gov/safeharbor/shlist.nsf/webPages/safe+harbor+list (accessed Nov. 6, 2003).

[142]Decision 2000/520/EC of July 26, 2000, pursuant to Directive 95/46/EC of the European Parliament and of the Council on the adequacy of the protection provided by the safe harbor privacy principles and related frequently asked questions issued by the U.S. Department of Commerce (O.J. L 215, Aug. 25, 2000, p. 7 et seq.).

[143]Law for the Protection of Personal Data of 2000.

[144]See further Electronic Privacy Information Center and Privacy International, *Privacy and Human Rights*, 2003, pp. 132-139 (hereinafter cited as Electronic Privacy Information Center and Privacy International, *Privacy and Human Rights 2003*, 2003). The right of habeas data is, in general, designed to protect the image, privacy, honor, information self-determination, and freedom of information of a person. Enforcement of the right is provided by granting an individual the right to petition a court to find out what information is being held or to request the correction, updating, or destruction of the personal information being held.

[145]Decision C (2003) 1731 of June 30, 2003, pursuant to Directive 95/46/EC of the European Parliament and of the Council on the adequate protection of personal data in Argentina (O.J. L 168, July 5, 2003).

[146]See further, Electronic Privacy Information Center and Privacy International, *Privacy and Human Rights 2003*, 2003, pp. 167-171, 195-197.

Australia, New Zealand, Hong Kong, Korea, and Japan.[147] Most of these jurisdictions—but not Japan—have also established data privacy agencies. New Zealand has been the fastest and perhaps most ambitious of these jurisdictions in the data privacy field; it was the first to enact data privacy legislation spanning the public and private sectors.[148] Australian, Korean, and Japanese legislation in the field was initially limited largely to regulating the data-processing activities of government agencies,[149] but it has recently been extended to cover the private sector as well.[150] However, some of these extensions still leave large gaps in private sector coverage.[151] Other aspects of the laws in question also diverge from the E.U. model(s).[152] Not surprisingly, none of the countries concerned has yet been formally recognized by the European Commission as offering adequate protection pursuant to the E.U. Directive.

Data privacy regimes in other Asia-Pacific jurisdictions tend to be rather patchy in coverage and enforcement levels. Thailand, for instance,

---

[147]Further on Australian law, see, e.g., G.L. Hughes and M. Jackson, *Hughes on Data Protection in Australia*, 2001; on New Zealand law, see E. Longworth and T. McBride, *The Privacy Act: A Guide*, GP Publications, Wellington, 1994 (hereinafter cited as Longworth and McBride, *The Privacy Act*, 1994); and P. Roth, *Privacy Law and Practice*, Butterworths/LexisNexis, Wellington, 1994 (looseleaf, regularly updated) (hereinafter cited as Roth, *Privacy Law and Practice*, 1994); on Hong Kong law, see M. Berthold and R. Wacks, *Hong Kong Data Privacy Law: Territorial Regulation in a Borderless World*, 2nd Edition, Sweet and Maxwell, Asia, 2003; on Korean law, see C.B. Yi and K.J. Ok, "Korea's Personal Information Protection Laws," *Privacy Law and Policy Reporter* 9:172-179, 2003; and H.-B. Chung, "Anti-Spam Regulations in Korea," *Privacy Law and Policy Reporter* 10:15-19, 2003; on Japanese law, see D. Case and Y. Ogiwara, "Japan's New Personal Information Protection Law," *Privacy Law and Policy Reporter* 10:77-79, 2003.

[148]See Privacy Act of 1993. Further on the act, see Longworth and McBride, *The Privacy Act*, 1994; and Roth, *Privacy Law and Practice*, 1994.

[149]For Australia, see Privacy Act of 1988; for Japan, see Act for Protection of Computer-Processed Personal Data Held by Administrative Organs of 1988; for Korea, see Act on Protection of Personal Information Maintained by Public Agencies of 1994.

[150]For Australia, see Privacy Amendment (Private Sector) Act of 2000; for Japan, see Privacy Law of 2003; for Korea, see Act on Promotion of Information and Communications Network Utilization and Information Protection . . . of 1999. Note, too, that several of the Australian states have enacted data privacy laws covering their respective government agencies and, to a lesser extent, the health sector. See, for example, Victoria's Information Privacy Act of 2000 and Health Records Act of 2001.

[151]For example, with a few exceptions, the Australian legislation does not apply to "small business operators," that is, businesses with an annual turnover of AUD$3 million or less (see federal Privacy Act, Sections 6C1, 6D, 6DA, and 6E). Another major gap is that the legislation does not cover the processing of data by employers about their present and past employees (as long as the processing is directly related to the employment relationship) (Section 7B(3)).

[152]The Japanese laws, for example, do not formally operate with a distinction between sensitive and nonsensitive data, and they make relatively extensive use of "opt-out" consent mechanisms.

has inserted data privacy rules covering the government sector in legislation dealing primarily with freedom of government information.[153] Singapore has so far decided to establish a data privacy regime based on voluntary, self-regulatory schemes that are linked with its national trust mark program.[154] The primary catalyst for the schemes seems to be commercial concerns.[155] The People's Republic of China lacks any credible data privacy regime. Some legal rules have been adopted that potentially provide indirect protection for data privacy,[156] but their operational potential is rendered nugatory by a political culture that traditionally shows scant respect for personal privacy.[157] Moreover, there is little, if any, sign that China is ready to adopt more effective data privacy rules in order to meet E.U. adequacy standards. By contrast, India is reported to be considering the enactment of a data privacy law modeled on the E.U. Directive largely owing to a fear that its burgeoning outsourcing industry will flounder without such legislation in place.[158]

Legal regimes for data privacy are least developed in the African countries, taken as a whole. As noted above, the African Charter on Human and People's Rights of 1981 omits mentioning a right to privacy in its catalog of basic human rights. Moreover, none of the African countries has enacted comprehensive data privacy laws.

Nevertheless, some countries display increasing interest in legislating on data privacy. This interest is partly due to the obligations imposed by ICCPR Article 17. It is also probably due partly to a desire to meet the adequacy requirements of E.U. Directive Articles 25 and 26. In some cases, stimulus is also provided by recent firsthand experience of mass oppression. The Republic of South Africa has come farthest along the path to establishing a comprehensive legal regime on data privacy. Express provision for a right to privacy is made in Section 14 of the South African Bill of Rights set out in Chapter 2 of its Constitution of 1996. Also included (in Section 32) is a broad right of access to information held in both the public and private sectors. Freedom-of-information legislation

---

[153]See Official Information Act of 1997, described in C. Opassiriwit, "Thailand: A Case Study in the Interrelationship Between Freedom of Information and Privacy," *Privacy Law and Policy Reporter* 9:91-95, 2002.

[154]See Model Data Protection Code for the Private Sector of 2002; Industry Content Code of 2002.

[155]For criticism of the schemes, see G. Greenleaf, "Singapore Takes the Softest Privacy Options," *Privacy Law and Policy Reporter* 8:169-173, 2002.

[156]See further, Electronic Privacy Information Center and Privacy International, *Privacy and Human Rights 2003*, 2003, pp. 197-200.

[157]Electronic Privacy Information Center and Privacy International, *Privacy and Human Rights 2003*, 2003, pp. 200-210.

[158]See A. Pedersen, "India Plans EU-Style Data Law," *Privacy Laws and Business*, May/June, No. 68, pp. 1, 3, 2003.

based on the latter right was enacted in 2002,[159] and work is proceeding on a bill for separate data privacy legislation.[160] Kenya is also drafting a new constitution containing rights similar to those in the South African Constitution.[161]

B.4.3 Relative Impact of Regulatory Regimes

A comparative evaluation of the impact of the various regulatory regimes canvassed above is both complex and beset by numerous potential pitfalls. The complexity of the task arises partly from the multiple facets of impact measurement: impact needs to be evaluated in terms of economy (i.e., the cost of setting up the regime), efficiency (i.e., the cost of the regime measured against its practical results), effectiveness (i.e., the extent to which the practical results of the regime fulfill its ultimate aims), and equity (i.e., the extent to which the regime extends protection equitably across social groups).[162]

Further complicating matters is that each country's data privacy regime consists of more than formal legal rules. While the latter, together with formal oversight mechanisms, are important constituents of a data privacy regime, they are supplemented by a complex array of other instruments and institutions—information systems, industry codes, standards, and so on—that concurrently influence the practical impact of the legal rules. The functioning of a data privacy regime (including, of course, the extent to which "law in books" equates with "law in practice") will also be shaped by a myriad of relatively informal customs and attitudes that prevail in the country concerned—for example, the extent to which the country's administrative and corporate cultures are imbued with a respect for authority or respect for "fair information" principles.[163] It goes without saying that many of these factors can be easily overlooked or misconstrued. Their existence means, for instance, that it cannot be assumed that a data privacy agency with strong formal powers will necessarily have

---

[159]See I. Currie and J. Klaaren, *The Promotion of Access to Information Act Commentary*, Siber Ink, South Africa, 2002, pp. 11, 18 (hereinafter cited as Currie and Klaaren, *The Promotion of Access to Information Act*, 2002). A unique feature of the legislation is that it provides, as a point of departure, for freedom-of-information rights not just in relation to information held by government agencies but also information held in the private sector.

[160]See Currie and Klaaren, *The Promotion of Access to Information Act*, 2002. See also Electronic Privacy Information Center and Privacy International, *Privacy and Human Rights 2003*, 2003, p. 450.

[161]See Sections 14 (right of privacy) and 47 (rights of information access and rectification) of the Draft Bill for the Constitution of the Republic of Kenya (version of Sept. 27, 2002).

[162]This classification of criteria is based on Bennett and Raab, *The Governance of Privacy*, 2003, p. 193 et seq.

[163]See generally, Flaherty, *Protecting Privacy in Surveillance Societies*, 1989.

greater success in fulfilling its objectives than that achieved by an agency with weaker formal powers.[164]

Yet another complicating element is that the regulatory approach of many data privacy agencies can obscure their positive achievements. Agencies frequently prefer to resolve conflict in a relatively quiet way, through "backroom" negotiation rather than by publicly striking out with the threatened use of punitive sanctions.[165] Further, agencies are often equally concerned, if not more so, about curbing an unrealized potential for privacy-invasive activity as about providing a remedy after such activity occurs. Measuring the impact of anticipatory forms of control can be more difficult than for reactive, ex post facto control forms.[166]

These problems notwithstanding, a large degree of consensus exists among experts in the field regarding the relative strengths of certain data privacy regimes. Part of this consensus is a view that the U.S. data privacy regime is weaker in fundamental respects than the equivalent regimes in many other countries, particularly those in Europe, which have had some influence in restricting certain data-processing practices and raising awareness of the importance of privacy safeguards.[167] For example, one conclusion of a comparative study of the data privacy regimes of Germany, the United Kingdom, Sweden, Canada, and the United States is that "the United States carries out data protection differently than other countries, and on the whole does it less well."[168] The major reasons for this finding are the lack of a U.S. federal data privacy agency, together with the paucity of comprehensive data privacy legislation covering the U.S. private sector. While the finding stems from the late 1980s, it is still pertinent and is supported by more recent analyses.[169] A basic premise of all these analyses is that the gaps in the U.S. regime are not adequately

---

[164]Again, see Flaherty, *Protecting Privacy in Surveillance Societies*, 1989. Note particularly Flaherty's finding that the German Federal Data Protection Commissioner (Bundesdaten-schutzbeauftragter)—which has only advisory powers—had, at least up until the late 1980s, a more profound impact on the federal public sector in (West) Germany than Sweden's Data Inspection Board (Datainspektionen)—which can issue legally binding orders—had on the Swedish public sector (Flaherty, *Protecting Privacy in Surveillance Societies*, 1989, p. 26).

[165]Flaherty, *Protecting Privacy in Surveillance Societies*, 1989.

[166]For further discussion on the difficulties of comparative assessment of data privacy regimes, see Bennett and Raab, *The Governance of Privacy*, 2003, Chapter 9; C.D. Raab and C.J. Bennett, "Taking the Measure of Privacy: Can Data Protection Be Evaluated?," *International Review of Administrative Sciences* 62:535-56, 1996.

[167]See, for example, Bygrave, *Data Protection Law*, 2002, Chapter 18 and examples cited therein; see also Flaherty, *Protecting Privacy in Surveillance Societies*, 1989, particularly Part 1.

[168]Flaherty, *Protecting Privacy in Surveillance Societies*, 1989, p. 305.

[169]The most extensive being Schwartz and Reidenberg, *Data Privacy Law*, 1996—see especially their conclusions at pp. 379-396.

filled by other measures, such as industry self-regulation and recourse to the courts.[170]

By contrast, the German data privacy regime is often viewed as one of the most successful.[171] It has a comprehensive, well-established legislative platform with a firm constitutional footing. One such feature is a legal requirement that organizations appoint internal privacy officers.[172] Another such feature is the regime's extensive encouragement of "systemic data protection" (Systemdatenschutz): that is, integration of data privacy concerns in the design and development of information systems architecture.[173]

German privacy legislation is backed up by comparatively effective oversight and enforcement mechanisms. The effectiveness of these mechanisms appears to be the result of a combination of factors, most notably the seriousness with which Germans generally take data privacy issues; the relatively conformist, legalistic nature of German administrative and corporate cultures; and the strong, persuasive personalities of the individuals who have been appointed data privacy commissioners, together with the considerable talents of their staff.[174]

All this said, the data privacy regime in Germany does have weak points. One weakness is the Federal Data Protection Commissioner's lack of authority to issue legally binding orders—a feature that is arguably at odds with the thrust of Directive 95/46/EC. Another, more significant, weakness is the sheer mass of rules on data privacy; the regulatory framework is so dense as to be confusing, nontransparent, and unwieldy.[175] These weaknesses mean that, despite its relative success, the German regime still falls short of meeting its policy objectives.

Data privacy regimes in most other, if not all, jurisdictions display a

---

[170]See, for example, D.A. Anderson, "The Failure of American Privacy Law," pp. 139-167 in B.S. Markesinis, ed., *Protecting Privacy*, Oxford University Press, Oxford, 1999.

[171]See, e.g., Flaherty, *Protecting Privacy in Surveillance Societies*, 1989, especially pp. 21-22.

[172]See Federal Data Protection Act, Sections 4f-4g.

[173]See particularly, Federal Data Protection Act, Sections 3a, 9; Federal Teleservices Data Protection Act of 1997 (*Gesetz über den Datenschutz bei Telediensten vom 22. juli 1997*) (as amended in 2001). For further discussion, see Bygrave, *Data Protection Law*, 2002, particularly pp. 346, 371.

[174]See generally, Flaherty, *Protecting Privacy in Surveillance Societies*, 1989, Part 1.

[175]See generally, A. Rossnagel, A. Pfitzmann, and H. Garstka, *Modernisierung des Datenschutzrechts* [Modernization of Data Protection Law], report for the German Federal Ministry of the Interior (Bundesministerium des Innern), September 2001, available at http://www.bmi.bund.de/downloadde/11659/Download.pdf (accessed Aug. 20, 2003). See also, e.g., S. Simitis,"Das Volkzählungsurteil oder der lange Weg zur Informationsaskese—(BVerfGE 65, 1)" [The Census Judgment or the Long Road to Information Asceticism], *Kritische Vierteljahresschrift für Gesetzgebung und Rechtswissenschaft* 83:359-375, 2000 (highlighting gaps between legal principle and practice in the data privacy field).

similar shortfall. European regimes in general are a case in point. There is sporadic evidence that many of these do not outperform the U.S. regime in all respects even if they are, on paper at least, far more comprehensive and stringent than their U.S. counterpart.[176] More significantly, the European Commission has recently found that while the E.U. Directive (95/46/EC) has created a "high level" of data privacy in Europe, implementation of the directive is afflicted by major problems. Not only has national transposition of the directive often been slow,[177] there appear to be—even after transposition—low levels of enforcement, compliance, and awareness with respect to the national regimes. Data privacy agencies in Europe are found, in general, to be underresourced, leading in turn to the underresourcing of enforcement efforts. Concomitantly, the commission finds that compliance by data controllers is "very patchy," while data subjects apparently have "low" awareness of their data-protection rights. Moreover, there remain differences between the various national laws that run counter to the harmonizing objective of the E.U. Directive.[178] Particularly problematic from an international perspective is that E.U. member states' respective implementation of Articles 25 and 26 in the E.U. Directive is found to be very broadly divergent; indeed, in many cases, it is inconsistent with the directive. Further, the commission finds that a substantial amount of transborder data flow is not being subjected to regulation at all.

Finally, account should be taken of several strands of criticism of data privacy regimes generally. One line of criticism concerns the regimes' underdevelopment of a systemic focus—as manifested, for instance, in the paucity of direct legislative encouragement for privacy-enhancing technologies.[179] Another line of criticism relates to marginalization of the

---

[176]For example, a survey in 2000 of privacy policies posted on U.S.- and E.U.-based Internet sites that sell goods or services to consumers found the policies on the E.U. sites to be no better than the policies on U.S. sites; indeed, some of the latter sites displayed the best policies. See K. Scribbins, *Privacy@net: An International Comparative Study of Consumer Privacy on the Internet*, Consumers International, 2001, available at http://www.consumersinternational. org/document_store/Doc30.pdf (accessed Oct. 20, 2003). See, too, results of a more recent survey published in April 2003 by World IT Lawyers. This survey canvassed 420 commercial Web sites across seven countries (France, Germany, the Netherlands, Portugal, Switzerland, Spain, and the United Kingdom) and found that approximately half of these sites did not display a privacy policy; see ZDNet UK, "UK Web Sites Fare Badly on Consumer Rights," April 30, 2003, available at http://news.zdnet.co.uk/business/0,39020645,2134138,00.htm (accessed Oct. 29, 2003).

[177]Several E.U. member states have been tardy in transposing the E.U. Directive into national law, the principal ones being France, Ireland, Luxembourg, and Germany. Further on implementation status, see http://europa.eu.int/comm/internal_market/privacy/law/ implementation_en.htm (accessed Oct. 25, 2003).

[178]See also Charlesworth, "Information Privacy Law in the European Union," 2003.

[179]See especially Bygrave, *Data Protection Law*, 2002, Part IV.

judiciary; in many countries, the courts have played little, if any, direct role in developing and enforcing data privacy norms. This situation not only results in a scarcity of authoritative guidance on the proper interpretation of the relevant legislation, but it contributes to the marginalization of data privacy as a field of law.[180]

Still another line of criticism is that data privacy regimes so far have tended to operate with largely procedural rules that do not seriously challenge established patterns of information use but seek merely to make such use more efficient, fair, and palatable for the general public. In this view, legislators' motives for enacting data privacy laws are increasingly concerned with engendering public acceptance for new information systems, particularly in the area of electronic commerce. Concomitantly, it is argued that the regimes are incapable of substantially curbing the growth of mass surveillance and control.[181]

---

[180]See especially Bygrave, "Where Have All the Judges Gone?," 2001.
[181]See especially J. Rule, D. McAdam, L. Stearns, and D. Uglow, *The Politics of Privacy: Planning for Personal Data Systems as Powerful Technologies*, Elsevier, New York, 1980; see also Flaherty, *Protecting Privacy in Surveillance Societies*, 1989.

C

Biographies

C.1 COMMITTEE MEMBERS

William H. Webster, *Chair,* is a senior partner at Milbank, Tweed, Hadley and McCloy LLP's Washington, D.C., office and heads the Litigation Department there. He is also involved in the firm's international corporate, banking, trade, and administrative law practices. Prior to joining Milbank, Tweed in 1991, Judge Webster had been, since 1987, director of Central Intelligence, where he headed all the foreign intelligence agencies of the United States and directed the Central Intelligence Agency. Earlier, he had served as director of the Federal Bureau of Investigation, from 1978 to 1987; judge of the U.S. Court of Appeals for the Eighth Circuit, from 1973 to 1978; and judge of the U.S. District Court for the Eastern District of Missouri, from 1970 to 1973. A practicing attorney with a St. Louis law firm from 1949 to 1959, Judge Webster served as U.S. Attorney for the Eastern District of Missouri from 1960 to 1961. He returned to private practice in 1961. From 1964 to 1968, he was a member of the Missouri Board of Law Examiners. Judge Webster graduated from Amherst College and received his Juris Doctor from Washington University Law School. He is a member of the American Bar Association, the Council of the American Law Institute, Order of the Coif, and a fellow of the American Bar Foundation. He has received numerous honorary degrees and awards, including the Freedoms Foundation National Service Medal (1985), the Presidential Medal of Freedom (1991), the National Security Medal (1991), and the 2001 Justice Award of the American Judicature Society. He is a past chair of the American Bar Association Business Law

Section and past president of the Institute of Judicial Administration. He is a trustee of Washington University in St. Louis.

James Waldo, *Vice Chair*, is the lead architect for Jini, a distributed programming system based on Java. Before joining Jini, Dr. Waldo worked in JavaSoft and Sun Microsystems Laboratories, where he did research in the areas of object-oriented programming and systems, distributed computing, and user environments. Before joining Sun, Dr. Waldo spent 8 years at Apollo Computer and Hewlett-Packard (HP) working in the areas of distributed object systems, user interfaces, class libraries, text, and internationalization. While at HP, he led the design and development of the first Object Request Broker and was instrumental in getting that technology incorporated into the first OMG CORBA specification. He edited the book *The Evolution of C++: Language Design in the Marketplace of Ideas* (MIT Press), and was the author of the "Java Advisor" column in *Unix Review's Performance Computing* magazine. Dr. Waldo is an adjunct faculty member of Harvard University, where he teaches distributed computing in the Department of Computer Science. He received his Ph.D. in philosophy from the University of Massachusetts (Amherst). He also holds M.A. degrees in both linguistics and philosophy from the University of Utah. He is a member of the Institute of Electrical and Electronics Engineers (IEEE) and the Association for Computing Machinery (ACM). He served on the Computer Science and Telecommunications Board's (CSTB's) Committee on Networked Systems of Embedded Computers, which produced the report *Embedded, Everywhere: A Research Agenda for Networked Systems of Embedded Computer* (National Academy Press, Washington, D.C., 2001).

Julie E. Cohen is a professor of law at the Georgetown University Law Center. She teaches and writes about intellectual property law and information privacy law, with particular focus on digital works and on the intersection of copyright and privacy rights. She is a member of the Advisory Board of the Electronic Privacy Information Center and the Advisory Board of Public Knowledge. Prior to joining the Law Center faculty, Professor Cohen was an assistant professor of law at the University of Pittsburgh School of Law. She previously practiced with the San Francisco firm of McCutchen, Doyle, Brown and Enersen, where she specialized in intellectual property litigation. Professor Cohen is a graduate of Harvard University (A.B., 1986) and the Harvard Law School (J.D., 1991). She is a former law clerk to the Hon. Stephen Reinhardt of the United States Court of Appeals for the Ninth Circuit.

Oscar Gandy, Jr., is professor emeritus at the Annenberg School for Communication at the University of Pennsylvania. Previously he was director of the Center for Communication Research at Howard University. His Ph.D. in public affairs communication was awarded by Stanford University in 1976. He is author of *The Panoptic Sort* and *Beyond Agenda Setting*, two books that explore issues of information and public policy. His most recent work is in the area of communication and race and the ways in which the media frame racial comparisons. His most recent book, *Communication and Race*, explores the structure of media and society, as well as the cognitive structures that reflect and are reproduced through media use. A book in progress, *If It Weren't for Bad Luck*, explores the ways in which probability and its representation affect the lives of different groups in society. He has been an active member of several professional organizations, serving as head of the Minorities and Communication Division and chair of the Standing Committee on Research for the Association for Education in Journalism and Mass Communication, and as a member of the International Council of the International Association for Media and Communication Research. He also served as chair of the board of directors of the Electronic Privacy Information Center. He was awarded the Dallas Smythe Award in 1999 from the Union for Democratic Communication.

James Horning is chief scientist and director of West Coast operations at Network Associates Laboratories. He was the founder of InterTrust's Strategic Technologies and Architectural Research Laboratory (STAR Lab) in 1997 and its director through October 2001. Previously, he was a founding member and senior consultant at Digital's Systems Research Center (DEC/SRC), a research fellow at Xerox's Palo Alto Research Center (PARC), and a founding member and chair of the University of Toronto's Computer Systems Research Group (CSRG). He is a member and past chair of the International Federation for Information Processing's (IFIP's) Working Group 2.3 (Programming Methodology). He is a coauthor of two books, *Larch: Languages and Tools for Formal Specification* (1993), and *A Compiler Generator* (1970). He wrote his first computer program in 1959 and received his Ph.D. in computer science from Stanford University 10 years later. He is a fellow of the ACM.

Gary King is the David Florence Professor of Government at Harvard University. He also serves as director of the Institute for Quantitative Social Science. Dr. King has been elected fellow of the American Association for the Advancement of Science (AAAS) (2004), fellow of the American Academy of Arts and Sciences (1998), fellow of the American Academy of Political and Social Science (2004), president of the Society for Political Methodology (1997-1999), and vice president of the American Political Science Association (APSA) (2003-2004). He was also appointed a fellow of the Guggenheim Foundation (1994-1995), visiting fellow at Oxford (1994), and senior science adviser to the World Health Organization (1998-2003). Dr. King has won the McGraw-Hill Award (2006), the Durr Award (2005), the Gosnell Prize (1999 and 1997), the Outstanding Statistical Application Award (2000), the Donald Campbell Award (1997), the Eulau Award (1995), the Mills Award (1993), the Pi Sigma Alpha Award (2005, 1998, and 1993), the APSA Research Software Award (2005, 1997, 1994, and 1992), the Okidata Best Research Software Award (1999), and the Okidata Best Research Web Site Award (1999), among others. His more than 100 journal articles, 10 public domain software packages, and 7 books span most aspects of political methodology, many fields of political science, and several other scholarly disciplines. Dr. King's work is cited widely across scholarly fields and beyond academia. His work on legislative redistricting has been used in most American states by legislators, judges, lawyers, political parties, minority groups, and private citizens, as well as by the U.S. Supreme Court. His work on ecological inference has been used in as many states by these groups, and in many other practical contexts. His contributions to methods for achieving cross-cultural comparability in survey research have been used in surveys in more than 80 countries by researchers, governments, and private concerns. The statistical methods and software that he developed for addressing many problems are used extensively in academia, government, consulting work, and private industry.

Lin E. Knapp is currently an independent consultant. Previously, she was the vice chair of PricewaterhouseCoopers (and one of its predecessor firms) for 10 years and, before that, a senior partner in the management consulting practice. As a vice chair, Ms. Knapp has held the positions of Global Chief Information Officer (CIO) and Global Chief Knowledge Officer (CKO). A well-known authority on the strategic use of both intellectual capital and technology, she has been a member of the firm's global leadership team—its Management Committee and Board of Partners. Ms. Knapp has received worldwide recognition for her work in technology, knowledge management, and the new economy. She served as a member of the National Research Council's study team examining Computer Technology and Its Impact on Service Sector Productivity. She is a frequent keynote speaker; her recent addresses include those at the European Business Information Conference, Harvard University's Women In Leadership Conference, the World Congress on Information Technology, and the White House-sponsored Critical Infrastructure Assurance Conference. She is a member of Harvard University's global Women's Leadership

Board and was recently recognized by *Crain's New York Business* as one of New York's 100 most influential women in business.

Brent Lowensohn has served, during the course of this study, as director of the IT Advanced Technologies Department and director of IT Research at the Kaiser Permanente Medical Care Program, the largest health maintenance organization in the country, with more than 100,000 employees serving 9 million members from a $28 billion annual budget. Dr. Lowensohn has also served as a visiting scientist at the Massachusetts Institute of Technology's (MIT's) Media Laboratory. His Ph.D. in social psychology was awarded by Syracuse University in 1976. His research, which opened up a new area in environmental psychology, won his induction into Sigma Xi, the Scientific Research Society. Dr. Lowensohn led his department in the identification, creation, evaluation, and implementation of innovative, high-technology applications for health care management and operations. As a result, the department has been on the forefront of many technology-based issues such as electronic clinical information systems, biometrics, intelligent spaces, and automated authentication systems. His current activities are focused on social and technological support for home-based health monitoring and chronic disease management. Dr. Lowensohn is a founding member of the Gartner Group Advanced Technologies Best Practices Group; was a member of three MIT consortia (Things that Think, Center for Bits and Atoms, and Changing Places), a member of the Biometrics Working Group of the Biometrics Consortium, and a member of Cross Industry Working Team of the Center for National Research Initiatives. His background in the social sciences, health care, and technology provides a unique perspective on contemporary issues.

Gary T. Marx is professor emeritus at the Massachusetts Institute of Technology. He has written, among other works, *Protest and Prejudice: A Study of Belief in the Black Community; Undercover: Police Surveillance in America;* and *Undercover: Police Surveillance in Comparative Perspective.* His work has appeared or has been reprinted in more than 250 books, monographs, and periodicals and has been translated into many languages. He received his Ph.D. from the University of California at Berkeley. He has taught there, at Harvard University, at the University of Colorado, and in Belgium, Spain, Austria, and China. He has lectured throughout the world. He has served in an advisory capacity for many government and nonprofit organizations and on many editorial boards. He has a book in progress on new forms of surveillance.

Helen Nissenbaum is associate professor in the Department of Culture and Communication and a senior fellow of the Information Law Institute at New York University. She specializes in social, ethical, and political dimensions of technology, with a focus on information technology. Her published works on privacy, property rights, electronic publication, accountability, the use of computers in education, and values embodied in computer systems have appeared in scholarly journals of philosophy, applied ethics, law, and computer science. She is the author of *Emotion and Focus* (University of Chicago Press), coeditor (with D.J. Johnson) of *Computers, Ethics and Social Values* (Prentice-Hall), and a founding coeditor of the journal *Ethics and Information Technology* (Kluwer Academic Press). Grants from the National Science Foundation (NSF) and the Ford Foundation have supported her work, including an interdisciplinary study of human values in Web-browser security with Batya Friedman and Edward Felten, and an internship for undergraduates to promote the public interest in information technology. She has served on committees of the National Research Council, NSF, UNESCO, AAAS, and ACM. Professor Nissenbaum was a member of the School of Social Science, Institute for Advanced Study (2000-2001); served as associate director of Princeton University's Center for Human Values; and held a postdoctoral fellowship at the Center for the Study of Language and Information at Stanford University. She earned a B.A. (honors) from the University of the Witwatersrand, Johannesburg, and a Ph.D. in philosophy from Stanford University.

Robert M. O'Neil became the founding director of the Thomas Jefferson Center for the Protection of Free Expression in August 1990, after serving 5 years as president of the University of Virginia. He continues as a member of the university's law faculty, teaching courses in constitutional law and a new course on free speech and cyberspace. In 1963, after serving as law clerk to Supreme Court Justice William J. Brennan, Jr., Professor O'Neil began three decades of teaching about free speech and press at the University of California, Berkeley, and the Universities of Cincinnati, Indiana, Wisconsin, and Virginia. In addition to teaching, he has had a distinguished career in higher-education administration, serving as provost of the University of Cincinnati, vice president of Indiana University for the Bloomington Campus, and president of the University of Wisconsin, before coming to Virginia. He has chaired the National Association of State Universities and Land-Grant Colleges and served on the executive committee of the Association of American Universities. From 1992 to 1999, he chaired Committee A (Academic Freedom and Tenure) of the American Association of University Professors (AAUP), of which he was general counsel from 1970 to 1972 and again from 1990 to 1992. He has also served as a trustee or director of the Commonwealth Fund, the Fort James Corporation, the Media Institute, and Teachers Insurance and Annuity Association (TIAA). He chairs special committees of the AAUP on Academic Freedom and National Security in Time of Crisis, and on Hurricane Katrina and New Orleans Universities, and directs the Ford Foundation's Difficult Dialogues Initiative. In Virginia he serves as chairman of the board of WVPT-Public Television, as a trustee and former president of the Council for America's First Freedom, and is the first president of Virginia's Coalition for Open Government. He is the author of several books, including *Free Speech: Responsible Communication Under Law*, *The Rights of Public Employees* (2nd edition, 1993), and *Classrooms in the Crossfire*, as well as many op-ed pieces and articles on free speech and press in law reviews and other journals. His latest book, *Free Speech in the College Community* (March 1997), is published by the Indiana University Press. On numerous occasions, Professor O'Neil has testified before state legislatures and congressional committees on the First Amendment implications of proposed legislation.

Janey Place is CEO of DigitalThinking, a business strategy, technology, innovation, and payment systems consulting company based in New York and Los Angeles. Prior to starting DigitalThinking in 2004, she was executive vice president of eCommerce Strategy for Mellon Financial Corporation, responsible for Mellon's eCommerce strategy and customer information management. She was president of MellonLab and a member of Mellon's Senior Management Committee. Formerly, she was the executive vice president for Bank of America's Strategic Technology Group, which was responsible for Internet initiatives, advanced technology research and development, and information technology architecture. Previously, Ms. Place was senior vice president in charge of Internet strategy and research and development at Wells Fargo Bank. She was information technology manager at Hughes Aircraft Company and served as corporate manager of Strategic Technology Planning for Tosco Corporation. Ms. Place also was a lecturer in systems and communication theory at the University of California, Santa Cruz. She is a published author of two books and many articles, editor of a communications magazine, producer and director of film and video programs, and a frequent speaker. She has served on a number of corporate boards and currently is a director for PortBlue, an information management company. Ms. Place earned a bachelor's degree from the University of California at Los Angeles. She holds a master's degree and a doctorate in systems theory and attended the Graduate School of Management at the University of California at Los Angeles.

Ronald L. Rivest is a member of the Massachusetts Institute of Technology's Computer Science and Artificial Intelligence Laboratory, a member of the laboratory's Theory of Computation Group, and a leader of its

Cryptography and Information Security Group. He is also a founder of RSA Data Security. (RSA was bought by Security Dynamics; the combined company has been renamed RSA Security.) Professor Rivest has research interests in cryptography, computer and network security, and algorithms. He is a fellow of the Association for Computing Machinery and of the American Academy of Arts and Sciences and is also a member of the National Academy of Engineering. Together with Adi Shamir and Len Adleman, he was awarded the 2000 IEEE Koji Kobayashi Computers and Communications Award and the Secure Computing Lifetime Achievement Award. Professor Rivest received an honorary degree (the "laurea honoris causa") from the University of Rome. He is an inventor of the RSA public-key cryptosystem. He has extensive experience in cryptographic design and cryptanalysis and has published numerous papers in these areas. He has served as a director of the International Association for Cryptologic Research, the organizing body for the Eurocrypt and Crypto conferences, and as a director of the Financial Cryptography Association.

Teresa Schwartz is the J.B. and Maurice C. Shapiro Professor Emeritus of Public Interest Law at the George Washington University Law School. From 1995 to 2001, she was deputy director of the Federal Trade Commission's Bureau of Consumer Protection. At the commission, she participated in and oversaw critical, growing work on privacy policy as a consumer protection issue. Prior to joining the commission, she was a member of the law faculty at George Washington University Law School. During her 25 years on the faculty, she served as the academic dean; taught and published in the areas of administrative law, torts, and product liability; and was named the J.B. and Maurice C. Shapiro Professor of Public Interest Law. Ms. Schwartz began her legal career in 1971 as an attorney adviser to Federal Trade Commissioner Mary Gardiner Jones. In 1978, she was awarded a White House Fellowship. Ms. Schwartz has served on the board of directors of Consumers Union, the Food and Drug Law Institute, and the District of Columbia Bar. She also has served on the editorial advisory board of the *Administrative Law Review*. Ms. Schwartz earned her B.A. from Stanford University in 1965 and her J.D. (with highest honors) from George Washington University in 1971. She is a member of the Bar of the District of Columbia.

Lloyd N. Cutler, of Wilmer, Cutler and Pickering, was co-chair until he passed away on May 8, 2005.

Robert W. Crandall, Brookings Institution, resigned on April 4, 2006.

C.2 STAFF MEMBERS

Herbert S. Lin is senior scientist and senior staff officer at the Computer Science and Telecommunications Board (CSTB), National Research Council (NRC) of the National Academies, where he has been the study director for major projects on public policy and information technology. These studies, published by the National Academy Press, include a 1991 study on the future of computer science (*Computing the Future*), a 1996 study on national cryptography policy (*Cryptography's Role in Securing the Information Society*), a 1999 study of Department of Defense systems for command, control, communications, computing, and intelligence (*Realizing the Potential of C4I: Fundamental Challenges*), and a 2000 study on workforce issues in high-technology (*Building a Workforce for the Information Economy*). Prior to his NRC service, he was a professional staff member and staff scientist for the House Armed Services Committee (1986 to 1990), where his portfolio included defense policy and arms control issues. He also has significant expertise in math and science education. He received his Ph.D. in physics from MIT in 1979. Avocationally, he is a long-time folk and swing dancer and a poor magician. Apart from his CSTB work, a list of publications in cognitive science, science education, biophysics, and arms control and defense policy is available on request.

Lynette I. Millett is a senior program officer at the Computer Science and Telecommunications Board of the National Research Council. She is currently involved in several CSTB projects, including a comprehensive exploration of privacy in the information age, a study on certification and dependable software systems, an assessment of biometrics technologies, and an examination of the Social Security Administration's electronic services strategy. Her portfolio includes significant portions of CSTB's recent work on software and on identity systems and privacy. She was the study director for the CSTB project that produced the reports *Who Goes There? Authentication Through the Lens of Privacy* and *IDs—Not That Easy: Questions About Nationwide Identity Systems*. She has an M.Sc. in computer science from Cornell University, along with a B.A. in mathematics and computer science with honors from Colby College, where she was elected to Phi Beta Kappa. Her graduate work was supported by both an NSF graduate fellowship and an Intel graduate fellowship.

Kristen Batch is an associate program officer with the Computer Science and Telecommunications Board of the National Research Council. She is currently involved with several projects focusing on emerging wireless technology and spectrum policy, biometrics technologies, and privacy in the information age. While pursuing an M.A. in international communications from American University, she interned at the National Telecommunications and Information Administration in the Office of International Affairs and at the Center for Strategic and International Studies in the Technology and Public Policy Program. She also earned a B.A. from Carnegie Mellon University in literary and cultural studies and Spanish, and received two travel grants to conduct independent research in Spain.

David Padgham (re)joined CSTB as an associate program officer in the spring of 2006, following nearly 2 years as a policy analyst in the Association for Computing Machinery's (ACM's) Washington, D.C., Office of Public Policy. While at ACM, he worked closely with that organization's public policy committee, USACM. Previously, he spent nearly 6 years with CSTB in positions ranging from project assistant to research associate working on, among other things, the studies that produced *Trust in Cyberspace*, *Funding a Revolution*, and *Realizing the Potential of C4I*. More recently, he has assisted with the research and production of *Broadband: Bringing Home the Bits*, *LC21: A Digital Strategy for the Library of Congress*, *The Internet's Coming of Age*, *Looking Over the Fence at Networks*, and *Information Technology Research, Innovation, and E-Government*. He holds a master's degree in library and information science (2001) from the Catholic University of America in Washington, D.C., and a bachelor of arts degree in English (1996) from Warren Wilson College in Asheville, N.C.

Jennifer M. Bishop, program associate, began working with the Computer Science and Telecommunications Board of the National Research Council in 2001. She was involved in several studies, including those on telecommunications research and development, digital archiving and the National Archives and Records Administration, and information technology and creativity. She also maintained CSTB's contact database, handled updates to the CSTB Web site, coordinated the layout and design of *Update*, the CSTB newsletter, and designed book covers and promotional materials. Prior to her move to Washington, D.C., she worked for the City of Ithaca, New York, coordinating the Police Department's transition to a new SQL-based time accrual and scheduling application. Her other work experience includes designing customized hospitality industry performance reports for RealTime Hotel Reports, LLC.; maintaining the police records database for the City of Ithaca; and freelancing in publication design. She is a visual artist working in oil and mixed media. She holds a B.F.A. from Cornell University.

Janice M. Sabuda is a senior program assistant at the Computer Science and Telecommunications Board of the National Research Council. She currently supports all board activities and is involved in several studies, including Improving Cybersecurity Research in the United States,

Information Technology and the States: Public Policy and Public Interests, Planning Meeting on Fundamental Research Challenges in Computer Graphics, Privacy in the Information Age, and Radio Frequency Identification (RFID) Technologies: A Workshop. Previously, she focused on the congressionally requested study that resulted in *Youth, Pornography, and the Internet* (2002) and the project that resulted in *Global Networks and Local Values* (2001). Prior to joining CSTB in August 2001, she worked as a customer service representative at an online fundraising company and as a client services analyst at a prospect research firm. She is currently pursuing a certificate in event management from the George Washington University Center for Professional Development. She received her bachelor of science degree (1999) in business administration from the State University of New York College at Fredonia.

Index